ROYAL HISTORICAL SOCIETY

STUDIES IN HISTORY

New Series

FRANCO-IRISH RELATIONS, 1500–1610

POLITICS, MIGRATION AND TRADE

TO COLM LENNON, MENTOR AND FRIEND

Publication of this volume was aided by a generous grant from the Fondation Irlandaise, Collège des Irlandais, Paris

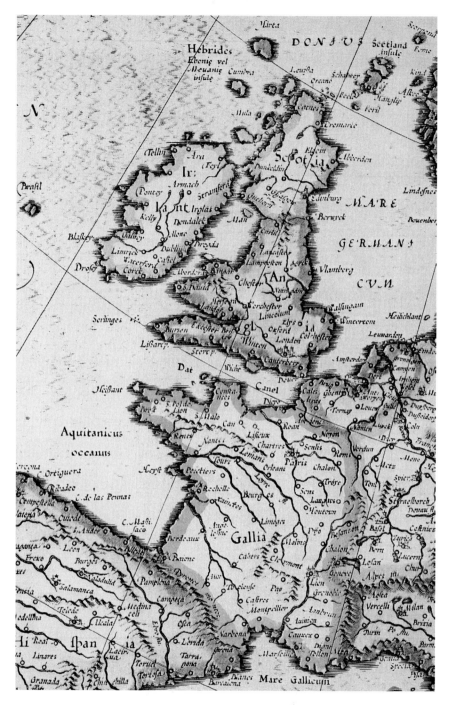

Extract from the late sixteenth-century Mercator-Hondius map of Europe,
reproduced from *Landmarks of mapmaking*, maps chosen and displayed by
R. V. Tooley, Oxford 1976.

FRANCO-IRISH RELATIONS, 1500–1610
POLITICS, MIGRATION AND TRADE

Mary Ann Lyons

THE ROYAL HISTORICAL SOCIETY
THE BOYDELL PRESS

First published 2003

A Royal Historical Society publication
Published by The Boydell Press
an imprint of Boydell & Brewer Ltd
PO Box 9, Woodbridge, Suffolk IP12 3DF, UK
and of Boydell & Brewer Inc.
PO Box 41026, Rochester, NY 14604–4126, USA
website: www.boydell.co.uk

ISBN 0 86193 266 8

ISSN 0269–2244

1003586792

A catalogue record for this book is available
from the British Library

Library of Congress Cataloging-in-Publication Data
Lyons, Mary Ann.
   Franco-Irish relations, 1500–1610 : politics, migration, and trade /
Mary Ann Lyons.
   p. cm. – (Royal Historical Society studies in history. New series,
ISSN 0269–2244)
Includes bibliographical references and index.
   ISBN 0–86193–266–8 (alk. paper)
1. Ireland – Relations – France.   2. Ireland – History – 16th century.
3. Ireland – Foreign relations – France.   4. Ireland – Civilization –
French influences.   5. Ireland – Foreign economic relations – France.
6. France – Foreign economic relations – Ireland.   7. France – Foreign
relations – 16th century.   8. France – Foreign relations – Ireland.
9. France – Relations – Ireland.   I. Royal Historical Society (Great
Britain) II. Title. III. Series.
   DA964.F8L96 2003
   303.48'2415044'09031 – dc21   2003005336

This book is printed on acid-free paper

Printed in Great Britain by
St Edmundsbury Press Ltd, Bury St Edmunds, Suffolk

Contents

List of Illustrations

Frontpiece/jacket illustration: Extract from the late sixteenth-century Mercator-Hondius map of Europe, reproduced from *Landmarks of mapmaking*, maps chosen and displayed by R. V. Tooley, Oxford 1976. Despite successive attempts to secure copyright permission to reproduce this map, no reply was forthcoming prior to this book going to press.

Photographic Acknowledgements

Plates 1 and 2 are reproduced by kind permission of the Bibliothèque Nationale de France, Paris.

Acknowledgements

This book is based upon my doctoral dissertation, completed at the National University of Ireland, Maynooth, in 1997. The following deserve thanks for their role in helping to bring about its publication.

My sincere thanks to the members of the history department, NUI Maynooth for their support since my undergraduate years. In particular, I wish to thank Professor Vincent Comerford for his advice and encouragement, Dr Raymond Gillespie for his valuable comments on drafts of this work, Dr Thomas O'Connor for direction regarding French archival collections, and Professor Jackie Hill and Ms Mary Cullen for their constant interest in my work. My thanks also to the former head of department, Professor Patrick J. Corish, for his ongoing support of my endeavours. Professor Joe Bergin (University of Manchester), Professor John Morrill (Cambridge University) and Professor Colin Jones (University of Warwick) have, in various ways, been instrumental in bringing this book to fruition and I am grateful to them for their interest and advice. Éamon Ó Cíosain (French Department, NUI Maynooth) gave me valuable guidance regarding French provincial archival collections for which many thanks. I am especially indebted to Monsignor Breandán Ó Doibhlin, William Glynn and the Fondation Irlandaise for facilitating me in my work in French archives and for a generous grant towards the publication of this book. Thanks are also due to Professor Michel Zylberberg (Université de Rouen), for illuminating relevant aspects of early modern French historiography and for guidance regarding archival sources during my period of study in France. Thanks to Dr John Logan, Dr Bernadette Whelan, Dr Rúan O'Donnell, and Dr Pádraig Lenihan, my former colleagues at the University of Limerick who were immensely supportive while I worked on preparing the text for publication. More generally, I wish to acknowledge the support of Professor Nicholas P. Canny, Professor Steven G. Ellis (National University of Ireland, Galway), Dr Hiram Morgan (National University of Ireland, Cork) and Dr Mary O'Dowd (Queen's University, Belfast). I am particularly indebted to Dr Phil Kilroy, Dr Ciaran Brady, Professor Louis M. Cullen (Trinity College, Dublin), Dr Declan Downey, Dr Tadhg Ó hAnnracháin (University College Dublin), Dr Vincent Carey (State University of New York at Plattsburgh) and Dr Enda Delaney (Queen's University, Belfast) who read full or partial drafts of this book and made incisive critical comments. None of the above listed are responsible for any errors or omissions in this work.

I wish to acknowledge the support of the staff at St Patrick's College, Drumcondra and that of the president, Dr Pauric Travers. My colleagues in the history department – Dr Daire Keogh, Dr Carla King, Dr Diarmuid

Ferriter, and Dr Matthew Stout – deserve special thanks for their interest and encouragement and for providing me with such a pleasant environment in which to work. I am particularly indebted to Dr James Kelly, head of department, who has been a constant source of support in all my endeavours and who commented extensively on earlier drafts of this study. I am very grateful to Professor David Eastwood and the editorial board of Royal Historical Society for publishing this book as part of the Society's Studies in History series. A special word of thanks to Ms Christine Linehan for her painstaking editorial work and also to Ms Pru Harrison at Boydell and Brewer Ltd for efficiently handling the production of this book. Thanks to Rev Sean Lyons for his translation of Latin texts, to Rev Benignus Millett, O.F.M. for providing me with references in the course of my research, to Jim Keenan (Geography Department, NUI Maynooth) for drawing the map featured in this publication and to the Bibliothèque Nationale de France for permission to reproduce images of Jean de Monluc and Antoine de Noailles.

I have been very fortunate in having much valued friends who have been a constant source of encouragement over many years. Pauline Mooney, Kathryn Moore, Anna-Marie MacCleary, Paula Coonerty, Catherine Leech, Geraldine Dixon, Patricia Duffy, Priscilla O'Connor, and Alan English deserve special thanks. Your friendship has always buoyed me up and is deeply appreciated. In this, as in so many things, I am indebted to my parents, Brendan and Ann, and my brother, Sean for whose unfailing support, assistance and interest, my sincere thanks. Finally, since my earliest years as an undergraduate student at Maynooth, Professor Colm Lennon, who supervised my doctoral dissertation, has been a constant source of gentle encouragement and quiet affirmation. In recognition of his valued enthusiasm, confidence, advice and friendship over the years, I dedicate this book to him.

Abbreviations

AE, CP	Ministère des Affaires Étrangères, Quai d'Orsay, Paris, Correspondance politique
AHA	*American Historical Association*
AHR	*American Historical Review*
ASHAA Saint-Malo	*Annales de la Société d'histoire et d'archéologie de l'arrondissement de Saint-Malo*
BIHR	*Bulletin of the Institute of Historical Research*
BN	Bibliothèque Nationale, Paris
CPR Henry VII	*Calendar of the patent and close rolls preserved in the Public Record Office, Henry VII, 2 vols, London 1914–16*
CPR Ireland Hen. VIII–Eliz.	*Calendar of the patent and close rolls of chancery in Ireland, ed. James Morrin, 3 vols, Dublin 1861–3*
CSP Domestic	*Calendar of state papers preserved in the Public Record Office, London, domestic series, 12 vols, London 1855–72*
CSP Foreign	*Calendar of state papers preserved in the Public Record Office, foreign series, 1547–89, 23 vols, London 1896–1950*
CSP Ireland	*Calendar of the state papers relating to Ireland, 1509–1670, 24 vols, London 1860–1912.*
CSP Scotland	*Calendar of state papers relating to Scotland and Mary, Queen of Scots, 1547–1603 preserved in the Public Record Office, the British Museum and elsewhere in England, 13 vols, London 1898–1969*
CSP Spain	*Calendar of state papers, Spanish, London 1862–95*
DNB	*Dictionary of national biography*
EHR	*English Historical Review*
HJ	*Historical Journal*
HMC	Historical Manuscripts Commission
IER	*Irish Ecclesiastical Record*
IESH	*Irish Economic and Social History*
IHR	*International History Review*
IHS	*Irish Historical Studies*
JMH	*Journal of Modern History*
LP Henry VIII	*Letters and papers, foreign and domestic, Henry VIII, 21 vols, London 1862–1932*
NLI	National Library of Ireland
PRIA	*Proceedings of the Royal Irish Academy*
PRO	Public Record Office, London
PROI	Public Record Office, Ireland
RH	*Revue Historique*
SP	*State papers*
TRHS	*Transactions of the Royal Historical Society*

Introduction

The historiography of Franco-Irish relations in the sixteenth and early seventeenth centuries has traditionally concentrated on commercial connections between the two countries and on the embryonic development of the Irish, and specifically the clerical, diaspora in France.[1] Ireland's commercial ties with France in the late Middle Ages have been the subject of a substantial amount of specialised scholarly research that has broadly traced the principal trade routes, identified both Irish and French families involved in commercial networks and provided an insight into the practicalities of their business transactions.[2] Arising from this exposition it is clear that Ireland had established trade links with the main ports of Normandy and those of the French Atlantic seaboard by the late fifteenth century. This trade survived the disruptions of legislative restrictions, war and piracy throughout the sixteenth century and increased in the early 1600s. While existing studies have examined Ireland's commerce with France in isolation, this study shows that when

[1] For a valuable survey of the historiography of Irish migration to Europe and specifically France in the early modern period see Thomas O'Connor, 'Ireland and Europe, 1580–1815: some historiographical remarks', in Thomas O'Connor (ed.), *The Irish in Europe, 1580–1815*, Dublin 2001, 9–26.
[2] A. F. O'Brien, 'Commercial relations between Aquitaine and Ireland, c. 1000 to c. 1550', in Jean-Michel Picard (ed.), *Aquitaine and Ireland in the Middle Ages*, Dublin 1995, 31–80; Jacques Bernard, 'The maritime intercourse between Bordeaux and Ireland, c. 1450–c. 1520', *IESH* vii (1980), 7–21; Mary Ann Lyons, 'Franco-Irish relations in the sixteenth century', unpubl. PhD diss. National University of Ireland 1997, ch. i; André l'Éspagnol, 'Les Relations commerciales entre l'Irlande et la Bretagne aux temps modernes, XVe et XVIIIe siècles: complémentarité ou concurrence?', in Catherine Laurent and Helen Davis (eds), *Irlande et Bretagne: vingt siècles d'histoire*, Rennes 1994, 169–77; Mary Ann Lyons, 'Maritime relations between France and Ireland, c. 1480–c. 1630', *IESH* xxvii (2000), 1–21. A useful though dated survey of Franco-Irish commercial relations is to be found in A. K. Longfield, *Anglo-Irish trade in the sixteenth century*, London 1929. For more modern interpretations of economic change in Ireland between 1550 and 1700 see Aidan Clarke, 'The Irish economy, 1600–60', in T. W. Moody, F. X. Martin and F. J. Byrne (eds), *A new history of Ireland*, III: *Early modern Ireland, 1534–1691*, Oxford 1976, 168–86, and Raymond Gillespie, *The transformation of the Irish economy, 1550–1700*, Dundalk 1991. Also useful are Wendy Childs, 'Ireland's trade with England in the later Middle Ages', *IESH* ix (1982), 5–33; Wendy Childs and Timothy O'Neill, 'Overseas trade', in Art Cosgrove (ed.), *A new history of Ireland*, II: *Medieval Ireland, 1169–1534*, Oxford 1987, 492–524; L. M. Cullen, *An economic history of Ireland since 1660*, 2nd edn, London 1987. Related studies include Jacques Bernard, *Navires et gens de mer à Bordeaux vers 1400–vers 1550*, 3 vols, Paris 1968; Pauline Croft, 'Trading with the enemy, 1585–1604', *HJ* xxxii (1989), 281–302; Karin Schüller, *Die beziehungen zwischen Spanien und Irland im 16. und 17. Jahrhundert: diplomatie, handel und die soziale integration Katholischer exulanten*, Münster 1999, 75–99.

set within the wider context of sixteenth-century Franco-Irish relations, these connections, combined with Irish seafarers' familiarity with French ports, proved critical in facilitating the flight and safe harbouring of Ireland's political dissidents who sought asylum or assistance in France from 1540 onwards. Later they were to determine the destinations of the thousands of Irish migrants who fled to France during and in the immediate aftermath of the final contest in the Elizabethan conquest of Ireland, the Nine Years' War (1594–1603).

Since the late nineteenth century both French and Irish scholars have explored the experience of clerical and lay Irish migrants in Brittany, Normandy and elsewhere in *ancien régime* France. However, the treatment of the migrants' experiences in these early studies is largely anecdotal and the analysis is typically very general and simplistic, concentrating mainly on clerics who fled the Elizabethan *régime* and the short-lived wave of post-war migration in the early years of the seventeenth century. Even these migrants are frequently only afforded the briefest comment as a prelude to more detailed analysis of the formation of Irish colonies in French cities and towns that, until recently, has focused on the late seventeenth and eighteenth centuries.[3] However, there are exceptions, notably accounts of the establishment of Irish colleges in Paris and Bordeaux published by Patrick Boyle, George Daumet and James O'Boyle in the early 1900s that in turn spawned a series of scholarly studies of the Irish colleges.[4] More recently, Lawrence Brockliss and Patrick Ferté have made a very significant contribution towards enabling historians to ascertain the extent and composition of the wider Irish clerical diaspora in France through their compilation of an extensive list of Irish clerics educated in French universities in the seventeenth and eighteenth centuries.[5]

3   A. Walsh, 'Irish exiles in Brittany', *IER* 4th ser. i (Jan.–June 1897), 311–22; Charles de Beaurepaire, 'Expulsion des irlandais, 1606', *Bulletin de la Société de l'histoire de Normandie* ix (1900–4), 42–4; Jules Mathorez, *Notes sur la colonie irlandaise de Nantes du XVIe au XVIIIe siècles*, Nantes 1913; F. Gourvil, 'Familles irlandaises en Bretagne aux XVIIe et XVIIIe siècles', *Nouvelle Revue de Bretagne* i (jan.–fév. 1949), supplément, 125–31.

4   See Patrick Boyle, *The Irish college in Paris, 1578 to 1901*, Dublin 1901; 'The Irish college at Paris, 1578–1901', *IER* 4th ser. xi (Jan.–June 1902), 193–210; and 'The Irish college at Bordeaux, 1603–1794', ibid. 4th ser. xxii (July–Dec. 1907), 127–45; George Daumet, 'Notices sur les établissements religieux anglais, écossais et irlandais fondés à Paris avant la révolution: fin', *Mémoires de la Société de l'histoire de Paris et de l'île de France* xxxix (1912), 88–124; Jules Mathorez, 'Notes sur les prêtres irlandais réfugiés à Nantes aux XVIIe et XVIIIe siècles', *Revue d'histoire de l'église de France* xiii (jan.–fév. 1912), 164–73; James O'Boyle, *The Irish colleges on the continent*, Dublin 1935; T. J. Walsh, *The Irish continental college movement: the colleges at Bordeaux, Toulouse and Lille*, Dublin 1973; Tomás Ó Fiach, *The Irish colleges in France*, Paris 1990; Liam Swords, *Soldiers, scholars, priests: a short history of the Irish college, Paris*, Paris 1985; T. S. Flynn, *The Irish Dominicans, 1536–1641*, Dublin 1993, 210–12.

5   L. W. B. Brockliss and Patrick Ferté, 'A prosopography of Irish clerics who studied in France in the seventeenth and eighteenth centuries, in particular at the universities of Paris and Toulouse', unpubl. typescript, Royal Irish Academy Library, Dublin, and Russell

Soldiers represent a significant cohort of the Irish who migrated to France in the sixteenth century. Yet the experiences of these men has received virtually no scholarly attention since the majority of Irish soldiers who sought employment on the continent were recruited into Spanish regiments, particularly in Flanders, from the 1580s.[6] D. G. White's essay on the Irish kerne (Gaelic professional foot-soldiers) who served in Henry VIII's campaign at Boulogne in 1544–6 represents the only sustained exploration of the experience of Irish soldiers in France. Even this study is primarily an analysis of the peculiar political significance of Gaelic kerne rendering their services in the forces of the English crown rather than an examination of the experiences of migrant soldiers and their families seeking employment abroad.[7]

In the 1930s and 1940s Richard Hayes made a pioneering contribution to our understanding of relations between the two countries, his achievements being a survey of long-standing Irish associations with the cities and towns of Nantes, Rouen, Paris and Bordeaux and his assembling of biographical compilations. These too were of greatest value and interest to the genealogist and the general reader.[8] Since then the history of the Irish, both clerics and laity, in France in the sixteenth and early seventeenth centuries has become the subject of increasingly rigorous examination. A growing number of scholars are currently engaged in research which involves systematic trawling through French archives, and their findings are not only revolutionising our understanding of the history of the Irish diaspora in France but also challenging accepted interpretations of Irish history and of Irish nationality.[9] Increasingly studies have become more narrowly focused with scholars

Library, Maynooth, County Kildare, and 'Irish clerics in France in the seventeenth and eighteenth centuries: a statistical survey', *PRIA* lxxxviiC (1987), 527–72.
[6] For studies of the formation of an Irish military community in Spanish Flanders from the 1580s see Brendan Jennings, 'Irish swordsmen in Flanders, 1586–1610', *Studies* xxxvi (1947), 402–10; xxxvii (1948), 189–202; Jerrold Casway, 'Henry O'Neill and the formation of the Irish regiment in the Netherlands, 1605', *IHS* xviii (Sept. 1973), 481–8; Gráinne Henry, *The Irish military community in Spanish Flanders, 1586–1621*, Dublin 1992. For allusions to Irish soldiers serving in French and Spanish regiments during the wars of the Catholic League see *CSP Ireland, 1592–6*, 64, and *Correspondance du duc de Mercoeur et des Ligeurs bretons avec l'Éspagne extraite des archives nationales*, ed. Gaston de Carné, 2 vols, Vannes 1899, i. 105–8.
[7] D. G. White, 'Henry VIII's Irish kerne in France and Scotland, 1544–5', *Irish Sword* iii (1957–8), 213–24.
[8] Richard Hayes, 'Irish footprints in Rouen', *Studies* xxvi (1937), 418–28; 'Irish links with Bordeaux', ibid. xxvii (1938), 291–306; *Old Irish links with France*, Dublin 1940; 'Irish associations with Nantes', *Studies* xxxvii (1948), 115–26; and *Biographical dictionary of Irishmen in France*, Dublin 1949. See also Hayes's later work, collaboratively edited with Christopher Preston and J. Weygand, *Les Irlandais en Aquitaine*, Bordeaux 1971. Other valuable contributions include 'The Irish at Paris', ed. David Buisseret, *IHS* xiv (1964–5), 58–60, and J. J. Silke, 'The Irish abroad, 1534–1691', in Moody, Martin and Byrne, *A new history of Ireland*, iii. 587–633.
[9] See, for example, Eamon Ó Ciosáin, 'Les Irlandais en Bretagne, 1603–1780: "invasion", accueil, intégration', in Laurent and Davis, *Irlande et Bretagne*, 152–66; Mary Ann Lyons,

confining their attention to particular migrant groups such as clerics, students, soldiers, indigents and criminals amongst others. Apart from the wealth of genealogical information that is being uncovered, scholars are gaining a much greater appreciation of the scale, patterns and periodisation of Irish migration to France in this era as well as exploring the motivations of migrants for travelling to France.[10] Advances in the study of immigration into France in the early modern period have also provided valuable insights into the processes whereby Irish immigrants became naturalised French subjects and were gradually integrated into their host society.[11] The work of Patrick Fitzgerald, Louis Cullen, Brendan Jennings, Jerrold Casway, Gráinne Henry, Thomas O'Connor, Ciaran O'Scea, T. C. Smout and others has greatly contributed to the formation of a comparative interpretative framework within which Irish migration in the early modern period can be studied properly.[12]

The most neglected sphere of Franco-Irish relations in this period is political association. In the historiography of sixteenth-century Ireland, recognition of Gaelic success in securing Spanish military support during the Nine Years' War has overshadowed any sustained examination of Irish intrigue with the French court. There have, however, been some significant advances towards addressing this *lacuna* in the historiography not only of Ireland but of France and the British Isles.[13] James Hogan's pioneering work, *Ireland in the*

' "Vagabonds", "mendiants", "gueux": French reaction to Irish immigration in the early seventeenth century', *French History* xiv (2001), 363–82; O'Connor, *The Irish in Europe*.

10 See Patrick Fitzgerald, ' "Like crickets to the crevice of a brew-house": poor Irish migrants in England, 1560–1640', in Patrick O'Sullivan (ed.), *Patterns of migration*, i, London 1992, 13–35; L. M. Cullen, 'The Irish diaspora of the seventeenth and eighteenth centuries', in Nicholas Canny (ed.), *Europeans on the move: studies on European migration, 1500–1800*, Oxford 1994, 113–49; T. C. Smout, 'The culture of migration: Scots as Europeans, 1500–1800', *History Workshop Journal* xl (1995), 108–17; T. C. Smout, N. C. Landsman and T. M. Devine, 'Scottish emigration in the seventeenth and eighteenth centuries', in Canny, *Europeans on the move*, 76–112. These and other works have contributed to the formation of a comparative interpretative framework within which Irish migration can best be studied.

11 Fernand Gueriff, 'Recherches sure les "étrangers" à Saint-Nazaire sous l'ancien régime', *Bulletin de la Société archéologique et historique de Nantes et de Loire-Atlantique* cii (1964), 15–34; Yves Lequin, *La Mosaïque France: histoire des étrangers et de l'immigration en France*, Paris 1988; Jean-François Dubost, *Les Étrangers en France, XVIe siècle–1789*, Paris 1993, and *La France italienne, XVIe–XVIIe siècle*, Paris 1997; Jean-François Dubost and Peter Sahlins, *Et si on faisait payer les étrangers? Louis XIV, les immigrés et quelques autres*, Paris 1999.

12 See Fitzgerald, 'Poor Irish migrants in England'; Cullen, 'The Irish diaspora'; Jennings, 'Irish swordsmen in Flanders'; Casway, 'O'Neill and the Irish regiment'; Henry, *The Irish military community*; Ciaran O'Scea, 'The devotional world of the Irish Catholic exile in early modern Galicia, 1598–1666', in O'Connor, *The Irish in Europe*, 27–48; Smout, 'The culture of migration'; Smout, Landsman and Devine, 'Scottish emigration'.

13 'British Isles' is used in this work as it was in regular use by cartographers and geographers by the late sixteenth century.

European system, published in 1920, represented a radical departure from the introspective approach to writing Irish history that was characteristic of his time and it is a measure of his achievement that his study has endured. Hogan sought to locate Ireland's history within the broader western European context and for the first time traced the French dimension to Geraldine intrigue and recognised the significance of the Guise faction at the French court for that intrigue. However, his study is now dated, and his interpretation and methodology are not without problems, not least being his heavy reliance on English official sources, errors in dating documents, a tendency to take liberties in interpreting sources and insufficient discrimination between episodes of futile intrigue and real threats of invasion. Since then D. L. Potter's scholarly article on French intrigue in Ireland during the reign of Henri II has made a significant contribution to our understanding of the complex dynamics governing the tentative political relationship between Irish dissidents and the French crown.[14] Potter presents a thorough analysis based upon the systematic study of a substantial and diverse collection of French, Irish, English and Scottish sources which serves as a valuable corrective to certain errors featured in Hogan's work. More important, it sets the analysis of Franco-Irish political relations within the wider British and west European contexts which are fundamental to understanding the tentative and fickle nature of those relations.

William Palmer's *The problem of Ireland in Tudor foreign policy, 1485–1603*, which argues that English policy in Ireland was profoundly shaped by foreign policy concerns and by the power politics of the Counter-Reformation has proved valuable in broadening parameters for studying the Tudors' governance of their Irish kingdom. However, Palmer's analysis fails to elaborate sufficiently upon the significance of the pursuit of French interests in Scotland in determining the balance of relations within the British Isles. Little attention is afforded the formation of political ties between individual Gaelic and Anglo-Irish lords on the one hand and members of the political elite of France on the other. Nor is there any critical evaluation of the substance of either Franco-Irish or Franco-Scottish intrigue that exerted a significant if variable catalytic influence on Tudor policy in respect of Ireland.

C. R. Sasso's unpublished doctoral dissertation, 'The Desmond rebellions, 1569–73 and 1579–83', has greatly illuminated our understanding of the tortuous progress of Irish negotiations at the French, Spanish and papal courts in an effort to secure military and financial support for James Fitzmaurice's campaign in opposition to Elizabeth in the 1570s. Sasso's assessment of the import of these negotiations for the prosecution of the Desmond rebellions in Ireland, and his commentary on the occasionally conflicting responses of the Dublin and Whitehall administrations to reported develop-

---

[14] D. L. Potter, 'French intrigue in Ireland during the reign of Henri II, 1547–59', *IHR* v (May 1983), 159–80.

ments in the negotiations, are especially complementary to this study. Micheline Kerney Walsh's account of the Ulster lords' sojourn in France while *en route* to Italy after their flight from Ireland in 1607 has also been valuable in informing the discussion that follows.[15]

Despite these advances in the historiography of sixteenth-century Irish politics, the present work would have been impossible were it not for parallel development in British history since the mid-1970s. Further to J. G. A. Pocock's[16] recommendation that a British framework ought to be adopted for studying the history of the kingdoms of England and Wales, Scotland and Ireland, a growing corpus of literature has deepened our understanding of various relationships between the constituent realms and also between the British Isles and continental Europe.[17] As John Morrill[18] and Pocock have independently argued, much of the story of the sixteenth-century interactions of England, Ireland and Scotland only makes sense in a dynastic or a European geo-political/geo-religious context within which the three kingdoms 'interacted so as to modify the conditions of one another's existence'.[19] As a subordinate to the English crown, Ireland's relations with France can therefore only be properly analysed and understood within this broader milieu. Moreover, several studies of Franco-Scottish and Anglo-French political relations, especially those completed since the early 1970s, have significantly enhanced efforts to understand the dynamics governing Anglo-Scottish, Anglo-Irish and Hiberno-Scottish political relations.[20] Recent studies of sixteenth-century French politics, most notably those focused on

---

[15] Micheline Kerney Walsh, *'Destruction by peace': Hugh O'Neill after Kinsale*, Monaghan 1986, and *An exile of Ireland: Hugh O'Neill, prince of Ulster*, Dublin 1996. See also C. P. Meehan, *The fate and fortunes of Hugh O'Neill, earl of Tyrone and Rory O'Donnel, earl of Tyrconnell: their flight from Ireland and death in exile*, 3rd edn, Dublin 1886. For a more recent interpretation see Mary Ann Lyons, 'Reluctant collaborators: French reaction to the Nine Years' War and the flight of the earls, 1594–1608', *Seanchas Ard Mhacha* xix (2002), 70–90.

[16] J. G. A. Pocock, 'British history: a plea for a new subject', *JMH* xlvii (1975), 601–28, and 'The limits and divisions of British history', *AHR* lxxxviii (1982), 311–36.

[17] S. G. Ellis, 'England in the Tudor state', *HJ* xxvi (1983), 201–12; Jenny Wormald, 'The creation of Britain: multiple kingdoms or core and colonies?', *TRHS* 6th ser. no. 2 (1992), 175–94; S. G. Ellis and Sarah Barber (eds), *Conquest and union: fashioning a British state, 1485–1725*, London 1995; A. Grant and K. Stringer (eds), *Uniting the kingdom? The enigma of British history*, London 1995; S. G. Ellis, *Tudor frontiers and noble power: the making of the British state*, Oxford 1995; Brendan Bradshaw and John Morrill (eds), *The British problem, c. 1534–1707: state formation in the Atlantic archipelago*, London 1996, esp. Hiram Morgan's 'British policies before the British state'; S. J. Connolly (ed.), *Kingdoms united? Great Britain and Ireland since 1500*, Dublin 1999; Mark Nicholls, *A history of the modern British Isles, 1529–1603*, Oxford 1999; S. G. Ellis, *Ireland in the age of the Tudors, 1447–1603: English expansion and the end of Gaelic rule*, Harlow 1999.

[18] John Morrill, 'The British problem, c. 1534–1707', in Bradshaw and Morrill, *The British problem*, 14–15.

[19] Pocock, 'Limits', 317.

[20] See Glenn John Richardson, 'Anglo-French political and cultural relations during the reign of Henry VIII', unpubl. PhD diss. London 1995; D. L. Potter, 'Diplomacy in the

the Guise dynasty which played a central role in Franco-Irish intrigue in this period, have likewise been indispensable to a study of this kind.[21] In short, the historiographical advances that have occurred in each of these spheres in the last generation have been vital to the creation of the integrated, inclusive interpretative framework necessary for the analysis of Franco-Irish political relations in the sixteenth century.

The present study aims to address two *lacunae* in the political and demographic history of the British Isles and France. First, it presents a detailed exploration of the development of Franco-Irish political relations during the period 1523–84. This takes the form of a systematic exposition of Franco-Irish political engagement, episode by episode, and analysis of the circumstances that precipitated the onset of the decline in France's role as a refuge and possible source of aid for Ireland's political exiles in the 1570s. Second, the examination of the first wave of Irish migration to France in the 1590s and early 1600s contributes to furthering our understanding of the wider phenomenon of migration from Ireland and indeed from the British Isles to continental Europe in the early modern period.

mid-sixteenth century: England and France, 1536–1550', unpubl. PhD diss. Cambridge 1973; E. H. Harbison, 'French intrigue at the court of Queen Mary', *AHA* xlv (1940), 533–51, and *Rival ambassadors at the court of Queen Mary*, London 1940; Charles Giry Deloison, 'La Naissance de la diplomatie moderne en France et en Angleterre du XVIe siècle, 1475–1520', *Nouvelle Revue du seizième siècle* v (1987), 41–58; Elizabeth Bonner, 'The first phase of the politique of Henri II in Scotland', unpubl. PhD diss. Sydney 1993; Marie-Noëlle Baudouin-Matuszek, 'Henri II et les expéditions françaises en Écosse', *Bibliothèque de l'École de chartes* cxlv (1987), 339–82, and 'Un Ambassadeur en Écosse au XVIe siècle: Henri Clutin d'Oisel', *RH* cclxxxi (1989), 77–131; J. D. Mackie, 'Henry VIII and Scotland', *TRHS* 4th ser. xxix (1947), 93–114; P. Holte, 'Tradition, reform and diplomacy: Anglo-Scottish relations, 1528–42', unpubl. PhD diss. Cambridge 1992; J. H. Burns, 'Scotland and England: culture and nationality, 1500–1800', in J. S. Bromley and E. H. Kossman (eds), *Metropolis, dominion and province, Britain and the Netherlands*, iv, The Hague 1971; David Head, 'Henry VIII's Scottish policy: a reassessment', *SHR* lxi, i, no. 171 (1982), 1–24; B. P. Levack, *The formation of the British state: England, Scotland and the Union, 1603–1707*, Oxford 1987; Jane Dawson, 'Sir William Cecil and the British dimension of early Elizabethan foreign policy', *History* lxxiv (1989), 196–216; 'Two kingdoms or three? Ireland in Anglo-Scottish relations in the middle of the sixteenth century', in R. A. Mason (ed.), *Scotland and England, 1286–1815*, Edinburgh 1987, 113–38; and 'The fifth earl of Argyle, Gaelic lordship and political power in sixteenth-century Scotland', *SHS* lxvii (1988), 1–27; Ciaran Brady, 'Shane O'Neill departs from the court of Elizabeth: Irish, English, Scottish perspectives and the paralysis of policy, July 1559 to April 1562', in Connolly, *Kingdoms united?*, 13–28.

[21] See, for example, Jean-Marie Constant, *Les Guise*, Paris 1984, and Stuart Carroll, *Noble power during the French wars of religion: the Guise affinity and the Catholic cause in Normandy*, Cambridge 1998.

I

In so far as it can be said that the French had a policy in respect of Ireland in the sixteenth century, it only ever constituted a lesser dimension to their more crucial policy in relation to England which had as its aim the prevention of the latter's absorption into the Habsburg dominion. The French crown's dealings with Irish dissidents cannot therefore be studied in isolation. By virtue of Ireland's political and constitutional subjugation to the English crown, all intrigue, however harmless, between the French and Anglo-Irish or Gaelic parties necessarily exercised the attention of the Tudor monarchs and their English and Irish councils. Critical to any examination of Franco-Irish intrigue is the evaluation of reaction to it within the Dublin and Whitehall administrations that governed Ireland in the name of the English crown. The full significance of various episodes of Franco-Irish intrigue can only be appreciated in terms of their ramifications for the security of the wider British polity. It was precisely because the tenth earl of Desmond, Gerald Fitzgerald, and Shane O'Neill presented themselves as rebels against the English crown and coincided, if not collaborated, with the Scots in their challenges to the Tudors, that these otherwise inconsequential lords in a distant polity attracted disproportionate attention from English, Scottish and continental rulers and diplomatic personnel. The British dimension was therefore central to French motivation for designs on Ireland. While the plans of Irish dissidents were not entirely contingent upon Hiberno-Scottish collaboration with the French, they invariably sought to exploit opposition to the Tudors in Scotland in their solicitations for French military intervention in Ireland. Ironically, hopes for a French invasion of Ireland via Scotland, which appeared the most promising option to successive Irish malcontents for a period of over sixty years, were doomed. When foreign aid eventually arrived in Ireland in 1600 it came not through Scotland but directly from Spain.

Ireland's dependent constitutional and political status also resulted in the Dublin administration, the loyal Anglo-Irish minority and the Gaelic Irish majority having no access to formal diplomatic structures and personnel through which to conduct independent political relations with continental Europe. English ambassadors at the French court and their French counterparts in England served as the only official channel by which the Irish council and compliant Anglo-Irish and Gaelic Irish subjects could access the European diplomatic network. Consequently, disaffected Anglo-Irish lords and Gaelic chiefs operated outside conventional structures in forging links with the French court in their efforts to secure support.

The character of the surviving source material and the covert nature of intrigue creates obvious problems for the historian when endeavouring to trace the often-labyrinthine manoeuvres of those involved and complicates attempts to gauge the substance, intention and course of the intrigue. The success of those involved in concealing their seditious schemes from the eyes of the Dublin and Whitehall administrations, from English and imperial agents and also from English seafarers during their stays in France renders the historian's task particularly difficult. In the case of the most serious engagements, negotiations were conducted through individual emissaries or by the Irish lords themselves who escaped under cover to France. Their reliance upon personal contacts to prevent the interception of letters lessened the need for written correspondence and ensured that little material survives. The scarcity of surviving documentary evidence is also explained by the emissaries' retention of all correspondence in their personal possession. Both French and Irish envoys were keenly aware of the consequences of their being found in possession of incriminating documentation which in turn has minimised the chances of survival of this correspondence. Moreover, given that both the Irish and French emissaries employed to make representations on their masters' behalf were of modest means, there are no private papers of significance, and only a handful of letters written by French and Irish conspirators, confiscated by English and Anglophile Scottish officials, has survived.

Ascertaining the actual as opposed to the reported course of the contacts between successive Irish dissidents and the French court is problematic, being necessarily impeded by the need to rely on the papers generated by parties other than those directly involved in the intrigue for evidence of what transpired. The correspondence of French ambassadors in England and Scotland and that of their English counterparts in France (all of whom played a vital role in the purveyance of intelligence concerning Irish engagement with the French) serves as the main source of information, though it is not without serious limitations. Such material is often linguistically obscure, making only veiled allusions to parties involved in intrigue. It can be difficult to ascertain the degree of discretion being exercised by a French ambassador, who was party to conspiracy, in the interests of protecting his monarch's reputation. Certain individual French ambassadors to England and Scotland acted with more independence than others, giving rise to ambiguity as to whether their opinions and actions can rightly be equated with those of their monarch. French ambassadorial correspondence also exhibits a heavy dependence upon the reports of English officials in the Dublin and Whitehall administrations concerning affairs in Ireland. This has obvious ramifications in terms of the assessment of the Irish situation conveyed to the French crown.

In the absence of a substantial corpus of Gaelic source material on the subject, historians are obliged to rely on glimpses of episodes in Franco-Irish political engagement as seen through the eyes of members of the Dublin administration. Almost invariably these correspondents described the protagonists from a very remote vantage point, often only discovering the dissidents' involvement in intrigue when they had already fled Ireland for France or Scotland. By virtue of their isolation from the European diplomatic nexus, Dublin officials were reliant upon hearsay and the interrogation of captured suspects, mariners or travellers recently returned from the continent in their search for information regarding the progress of Irish intrigue there. Factional divisions within and between the two administrations, rivalry between Old and New English office-holders and competition to secure the crown's backing for particular policies in governing Ireland and for responding to foreign threats also contributed to exaggerated reporting of the substance and gravity of Franco-Irish associations.

Furthermore, the study of political intrigue is itself a problematic task. Like all early modern intrigue, that between the French and Irish was comprised of a mixture of serious negotiations, talks, requests for aid presented in letters or in person, and a great deal of supposition, extrapolation, hearsay, dissembling, conjecture and falsification, deliberate or otherwise. It featured intentional manipulation of intelligence as all parties contrived to present and interpret events in a manner that suited their own particular purposes. As a consequence, it can be difficult to distinguish between substantial and fanciful intrigue. While often of ephemeral consequence and questionable reliability, rumours and reports are useful none the less, providing immediate insights into the responses of contemporaries to political circumstances as they unfolded. The manipulation by conspirators of the uncertainty that was a precondition for their intrigues had a discernible impact on the course of political events in Ireland, England, Scotland and to a much lesser extent, France.

In this study, all reported episodes of Franco-Irish intrigue in the sixteenth century are examined; the broadly defined term 'intrigue' is deliberately used to denote all political engagement. However, as will become apparent, there were marked qualitative differences and gradations in the seriousness of the various rounds of intrigue, the most significant of which occurred in 1522–3, 1540 and the mid-1540s, 1549–50, 1565–7, 1569–79 and 1582–4. Each had been singled out for in-depth analysis and its relative importance assessed within the broader context of evolving political relations between the two countries. In some cases, most notably in the mid-1540s, the intrigue was nothing more than speculation, unfounded allegations and deliberate scaremongering designed to apply pressure on the Tudor *régime* in time of war. Mostly it involved the Irish directing appeals to the French monarch, the Guise faction, other influential courtiers or French ambassadors in England and Scotland for financial or military support for their causes. However, on certain rare occasions, notably in 1522–3 and again in 1549–50, both the French and the Irish parties were especially earnest in their engagement and pursued serious negotiations. In the first case this ended in an indentured treaty between François I and James Fitzgerald, tenth earl of Desmond. This study explores the reasons for the relative seriousness of each round of intrigue, and investigates the differences in the ranks, motives and commitment of those involved. The timing and substance of reported French designs on Ireland is examined and the likelihood of French military intervention is assessed within the broader *milieu* of British and continental politics and diplomacy.

II

Prior to the early 1520s Ireland and France had no political engagement of consequence. Before tentative political relations began in 1522–3, virtually all contact between the two countries revolved around trade. This remained the case throughout the sixteenth and early seventeenth centuries. Independent of the vicissitudes of politics, commerce remained the main channel of Franco-Irish contact.[22] Indeed, even Ireland's trade links with France were small-scale and uncertain by contemporary standards in this period, though trade did increase in the early 1600s. In the late fifteenth century the widespread perception of Ireland as a peripheral, underdeveloped country with a dangerous coastline and rough seaways inhibited most continental mariners from venturing to trade there on a regular basis, and the Bretons and French were no different. Merchants from Normandy were reluctant to travel to a country they described as 'étrange et sauvage'.[23] Those who did venture there complained of the difficulties they encountered while conducting business in the ports of Cork, Drogheda and Limerick. Ireland's inhospitable reputation was reinforced in the late fifteenth century when several French merchants and their factors returned with reports of having been imprisoned in foul Irish jails. The country was viewed with some trepidation by French mariners who did not dare to trade there for fear of the 'sauvages' or Gaelic Irish.[24] English seafarers shared some of these concerns. In an anonymous tract, written after 1580 and entitled 'A special direction for diverse trades of merchandise', the author advised traders travelling to the north of Ireland to 'take heed of the people, because they are false and full of treachery'.[25] However, such anxieties were offset by the more widespread availability of increasingly accurate maps, charts, rutters and navigational guides during the sixteenth and early seventeenth centuries which helped French, Flemish, Spanish and English mariners negotiate the difficulties of the Irish coastline and harbours.

Ireland's comparatively poor commercial enticement to French merchants and their continental counterparts was a more crucial disincentive to foreign seafarers as, apart from the abundant fish supplies, there was little reason for them to frequent Ireland's ports in preference to continental or British ones. In Ireland they were obliged to conduct business in an uncommercialised economy that was backward even by contemporary rural European standards, that relied at least in some regions on barter exchange, and that offered

---

[22] This discussion draws heavily on Lyons, 'Maritime relations', and 'Franco-Irish relations', ch. i.

[23] Quoted in Michel Mollat, *Le Commerce de la Haute Normandie au XVe siècle et au début du XVIe siècle*, Paris 1952, 155.

[24] Ibid. O'Brien, 'Commercial relations', 42.

[25] Quoted in Conyers Read, 'English foreign trade under Elizabeth', *EHR* xxix (1914), 517.

products that were at best only comparable to those available at markets closer to home.

These obstacles notwithstanding, throughout the sixteenth and early seventeenth centuries Ireland maintained significant if small-scale commercial relations with the ports of Normandy, Brittany, Pays-de-la-Loire, Charante-Poitou and Aquitaine. Normandy's trade with the British Isles and Ireland steadily increased from the 1490s onwards, largely owing to France's economic recovery in the aftermath of the Hundred Years' War.[26] Merchants from Limerick, Drogheda, Cork, Youghal and Waterford dominated Irish trade with Normandy's principal port of Rouen. In the late fifteenth and early sixteenth centuries, Irish merchants regularly chartered ships from Normandy, and specifically Rouen, in order to transport wine to Ireland from the Algarve, Andalusia, the upper Seine, Burgundy and, to a lesser extent, Bordeaux.[27] Corn and iron were imported from Rouen which in turn became an outlet for Irish hides.[28] Normandy's other major port, Dieppe, had regular commercial contact with Ireland, particularly with Limerick-based merchants who chartered ships from the French port to transport cargoes to Ireland, although Dieppe's commercial ties with Ireland appear to have lapsed from the 1530s.[29] The smaller Normandy ports of Honfleur and Harfleur had modest links with Cork, Limerick and Galway in the late fifteenth and early sixteenth centuries.[30]

Breton trade with Ireland had likewise steadily intensified from the mid-fifteenth century, though it too only ever accounted for a small proportion of the province's commerce as a whole. Since the late fifteenth century Breton merchants had frequented the ports of the south-eastern coast of Ireland, between Drogheda and Baltimore, only occasionally venturing to Dingle, Limerick or Galway.[31] In the early 1500s in particular, the abundant

---

[26] Michel de Boüard, *Histoire de la Normandie*, Toulouse 1970, 289–90; O'Brien, 'Commercial relations', 42.

[27] O'Brien, 'Commercial relations', 40.

[28] Mollat, *Le Commerce de la Haute Normandie*, 105, 156; Ernest de Fréville, *Mémoire sur le commerce maritime de Rouen depuis les temps les plus reculés jusqu'à la fin du XVIe siècle*, 2 vols, Rouen 1857, ii. 418; C. de Robillard de Beaurepaire, *Inventaire-sommaire des archives communales antérieures à 1790, ville de Rouen*, I: *Délibérations*, Rouen 1887, A. 10 (13 juin 155), A. 11 (16 avril 1616).

[29] M. de Noailles to the admiral of France, 16 août 1559, AE, CP Angleterre, copies des dépêches et mémoires des ambassades de MM Antoine, Francois et Gilles de Noailles, xiv. 62–3; Bernard, *Navires et gens de mer*, iii. 366–7, 388; Mollat, *Le Commerce de la Haute Normandie*, 161; Lord Deputy Sir Henry Sidney to the privy council, 17 June 1576, CSP Ireland, 1574–5, 95.

[30] *Calendar of material relating to Ireland from the High Court of Admiralty examinations, 1536–1641*, ed. John C. Appleby, Dublin 1992, nos 697, 701, 1319; Mollat, *Le Commerce de la Haute Normandie*, 138, 156n.; Bernard, *Navires et gens de mer*, iii. 136–7.

[31] Arthur E. J. Went, 'Foreign fishing fleets along the Irish coasts', *Journal of the Cork Historical Society* liv (1949), 17–20; Henri Touchard, *Le Commerce maritime breton à la fin du moyen âge*, Paris 1967, 138, 237; Timothy O'Neill, *Merchants and mariners*, Dublin 1987, 49.

fish supplies off the Irish coasts attracted increasing numbers of fishing vessels from that province. Of all the Breton ports, Ireland's trade links were strongest with Saint-Malo throughout the sixteenth and early seventeenth centuries, with Galway, Cork, Dublin, Donegal, Kinsale, Limerick, Carrickfergus, Dundalk and, to a lesser extent, Drogheda, each having strong commercial ties with this port. Trade between Nantes and Ireland was inconsequential by comparison.[32] As was the norm, merchants from Nantes visited various ports in Ireland according to the dictates of the market, though Dublin, Waterford and Cork appear to have been their main destinations.

In the late fifteenth and early sixteenth centuries La Rochelle maintained commercial ties with Drogheda, Dundalk, Dublin, Arklow, Waterford, Cork, Kinsale, Baltimore, Bantry and Galway.[33] Similarly, Bordeaux was involved in trade with all Ireland's major ports, from Drogheda and Dublin to Limerick, Galway, Sligo, Lough Foyle and Carrickfergus, with Cork, Waterford and Youghal ranking as the principal destinations. Unlike those merchants based at Bordeaux and La Rochelle who travelled only very infrequently to Ireland, their Irish counterparts continued to operate as seafaring merchants throughout the sixteenth and early seventeenth centuries, conducting their transactions in person in French ports, especially Saint-Malo and Bordeaux. Typically they found lodgings either in private *oustaus* owned by native merchants or in the town's hostelleries where they were able both to conduct business and to enjoy gambling and drinking within the tight-knit circle of Irish and English merchants and mariners during their short sojourns. In ports such as Calais and Saint-Malo, they employed both Englishmen and Irishmen as resident factors.[34] Merchants from Ireland who traded in Bordeaux tended to spend a few weeks at most bargaining, chartering and loading ships in the port. One gains a sense of the scale of Irish trade at Bordeaux from the annual attendance of between 7,000 and 8,000 Irish, Scottish and English merchants at its autumn fairs.[35] Similarly, when Irish merchants from the ports of Drogheda, Dublin, Galway, Waterford and Limerick frequented La Rochelle throughout the 1580s and 1590s, they tended not to remain in the town for extended periods. Typically they arrived

---

[32] Jean Tanguy, *Le Commerce du port de Nantes au milieu du XVIe siècle*, Paris 1956, 71.

[33] *Rochelais* merchants and mariners who were unfamiliar with Ireland were advised by their more experienced compatriots that Youghal was the port which was most suitable for unloading their cargo: O'Brien, 'Commercial relations', 50–2.

[34] *High Court of Admiralty examinations*, no. 706. For discussions of the practical aspects of the commercial transactions of foreign merchant colonies in French ports see P. Jeannin, 'Les Pratiques commerciales des colonies marchands étrangères dans les ports français, XVIe–XVIIIe siècles', in L. M. Cullen and Paul Butel (eds), *Négoce et industrie en France et en Irlande aux XVIIIe et XIXe siècles*, Paris 1980, 9–16, and Mary Ann Lyons, 'The emergence of an Irish community in Saint-Malo, 1550–1710', in O'Connor, *The Irish in Europe*, 107–26.

[35] Prosper Boissonnade, 'Le Mouvement commerciale entre la France et les Îles Britanniques au XVIe siècle', *RH* cxxxiv (mai–aôut 1920), 214.

in small groups, occasionally in flotillas comprised of Flemish, French, Scottish and other ships, and having bargained with local merchants, they loaded their ships without delay for the return journey.[36]

In spite of the fact that individual Irish merchants resided permanently in Bordeaux, Saint-Malo, Rouen and elsewhere in France in the fifteenth and early sixteenth centuries, there is little evidence to suggest the existence of permanent Irish communities in any of the French Atlantic ports prior to the 1640s.[37] This pattern was mirrored by French merchants and mariners, only a handful of whom settled in Ireland during this period. More commonly, they operated from their native ports and established regular business contacts with individual families in Ireland, the White family of Limerick who were actively involved in trade with Dieppe in the 1500s being a case in point. French merchants negotiated with their Irish counterparts to transport cargoes to and from Ireland on their behalf.[38] When in Ireland, they regularly exchanged commodities in a number of ports during the course of one journey and it was common practice for merchants to disembark in Irish harbours and dispatch their ships back to their port of origin while they sold their produce, before summoning the vessels to bring them back to France.[39]

These maritime associations, which were firmly established between merchants and mariners in both countries by the beginning of the sixteenth century, formed the crucial foundations on which all other connections gradually developed. While the traditional basis for relations between the two countries was expanded by the unprecedented and ultimately short-lived development of tentative political ties from the early 1520s, it was these commercial contacts which proved most durable in sustaining Franco-Irish relations throughout the sixteenth century, despite the disruptions of legislative restrictions, warfare and piracy. In the era before the establishment of permanent resident embassies in France, England and Scotland, it was Irish, Breton and French seafarers who were the main purveyors of intelligence on current affairs to the countries they frequented. Throughout the sixteenth century they were a source of vital information for the Dublin and Whitehall administrations concerning the progress of Irish efforts to secure financial and military aid at continental courts. They also carried home rumours of intrigue between Irish dissidents and supposed continental collaborators that were seized upon by the Dublin administration as it sought to gauge the gravity of recurrent threats of foreign invasion. As this study shows, Irish,

---

[36] Richard Proudfoot, intelligence, 5 May 1593, PRO, SP 63/169/214 (enclosure); Etienne Trocmé and Marcel Delafosse, *Le Commerce rochelais de la fin du XVe siècle au début du XVIIe*, Paris 1953, 84.
[37] See Robert Boutruche, *Histoire de Bordeaux de 1453 à 1715*, Bordeaux 1966, 182; Bernard, 'Maritime intercourse', 13. For the establishment of Irish communities in seventeenth-century France see Ó Ciosáin, 'Les Irlandais en Bretagne, 1603–1780', and Lyons, 'An Irish community in Saint-Malo'.
[38] Lyons, 'Maritime relations', 17–18.
[39] Ibid. 18.

Breton and French mariners, by virtue of their intimate acquaintance with Breton and French ports, were invaluable in expediting the safe passage to France of a succession of Irish political dissidents and religious refugees in the 1500s and the Ulster lords in 1607. Moreover, established commercial contacts between Ireland and the ports of Saint-Malo, Rouen and Nantes in particular were harnessed as migrant paths for transporting several thousand Gaelic soldiers, peasants and their families out of Ireland into France during and in the aftermath of the Nine Years' War.

III

Prior to the development of political relations between the two countries, apart from merchants and mariners, the only other group of Irishmen whom the French directly encountered in significant numbers were Gaelic soldiers serving in continental armies. Their formidable military reputation ensured that Gaelic servicemen were amongst the most sought-after soldiers to serve in European and Scandinavian campaigns. Quite apart from the unquantifiable number of individuals who enlisted in French armies throughout the late medieval period, French forces were not unfamiliar with entire companies of Irish soldiers. In 1418 they encountered an army comprised of 1,600 Irishmen who participated in the siege of Rouen under the command of Thomas Butler, prior of Kilmainham.[40] Consequently, while Henry VIII's deployment of 600 Gaelic soldiers in the Boulogne campaign in 1544–6 represented an important symbolic and practical demonstration of Irish confidence in and support for the English crown, it was neither unprecedented nor unique.

Irish involvement in the siege of Boulogne was particularly important in Franco-Irish relations because it educated the French in the military tactics of Gaelic soldiers at a time when they were developing political ties with the Irish and when plans to stage a French invasion of Ireland featured prominently in French propaganda. Whereas previously the French assessed Irish soldiers in terms of their ability to serve in their armies, from the mid-sixteenth century, as Franco-Irish political intrigue intensified, they began to assess the suitability of the Gaelic Irish in an entirely new light, that is, as potential military allies in an offensive against England. Following their performance at Boulogne, Henri II (1547–59) who, of all the Valois monarchs, demonstrated the strongest interest in Ireland, held Gaelic soldiers in high esteem owing to their valour and endurance. When Henri's political interests in Scotland caused him to contemplate the extension of the French military campaign in Scotland into Ireland in 1549–50, the baron de Fourquevaux, a commander of the French army deployed in the Scottish campaign of 1548, was dispatched on a reconnaissance mission to Ulster to

---

40 See Hayes, *Old Irish links with France*, 114–16.

ascertain the military capabilities of the Irish. However, Fourquevaux's discouraging report confirmed Henri's doubts regarding the suitability of the Irish as allies. This summation proved significant, though not ultimately decisive, in causing Henri to shelve his designs for a French invasion of Ireland at that time. None the less, as this study shows, the unreliability of the Irish as allies did not dissuade the French from continuing to hold Gaelic servicemen in high regard and to recruit them into their companies on an informal basis throughout the sixteenth century and officially from 1637.[41]

IV

The coincidence of the development of an apparatus of international diplomacy, a reorientation in French foreign policy and changes in domestic political organisation in France, England, Scotland and Ireland, particularly from the 1530s onwards, resulted in the French monarchy and a small cohort of France's political elite becoming very slowly but steadily more attuned to the nuances of domestic Irish politics. In the process they were afforded unprecedented opportunities for conspiratorial engagement with disaffected Irish lords. As the operation of the French diplomatic machinery became more professionalised, diplomats stationed in England and Scotland corresponded with their government more regularly and copiously than ever before. This study shows that from the 1540s in particular French awareness of the Irish polity was very gradually cultivated by means of the increasing volume of intelligence that filtered through to the French crown and political elite via the channels of the ever-tightening diplomatic network connecting Paris, Whitehall, Edinburgh and, by extension, Dublin. French ambassadors based at the English and Scottish courts began to apprise their monarch of the most potent magnates and promising allies within the Irish polity. They furnished details of the location of Gaelic and Anglo-Irish lordships, identified their most accessible ports and assessed the military capabilities of individual lords. On rare occasions, ambassadors presented their considered opinion on the feasibility of staging a French attack on Ireland.[42]

While the ambition of vindicating the French monarchy's rights in the

41 See *Correspondance du duc de Mercoeur*, ii. 105–8; Pierre Gouhier, 'Mercinaires irlandais au service de la France, 1635–1664', *Revue d'histoire moderne et contemporaine* xv (jan.–mars 1968), 672–90.
42 Garrett Mattingly, *Renaissance diplomacy*, London 1955, 151–2; Deloison, 'La Naissance de la diplomatie moderne', 41–58; Gary Bell (comp.), *A handlist of British diplomatic representatives, 1509–1688*, London 1990, 68; Janine Garrisson, *A history of sixteenth-century-France, 1483–1598: Renaissance, Reformation and rebellion*, trans. Richard Rex, Basingstoke 1998, 136, 140–69; David Potter, *A history of France, 1460–1560: the emergence of a nation state*, Basingstoke 1995, 256, 264, 269, 298. Particularly useful are M. S. Anderson's works, *The rise of modern diplomacy, 1450–1919*, Harlow 1993, ch. i, and *The origins of the modern European state system, 1494–1618*, Harlow 1998, ch. iii.

Italian peninsula moulded French foreign policy until the mid-sixteenth century, a combination of the crown's realisation of the futility of pursuing French interests there, and the Habsburg-Valois struggle (1519–56), prompted a reorientation that paved the way for fostering political relations with Ireland. This turnabout became apparent in the Valois's increased prioritisation of the northern and north-eastern frontiers of their kingdom and in their efforts to win allies opposed to France's aggrandising Habsburg rivals. It was also evident in French intervention in Scottish affairs and in an unprecedented, utilitarian and expedient French interest in Gaelic Irish politics. Consequently England, Scotland and, by extension, Ireland, were drawn into the tentacles of French diplomacy and politics as permanent ambassadors were exchanged between the French, English and Scottish courts, though Ireland remained on the periphery of that network having no distinct diplomatic channel of contact with France.

The emergence of an increasingly centralised state system within François's and Henry VIII's realms also facilitated the development of Franco-Irish political relations.[43] Prior to the 1530s, when the drive towards centralisation and bureaucratisation in Whitehall and in Dublin got under way in earnest, the jurisdiction of the English king as lord of Ireland was effective in the Pale and south-eastern regions and in those outlying areas which retained residual structures of feudalism from the period of the Anglo-Norman settlement. Beyond these districts, the political, legal and landholding systems remained autonomous, and were dominated by the traditionally sovereign Gaelic rulers, the strongest of whom were the O'Neills and the O'Donnells in Ulster. The heads of Ireland's three leading Anglo-Irish families, the Fitzgeralds, earls of Kildare and Desmond, and the Butlers, earls of Ormond, were relied upon by the Dublin administration to maintain the colonial presence in their patrimonies and to varying extents they co-operated with the government by allowing English common law to be practised and crown revenues to be collected in their lordships. Down to the 1520s the lordship of Ireland, like the English northern marches, was ruled by aristocratic delegation. The office of lord deputy was almost continually occupied by the earls of Kildare who enjoyed powers which were commensurate with their being delegated royal jurisdiction in respect of Ireland and who exercised considerable authority over Gaelic regions.

However, the failure of the Kildare dynasty's violent resistance to Sir Thomas Cromwell's initiatives to reform the Dublin administration in line with the more centralised, bureaucratised *régime* in England in 1534–5 removed them from the premier position in the Dublin administration and paved the way for what Brendan Bradshaw has termed 'the Irish constitutional revolution'. Further to Cromwell's reform of the Irish administration

---

[43] See R. R. Betts, 'Constitutional development and political thought in western Europe', in G. R. Elton (ed.), *The new Cambridge modern history*, II: *The Reformation, 1520–59*, Cambridge 1958, 446–7.

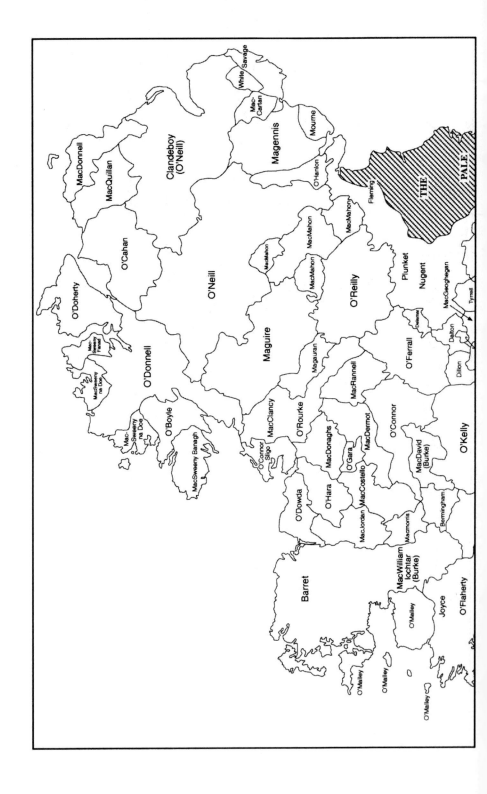

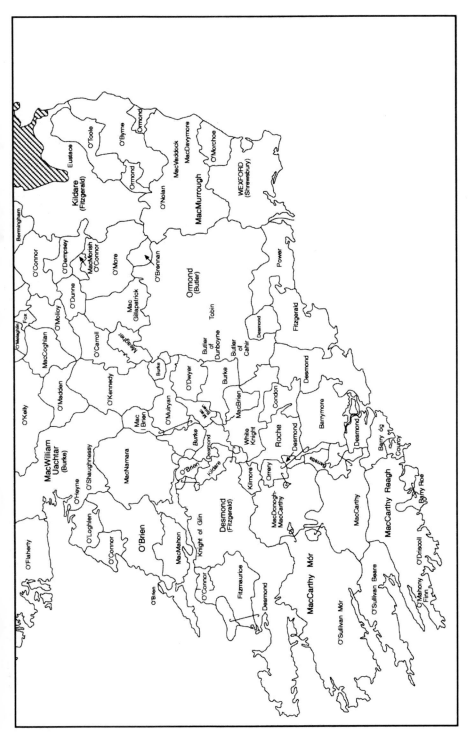

Gaelic lordships, c. 1534, with prominent English marchers

and the appointment of a resident English lord deputy to preside over the Irish council from the late 1530s onwards, successive lords deputy made inroads into Gaelic quarters of the island as the slow and tortuous process of anglicisation of those areas beyond the Pale got under way.[44]

As the arm of the Dublin administration extended further into previously alien Gaelic territories, the Irish council, which had previously left the business of negotiations and campaigns in Gaelic Ireland to the earls of Kildare, became better acquainted with the complexities that characterised Gaelic politics. In the modern style of reformed government, the deputy and councillors regularly reported their findings to Whitehall. In so doing they increased the efficient transmission of intelligence concerning Irish affairs through the artery of the Dublin administration to Whitehall and from there through diplomatic channels to the French court. The French crown's expanded knowledge of Gaelic politics and of the capabilities and grievances of leading Gaelic and Anglo-Irish magnates was therefore paradoxically attributable to these reforms in the Irish administration.

V

For a period of over sixty years, between 1522 and 1584, a succession of Irish political malcontents importuned the French court with requests for assistance, gradually redirecting their efforts to the Escorial and the papal court from the 1570s onwards. Ireland's evolving political relationship with France took shape through the medium of ongoing intrigue that peaked in a number of particularly significant episodes. In the early 1520s, when France was at war with England, the tenth earl of Desmond initiated the first substantive political engagement with François I in a round of negotiations that ended in a ratified treaty. That tentative political relationship was significantly advanced in 1540 when Desmond's kinsman, Gerald Fitzgerald, became the first Irish aristocrat to seek political refuge in France, generating intrigue and lively diplomatic response in the process. Throughout the mid-1540s, during the next Anglo-French war, the intrigue amounted to little more than unsubstantiated rumours of collusion between the French and Gerald Fitzgerald to launch a French invasion on Ireland which ran rife in both countries.

Then, in the winter of 1549–50, the whole nature of Franco-Irish intrigue suddenly grew profoundly serious as two senior-ranking French diplomats met in Ulster with the province's leading Gaelic lord, Con O'Neill amongst others, and engaged in several weeks of intense negotiations to discuss the

---

[44] See Brendan Bradshaw, *The Irish constitutional revolution of the sixteenth century*, Cambridge 1979.

logistics of extending the French campaign in Scotland into Ireland. In the event, nothing came of these talks. While a number of 'diehards' strove to maintain the momentum that had preceded the 1549–50 Ulster negotiations by continually lobbying Henri II for support, within two years they realised that their efforts were in vain. Consequently, throughout the 1550s and early 1560s, Franco-Irish intrigue reverted to speculation and scaremongering as manifest in constant rumblings of imminent French or joint French-Scottish attacks on Ireland. These reports assumed significantly graver proportions in 1566–7 when Shane O'Neill, at the height of his power, posing a serious threat to English authority in Ireland and to British security, addressed formal solicitations for military support to the French crown and the Guise faction. However, O'Neill's assassination in 1567 immediately and decisively terminated that engagement.

Following his declaration of rebellion in 1569, James Fitzmaurice Fitzgerald, like Shane O'Neill, sought the backing of the French crown and the Guise faction, initially through the agency of envoys and later by personal representations at the court. Supporters of the Guise dynasty provided him with the only significant assistance given an Irish lord by any French party. The fact that Fitzmaurice and his team of emissaries proved such able negotiators, capable of persuading Catholic continental leaders to lend military support to his cause, taught Elizabeth I and her councillors that they could no longer afford to dismiss reports of continental intrigue as unsubstantiated propaganda. By the time Brian Macgeoghegan and William Nugent, two exiled Irish conspirators, made personal representations for their cause at the French court in the early 1580s it was already clear that the Escorial was the more promising source of help for disaffected elements in Ireland.

This study shows that, although ultimately fruitless in real military or financial terms, those decades of varying intensity of intrigue between France and Ireland cultivated a very significant, tentative political association between the two countries against formidable odds. Their contacts expanded mutual awareness and knowledge in terms of their respective political *milieus*. They brought the French and Bretons into direct personal contact with Anglo-Irish and Gaelic lords who for the first time were given a hearing as they articulated in person their causes and grievances. They trained these lords and their envoys in the protocol that governed bargaining for assistance at the French court. As the sixteenth century progressed, the Anglo-Irish and the Gaelic Irish also realised the indispensable value of harnessing the Catholic Counter-Reformation cause and its rhetoric as a means of generating continental support for their campaigns of resistance against a Protestant monarch.

For their part, successive French monarchs, along with leading government, ambassadorial and military officials were awakened to the potential usefulness of the Irish as levers with which to apply pressure on the Tudor *régime*, particularly during the various wars with England. In their involvement with Irish dissidents, they also demonstrated a rudimentary though fundamentally accurate grasp of the essentials of Irish politics and society by harnessing two potent propaganda weapons in negotiations, namely, the Geraldine cause and the preservation of the Catholic faith. In response to the approaches of these lords and their emissaries, the French were forced to consider seriously the logistics of an invasion and in all but one case, they were ultimately resigned to the political and military impracticality of such designs. Moreover, as this study illustrates, a variety of 'external' factors impinged upon Ireland's evolving political relationship with France. The most important of these were the fluctuating strength of the Auld Alliance between Scotland and France, the vicissitudes of the Guise faction, variations in French interest and involvement in Scotland, the strength of alliances between Gaelic elements in Ulster and the Scottish Highlands, and changes in relations within the British and wider international contexts. The ramifications of each of these contingencies for determining the outcome to Irish complicity with the French are therefore assessed.

In its most serious manifestations Franco-Irish intrigue may also be seen to have exerted a significant catalytic effect on English strategies in respect of the governance and defence of Ireland and, by implication, the British Isles. When it took the form of direct substantive negotiations for orchestrating a French invasion as in 1522–3, 1549–50 and the mid-1570s, it spurred lords deputy and members of the Irish council to appeal for additional revenue and naval forces in the event of a French attack and provided them with added impetus to suppress associated domestic uprisings or conspiracies quickly and effectively. When the privy council and the lord deputy and council in Ireland assumed different stands in response to threats of French invasion, as occurred most dramatically during the crisis of the Desmond rebellions in the 1570s in particular, Franco-Irish intrigue became a divisive issue in the increasingly antagonistic factional politics of the English court and of the Dublin administration.

VI

This study of Franco-Irish relations in the sixteenth century incorporates a limited examination of the formation of the French elite's perceptions of Ireland and of its inhabitants over the course of the century. Apart from a handful of French pilgrims, including aristocrats and ecclesiastics, who visited St Patrick's Purgatory at Lough Derg in north-west Ulster in the sixteenth century, French elite society in general had little knowledge of Ireland or of its inhabitants beyond that garnered from scholarly works.[45] The

---

[45] *Annála ríoghachta Éireann: Annals of the kingdom of Ireland by the Four Masters from the earliest period to the year 1616*, ed. and trans. John O'Donovan, 5 vols, Dublin 1846–51, iii. 1335; *Annála Uladh: Annals of Ulster . . . : a chronicle of Irish affairs, 431–1131, 1155–1541,*

superficial and impressionistic character of the representations of Ireland and the Irish in circulation within French literate society is exemplified in an account penned by Gilles le Bouvier in the 1450s.[46] His description projected an image of a country that was wild, alien and utterly peripheral to the rest of western Europe. Ireland was, he believed, a country of marshes and without roadways.

Yet le Bouvier did have a grasp of some of the more salient features of Gaelic society. He was aware, for example, of the clear distinction that existed between the large number of independent lords and the handful of 'rois' in Gaelic Ireland, and observed the importance of cattle and land as measures of a lord's wealth. He was also apprised of the hostility that prevailed between Gaelic and English elements on the island, and remarked that English merchants tended to limit their commercial transactions to the Pale towns since the greater part of the country was, as he put it, at war with the English. The Gaelic population was portrayed as primitive, living only on meat and fish and having no use for clothes, plates, pots, pans or money. They were also believed to have had no profession by which to earn a living and Le Bouvier was acquainted with the Gaelic practice of booleying whereby families lived in temporary 'houses' while they accompanied their cattle herds in search of grazing.

The works of François Rabelais and Michel de Montaigne, two of France's most celebrated literary figures of the sixteenth century, exposed the French elite to cameo representations of the Gaelic Irish that affirmed such broadly negative perceptions. Rabelais deliberately seized upon the figure synonymous with Ireland in French consciousness, the Gaelic soldier. The reader was presented with a caricature of Irishmen as valiant but vile soldiers while Montaigne depicted the Irish as quasi-barbaric by virtue of their penchant for going naked.[47] However, in tandem with increasingly detailed diplomatic intelligence concerning Ireland, the sixteenth- and early seventeenth-century vogue for commentaries on foreign cultures was instrumental in beginning the process of deepening the French elite's awareness and knowledge of the Gaelic Irish. Since there is no record of any French scholar having visited Ireland in this period, French readers appear to have relied upon works written about Ireland by English authors. Yet their dependence upon

ed. W. M. Hennessy and Bartholomew MacCarthy, 4 vols, Dublin 1887–1901, iii. 521; Annála Connacht: the Annals of Connacht, A.D. 1224–1544, ed. A. M. Freeman, Dublin 1944, 630; François Rabelais, Les Oeuvres de maistre François Rabelais, ed. Ch. Marty-Laveaux, 6 vols, Paris 1868–1903, i. 13; iii. 138; iv. 70–7.
46 'Le livre de la description des pays de Gilles Le Bouvier, dit Berry', BN, MS Fr. 5873 (ancien fonds); Le Livre de la description des pays de Gilles Le Bouvier, dit Berry, ed. E. T. Hamy, Paris 1908, 122–3.
47 Oeuvres de Rabelais . . ., ii. 510; Michel de Montaigne, Les Essais, ed. Fortunat Strowski, 5 vols, New York 1981, i. 164.

translations of works by such celebrated English writers as William Camden was not without its problems. In addition to learning about the physique, temperament, morality, personal hygiene, marital arrangements, child-rearing practices and military prowess of the Gaelic Irish, the French reader inherited the moralistic ideological overtones of these English authors, most of whom viewed Gaelic civilisation in purely negative terms as is evident in their lengthy commentaries on the supposedly idle, immoral, superstitious, uncouth and un-Christian features of the Gaelic character.[48]

The period 1500 to 1610 witnessed Franco-Irish relations evolve from being exclusively and traditionally based on trade and the small-scale migration of soldiers and pilgrims which continued at a modest level, through a short phase of unprecedented political intrigue between the 1520s and 1580s, to a reversion to traditional contacts in the early seventeenth century with an increase in trade and the French population's engagement with an unprecedented influx of Irish migrants into France. In spite of the greater exposure of French elite society to the Gaelic Irish and the Anglo-Irish that came about as a result of increased trade, the development of political contacts and more ready access to scholarly commentaries on contemporary Ireland, the vast majority of the French elite still knew very little about the country or its inhabitants in the early seventeenth century. Fragmentary details that filtered through to elite circles from mariners' intelligence reports, from direct contacts with Irish mariners in the French courts of admiralty or from encounters with individual Irish soldiers, pilgrims, visitors or criminals over the course of the sixteenth century, and the urban authorities' dealings with large bands of Irish immigrants in the early 1600s, only served to corroborate the negative impression conveyed in late medieval scholarly tracts and perpetuated in sixteenth- and seventeenth-century commentaries that typically drew heavily on the twelfth-century Welsh commentator, Giraldus Cambrensis's hostile portrayal of Ireland and the Irish.[49]

During and in the immediate aftermath of the Nine Years' War in Ireland the unprecedented arrival of several thousand Irish migrants in France represented a watershed in Franco-Irish relations in the early modern period. Previously the French elite relied on scholarly works and isolated encounters with individual Irish persons to satisfy their anthropological curiosity regarding the lifestyle of the Irish whom they viewed at a distance with superior fascination as an alien, exotic race. Suddenly, within the space of a decade, France's municipal, provincial and national authorities, its urban-based aristocracy, and even members of the royal family and some of the populace at large were exposed to unprecedented direct contact with large numbers of Gaelic men, women and children, all of whom lived in

[48] For a detailed discussion of French exposure to English commentaries on Gaelic Ireland and its inhabitants see Lyons, 'Franco-Irish relations', ch. vi.
[49] Ibid.

squalor on the streets of their cities and towns. What was remarkable about the elite's response was the extent to which, in spite of the development of Franco-Irish relations during the preceding century, their impressions corroborated the negative image of Ireland and of the Irish that had long been in circulation in *ancien régime* France.

1

'Vain Imagination': The French Dimension to Geraldine Intrigue, 1523–1539

The first half of the sixteenth century witnessed the tentative beginnings of direct political relations between Ireland and France in the form of a French dimension to the intrigues of the Anglo-Irish Geraldine dynasty. During this period, leading members of the Geraldine family of Desmond and Kildare mounted campaigns in opposition to the English crown and in the process sought the assistance of François I (1494–1547). James Fitzgerald, tenth earl of Desmond (d. 1529), was the first Irish magnate to engage in serious intrigue with the French crown in the early 1520s. In 1540 his kinsman, Gerald Fitzgerald, heir to the earldom of Kildare then in abeyance following his half-brother's rebellion (1534–5), sought temporary asylum in France. His status as a leading Anglo-Irish magnate and as a figurehead of Ireland's first nation-wide coalition gained him an hospitable reception at the hands of the French authorities and ensured his safe passage through France into Flanders while exerting a modest strain on Anglo-French relations. In the longer term, it gave rise to his being invested with a pivotal role in French war propaganda during the 1540s. This deliberately contrived scaremongering was effective in playing upon one of the greatest fears of the Whitehall and Dublin administrations in relation to Ireland – a revival of the Geraldine interest, backed by the French and possibly the Scots. Through their intrigues the Fitzgeralds therefore furnished the French with legitimising causes for possible intervention in Ireland during the two Anglo-French wars in the 1520s and in the mid-1540s.

I

When François I ascended to the French throne on New Year's Day 1515, the politics of the British Isles were the least of his concerns. Rather, his immediate preoccupation was the vindication of the French crown's rights in Italy. Yet seven years later, the exigencies of continental politics propelled him to engage in intrigue with the tenth earl of Desmond amongst others to undermine the Tudor *régime* in England. The death of King Ferdinand of Aragon in 1516 and of the Holy Roman Emperor, Maximilian I, in 1519 created the prospect of a vast accumulation of territories under the sceptre of one ruler with ancestral claims to Burgundy. Following the accession of Charles of

Habsburg, duke of Burgundy and heir to Castille, as Holy Roman Emperor in 1519, François suspected the emperor of aiming at universal domination, a *monarchie* of all Christendom. Consequently, between Charles's election in 1519 and his abdication in 1556, European politics revolved around the single axis of the Habsburg–Valois diplomatic and military struggle, into which England, Italy, Germany and even the Turks were drawn. François turned his attention northwards to England and in 1518 actively sought Henry VIII's support. However, with the balance of power favouring Charles, Henry resolved to throw in his lot with the emperor and in 1522, a year after François deliberately provoked war with Charles, an Anglo-French war commenced.[1]

François I adopted a 'British strategy' in planning the French offensive against England. He identified England's strategically vulnerable peripheral possessions of Scotland and Ireland as the Tudors' Achilles' heel: while he would aim to reclaim England's possessions in France, the Scots and the French would invade England and the Irish would stage a rebellion. From 1522 onwards Henry VIII and François I each sought to undermine the other's authority by cultivating the allegiance of disaffected subjects within the other's realm. Henry cultivated the French constable, Charles, duc de Bourbon. The French king looked to Scotland and Ireland in an effort to capitalise on the reinvigorated Auld Alliance in the case of the first and on internecine dissension in the second.[2] His first step was to reaffirm the Auld Alliance with Scotland in November 1521 by granting the duke of Albany (the heir presumptive to the Scottish throne) permission to return to Scotland.[3] Upon the duke's arrival, the queen mother, Margaret, sister to Henry VIII, defected to his party, leaving the English king without support at the Scottish court. In the summer of 1522 Albany mustered an army to invade England, but a lack of support from the Scottish nobility forced him to abandon his campaign and sign a truce with Lord Dacre in September. Frustrated by the failure of his designs, Albany left for France, intent upon raising an army and the necessary finance to launch a second offensive on England.

[1] G. R. Elton, *England under the Tudors*, 2nd edn, London 1989, 92–3; F. C. Spooner, 'The Hapsburg–Valois struggle', in Elton, *New Cambridge modern history*, ii. 334–58; Peter Gwyn, 'Wolsey's foreign policy: the conferences at Calais and Bruges reconsidered', *HJ* xxiii (1980), 755–72; Head, 'Henry VIII's Scottish policy', 5; R. J. Knecht, *French Renaissance monarchy: Francis I and Henry II*, New York 1984, 35–6; Richard Bonney, *The European dynastic states, 1494–1660*, Oxford 1991, 100–1; Garrisson, *Sixteenth-century France*, 137–45; Potter, *History of France*, 264–7.
[2] J. J. Scarisbrick, *Henry VIII*, 4th edn, London 1970, 127–30; Head, 'Henry VIII's Scottish policy', 7; William Palmer, *The problem of Ireland in Tudor foreign policy, 1485–1603*, Woodbridge 1994, 35.
[3] The Auld Alliance was reaffirmed by James IV in 1492 and had been renewed in 1512. See Norman MacDougall, *The Stewart dynasty in Scotland: James IV*, East Lothian 1997, 82–3, 87, 91, 192, 200, 207–8, 250, 252–3, 256.

Following Albany's failure in the autumn of 1522, François I gave serious consideration to overtures which he had received from the Anglo-Irish lord, James Fitzgerald, tenth earl of Desmond. In several respects Desmond appeared a suitable ally. He was head of the Munster branch of the Anglo-Irish Geraldine dynasty that had been staunch Yorkist supporters throughout the fifteenth century. He enjoyed a reputation in continental circles as one of the principal magnates in Ireland. Although the French political elite's knowledge of Ireland was extremely limited in the early 1500s, Desmond was one of the few lords known to a minority of them. More pertinently, he was known to have had an extensive patrimony and considerable resources. The French were aware of the strategic potential of Desmond's lordship and especially the ports of Youghal, Kinsale and Cork in the event of their launching an attack on England via Ireland. They also knew that having been alienated from the Irish council since 1520, when he had been accused of excessive reliance on the advice of Irishmen and of being in breach of terms agreed with the council, Desmond was eager to exploit the recent outbreak of hostilities between England and France by initiating serious negotiations with François I.[4] The earl's motive for involvement in this and subsequent continental intrigue was his desire to end English rule in Ireland, to remove Henry VIII from the throne and to have his seigneurial grievances addressed, while François used the threat of rebellion in Ireland as part of his strategy to win the Anglo-French war.

As this engagement with François I and his subsequent negotiations with Charles V demonstrate, Fitzgerald displayed an aptitude for framing his solicitations in a manner that made an alliance with him appear an advantageous strategic move in the interests of François or Charles. He was also keenly sensitised to the need to present continental rulers with well-formulated proposals to invade Ireland in terms that would convince them that to do so would be vital in a strategy for a large-scale invasion of the British Isles. The earl initiated contact by dispatching his emissary, Anthony Daly, to the French court, probably in 1522.[5] Desmond directly requested that a French army be sent to Ireland and promised that, with their combined forces, they would subjugate the entire country to the French crown. In response,

---

[4] The earl of Surrey and the council of Ireland to Henry VIII, *LP Henry VIII*, iii/1 (1519–23), 989; *SP Henry VIII*, ii. 46–7; Surrey to Cardinal Thomas Wolsey, 25 Sept. 1520, *LP Henry VIII*, iii/1 (1519–23), 990; *SP Henry VIII*, ii. 47; Surrey and the council of Ireland to Wolsey, 6 Oct. 1520, *LP Henry VIII*, iii/1 (1519–23), 1011; *SP Henry VIII*, ii. 50; Surrey to Wolsey, 3 Nov. 1520, *LP Henry VIII*, iii/1 (1519–23), 1037; *SP Henry VIII*, ii. 57. See also 'Annales breves Hiberniae, auctore Thaddaeo Dowling', in *The annals of Ireland by Friar John Clyn and Thady Dowling, together with the Annals of Ross*, ed. Richard Butler, Dublin 1849, 34.

[5] Declaration of Robert Cowley, 1538, *Calendar of the Carew manuscripts preserved in the archiepiscopal library at Lambeth, 1515–1624*, 6 vols, London 1867–73, 144; Richard Bagwell, *Ireland under the Tudors: with a succinct account of the earlier history*, 3 vols, London 1885–90. i. 181.

François dispatched an envoy to Ireland on three occasions. Posing as a merchant, he made arrangements with Desmond to supply an army with victuals and the French king was reported to have lent his financial support to this venture.[6] François I had four French commissioners draw up a formal treaty at Saint-Germain-en-Laye on 4 March 1523, setting out his terms and those of the earl of Desmond. He then dispatched François de Candale, comte d'Oisy, and François de Bergagni to meet with Desmond in his castle at Askeaton, where the earl sealed the agreement on 20 June.[7]

By the terms of this, the only treaty to come of sixty years of Franco-Irish intrigue, Desmond bound himself to declare war against Henry VIII, on condition that François I would not finalise any peace pact with England that did not provide for the earl, Theodoric O'Brien, and his nephews.[8] In the event of an English attack on Ireland, the French king pledged to defend his Irish allies. The French were also to acquire the southern ports of Youghal, Kinsale and Cork as guarantees of Desmond's *bona fides*. The earl was intent upon harnessing French backing for his own agenda, requiring that François I should support him in punishing those within his patrimony who refused to pay their seigneurial dues. The king was also expected to provide Desmond and his seneschal, David MacMorice, with pensions. For his part, Desmond agreed to field and command 4,000 horse and 10,000 foot soldiers. If the earl managed to muster 15,000 infantry, François would provide two angelots of gold for all properly armed troops, and one angelot each for the kerne (Gaelic foot soldiers) equipped with a sword and a lance. Desmond was obliged to supply the horses for the artillery. Significantly, although the earl had requested that French troops be dispatched to Ireland, François gave no such undertaking in the agreement, limiting his commitment to financial support.[9]

François needed a rationale for invading Ireland as part of his grander British strategy for staging an attack on England and replacing Henry Tudor. He therefore revived the cause of Richard de la Pole, the much-feared Yorkist claimant to the English crown, just as Louis XII had done during the war with England in the early 1510s.[10] As distinct from subsequent contacts between Irish lords and the French crown, this first engagement was a closing chapter

---

6 'A letter of news', n.d., *LP Henry VIII*, iii/2 (1519–23), 2799.
7 'Articles agreed upon between François Ier, king of France and James, earl of Desmond for making war against Henry VIII', BL, MS Cotton Titus B.XI (extract) (NLI, n. 3642, p. 3260); 'Traité d'alliance entre le roy François premier et Jacques, comte de Eymonie [Desmond], prince en Hybernie, contre le roy d'Angleterre', 1523, MS Add. 30,666 (NLI, n. 861, p. 743); pact between Francis I and earl of Desmond, 20 June 1523, *LP Henry VIII*, iii/2 (1519–23), 3118. See also William Wise to Thomas Cromwell, 12 July 1534, *LP Henry VIII*, vii (1534), 971; *SP Henry VIII*, ii/3, 198–9n.
8 Desmond tabled a similar condition in his negotiations with Charles V in April 1529: Gonçalo Fernandez to Charles V, 28 Apr. 1529, *LP Henry VIII*, iv/3 (1529–30), 5501.
9 Ibid.
10 See *DNB* xlvi (1896), 46–7.

in late medieval dynastic politics, aimed at the assertion of the Yorkist claims to the English throne to which the father of the tenth earl of Desmond had been a party in lending support to Perkin Warbeck in the 1490s.[11] Yet the 1522–3 plot was distinct from previous Yorkist challenges to the Tudors in that it drew the French crown and a leading Anglo-Irish lord into a direct formal alliance, the first and only one of its kind in the sixteenth century.

In 1522 François received Pole at court in Paris, whilst he entertained the Scottish agent, the duke of Albany, at that time actively engaged in preparations for what turned out to be another unsuccessful attack on England from Scotland.[12] The centrality of Pole as a figurehead in François I's 'British strategy' is clearly evident in his deployment of Pole's kinsman, François de Foix, comte de Candale (Kendalle), to officiate at the signing of the Franco-Irish treaty at Askeaton in June 1523.[13] In summer 1523, while Desmond awaited a signal from François I to commence hostilities, preparations were afoot in France for Pole and the duke of Albany to launch a two-pronged joint invasion of England, aimed at dethroning Henry Tudor and crowning Pole as Richard IV, the legitimate king of England. Albany was to lead the offensive from Scotland while Pole launched a direct attack from Brittany but although both departed France in September, neither campaign was ultimately successful.[14]

Meanwhile in Ireland, Desmond was left without any direction from the French king who refused to advance plans for an invasion of Ireland unless at the very least a simultaneous invasion of England via Scotland could be arranged. This delay had a detrimental effect on the prospect of French intervention in Ireland. While Desmond remained eager to press ahead with his own campaign, backed by the French, it became increasingly difficult for him to do so as he came under severe pressure from the lord deputy, Piers Butler, eighth earl of Ormond, who led a campaign against the rebel earl. This caused Desmond to divert his financial and military resources into a defensive

---

11 Jean-Didier Chastelain, *Imposture de Perkin Warbeck*, Brussels 1952, 29; Ellis, *Ireland in the age of the Tudors*, 87–92. While the earl of Desmond publicly demonstrated his support for Warbeck, the eighth earl of Kildare was much more covert in his backing for the pretender.

12 *DNB* xlvi (1896), 46–7.

13 Fernandez to Charles V, 28 Apr. 1529, *LP Henry VIII*, iv/3 (1529–30), 5501; *Dictionnaire de la noblesse*, comp. François-Alexandre Aubert de la Chenaye-Desbois and [?] Badier, 3rd edn, viii, Paris 1866, 180–1. According to the imperial envoy, Gonçalo Fernandez, Desmond regarded Candale as his Breton kinsman and the envoy described Candale as being from near Bordeaux and a member of the French king's army (he had served in the Italian wars). Candale was a direct descendent of Jean de Foix, comte de Candale (d. 1485) who was married to Marguerite de la Pole-Suffolk, countess of Candale in England and daughter of Richard, duke of Suffolk and of Marie of Sicily: *Dictionnaire de la noblesse*, viii. 176ff; *Dictionnaire de la biographie française*, comp. Prevost d'Amat and Roman d'Amat, fasc. xxxvii, Paris 1954, 1027.

14 *DNB* xlvi (1896), 47; Head, 'Henry VIII's Scottish policy', 7–8.

campaign.[15] The protracted nature of Desmond's negotiations with the French was also harmful as it led to the discovery by the Irish council of the planned attack on Ireland which deprived the latter of its essential element of surprise. It also exerted a catalytic impact on the council's dealings with the earl, affording the lord deputy and council a vital opportunity to monitor his manoeuvres from a relatively early stage in his negotiations with the French.[16]

Notwithstanding this diversion of his attention and resources and his awareness of the mounting stakes hinging on his involvement in this intrigue, Desmond continued to hold out vain hopes of French assistance. However, a series of events overtook François's crumbling scheme for launching a three-pronged attack on England via Ireland, France and Scotland. In May 1524, nine months after his second abortive offensive against England, a disillusioned duke of Albany again left Scotland for France. The following February Richard de la Pole, the legitimising focus for French designs against England, was killed at the battle of Pavia.[17] More critically, in August 1525, the Anglo-French war ended and in May of the following year, that peace was copper-fastened by the Treaty of Cognac. Throughout the following seventeen years Anglo-French relations remained stable and relatively amicable. The French immediately abandoned all designs on England, leaving Desmond cut adrift to face the censure of the English king and to seek assistance from an alternative source. The earl proved equally swift, pragmatic and utilitarian in his response to the failed outcome to this episode. Undeterred by his having been attainted for his conspiratorial involvement with the French, in April 1529 he redirected his solicitations to the imperial court and promised Charles V's emissary, Conçalo Fernandez, 'henceforth to hold the French as enemies, as they were enemies to the emperor'.[18]

François may genuinely have hoped to realise his ambition of overthrowing Henry VIII by means of a grand 'British strategy'. However, it is more likely that his true intentions only stretched so far as using Desmond, Albany and Pole as parties to his more limited and realistic strategy, the object of which was to help achieve victory in war by preying on English inse-

---

[15] Articles alleged by the earl of Ormond against the earl of Desmond, 23 May 1525, *LP Henry VIII*, iv/1 (1524–6), 1352; *SP Henry VIII*, ii. 120–4.

[16] Palmer, *Problem of Ireland*, 37.

[17] *DNB* xlvi (1896), 47; Head, 'Henry VIII's Scottish policy', 8.

[18] The lord deputy and council to the king, Wolsey and others (after 10 Nov. 1522 and before 18 June 1529), *CSP Ireland, 1509–1573*, 7; act of attainder against James, earl of Desmond (to take effect from 10 Nov. 1523), *LP Henry VIII*, iv/2 (1526–8), 3818; Fernandez to Charles V, 28 Apr. 1529, *LP Henry VIII*, iv/3 (1529–30), 5501. For discussions of French relations with England during this period see Potter, 'Diplomacy in the mid-sixteenth century', and Richardson, 'Anglo-French relations'. See also D. M. Downey, 'Culture and diplomacy: the Spanish–Habsburg dimension in the Irish counter-Reformation movement, *c.* 1529–*c.* 1629', unpubl. PhD diss. Cambridge 1994, 3–32, which examines in detail Desmond's negotiations with Fernandez, and the earl's correspondence with Charles V.

curities regarding the defence of the British Isles. This is evident in the poor planning of Albany's and Pole's expeditions. More significantly, it is apparent in François I's half-hearted readiness to proceed with his plans in the naive belief that only Desmond and a handful of his allies could stage a rebellion in Ireland, and in his abandoning of his seditious designs against Henry once the peace treaty was signed in 1526.

In spite of its failure, when set within the context of broader Franco-Irish relations in the sixteenth century, the 1522–3 negotiations and agreement represented a significant point of departure in several key respects. This was the first and only occasion on which a formal enrolled treaty was agreed between the Irish and the French in the sixteenth century. It was the first of only three occasions during that century when French envoys are known to have been dispatched officially to conduct negotiations with Irish lords.[19] Desmond's active collusion with the French was distinctive by virtue of the fact that he and Albany undertook to mount simultaneous though separate offensives against England from Ireland and Scotland respectively. He negotiated directly with François I rather than under the aegis of French officials in Scotland and although he was apprised of plans for the invasion of England from Scotland, Desmond's plans were not predicated on a co-ordinated extension of a campaign from Scotland into Ireland as envisaged in the late 1540s, the early 1550s and the mid-1560s. Desmond's presentation of his proposals is also unique when compared with later episodes of Franco-Irish intrigue. At a time when the Guise faction, which was to be the key target of Irish solicitations for aid in subsequent decades, was as yet unheard of at the French court, it was the French king and French Yorkist sympathisers to whom he addressed his appeals for assistance.

Desmond's strategy was also unusual and particularly farsighted in that he only admitted a handful of Irish lords as parties to the 1523 agreement. This had the advantage of presenting François with a coterie of Irish lords, united under Desmond's control, with whom the French could readily collaborate. In so doing, he avoided the problem later encountered by the O'Connors, the O'Neills and the O'Donnells who failed to overcome French reservations regarding irreconcilable divisions within the ranks of the Gaelic Irish during the intrigues of 1549–50 and 1566–7. Furthermore, by virtue of its timing, the 1522–3 episode bore the last vestiges of medieval intrigue, as its propaganda lacked the invocation of a religious cause that characterised encounters between the French and the Irish from the early 1540s onwards. Finally, François's dalliance with Desmond had long-term ramifications for France's political relations with Ireland as it acquainted the French with the country's most powerful Anglo-Irish dynasty, the Geraldines of Desmond and of

---

[19] The second occasion was when a French nobleman, Theobald de Bois, visited Tyrconnell in 1543, and the third was a diplomatic mission to Ulster led by Jean de Monluc and Beccarie de Pavie, baron de Fourquevaux, in 1549–50.

Kildare, who remained central parties to French intrigue down to the mid-1580s.

François's engagement with the earl of Desmond also manifested the characteristics of subsequent episodes in Franco-Irish intrigue in several key respects. During the Anglo-French war François adopted a British offensive strategy in applying pressure on England, which, its failure notwithstanding, was continued and brought even closer to realisation by François's successor, Henri II, in the late 1540s and 1550s. Desmond's failure to realise his plans for a French invasion of Ireland taught him the paramount importance of continental politics in dictating the outcome of Irish intrigue with continental rulers. The French dimension to Desmond's designs in 1522–3 exerted a significant catalytic impact on the Irish council's treatment of the disaffected earl. As this study has shown, the lord deputy and council took immediate steps to suppress the earl's seditious activities by resorting to what were to become tried and tested methods, namely isolating the main conspirator and adopting expedient and relatively inexpensive defence measures to tide them over the crisis. Finally, Desmond's resolve to use French backing to boost his assertion of his seigneurial rights points to the conditional nature of his involvement with the French and intimates that he viewed himself as more than a mere pawn at the hands of continental rulers. The earl's insistence upon the preservation of his privileges as a condition for collaboration with the French was replicated in the agendas of every other Irish lord who sought French intervention in Ireland down to the mid-1580s.

II

Following a seventeen-year period of inactivity, a second phase in Franco-Irish political relations commenced in early 1540 when Gerald Fitzgerald fled to France.[20] The dramatic circumstances that prompted Gerald's exile represent a milestone in the history of the lordship and were well known at both the French and imperial courts.[21] When François learned that Gerald Fitzgerald's half-brother, Silken Thomas, had staged a rebellion in 1534, he was said to have been 'not sorry that the Irish make war upon the king of England', though he was not prepared to fracture his peace with Henry VIII on Fitzgerald's account.[22] Following the capture of the Geraldine fortress at Maynooth in March 1535 Silken Thomas and his five uncles were executed at Tyburn in February 1537, at which time Gerald, who had been ill with

---

[20] See Vincent Carey, *Surviving the Tudors: the 'Wizard' earl of Kildare and English rule in Ireland, 1537–1586*, Dublin 2002, for a detailed account of the life and *milieu* of Gerald Fitzgerald, eleventh earl of Kildare.

[21] See Laurence McCorristine, *The revolt of Silken Thomas: a challenge to Henry VIII*, Dublin 1987.

[22] Quoted ibid. 78.

smallpox at Donore, County Kildare, became heir to his dynasty's shattered inheritance.[23] Having recovered, he was spirited away from Kildare by his tutor, Thomas Leverous, and sought refuge in the homes of Lady Mary O'Connor, Lady Mary O'Carroll and in the O'Dunnes country before being moved on to Thomond where he stayed for several months under the protection of Conor O'Brien. There he was joined by James Delahide, a priest named Robert Walsh who subsequently accompanied him to the continent, and other supporters. Fearing for the boy's safety, O'Brien dispatched him along with Leverous and Delahide to Kilbrittan castle in Desmond's patrimony where he came directly under the protection of his aunt, Lady Eleanor MacCarthy. In the summer of 1538 Eleanor took Gerald, Leverous, Delahide and Walsh with her to Donegal and from there he escaped to France in late February or early March 1540.[24]

Convinced that the aggressive campaign of the new lord deputy, Leonard Grey, to extend royal authority throughout Gaelic quarters of the country during the period 1537–40 heralded the king's intention to undertake widespread conquest, the leading Gaelic magnates of the lordship reacted by forming a loose confederation, led by Eleanor MacCarthy's new husband, Manus O'Donnell, that has been misleadingly called the Geraldine League. Though Gerald's restoration and Grey's recall were its ostensible objectives, the confederation was essentially a Gaelic movement. The emergence of the league was a cause of serious concern to Grey and the Irish council, not least because the alliance between Con O'Neill, O'Connor Sligo and Manus O'Donnell represented a departure from the traditional dynastic alignments within Gaelic politics. The involvement of O'Brien of Thomond, O'Connor Faly and several other lesser chiefs resulted in the league assuming the proportions of a 'national' movement.[25]

In the historiographical treatment of this league Gerald Fitzgerald's departure in spring 1540 is typically referred to, and thereafter any discussion of his continental exile is relegated to biographical accounts, the narrative resuming with his return to Ireland as an adult in the 1550s.[26] While recent

---

[23] See Colm Lennon, *Sixteenth-century Ireland: the incomplete conquest*, Dublin 1994, chs iii–iv; Ellis, *Ireland in the age of the Tudors*, chs iv-vi; Mary Ann Lyons, *Gearóid Óge Fitzgerald, ninth earl of Kildare*, Dundalk 1998, and *Church and society in county Kildare, c. 1470–c. 1547*, Dublin 2000.

[24] See Brian Fitzgerald, *The Geraldines: an experiment in Irish government, 1169–1601*, London 1951, 230–4.

[25] Ellis, *Ireland in the age of the Tudors*, 148–9.

[26] For discussions of the league see Bagwell, *Tudors*, i. 248; Philip Wilson, *The beginnings of modern Ireland*, Dublin 1912, 225–7; Fitzgerald, *The Geraldines*, 236; Augustine Valkenburg, 'A study in diplomacy: Gerald eleventh earl of Kildare, 1525–85', *Journal of the Kildare Archaeological Society* xiv (1968), 296; Bradshaw, *Irish constitutional revolution*, 174–85; Ellis, *Ireland in the age of the Tudors*, 148–9; Ciaran Brady, *The chief governors: the rise and fall of reform government in Tudor Ireland, 1536–88*, Cambridge 1994, 16–23; Lennon, *Sixteenth-century Ireland*, 149–51.

scholarship has shed new light on the composition and motives of the league, Gerald's flight to France had continued to be regarded as essentially tangential to mainstream Irish politics in the 1540s. Analyses of his activities on the continent and those of the league membership in Ireland are divorced from each other. The Geraldine heir is regarded as a figurehead for the league and it is assumed that he automatically lost his status as a potential leader of the confederation once he fled to France. The examination of Gerald's exile has been isolated from analysis of the independent survival of the league in Ireland with the result that there has been no assessment of his role as a propaganda tool in the Franco-Irish intrigue that exerted a catalytic impact on English policy in relation to Ireland in the 1540s and later.

It is certain that a divergence occurred in the objectives pursued by the exiled Geraldine party and those of their former allies in the league in the aftermath of Gerald's flight to France and especially following the withdrawal from the league of the Anglo-Irish Desmond pretender, James FitzJohn. Thereafter, the movement became purely Gaelic in its composition.[27] However, immediately after Gerald's departure for Brittany, the Irish council had no way of knowing that such a split was to occur. Although defeated at Bellahoe in August 1539, the league survived and with Gerald at large seeking the intervention of Henry VIII's continental rivals in support of his cause, the threat to the crown assumed graver proportions. Fearing recriminations for his own botched handling of the Geraldine heir, the boy's uncle, Lord Deputy Leonard Grey, reflected the council's panic-stricken response to the news of his escape to France that broke in March 1540, declaring (however genuinely) that he wished Gerald 'were once in holt [sic], or right out of the word [world]. It should be for the quietness of the king's poor subjects here'.[28] The Dublin administration therefore faced challenges on two fronts, the real military threat posed by the league in the domestic context and the possibility of continental intervention arising from the league's collusion with Cardinal Reginald Pole, the papacy, François I or Charles V.

The resounding defeat inflicted on the league's forces at Bellahoe in August 1539 forced its adherents in Munster and Ulster, and particularly those most closely associated with the Geraldine heir, to recognise that a domestic campaign alone would not bring about the restoration of the boy to his dynastic inheritance.[29] Certainly, the confederation did not collapse following Gerald's departure to France, but instead modified its agenda to suit changing domestic and international circumstances. Equally the exiled Geraldine party did not immediately abandon the league's original ostensible

---

[27] James FitzJohn was recognised as thirteenth earl of Desmond in Janurary 1541: Ellis, *Ireland in the age of the Tudors*, 149.
[28] Lord Deputy Leonard Grey to Cromwell, 17 Mar. 1540, *LP Henry VIII*, xv (1540), 355; *SP Henry VIII*, iii. 193.
[29] Brady, *Chief governors*, 18–25.

key objective, in spite of the fact that soon after their arrival in France they realised that shifting trends in continental diplomacy militated against their achieving that goal in the short term. Gerald's flight to France therefore provided an opportunity for the Geraldine party within the league to pursue that end in other more promising circles while ensuring the young man's safety.

By 1541, however, the league was effectively defunct. Yet the Irish council's concern at a possible French invasion in the period 1544–5 and its efforts to settle terms with former members of that confederation, suggests that the divergence in the agenda of members of the disbanded league in Ireland and of the exiled Geraldine party, which has been clearly identified by historians, was not nearly so obvious to contemporaries. The Geraldine exiles' overtures to the Scottish, French and imperial courts, the hospitable reception afforded them during their sojourn in France, and the failure or refusal of both François and Charles to take adequate steps to ensure their arrest, gave cause for concern and suspicion in both Whitehall and Dublin. The modest diplomatic flurry that ensued once certain intelligence of Gerald's flight to France reached the Irish and English councils testifies to English anxiety concerning the ramifications of the Irish fugitives' appeals to Henry VIII's tenuously allied rivals, François and Charles. Fitzgerald's exile represented the first test of the efficacy of Anglo-French diplomacy in handling the contentious issue of the French monarch's affording refuge to Irish political dissidents and clearly demonstrated the superiority of the French over the English in facilitating his evasion of arrest.

The measures adopted by the administrations in Whitehall and Dublin to capture Gerald and his escorts suggest that Gerald's brief sojourn in France exerted a mild strain on the delicately balanced diplomatic relations between England, France and the Habsburg empire. Cautious handling of the situation by both the Irish and English councils, and their relief at Gerald's eventual resort to Italy following his sojourn in France and Flanders, reflected real concern at Fitzgerald's perceived potential to contribute to the de-stabilisation of the diplomatic balances that Henry VIII strove to maintain with both François and Charles. All three rulers shared that concern, though none more so than Henry. The realisation on the part of both the French king and the emperor of Gerald's potential value as a pawn and as a propaganda weapon in international politics marked an important development in Ireland's relations with France and the Holy Roman Empire in the early 1540s.

Hindsight has led historians automatically to dismiss any serious consideration of the prospect of a French intervention in support of Gerald's cause in the 1540s. Yet down to the mid-1540s, the Irish council's attentions were exercised by the prospect of Gerald's re-emergence as leader of a Gaelic resurgence. More intermittently, its members were apprehensive at the possibility of a French expedition to Ireland in support of the Geraldine cause. Having become acquainted with Gerald Fitzgerald, and having been unintentionally apprised of his importance as a result of the English government's anxiety to have him arrested, the French exploited all opportunities to apply pressure on Henry VIII during the Anglo-French war (1543–6) by encouraging intrigue focused on a French campaign to secure Gerald's restoration.

As this study is primarily concerned with the reaction generated by Gerald's sojourn in France, his flight to the imperial territories is only afforded brief notice. Yet it must be considered since Charles's manipulative representation to Henry VIII of François's handling of the Irish fugitives highlights his efforts to exploit Fitzgerald's refuge in France to undermine François's credibility in Henry's eyes at a time when the alliance between the continental rulers, forged by the truce signed at Nice (1538), was beginning to disintegrate. The change in the league's direction of its foreign solicitations between summer 1538 and 1540, the conduct of the exiled Geraldine party, and the reactions that they triggered in Ireland, England, Scotland and on the continent are only comprehensible within the wider context of continental and British politics prior to, and at the time of, Gerald's arrival in France in March 1540. It was the delicate nature of international relations at that precise juncture that caused Gerald's exile to be afforded such disproportionate importance.

III

Six months after war between France and Charles V ended with the signing of a truce at Nice in June 1538, Cardinal Reginald Pole set out from Rome on a mission to rally the Catholic powers of western Europe to participate in a military offensive against Henry VIII whom he termed a 'most cruel and abominable tyrant'. At the same time Cardinal David Beaton was dispatched from Rome to Scotland with instructions to cultivate the support of James V of Scotland for the planned pan-European Catholic alliance.[30] In the early months of 1539 the proposed offensive campaign against England seemed set to begin, but by late spring the most acute phase of the invasion scare had passed as Pole failed to secure the support of either Charles or François. Between 1538 and 1540 Anglo-French relations were cool though essentially amicable. By virtue of his *entente* with Charles, François was in a sufficiently strong position to spurn English interests while Henry's efforts to forge ties with both Charles and James V of Scotland in the hope of closing this postern gateway to England resulted in his reluctance to antagonise the French.

Within the *milieu* of shifting alliances in European politics during the period 1538–43, attempts by the Geraldines to secure the backing of the Scots, the French king and the emperor in turn became embroiled in a drive by Henry VIII's continental rivals to isolate England. However, their chances

---

[30] Scarisbrick, *Henry VIII*, 361–79.

of securing French backing were minimal as in 1540–1 François was at pains to ingratiate himself with Henry, particularly from April 1540 as French relations with Charles steadily deteriorated. The circumstances surrounding the fugitive Geraldine party's attempt to secure the support of François I therefore contrasted sharply with those that prevailed in the early 1520s when France was at war with England. Significantly, unlike the tenth earl of Desmond, who conducted his negotiations with François in an individual capacity, Gerald Fitzgerald was a figurehead of a near all-Ireland coalition; its object of securing his restoration to dynastic and political ascendancy had 'national' implications.

In Ireland, well before Gerald was spirited off to the continent, and before Cardinal Reginald Pole and Cardinal David Beaton formally commenced their negotiations with Charles, François, James V and others, the league's leadership endeavoured to attach their cause to Pole's scheme for a pan-European Catholic alliance in opposition to Henry. They did so by intensifying their contacts with their traditional allies, the Scots, between early 1538 and late 1539 and in the process caused considerable alarm to the Irish council. It was an opportune time to publicise their grievances as Ireland was high on the list of papal priorities. According to an anonymous account of papal intrigue from early 1538 the pope had resolved to

> mediate for peace between the emperor and the French king, after which he means to have a General council and desire all Christian princes to aid the good Christian people of Ireland . . . and will appeal to the Christian king of France and to the king of Scots for aid as their kingdoms are near Ireland; and whenever the fleet is assembled to go to Barbary, the greater part will go to Ireland to aid of the gentleman [probably Gerald Fitzgerald] who has written to his Holiness against the tyrant of England.[31]

In June Thomas Luttrell and William Brabazon expressed concern at the possibility of Gerald Fizgerald's recommencing war with the aid of Ulster and Scottish lords.[32] Other councillors closely monitored the movements of known Geraldine supporters throughout the summer of 1538, particularly of James Delahide and Bishop Roderick O'Donnell who regularly travelled between Ulster and Scotland.[33]

---

31 Ireland and Rome, 1538, PRO, SP 60/6/9; *LP Henry VIII*, xiii/1 (1538), 77.
32 Sir Thomas Luttrell to Sir Gerald Aylmer, 5 June 1538, SP 60/7/3; *LP Henry VIII*, xiii/1 (1538), 1138; Sir William Brabazon to Aylmer and Sir John Alen, 5 June 1538, *LP Henry VIII*, xiii/1 (1538), 1139; *SP Henry VIII*, iii/3, 18.
33 Grey to Henry VIII, 4 June 1538, *LP Henry VIII*, xiii/1 (1538), 1136; *SP Henry VIII*, iii. 15; Luttrell to Aylmer, 5 June 1538, *LP Henry VIII*, xiii/1 (1538), 1138; Ormond to the council of Ireland, 25 June 1538, *LP Henry VIII*, xiii/1 (1538), 1259; *SP Henry VIII*, iii. 44; Ormond to Cowley, 20 July 1538, *LP Henry VIII*, xiii/1 (1538), 1429; *SP Henry VIII*, iii. 52; Brabazon, Aylmer and Alen to Cromwell, 24 July 1538, *LP Henry VIII*, xiii/1 (1538), 1147; *SP Henry VIII*, iii. 57; Brabazon, Aylmer and Alen to Cromwell, 22 Aug. 1538, *LP Henry VIII*, xiii/2 (1538), 160; *SP Henry VIII*, iii. 87.

It is not clear precisely what plans were envisaged but late in November 1538 the lord chancellor in Ireland, Sir John Alen, was anxious about the intensity of recent contacts between the Scottish lords and Alexander Carragh, captain of the Scots. He was also disturbed by unconfirmed and, as it transpired, unsubstantiated reports that Gerald was in Scotland, planning an invasion of Ireland along with Alexander and Cahir Carragh, and that Con O'Neill and Manus O'Donnell were colluding with the Carraghs and the king of Scotland respectively. Alen's Scottish informer grasped the essence of the Geraldine party's strategy at that time, and his report is proof of a perception amongst contemporaries that the Geraldines were attempting to align themselves with the pan-European alliance aimed at the encirclement of England.[34]

A similar impression is conveyed in an anonymous and wholly impractical proposition presented to Henry VIII in 1538: designed to trap Gerald Fitzgerald, the artifice was predicated on the well-founded assumption that the Geraldines had close links with Cardinal Pole and the papacy.[35] Months before he embarked on his embassy to whip up the support of Catholic rulers against England immediately after Christmas 1538, Cardinal Pole's frequent contact with Gerald Fitzgerald and his Irish supporters had aroused the suspicion of the Irish council.[36] Then, in spring 1539, as Pole and Beaton lobbied for support in Spain, France and Scotland and Henry VIII failed to rupture the alliance between Charles V and François I, the threat to English defences reached its height. The English privy councillors immediately moved to adopt extraordinary defensive measures. Counties were mustered, defence works at Calais, Guines and on the Scottish borders were strengthened, stones from dissolved monastic sites were transported to the coast to build blockhouses, and beacons were prepared. Henry himself toured the coastal defences, supervised the construction of bulwarks and inspected his ships at Portsmouth in anticipation of invasion. Equally mindful of the allies' British strategy for invading England, the Irish council grew increasingly concerned at the overtly Scottish orientation of the Geraldine faction and the associated papal dimension to their intrigue. The situation was rendered all the more urgent by the fact that Gerald's uncle, Lord Deputy Leonard Grey, seemed no closer to capturing the fugitive, while reports circulated that the boy had in fact escaped to Scotland.[37]

[34] Alen to Cromwell, 29 Nov. 1538, *LP Henry VIII*, xiii/2 (1538), 937.
[35] Intrigue against the Fitzgeralds, July [?] 1538, *LP Henry VIII*, xiii/1 (1538), 1516.
[36] Gerald Fitzgerald to Cardinal Reginald Pole, 7 Dec. 1538, *LP Henry VIII*, xiii/2 (1538), 999.
[37] In December of the previous year it had been reported that Gerald Fitzgerald had escaped to Scotland: council of Ireland to Cromwell, 12 Dec. 1538, *LP Henry VIII*, xiii/2 (1538), 1032; *SP Henry VIII*, iii. 108. See also Scarisbrick, *Henry VIII*, 361–2; J. D. Mackie, *A history of Scotland*, 2nd edn, rev. Bruce Lenman and Geoffrey Parker, Middlesex 1978, 133; Head, 'Henry VIII's Scottish policy', 14.

Further fuel was added to the suspicions of Irish councillors in early March when Fitzgerald's personal envoy, Ruoric O'Spellan, was arrested on board a French ship forced to take refuge at South Shields on the north-east England coast.[38] O'Spellan and two other clerics were found to have in their possession 'slanderous letters' from the Irish rebels to the pope and to 'the traitor Pole' which were confiscated. O'Spellan had a letter from Gerald addressed to the cardinal in which Fitzgerald praised his 'uncle' for the kindness he and his associates had shown him, and requested that the cardinal pay close attention to O'Spellan's representations. Also confiscated were several letters from the 'traitor', Roderick O'Donnell, bishop of Derry, addressed to the pope, which expounded on 'the calamities of the papists in Ireland, with sundry traitorous lies' against Henry VIII's officials in Ireland amongst others. When questioned, O'Spellan admitted having previously travelled to Cambray in France to conduct talks with Pole.[39] Alarmed by the discovery of this proof of the suspected involvement of the Irish league in Pole's crusade against Henry, Thomas Cromwell rejoiced at the capture of Gerald's envoy in particular as 'a great hindrance to the Irish rebels'.[40]

To add to the league's difficulties arising from the arrest of one of its key negotiators with Pole and Henry's continental rivals and the associated discovery of their plans, the most acute phase of the invasion scare passed by late spring 1539 as Pole, and by extension, the league failed to secure even a promise of military assistance from either Charles V or François I. Consequently, throughout the early summer months of 1539, Scotland remained the principal target of Irish overtures for military assistance. Though the league's efforts to have its cause incorporated in Pole's intrigue through its alignment with the Scots were closely monitored by the Irish council, the abeyance of the threat of invasion of England was reflected in the councillors' relaxed response to the prospect of a Scottish invasion of Ireland. William Brabazon, the under-treasurer, receiver-general and treasurer at war in Ireland, recommended that a mere two war ships patrolling the sea between

---

[38] The earl of Westmoreland to Cromwell, 7 Mar. 1539, *LP Henry VIII*, xiv/1 (1539), 455; council of the north to Cromwell, 9 Mar. 1539, *LP Henry VIII*, xiv/1 (1539), 481; *SP Henry VIII*, v. 151; Cromwell to Henry VIII, 14 Mar. 1539, *LP Henry VIII*, xiv/1 (1539), 516; *SP Henry VIII*, i/1&2, 598.

[39] Council of the north to Cromwell, 9 Mar. 1539, *LP Henry VIII*, xiv/1 (1539), 481; *SP Henry VIII*, v. 151; Cromwell to Henry VIII, 14 Mar. 1539, *LP Henry VIII*, xiv/1 (1539), 516; *SP Hen. VIII*, i/1, 2, 598.

[40] Cromwell to Henry VIII, 17 Mar. 1539, *LP Henry VIII*, xiv/1 (1539), 538; *SP Henry VIII*, i/2, 601. On 28 April 1539 O'Spellan, Robert Moore and John Macyvaroill were attainted, O'Spellan having been 'set in the brake' in the Tower: attainder of John Macyvaroill, Robert Moore and Roger Aspelan, 28 Apr. 1539, *LP Henry VIII*, xiv/1 (1539), 867.

Ireland and Scotland would suffice to prevent the Scots from coming to the aid of the Irish.[41]

Nevertheless, on the domestic front, by July 1539 the Irish league posed a serious threat to the crown. The earl of Desmond had joined Manus O'Donnell and Con O'Neill in a campaign to 'bring in young Gerald and exclude the king from Ireland'.[42] Sir John Alen, who was acutely sensitised to the international connotations of that domestic threat, was convinced that 'the bishop of Rome is author of this, and the king of Scots an abettor, for messages daily pass from them [the Irish] to Scotland and from thence to Rome'. Disturbed by news that Bishop Roderick O'Donnell, a leading Geraldine supporter, had gone to Scotland and intended travelling from there to Rome, Alen feared that 'if they have outward aid they will also find assistance within the Pale, among Geraldines and papists, by enticement of Friars Obstinates and other religious persons'. A further source of irritation was Connor More O'Connor's boast that the leaders of the Irish league were claiming that the pope, the emperor and the king of France would invade England and that James V of Scotland was set to invade Ulster. Soon, they hoped, Ireland's liberation from English subjugation would be complete with Con O'Neill's proclamation as king of Ireland at Tara in County Meath, seat of the high kings of Ireland.[43]

Although the Geraldine forces continued to pursue their offensive after their defeat at Bellahoe in August 1539, thereafter decisive changes occurred that magnified the impact of that defeat and caused the league leaders to redirect their solicitations for assistance from Scotland to continental Europe, beginning with France.[44] To the detriment of their efforts, Anglo-French relations improved and by the end of the year it was also evident that the crusade proposed by Cardinal Pole and Cardinal David Beaton, leader of Scotland's militant papalist faction, would not materialise. The efforts of the league were further impeded when relations between James V and Henry VIII began to improve significantly towards the end of 1539. This commenced with their exchange of cordial letters, and advanced with Sir Ralph Sadler's visit to Edinburgh in early 1540 when Henry attempted to forge an alliance with James in the hope of sundering the Auld Alliance and foiling the military threat from the Scots in the event of war being declared between François and Charles.[45] Irish hopes for assistance from James were dealt a further blow when Manus O'Donnell, one of the pivotal figures in the

---

[41] Brabazon to Cromwell, 26 May 1539, *LP Henry VIII*, xiv/1 (1539), 1027; *SP Henry VIII*, iii. 133–4. See also Scarisbrick, *Henry VIII*, 362–3, and Palmer, *Problem of Ireland*, 52–3.

[42] Alen to Cromwell, 10 July 1539, *LP Henry VIII*, xiv/1 (1539), 1245; *SP Henry VIII*, iii. 136.

[43] Ibid.

[44] Cowley to Cromwell, 8 Sept. 1539, *LP Henry VIII*, xiv/2 (1539), 137; *SP Hen. VIII*, iii/3, 145.

[45] DNB xlvi (1896), 38; Elton, *England under the Tudors*, 156; Scarisbrick, *Henry VIII*, 364; Head, 'Henry VIII's Scottish policy', 15; Palmer, *Problem of Ireland*, 58.

confederation, abandoned the latter in the winter of 1539–40 by which time he could no longer exert effective control over its membership. O'Donnell's action had serious consequences. Apart from the impact of the loss of his leadership, the league was also cut adrift from the ties that he had established with the Scottish court.[46] Scotland was therefore effectively retired from direct involvement in international intrigue aimed at undermining the Henrician *régime* in England. As such it became a redundant source of military assistance for the league leadership intent on prolonging their campaign in Ireland.

Increasingly disillusioned by the failure of their domestic campaign and of their appeals for foreign aid dating from early 1538, and faced with James V's weakening position *vis à vis* Henry VIII, Gerald Fitzgerald's supporters were forced to turn to the key players on the continental stage as potentially more promising sources of assistance. By the beginning of 1540, a shift away from the Scottish court to those of François I and Charles V was discernible as the Irish were said to have been 'exciting the emperor, French king, and other foreign princes to take their part', though Leonard Grey dismissed their efforts as 'vain imagination'.[47] The league leaders kept abreast of changing alignments in continental politics in their attempts to harness continental support for the Geraldine and wider Irish cause. In this context, it was hardly surprising that France was chosen by the league's former leader, Manus O'Donnell and his wife, as a safe refuge for the exiled Gerald Fitzgerald.[48]

---

46 For Manus's associations with James V see *The letters of James V collected and calendared by the late Robert Kerr Hannay*, ed. Denys Hay, Edinburgh 1954, 275, 339; *Annála ríoghachta Éireann*, v. 1364–5. See also Brendan Bradshaw, 'Manus "The Magnificent": O'Donnell as Renaissance prince', in Art Cosgrove and Donal McCartney (eds), *Studies in Irish history presented to R. Dudley Edwards*, Dublin 1979, 22.

47 Grey and council to Henry VIII, 18 Jan. 1540, *LP Henry VIII*, xv (1540), 82; *SP Henry VIII*, iii/3, 176.

48 Grey to Cromwell, 17 Mar. 1540, *LP Henry VIII*, xv (1540), 355; *SP Henry VIII*, iii. 193. See also James Hogan, *Ireland in the European system*, London 1920, ch. iii, though care must be taken as a number of Hogan's statements are not adequately substantiated by the available evidence.

2

Gerald Fitzgerald's Sojourn in France, 1540

In spring 1540 fears for Gerald Fitzgerald's safety prompted Manus O'Donnell and his wife, Eleanor, to arrange the boy's escape to the continent. Thanks to Manus's characteristic duplicity in concealing his involvement in those arrangements, Eleanor has traditionally been credited with orchestrating her nephew's escape, supposedly on the grounds that she suspected her husband of intending to hand the boy over the English government following his abandonment of the league the previous winter. Manus deflected English suspicions of harbouring Gerald by giving a conditional undertaking to surrender Gerald and his close associate, James Delahide, to Henry VIII in return for a pardon for himself.[1] Yet all the while Gerald and his escorts enjoyed the covert support of the Gaelic chief who undermined the Irish council's efforts to capture them. It was alleged that several people who 'feigned themselves to seek diligently for him [Gerald] in the day time, . . . in the night time . . . were in his company and in O'Donnell's, his uncle, making good cheer and laughing merrily together'.[2] Alain Governors, the Breton shipmaster responsible for conveying the boy to France, testified to O'Donnell's direct input in finalising the travel arrangements.[3] While Governors was in Donegal Bay in late February or early March, Manus approached him, accompanied by several religious (including Leverous and Walsh), and requested that he convey Gerald to Brittany. In accordance with a formal agreement drafted and signed by both parties in the presence of a notary, Governors undertook to conduct Gerald and his escorts to his native port of Saint-Malo. The fugitive, then in his mid-teens, was smuggled on board Governors's ship by night, disguised as 'one of the wild Irish', being bareheaded and wearing only a saffron shirt.[4]

---

[1] Raphael Holinshed, *The historie of Irelande*, continued by Richard Stanihurst, London 1577, 102. See also C. W. Fitzgerald, *The earls of Kildare and their ancestors from 1057 to 1773*, 2nd edn, Dublin 1858, 181–2; Valkenburg, 'A study in diplomacy', 296.

[2] Thomas Barnaby to Henry VIII, 6 Feb. 1541, *LP Henry VIII*, xvi (1540–41), 525; *SP Henry VIII*, iii. 283.

[3] Notice regarding Manus O'Donnell, *LP Henry VIII*, xv (1540), 28; Bartholomew Warner to Sir John Wallop, 22 May 1540, *LP Henry VIII*, xv (1540), 704; *SP Henry VIII*, iii. 211. See also Fitzgerald, *The earls of Kildare*, 192–5, and *Collection of documents relating to Jacques Carrier and the sieur de Roberval*, ed. H. P. Biggar, Ottawa 1930, 84. Brian Fitzgerald (*The Geraldines*, 236) inaccurately states that it was Eleanor who had the contract for Gerald's conveyance drawn up by a notary.

[4] Warner to Wallop, 22 May 1540, *LP Henry VIII*, xv (1540), 704; *SP Henry VIII*, iii/3, 211.

Fitzgerald was accompanied by three men. One was his tutor, Thomas Leverous, 'a priest of fifty winter[s] of age' who 'hath governed him ever since the death of his father' and who exercised stern control over his ward to the extent that 'if he rebuke him never so little, he [Gerald] trembleth for fear'.[5] The second was Robert Walsh.[6] The third man, whom Governors never heard addressed by his name, was almost certainly Darby Gunning of Dublin.[7] The party spent several weeks in France in the late spring and early summer before proceeding to Flanders where they resorted to the imperial court at Brussels. In order to ensure that Gerald evaded capture by the English ambassador to the imperial court, Charles dispatched the party to the palace of the bishop of Liège where he remained for a period of six months and received a monthly allowance of 100 crown from the emperor. From there they travelled to Italy where Gerald and Leverous remained under the protection of Cardinal Pole and the papacy until the late 1540s.[8]

Fitzgerald's flight to France was dictated partly by chance and partly by design. Given that James V of Scotland was no longer sympathetic to the Geraldine cause, France, by virtue of its proximity, was the best alternative. Transportation to France was easy to organise given the regularity with which Breton ships in particular frequented the coast of Donegal and on the strength of Breton seafarers' reports, Brittany was deemed a safe refuge for Gerald. It was also a convenient point for disembarking in the event of the exiled party deciding to proceed to Flanders or Italy.[9] Fitzgerald's conveyance to Saint-Malo is more likely to have been the consequence of Governors's provenance rather than the premeditated destination designated by the O'Donnells. By early 1540 the league had redirected their solicitations away from Scotland to François I and Charles V and it is likely that the O'Donnells were more hopeful of French backing for Gerald's cause owing to that clan's contacts with the French court dating from the early sixteenth century.[10]

---

5   Ibid; Wallop to Cromwell, 18 Apr. 1540, *LP Henry VIII*, xv (1540), 543; *SP Henry VIII*, iii. 326.

6   Warner to Wallop, 22 May 1540, *LP Henry VIII*, xv (1540), 704; *SP Henry VIII*, iii/3, 211. See also Rowley Lascelles, *Liber munerum publicorum Hiberniae*, 2 vols, London 1852, pt v, 41; Michael Comerford, *Collections relating to the diocese of Kildare and Leighlin*, 3 vols, Dublin 1883–6, i. 24–5; Valkenburg, 'A study in diplomacy', 296–7.

7   Attainder of Darby Gunning, 12 Apr. 1540, *LP Henry VIII*, xv (1540), 498; Wallop's certificate for Gunning's capture and conveyance, 1 June 1540, *LP Henry VIII*, xv (1540), 739; John Story to Cromwell, 1 June 1540, *LP Henry VIII*, xv (1540), 741. For descriptions of Fitzgerald's protectors see Wallop to Cromwell, 18 Apr. 1540, *LP Henry VIII*, xv (1540), 543; *SP Henry VIII*, iii. 326–7, and Vincent Noblet's account contained in Barnaby's report to Henry VIII, 6 Feb. 1541, *LP Henry VIII*, xvi (1541), 525; *SP Henry VIII*, iii. 283.

8   See Fitzgerald, *The Geraldines*, 241–4; Valkenburg, 'A study in diplomacy', 297. Leverous was admitted to an English monastery in Rome and Robert Walsh returned to Ireland.

9   The lords of Ulster followed a similar route during the early stages of their exile in October 1607: see ch. 7 below.

10   *Annála ríoghachta Éireann*, iii. 1335; *Annála Uladh*, iii. 521; *Annála Connacht*, 630; AN,

Initially Gerald and his guardians disembarked at Morlaix for three or four days while *en route* to Saint-Malo.[11] During their brief sojourn the captain of Morlaix received them with a show of hospitality, leading the young man by the hand in a procession through the streets of the town. The captain immediately notified the province's lieutenant-general, Jean de Laval Montmorency, sieur de Châteaubriant, of the party's arrival and appointed a Breton, Vincent Noblet, as Gerald's guide prior to his departure for Saint-Malo. However, it soon became apparent that Morlaix was not a suitable refuge for Gerald as several English merchants attempted to gain access to him, forcing Thomas Leverous to insist that the town's captain prevent all Englishmen from approaching his ward.[12]

Gerald and his escorts proceeded to Saint-Malo where they arrived on Palm Sunday. They stayed for five or six days in Governors's house and were feasted every day. The celebrated overseas explorer, Jacques Cartier, who had been appointed their conductor at sea, presented Fitzgerald to the captain of the town who 'welcomed him according to his power'.[13] His being received by Cartier, who had by then attained an international reputation as an overseas explorer, is illustrative of the high regard with which the Geraldine heir was held in the Breton town.[14] Saint-Malo proved a suitable refuge for the exiled Irish aristocrat. Unlike Morlaix, where the young man was readily identified by English merchants, Saint-Malo was a much larger, busier port with more

Paris, J. 960 (3), anc. J. 960, no. 2 (payment to Balthazar Linch). See also *Catalogue des actes de François Ier*, 9 vols, Paris 1887–1907, ii. 33; vii, second supplement, p. 675; Lord Deputy Sir Anthony St Leger to Henry VIII, 29 Aug. 1541, *LP Henry VIII*, xvi. 1127n. The cleric alluded to by St Leger was Conaught O'Siagail, chaplain to O'Donnell. See St Leger to Sir Thomas Wriothesley, 26 Feb. 1545, *SP Hen. VIII*, iii. 506; *LP Henry VIII*, xx/1, 273. See also Lughaigh Ó Cléirigh, *Beatha Aodha Ruaidh Uí Domhnaill. The life of Hugh Roe O'Donnell, prince of Tirconnell (1586–1602)*, trans. with notes and illustrations by Denis Murphy, Dublin 1895, pp. xxvi–xxvii; Hogan, *Ireland in the European system*, 62–3; Bradshaw, 'Manus "The Magnificent" '; Lyons, 'Maritime relations'.

[11] Thomas Treffry to Cromwell, 31 Mar. 1540, *LP Henry VIII*, xv (1540), 426.

[12] Warner to Wallop, 22 May 1540, *LP Henry VIII*, xv (1540), 704; *SP Henry VIII*, iii/3, 211–12.

[13] Wallop to Cromwell, 18 Apr. 1540, *LP Henry VIII*, xv (1540), 543; *SP Henry VIII*, iii. 326–7; Warner to Wallop, 22 May 1540, *LP Henry VIII*, xv (1540), 704; *SP Hen. VIII*, iii/3, 212.

[14] For discussions of Cartier's career see P. F. X. de Charlevoix, *History and general description of New France*, trans. John Gilmary Shea, 6 vols, New York 1866–72, i. 111–14; Bernard Millier, 'Jacques Cartier et la découverte du Canada: le miracle canadien', *ASHAA Saint-Malo* (1973), 61–78; Olga Obry, 'Saint-Malo porte d'un monde nouveau', ibid. (1979), 223–9; Gilles Foucqueron, 'Jacques Cartier, témoin de son temps', ibid. (1984), 121–33; Michel Bideaux, 'Jacques Cartier, découvreur en mission', ibid. (1984), 205–16. On a familial level, and in the sphere of municipal administration, Cartier was a very prominent figure. He ranked among the influential forum of the general assembly of bourgeois of the town and his wife, Catherine des Granges, was the daughter of the constable of Saint-Malo: *Jacques Cartier: documents*, ed. F. Joüon des Longrais, Rennes 1888, Paris 1984 edn, and Philippe Petout, *Hôtels et maisons de Saint-Malo XVIe et XVIIIe siècles*, Paris 1985, 22–3.

far-flung commercial contacts and a cosmopolitan culture.[15] Consequently, Gerald's brief sojourn there went unnoticed by English observers. More significantly, the notables of Saint-Malo actively backed Fitzgerald, with the result that 'in all this country, where he [Gerald] passed, he was . . . named to be king of Ireland' by supporters who declared 'that . . . [Henry VIII] hath disinherited him of his right'.[16]

Having learned that Gerald had arrived at Saint-Malo, the sieur de Châteaubriant dispatched a messenger to Governors's residence along with a horse to convey the boy and his guardians to the town of Châteaubriant on the Tuesday of Easter week. Gerald was then escorted to Châteaubriant by the lieutenant-general's messenger, as well as Jacques Cartier, Alain Governors and several other notables from Saint-Malo.[17] Jean de Laval Montmorency, the sieur de Châteaubriant, was one of the wealthiest men in sixteenth-century France. He had strong ties with the French court which were strengthened by the fact that his wife, Françoise de Foix, countesse de Châteaubriant, was François I's mistress before being superseded by the duchesse d'Etampes.[18] As lieutenant-general he was obliged to interview Fitzgerald and his escorts who had stirred such an animated response within his jurisdiction, and in view of his office and connections with the court, he was an obvious figure to be cultivated by the Geraldines in their efforts to solicit French support for their cause.

Upon his arrival at Châteaubriant, Fitzgerald was afforded an hospitable welcome by municipal officials. The morning after his arrival, the procurator of the town called upon him at his lodgings to welcome him, and invited him to spend the day touring around the town and inspecting their local produce. The sieur de Châteaubriant's messenger, however, refused to allow the Irish party to accept the procurator's invitation as he had been issued with strict instructions to convey them directly to his master's residence where, for the duration of his stay, Gerald was 'well reserved, and served like as should appertain to a man of great estate'.[19] Following their departure from Châteaubriant, details of the Geraldine party's itinerary are obscure and their motives difficult to ascertain.

---

15 André L'Éspagnol, *Histoire de Saint-Malo et du pays malouin*, Toulouse 1984, 99.

16 Warner to Wallop, 22 May 1540, *LP Henry VIII*, xv (1540), 704; *SP Henry VIII*, iii/3, 212.

17 Ibid; Wallop to Cromwell, 18 Apr. 1540, *LP Henry VIII*, xv (1540), 543; *SP Henry VIII*, iii. 326–7.

18 *Biographie universelle (Michaud) ancienne et moderne*, new edn, 45 vols, Paris 1843– , viii (1854), 14–15; Guillotin de Corson, *Les Grands Seigneuries de Haute-Bretagne*, 3rd edn, Rennes 1899, 59.

19 Warner to Wallop, 22 May 1540, *LP Henry VIII*, xv (1540), 704; *SP Henry VIII*, iii/3, 212.

I

While the immediate object of Gerald's transportation to France was clearly to ensure his safety, his escorts' ongoing contacts with Cardinal Pole gave the English authorities cause for concern in respect of his potential involvement in continental conspiracy to undermine Henry VIII's position. On the basis of the available evidence it is virtually impossible to draw definitive conclusions regarding the fugitives' strategy or true intentions during this early phase in their exile. Aside from the fact that no documentary material generated by the Gerald or his escorts has survived, attempts to dispel the ambiguity surrounding their purpose are impeded by the duplicity of French and imperial officials, by their harnessing of the affair for continental diplomatic propaganda purposes completely independent of Gerald's 'cause', and by the clandestine nature of the exiles' itinerary and overtures. Moreover, it is highly likely that Leverous, Walsh and Fitzgerald changed their strategy over the course of the first few weeks of their exile in France and Flanders in response to their closer reading of the prevailing political and diplomatic climate and in reaction to their treatment in both countries.

When the party first arrived in France, their mood appeared optimistic. They were anxious to publicise Gerald's plight as the cause that had driven them into exile. In Saint-Malo Gerald was commonly held to be the rightful king of Ireland. The English agent, Bartholomew Warner, employed to locate Fitzgerald, alleged that this was propaganda generated 'of them of St Malo, [rather] than of the said Gareth or any of his, for they say they could speak scant a word of French'.[20] While Warner's assumption that Gerald did not claim to be king of Ireland is likely to have been correct, his explanation for the Geraldine party's failure to correct the *malouins* in their misguided understanding of his cause owing to their limited linguistic capabilities is wholly implausible. First, there is ample proof that the fugitives themselves communicated details of the circumstances that precipitated Gerald's flight from Ireland to *malouins* such as Alain Governors who provided them with assistance and also to the notables who received them at Morlaix, Châteaubriant and later in Flanders and Italy. Second, even if they wished to preserve the boy's anonymity in order to ensure his safety, it would have been impossible and counterproductive to conceal the circumstances that prompted their flight from figures such as Châteaubriant from whom they hoped to elicit support for the Geraldine cause.

Even while they were still in Brittany, there were conflicting reports as to their plans. Reports emanating from English mariners at Morlaix alleged that the fugitives had announced their intention to approach François I in person for assistance.[21] When they departed monsieur de Châteaubriant's residence

---

20 Ibid.
21 Treffy to Cromwell, 31 Mar. 1540, *LP Henry VIII*, xv (1540), 426.

they claimed that they were destined for the French court. Some parties in Brittany believed that they were intent upon targeting the dauphin, Henri (future Henri II), for aid, while others alleged that Gerald's guardians were hoping to seek Henri's intercession to secure a pardon for their ward from Henry VIII. Yet no concrete evidence exists to prove that they actually made direct personal or written representations to the king or to the dauphin.[22]

During a vital period between May 1540 and February of the following year, English agents in France lost track of the Irish fugitives who made their way northwards to the imperial court at Brussels. Although they had departed Châteaubriant in April at the latest, the party had not arrived at the French court by the third week of May. Bartholomew Warner speculated that 'perhaps he [Gerald] hath left that purpose and is gone to the bishop of Rome fearing the treaties of peace which is between the king our master and the French king'.[23] It was not until February 1541 that another English agent, Thomas Barnaby, intimated that Fitzgerald and his escorts had in fact attended the court in Paris while *en route* to Brussels. They had, he claimed, safely escaped from Paris to the nearby village of Makery, thanks to the connivance of the former French ambassador to England, Louis de Perreau, sieur de Castillon, who concealed all knowledge of Gerald's whereabouts from Sir John Wallop, the English ambassador, then at court.[24] Whether or not the fugitive party made representations directly to François I, there is no available evidence to suggest that the French provided them with any financial or military assistance.

Both the English agent, Thomas Barnaby, and Richard Pate, the imperial ambassador to the English court, viewed Gerald's escorts as incorrigible rebels whose purpose in escaping with the boy to the continent was to prolong and extend their opposition to Henry VIII by seeking the support of continental rulers. Consequently, Barnaby believed that in later years 'the child should curse the time that ever he knew them'.[25] Pate believed that 'the boy [was being] maintained in his parents' mischief'. This indicates that Gerald's escorts persisted in lobbying to have him reinstated to his dynasty's political position and estates by attempting to secure the backing first of François and later of Charles V rather than through solicitations that either ruler use his influence to obtain a royal pardon on their ward's behalf.[26] The fact that Pate perceived their stance during their sojourn in Flanders as defiant rather than

---

22 Warner to Wallop, 22 May 1540, *LP Henry VIII*, xv (1540), 704; *SP Henry VIII*, iii/3, 212. Fitzgerald (*The earls of Kildare*, 183–6) assumes, without proof of his point, that Gerald was thereafter summoned by François I to Paris and placed with the young dauphin, later Henri II. The evidence discussed hereafter contradicts this.
23 Warner to Wallop, 22 May 1540, *LP Henry VIII*, xv (1540), 704; *SP Hen. VIII*, iii/3, 212.
24 Barnaby to Henry VIII, 6 Feb. 1541, *LP Henry VIII*, xvi (1541), 525; *SP Henry VIII*, iii, 282.
25 Ibid.
26 Richard Pate to Henry VIII, 16 June 1540, *LP Henry VIII*, xv (1540), 793.

contrite strongly suggests that they adopted a similar stance during their stay in France. His observation on their demeanour also intimates that the outcome of their solicitations in France had not diminished their determined refusal to capitulate to Henry VIII.[27]

While Leverous and Walsh did not entirely dismiss the option of requesting that either François or Charles V make representations to Henry VIII for a royal pardon on the young man's behalf, Walsh in particular had serious reservations about the integrity of any pardon granted to Gerald by the English king unless it was fully validated by François and Charles.[28] However, all the available evidence points to the fact that both continental rulers, and especially François, went to great lengths to dissociate themselves entirely from suspicion of lending support to Fitzgerald on any basis. Equally there are no grounds for asserting that the Irish party in its own right had a concrete set of proposals for an independent offensive military strategy aimed at restoring Gerald to his dynastic inheritance for which they were seeking French or imperial backing.

What is clear, however, is that for the duration of their sojourn in France, the fugitives' focus was on meeting with Cardinal Pole, and to that end their main immediate objective was apparently to secure financial support.[29] Gerald's guide, Vincent Noblet, testified that Leverous and Walsh had said that as soon as they could 'recover any money into their hands, . . . they intend to go towards Cardinal Pole'.[30] At best, the Irish may have held out vain hopes for a realisation of Pole's grand scheme against Henry VIII. However, any news that they may have received from Ireland would have undermined their determination to persist with their solicitations. In June Gerald's uncle, Lord Deputy Leonard Grey, was arrested and imprisoned on a charge of treason that was partly based on his suspected collusion in ensuring Gerald's escape from arrest.[31] His successor, Sir Anthony St Leger, had set about rapidly pacifying the country, securing the compliant submissions of several of Gerald's former supporters.

Having received little more than a polite reception in both France and Flanders, and as English agents steadily closed in on the fugitives, capturing their two French guides and a fourth member of the party by February 1541, Leverous and Walsh are likely to have resigned themselves to the futility of

---

27 Ibid.
28 Barnaby to Henry VIII, 6 Feb. 1541, *LP Henry VIII*, xvi (1541), 525; *SP Henry VIII*, iii. 282.
29 Warner to Wallop, 22 May 1540, *LP Henry VIII*, xv (1540), 704; *SP Henry VIII*, iii/3, 212; Barnaby to Henry VIII, 6 Feb. 1541, *LP Henry VIII*, xvi (1541), 525; *SP Henry VIII*, iii. 282.
30 Barnaby to Henry VIII, 6 Feb. 1541, *LP Henry VIII*, xvi (1541), 525; *SP Henry VIII*, iii. 283.
31 See Aylmer and Alen's articles against Lord Leonard Grey [June 1538], *CSP Ireland, 1509–73*, 41–2; depositions of the council in Ireland against the late Lord Deputy Grey, Oct. 1540 (ibid. 55); Hogan, *Ireland in the European system*, 50; Brady, *Chief governors*, 23.

their persistence in clinging to their hopes.[32] They therefore proceeded to Italy, their endeavours to gain continental backing having failed owing to Pole's inability, and François's and Charles's refusal, to generate support for the Geraldine cause.

II

Gerald's seeking refuge and aid in France and Flanders while *en route* to meet Cardinal Pole in Italy exerted a modest impact on Anglo-French and Franco-imperial relations. The controversy surrounding his sojourn in France was merely one in a series of disputes between Henry VIII and François I that arose in the period between 1537 and 1542, all concerning the extremely sensitive issue of their assertion of royal honour.[33] The first centred on Cardinal Pole's arrival in France in April 1537, ostensibly to sponsor a joint Franco-imperial campaign against Henry VIII. Though Henry demanded that the cardinal be apprehended as a traitor under the terms of the Treaty of Cognac between England and France, François I received him politely and then sent him away from his court, claiming that the English ambassador had not demanded Pole's arrest. In 1539 the Rochepot and 'Matthew Bible' controversies became test cases in the expression of both monarchs' sovereign status. Relations were further compromised in late 1539 and in 1540 by disputes concerning the deportation of alleged criminals.[34]

Gerald Fitzgerald's stay in France was therefore construed and used by Henry VIII as further evidence of François's dishonourable behaviour towards him. In part, Henry castigated François for harbouring his enemies in an attempt to check the French king for his cavalier treatment of him. He also did so to remind François that it was he (Henry) and not Charles V who had helped him after his attempt to dominate Europe in 1525 ended in the ignominious defeat of the French at the battle of Pavia. Henry therefore used all evidence of François's support of his enemies (tacit or otherwise) as a pretext for reminding the French king that such behaviour was, in his view, evidence

---

[32] In a very significant *coup* for the English agents, Fitzgerald's servant, Darby Gunning, was captured in Normandy after the French king issued letters for the arrest of Gerald and each of his escorts. Acting in compliance with Wallop's order, Gunning was subsequently transported to England where he was interrogated about Fitzgerald's whereabouts and his plans. See Wallop's certificate for Gunning's capture and conveyance, 1 June 1540, *LP Henry VIII*, xv (1540), 739; John Story to Cromwell, 1 June 1540, *LP Henry VIII*, xv (1540), 741.

[33] See Potter, 'Diplomacy in the mid-sixteenth century', and Richardson, 'Anglo-French relations', for detailed discussions of these disputes.

[34] The most controversial case involved a Frenchman named Dick Hosier, alias Blanche Rose.

of the latter's debasement of the honour of the French crown arising from his collusion with Charles.[35]

When news of Gerald's escape to France broke in mid-March 1540 reaction in Whitehall was swift. Thomas Cromwell and the English privy council immediately alerted the English ambassador to France and enlisted several English agents including Bartholomew Warner and Thomas Barnaby to track down the fugitive party in Brittany. Within a month of Fitzgerald's arrival in France, the English ambassador, Sir John Wallop, sought the assistance of the sieur de Castillon, former French ambassador to England, who pledged to forward all relevant intelligence to Wallop, though the sincerity of his undertaking was subsequently called into question by Barnaby.[36]

At the outset, François I appeared unflinching in his loyalty to Henry and completely co-operative with the efforts of the English privy council and agents to ensure Gerald's speedy arrest. Until early June the greater problem seemed to be that posed by Charles V who agreed to banish the Irish fugitives but refused to deliver them to Henry on the grounds that to do so would be contrary to his own regal honour.[37] In an obvious ploy to apply pressure on Charles, the English ambassador at the imperial court, Richard Pate, asserted that he was confident that François would have had the fugitives arrested had Gerald not 'saved himself by flight' into the emperor's jurisdiction. However, Pate suspected his French counterpart at the imperial court of involvement with the Irish fugitives, claiming that they had frequent recourse to the French ambassador at his residence in Brussels.[38]

It was in late June, almost three months after Gerald's arrival in France, that doubts regarding François's credibility emerged, undermining his reputation as the more co-operative of the two continental rulers in his handling of the Irish dissidents. In the interests of cultivating Henry VIII's support, Charles's diplomatic personnel made political capital out of the Gerald Fitzgerald affair. They deliberately fanned growing suspicions that François had not been altogether as compliant with English officials in dealing with Fitzgerald's asylum in his jurisdiction as initially appeared to have been the case. On 23 June Castillon's successor as French ambassador to England, Charles de Marillac, notified François that Henry was aware of rumours of the French king's alleged sympathetic treatment of Gerald during his brief sojourn in France. Henry put it to Marillac that Charles V believed that the French had merely adopted the pretence of endeavouring to arrest Gerald as a cover to facilitate his escape from their jurisdiction.[39]

---

[35] Potter, 'Diplomacy in the mid-sixteenth century', and Richardson, 'Anglo-French relations'.

[36] Wallop to Cromwell, 18 Apr. 1540, *LP Henry VIII*, xv (1540), 543; *SP Henry VIII*, iii. 325–6.

[37] Pate to Henry VIII, 16 June 1540, *LP Henry VIII*, xv (1540), 793.

[38] Ibid.

[39] Charles de Marillac to François I, 23 juin 1540, *Correspondance politique de MM de*

The intelligence Henry had received from his agents in France suggested that there were real grounds for the emperor's insinuations regarding French misconduct. Henry was apprised of the warm reception afforded the fugitives in each of the ports and towns that they visited whilst in France. He learned how the most high-ranking royal official in that province, Lieutenant-General sieur de Châteaubriant, had entertained the young man at a time when he was aware that English agents were combing those very towns in pursuit of the Irish fugitives with arrest warrants issued by the French king. Henry was suspicious that the French had managed to close the gap sufficiently on the Geraldine party to have succeeded in capturing Gerald's servant, the least important member of the group, while failing to capture the boy and his influential guardians. He was also well aware of allegations that Gerald secretly enjoyed far greater support among the French than among Charles's subjects.[40]

Henry enlisted Marillac's services to transmit a heavily couched but clear message to François that he had grounds for suspecting the latter's honesty and co-operation in dealing with Fitzgerald, and that he had garnered incriminating 'evidence' of apparent French complicity with the Anglo-Irish lord. However, to counter the acerbic tenor of Marillac's *communiqué* to the French king, Henry emphasised that he attached little weight to Charles's allegations, which he recognised as an attempt on the emperor's part to stir up trouble between himself and François. The French king's response to Henry's view of the allegations levied against him by the emperor was typical of the reaction of successive French monarchs when accused of intrigue with Irish dissidents throughout the sixteenth century.[41] He assumed a posture of offended surprise and innocence and immediately jumped to his own defence. Within a week of having received Marillac's correspondence, François responded to Henry's aired suspicions. He attempted to exonerate himself from all allegations of subterfuge and demonstrated his palpable concern at the possible detrimental effect which either a discovery or distortion of his true handling of this affair might have on the amicable relations with Henry that he laboured to preserve at this vital time.

François expressed great surprise at the content of his ambassador's most recent advertisement concerning his handling of the Geraldine fugitives. He invoked the endorsement of Henry's ambassador at his court, Sir John Wallop, who could testify to the willing and liberal manner in which he had expedited all of the requisite procedures for Gerald's arrest as though he were a French subject. He countered Charles V's questioning of his earnestness in

Castillon et de Marillac, ambassadeurs de France en Angleterre (1537–42), ed. Jean Kaulek, Louis Farges and Gennain Léfèvre-Pontalis, Paris 1885, 192 (extract); *LP Henry VIII*, xv (1540), 803.

[40] Ibid.

[41] François I to de Marillac, 28 juin 1540, *Correspondance politique de MM de Castillon et de Marillac*, 196; *LP Henry VIII*, xv (1540), 816.

pursuing the fugitives while they were within his jurisdiction by citing the arrest of one of Fitzgerald's party, and he insisted that Gerald himself would have been captured had he been found.[42]

In support of these protestations of his impartiality, he dismissed the emperor's allegation that the French ambassador to the imperial court at Brussels had been implicated with the Geraldines. He declared emphatically that his ambassador, the bishop of Lavaur, had 'no charge' to receive the fugitives. Besides, according to François, even if the bishop were sympathetic to the dissidents' cause, he would have been too shrewd to have become involved with them, being aware of the amicable tenor of relations between France and England. François I therefore rejected the emperor's charges as being wholly at variance with the reality of his position vis-à-vis Henry VIII.[43]

It was the finely balanced state of diplomatic relations at the precise time of his flight to the continent that determined the sensitivity demonstrated by all parties in their handling of the problem posed by Gerald Fitzgerald in 1540–1. From early April 1540 French foreign policy had begun to manifest a departure from Anne de Montmorency's pro-imperialist line.[44] After the diplomatic coolness between England and France during the period 1538–40, a serious effort was now needed to win back Henry VIII in the light of François I's rapidly deteriorating relations with Charles V.[45] Although intent upon asserting his regal honour, François was in a decidedly deferential position in his contacts with Henry – hence his earnest desire to be exonerated from suspicion of partisanship in his dealing with the Geraldines.

Though Henry paid little attention to this matter during the summer of 1540 (much to the relief of Marillac), in October he again took the French ambassador to task concerning his master's alleged collusion with the Geraldine fugitives.[46] Henry declared that he had reason to believe that while Gerald and his guardians were in France, they had received warnings from the French and were assisted in escaping into Flanders. Whereas in June he had couched his suspicions and second-hand allegations of French collusion in terms that intimated his refusal to believe that François would undermine a fellow prince's position, he now appeared to believe these reports. Henry was convinced that after Gerald had crossed from France into Flanders, the French pretended that they wished to capture the boy and his attendants. Once again Marillac managed to allay Henry's suspicions concerning François's complicity in the affair.[47]

---

42 Ibid.
43 Ibid.
44 Bonney, The European dynastic states, 107–8; Garrisson, Sixteenth-century France, 161–2; Potter, History of France, 270–1.
45 Potter, History of France, 271.
46 De Marillac to Anne de Montmorency, 6 juill. 1540, Correspondance politique de MM de Castillon et de Marillac, 198; LP Henry VIII, xv (1540), 848; de Marillac to de Montmorency, 21 oct. 1540, LP Henry VIII, xvi (1540), 183.
47 De Marillac to de Montmorency, 21 oct. 1540, LP Henry VIII, xvi (1540), 183.

In spite of this innuendo, no agent or ambassador was able to present substantive evidence that François I, Châteaubriant, any member of the French court, French ambassadors to English or imperial courts, or the municipal officials at Morlaix or Rouen ever afforded the Geraldine party anything more than a welcome that could be justified on the grounds that it befitted the young man's standing as a displaced Irish aristocrat and member of the lordship's most formidable political dynasty. The only exceptions were the *malouins* who had been responsible for transporting the boy out of Ireland and who, in their euphoric reception of their guest, revered him as much more than an aristocrat. In Saint-Malo he had been hailed as a rebel and as rightful king of Ireland.[48] Consequently, in late May 1540, when it was clear that the fugitives had little prospect of receiving any form of substantive French aid, Fitzgerald's supporters at Saint-Malo feared recriminations from both the French and English kings on account of their involvement with the rebel. Yet at no point did even their support extend to their supplying Fitzgerald with any soldiers, ammunition or ships for a military campaign in Ireland.

Consequently, the issue of Gerald Fitzgerald's sojourn in France remained one of relatively minor importance in terms of relations between the two monarchs as evidenced by the very sporadic and short-lived attention afforded it by Henry VIII. Neither Henry nor François was prepared to countenance jeopardising their otherwise amicable relations over a solitary figure such as Fitzgerald, particularly since it was obvious that Cardinal Pole's plans for launching an offensive against England had collapsed well before the boy's arrival in France. None the less, it did serve a useful purpose at particularly delicate points in international relations such as occurred in October 1540, when Henry VIII was anxious about his rapport with his continental rivals and therefore revived this thorny issue to elicit assurances of French amity from François I.

In October the French king dispensed with his alliance with the emperor when Charles provocatively 'invested' his son, Philip, with the hotly contested prize of the duchy of Milan.[49] From mid-1540 opponents of the pro-imperialist French constable, led by the duchess d'Estampes and the admiral, Chabot de Brion, made steady progress in depriving Montmorency of his stranglehold on French foreign policy, thereby clearing the way for the French to forge an alliance with Henry VIII in preparation for the inevitable war against the emperor.[50] Notwithstanding Montmorency's efforts to balance France's imperial and English interests more equitably, the

---

[48] Warner to Wallop, 22 May 1540, *LP Henry VIII*, xv (1540), 704; *SP Henry VIII*, iii/3, 212.

[49] Spooner, 'The Hapsburg–Valois struggle', 353; Knecht, *French Renaissance monarchy*, 42; Bonney, *The European dynastic states*, 107; Garrisson, *Sixteenth-century France*, 161.

[50] Bonney, *The European dynastic states*, 107–8; Potter, *History of France*, 270; Garrisson, *Sixteenth-century France*, 161.

'Cowswade dispute' and the clashes over the refortification of Ardres reignited tensions between France and the emperor which were only temporarily defused early in 1541.[51]

Between autumn 1540 and the following February, even though Fitzgerald had long since crossed into Flanders, English agents continued their search for individuals involved in facilitating his passage through France. In an important *coup* they captured and interrogated Vincent Noblet, the Breton appointed as Gerald's guide following his arrival at Morlaix.[52] In the course of their investigations, these agents uncovered embarrassing evidence of the duplicity of François I's leading officials that lent substance to previous allegations and again called into question François's credibility in his dealings with Henry in the matter. For example, Barnaby made explicit accusations of deliberate procrastination on the part of Montmorency and Castillon in their handling of the affair. When he appeared in person at the French court and attempted to collect letters legislating for the arrest of the Geraldine party that were to be distributed in Paris and elsewhere throughout France, he was hindered by the manifest 'doubleness' of Montmorency and Castillon who 'trifled, and prolonged the matter for the obtaining of the said letters, until the child had warning, and so [was] conveyed' out of France.[53] Barnaby was especially censorious of Castillon's duplicity. He believed that Montmorency had summoned the French ambassador back from England to the French court at Paris. There, the former ambassador regaled Wallop with feigned protestations that he would have found Gerald though he knew the fugitive had already escaped from Paris. While at the French court, Barnaby was shocked by the audacity of Castillon who tried to convince him that his (Castillon's) Anglophile demeanour was so pronounced, it aroused Montmorency's suspicions that he was more favourably disposed to the English than to his own nation.[54]

III

Although Henry VIII was undoubtedly displeased by Barnaby's report, ultimately its timing diminished entirely its potential to upset Anglo-French relations. By early 1541 Gerald's exile in Europe and his association with Pole no longer gave Henry VIII significant cause for concern: there was no prospect of Pole orchestrating the pan-European alliance of the empire, France

---

[51] Potter, 'Diplomacy in the mid-sixteenth century', 47–53. Tensions grew out of a dispute over ownership of a small stretch of marshy land between Guisnes and Ardres in northern France ultimately necessitating the appointment of mediating commissioners.

[52] Barnaby to Henry VIII, 6 Feb. 1541, *LP Henry VIII*, xvi (1540), 525; *SP Henry VIII*, iii. 281–5.

[53] Ibid.

[54] Ibid. See also Potter, 'Diplomacy in the mid-sixteenth century', 342.

and Scotland that had caused a security alert in England two years previously. From having been in a position of diplomatic isolation during the period of François I's and Charles V's adherence to the terms of the truce signed at Nice (1538), Henry had re-emerged to become an active agent in mainstream European politics, negotiating alliances with both leaders early in 1541. While Gerald Fitzgerald was a source of political embarrassment to Henry, François and Charles in 1540, during the following year the three leaders had far greater challenges with which to contend.

Since the summer of 1540 significant changes in diplomatic personnel and foreign policy on a wider European level had brought about the gradual breach in the French-imperial alliance so sought after by Henry VIII whose sense of isolation was beginning to diminish.[55] Henry continued to court the favour of both François and Charles while the Estampes–Chabot faction strove to re-establish a French alliance with England after the diplomatic coolness of the period 1538–40.[56] The threat of war between France and Charles V escalated in spring 1541 while the French concentrated on securing English neutrality at the very least as a preliminary to the outbreak of war between a coalition of France, Cleves, Scotland, Denmark, Sweden and the Holy Roman Empire. By December French–imperial relations had seriously deteriorated as a result of the assassination of two French diplomats, Rinçon and Fregoso, in Lombardy by imperial forces the previous July, which engendered a widespread expectation of an imminent declaration of war. The French therefore trod a fine line in their relations with England, fearing that their close dealings with Henry VIII might precipitate the premature outbreak of war with the emperor.

In early 1542, while English negotiations with France were half-heartedly continuing, talks between the imperial ambassador to England, Eustace Chapuys, and members of the English privy council, got under way and Chabot's foreign policy of attempting to restrain England from moving into the imperial camp proved unsuccessful. In February of the following year Henry VIII concluded a treaty with Charles V and initiated preparations to join forces with the emperor in launching an offensive against France.[57]

Though in 1540 the exiled Irish party endeavoured to keep abreast of these

---

55 See Elton, *England under the Tudors*, 155–8; Spooner, 'The Hapsburg–Valois struggle', 352; Mackie, *A history of Scotland*, 133; Jean-Yves Mariotte, 'François Ier et la ligue de Smalkalde de la trêve de Nice à la paix de Crespy, 1538–44', *Schweizerische Zietschrift für Geschichte* xvi (1966), 215; Scarisbrick, *Henry VIII*, 361–79; Head, 'Henry VIII's Scottish policy', 14; Knecht, *French Renaissance monarchy*, 42; Bonney, *The European dynastic states*, 107; Garrisson, *Sixteenth-century France*, 160; Potter, *History of France*, 270–1.
56 Bonney, *The European dynastic states*, 107–8; Potter, 'Diplomacy in the mid-sixteenth century', 45, and *History of France*, 271; Garrisson, *Sixteenth-century France*, 161–2.
57 Potter, 'Diplomacy in the mid-sixteenth century', 53–68, and *History of France*, 271; Scarisbrick, *Henry VIII*, 427–8, 433–4; Head, 'Henry VIII's Scottish policy', 16; Knecht, *French Renaissance monarchy*, 42–3; Bonney, *The European dynastic states*, 107; Garrisson, *Sixteenth-century France*, 162.

shifts in continental politics in the hope of maximising their chances of securing continental backing for Gerald's cause, their peripheral importance to the cut and thrust of that political sphere, combined with their inopportune timing, minimised their chances of eliciting support from either of Henry VIII's rivals. By early 1541 the Geraldine element within the Irish league both at home and on the continent had resigned itself to the failed outcome of their effort to achieve that end through lobbying for continental aid. In spite of this, Gerald Fitzgerald's flight to France in 1540 represented a significant landmark in the evolution of political relations between Ireland and France. It brought the French authorities face to face with a leading Anglo-Irish noble who was at odds with the English king. For the first time, the French king was forced to tackle the delicate issue of dealing appropriately with a fugitive who was the figurehead of Ireland's first 'national' coalition in the early modern era. Most important, Gerald's sojourn in France and the anxious response that his escape triggered in English government circles alerted the French political elite to his importance in Irish politics. During the Anglo-French war in the mid-1540s Henry's French opponents used Gerald as a legitimising focus for their intrigue, propagating rumours of a French invasion of Ireland led by Fitzgerald, to play on the Irish and English councils' fears of a revival of the Geraldine interest in Ireland in efforts to secure victory in the war.

3

Irish Dimensions to the Anglo-French War, 1543–1546

In early August 1540 Lord Leonard Grey's successor, Sir Anthony St Leger, arrived in Ireland to begin an eight-year term of office as lord deputy. This led to a change in the tenor of domestic and Anglo-Irish political relations which in turn profoundly shaped the character of Franco-Irish relations. During the early and mid-1540s the altered dynamic of Ireland's contacts with France resulted in a temporary aberration in their relations in two key respects. First, thanks to the success of St Leger's conciliatory policy in handling the most powerful Gaelic and Anglo-Irish lords, the early and mid-1540s witnessed none of the opportunistic contrivance with the French that had character-ised previous decades. This was manifest in the refusal by both Anglo-Irish and Gaelic lords to respond to rumours of Gerald Fitzgerald leading a French invasion of Ireland that were little more than war propaganda deliberately circulated by Henry's French opponents in 1543–6 as one means of securing French victory over England. Second, in an unprecedented show of support for their newly-declared king, these lords mustered Gaelic soldiers for service in Henry's army in the Anglo-Scottish (1542–9) and Anglo-French (1543–6) wars at a time when his position and the security of the British Isles was particularly vulnerable.[1]

St Leger's occupancy of the lord deputyship was critical in maintaining the fragile peace and stability that resulted in both Irish abstinence from involve-ment in intrigue with France and consequent minimal demands for financial, military and naval resources from the English privy council to fortify Ireland's defences. His success, however, proved short-lived. Within months of the arrival in Ireland in May 1548 of St Leger's successor, Sir Edward Bellingham, his aggressive handling of the midland septs, led to insurrection. In the after-math, the dispossessed O'Connors embarked upon a sustained campaign to elicit military support from Henri II of France in support of their opposition to the English crown in what was the most serious episode in sixteenth-century Franco-Irish intrigue.[2]

During the early stage of his term as deputy, St Leger was guarded in his

---

[1] See White, 'Henry VIII's Irish kerne'; Lennon, *Sixteenth-century Ireland*, 159–64; Ellis, *Ireland in the age of the Tudors*, 155–7, and 'Tudor state formation and the shaping of the British Isles', in Ellis and Barber, *Conquest and union*, 56.
[2] See ch. 4 below.

hopes for his conciliatory policy 'so soon after the rebellion of Thomas Fitz-gerald, the entry made by young Gerald, assisted by O'Neill and O'Donnell, and the univers[al] combination of the Irishmen'.[3] Even after it was known that Gerald Fitzgerald had taken up residence in Italy, members of the Irish council harboured suspicions of French backing for the Geraldine heir, though there is little evidence to suggest that there was any substance to many of the rumours in circulation. Councillors' anxieties about French designs on Ireland were partly allayed by the consistently compliant behav-iour of both O'Neill and O'Donnell, formerly Fitzgerald's leading allies. None the less, they were acutely aware of the need to secure the island's defences, lest such an attack should occur.

In the early months of 1541, when war between François I and Charles V was inevitable, Henry VIII strove to neutralise the threat posed by his Scot-tish opponents by endeavouring to placate James V. When that strategy failed, he resorted to aggression. By the time hostilities broke out between François and the emperor in July 1542, plans were already afoot to stage an English invasion of France in the summer of the following year. In February 1543 Henry concluded a treaty with Charles, by which both rulers committed themselves to provide mutual aid and defence, and to launch a joint attack on France within two years.[4] However, before proceeding with the planned invasion of France in the spring of 1543, Henry was intent upon reducing the Scots to complete submission.[5]

From September 1542 the Irish council was acutely aware that Ireland was a likely target for a Scottish attack.[6] In the event, a series of disastrous developments, notably the resounding defeat of the Scots at Solway Moss in 1542 and the death of James V, seriously reduced the Scots' capacity to organise an invasion. This caused Henry to be sufficiently confident in Ireland's existing security measures to halt his plans for dispatching an army for the defence of the country. The defeat at Solway Moss prompted what John Morrill has termed the 'psychic numbing' of the Scots, leading them to believe that in order to maintain Scotland's identity, they would have to accept some form of union with another power. While the Scottish regent, James Hamilton, earl of Arran, hoped for a *rapprochement* with England, his rival, Cardinal Beaton, along with James V's influential widow, Marie de

---

3   Lord Deputy St Leger and council to Henry VIII, 24 Oct. 1541, *LP Henry VIII*, xvi (1541), 1284; *SP Henry VIII*, iii. 339.
4   Mackie, 'Henry VIII and Scotland', 11, and *A history of Scotland*, 133–4; Scarisbrick, *Henry VIII*, 427–8, 434–6; W. Croft Dickinson, *Scotland from the earliest times to 1603*, 3rd edn, rev. and ed. Archibald Duncan, Oxford 1977, 310; Head, 'Henry VIII's Scottish policy', 15–18; Knecht, *French Renaissance monarchy*, 43; Bonney, *The European dynastic states*, 108; Potter, *History of France*, 271.
5   Mackie, 'Henry VIII and Scotland', 107–9; Scarisbrick, *Henry VIII*, 435–6; Head, 'Henry VIII's Scottish policy', 18.
6   Henry VIII to the deputy and council of Ireland, 8 Oct. 1542, SP 60/10/282; *LP Henry VIII*, xvii (1542), 924; *CPR Ireland, Hen. VIII–Eliz.*, 78.

Guise, strongly favoured France as the least predatory guarantor of Scottish independence and of the Stuart dynasty. In the short term France was at war with the emperor and was therefore unable to come to the Scots' defence. Within the political vacuum that followed James's death, Henry was poised to realise his aim of subjugating Scotland through his reliance on a pro-English faction at the Scottish court, thereby enabling him to prepare for war with France.[7]

Henry's arrogant and exacting approach towards the governance of Scotland soon stirred the resentment of Scottish nobles. In late May 1543 he was adamant that no peace would be signed between England and Scotland unless the Scots severed their alliance with France.[8] Aware that Henry's declaration of war against France was imminent, St Leger anticipated the king's demand for military assistance by volunteering Irish forces for service either in Scotland or France. He proposed sending 500 horsemen to act as 'light scourers' in the belief that there were 'no properer [sic] horsemen in Christian ground'.[9] He recommended that the Gaelic kerne be trained in the use of morris pikes and handguns 'for, as for gunners, there be no better in no land than they be'. The deputy stressed the hardiness of the kerne and galloglas, declaring that 'there is no man that ever I saw, that will or can endure the pains and evil fare that they will sustain'.[10] While awaiting Henry's response to his proposal, St Leger took steps to secure Ireland's havens lest an attack should occur. He dispatched two ships to search the harbours in O'Donnell's country that were known to be frequented by Breton and French vessels, and had the chief's movements closely monitored. However, apprehension regarding a French or Scottish invasion compelled the lord deputy and council to be particularly diplomatic in their dealings with O'Donnell so as 'not to ruffle him without express command'.[11]

Throughout May and June 1543 St Leger monitored the movements of French and Scottish ships that did 'divers hurts' off the coast of Dublin and in the port of Carrickfergus in Antrim.[12] Even before the first hostile engagement between the English and French forces, the French and the Scots were out-manoeuvring the royal navy in the Irish Sea, stiffening the lord deputy's resolve that all French and Scots who anchored to any Irish port would be

---

7 Nicholls, *Modern British Isles*, 87–9; John Morrill, 'The fashioning of Britain,' in Ellis and Barber, *Conquest and union*, 19.
8 Head, 'Henry VIII's Scottish policy', 19–20.
9 St Leger to Henry VIII, 6 Apr. 1543, *LP Henry VIII*, xviii/1 (1543), 373; *SP Henry VIII*, iii/3, 443ff. See also White, 'Henry VIII's Irish kerne', 213–25.
10 Ibid.
11 Lord deputy and council of Ireland to the privy council, 5 June 1543, *LP Henry VIII*, xviii/1 (1543), 650; *SP Henry VIII*, iii/3, 470. See also Palmer, *Problem of Ireland*, 62; Nicholls, *Modern British Isles*, 87; Lyons, 'Franco-Irish relations', 102.
12 Lord deputy and council of Ireland to Henry VIII, 15 May 1543, *LP Henry VIII*, xviii/1 (1543), 553; *SP Hen. VIII*, iii. 459; St Leger to Henry VIII, 4 June 1543, *LP Henry VIII*, xviii/1 (1543), 646; *SP Henry VIII*, iii. 465. See also Scarisbrick, *Henry VIII*, 440.

restrained.[13] Having invaded France in June and concluded peace treaties with the Scots in July, Henry VIII instructed the Irish council to 'use Frenchmen as our enemies, and Scots entertain as our friends, so as they behave themselves accordingly'.[14] However, relations with the Scots rapidly deteriorated in early autumn when Henry's governor, the earl of Arran, deserted the pro-English faction and defected to the side of Reginald Pole's associate, Cardinal David Beaton, who had recently been released from prison.[15]

As part of their war strategy, the French sought in vain to incite disturbances in Ireland or at the very least to circulate rumours of their intention to invade this peripheral Tudor possession in a manner reminiscent of their engagement with Desmond during the Anglo-French war in the 1520s. With Henry forced to stretch his military and financial resources on a two-front war to the point of calling on reserves in Ireland, François sought to exploit England's vulnerability by capitalising on his contacts with the O'Donnells.[16] He secretly dispatched a French nobleman, Theobald de Bois, to offer money and arms to Manus O'Donnell as an enticement to stage an insurrection in Ireland though Manus declined his invitation.[17] Thereafter, significantly it was the French and particularly the Bretons, apparently without prompting from lords in Ireland, who circulated a series of ostensibly unsubstantiated rumours claiming that the French king had persuaded Gerald Fitzgerald to head a French invasion of Ireland, making this a unique episode in Franco-Irish intrigue. In October 1543 the first of these highly speculative reports of Gerald's alleged involvement in plans for an invasion of England backed by Pope Paul III and François I were brought to the attention of Henry VIII by his ambassador in Venice who admitted that he was unable to 'see what use such rascals can be'.[18] The French failed in their objective on this occasion as neither Henry nor the English privy council was particularly disturbed by this report. However, when similar rumours were circulated in May and June of the following year, the Irish council was compelled to treat the prospect of a foreign invasion of Ireland more seriously.

[13] St Leger to Henry VIII, 4 June 1543, *LP Henry VIII*, xviii/1 (1543), 646; *SP Henry VIII*, iii. 465.
[14] Henry VIII to the lord deputy and council of Ireland, Aug. 1543, *LP Henry VIII*, xviii/2 (1543), 105; *SP Henry VIII*, iii. 483.
[15] Mackie, 'Henry VIII and Scotland', 112; Scarisbrick, *Henry VIII*, 441–2; Head, 'Henry VIII's Scottish policy', 20–1.
[16] Manus's father, Aodh O'Donnell, had direct contacts with François I in the early 1530s. On 17 May 1531 François I ordered that a sum of *écus* was to be sent Aodh as a gift. On another unspecified date, Balthazar Lynch, a servant to O'Donnell, was to be given 50 *écus* to cover the cost of his return to Ireland bearing a dispatch from the king to the Gaelic lord: undated grant of 50 *écus* by François I to Balthazar Lynch, AN, Paris, J. 960³, no. 40, anc. J. 960, no. 2. See also *Catalogue des actes de François Ier*, ii. 33; vii, second supplement, 675.
[17] Hogan, *Ireland in the European system*, 62–3.
[18] Edmund Harvel to Henry VIII, 20 Oct. 1543, *LP Henry VIII*, xviii/2 (1543), 290; *SP Henry VIII*, ix. 521. See also Hogan, *Ireland in the European system*, 61.

Meanwhile Scotland remained Henry's primary concern. In December 1543 the Scottish parliament annulled the treaties of Greenwich and renewed all former treaties between Scotland and France.[19] The English privy council was confident not only of the neutrality but also of the active support of the Irish for the king.[20] Henry and St Leger were equally confident in their ability to rely on Irish troops to fight on the king's behalf in Scotland and in their apparent trustworthiness to launch a domestic offensive against the Scots in Ulster should the need arise. Henry VIII and Charles V agreed that each would field an army of 42,000 men against François I before 20 June 1544. Charles would invade France via Champagne and Henry would lead his companies along the Somme to Paris.[21]

By 11 March 1544 preparations for the deployment of Irish soldiers in France and Scotland were underway in London.[22] Initially, 3,000 men were requested, 2,000 for the French campaign and the remaining 1,000 for service in Scotland.[23] The lord justice and the Irish council expressed concern that enemy Breton ships looked set to control the waters between Brittany and Scotland if the English government did not take immediate steps to patrol the Irish Sea.[24] In response, the English privy council announced in March that upon further consideration of his original request for 3,000 Irish troops, Henry 'minding in no wise to have [Ireland] . . . disfurnished of men, as well for defence of the same in case of invasion' resolved to scale down his original request to a total of 1,000 men. Of these, 500 were to be ready for an immediate departure for service in France.[25]

By the end of May 600 of the soldiers were mustered for service in France in St James's Park, London, while the remaining 400 had arrived in Scotland. Those destined for France joined Henry's 42,000-strong force, and were divided into three detachments of 200 between the three divisions of vanguard, battle and rearguard.[26] Immediately after their arrival in France,

[19] Mackie, 'Henry VIII and Scotland', 112; Scarisbrick, *Henry VIII*, 442; Head, 'Henry VIII's Scottish policy', 21; Nicholls, *Modern British Isles*, 90.

[20] Privy council to the duke of Suffolk, 13 Dec. 1543, *LP Henry VIII*, xviii/2 (1543), 487, 521; *The Hamilton papers: letters and papers illustrating the political relations of England and Scotland in the XVI century*, ed. Joseph Bain, 2 vols, Edinburgh 1892, ii. 137.

[21] Scarisbrick, *Henry VIII*, 440–1; White, 'Henry VIII's Irish kerne', 213.

[22] White, 'Henry VIII's Irish kerne', 214.

[23] Lord justice and council of Ireland to St Leger, 24 Mar. 1544, *LP Henry VIII*, xix/1 (1544), 240; *SP Henry VIII*, iii. 490–2. See also White, 'Henry VIII's Irish kerne', 214–15.

[24] Ibid.

[25] The privy council to the justice and council in Ireland, 30 Mar. 1544, *LP Henry VIII*, xix/1 (1544), 261; *SP Henry VIII*, iii. 493–4; William Wise to St Leger, 22 Apr. 1544, *LP Henry VIII*, xix/1 (1544), 378. See also White, 'Henry VIII's Irish kerne', 215. Both the king and his councils in Dublin and Whitehall were vindicated in their concern over the menacing presence of Breton ships in the Irish Sea as within weeks of the departure of the Irish troops, the vessel carrying the royal treasure for their shipment was chased by Bretons.

[26] Edward Seymour, earl of Hertford, and others to Henry VIII, 25 May 1544, *LP Henry VIII*, xix/1 (1544), 575; *Hamilton papers*, ii. 244. See also Holinshed, *The historie of Irelande*,

the Irish were involved in action and distinguished themselves 'very gallantly' at the campaign in Ardres. As a result they gained a notorious reputation among the French as 'gens merveilleux sauvages' and 'experimentés à la guerre'.[27] On 29 July a number of Irish soldiers assisted the English commanders, Sir Thomas Poyns and Sir Nicholas Poynings, in the seizure of a strategic castle six miles from Boulogne.[28] Already acclaimed throughout western Europe for their unrivalled military capabilities, the Irish kerne earned particular notoriety during the siege, burning and spoiling all the villages within a radius of twenty or thirty miles of Boulogne and provoking strong protest from the French owing to their practice of beheading prisoners. After the siege had ended, and the English troops had been withdrawn from France, at least one company of Irish soldiers remained in the garrison of Boulogne.[29]

I

The participation of Irish kerne in the French campaign was, by all accounts, a resounding success. The speed with which they were mustered impressed upon the Dublin government the readiness of the Irish lords to render service to Henry VIII even under what the lord justice, Sir William Brabazon, and the Irish council considered an unreasonable amount of pressure. By raising troops for service abroad, the Dublin government cleared the country of disruptive elements, drew the Gaelic nobility in particular into more active involvement in the business of state, and provided the king with concrete proof of the potential value of a reformed Ireland.[30] Yet Henry was concerned at the continued presence of Breton ships off the Irish coast and was acutely sensitive to the island's vulnerability while a sizeable proportion of its armed forces was employed on foreign service. Meanwhile, in Scotland, a striking feature of the continuity that characterised the international diplomatic situations of summer 1540 and May 1544 was Cardinal Beaton's role as a persistent thorn in Henry's side while he attempted to coerce the recalcitrant Scots

---

110. For a detailed breakdown on Irish kerne serving in the various companies see 'The army against France', *LP Henry VIII*, xix/1 (1544), 274, and White, 'Henry VIII's Irish kerne', 218–19.

27 Duke of Norfolk to the privy council, 9 June 1544, *LP Henry VIII*, xix/1 (1544), 654; White, 'Henry VIII's Irish kerne', 219.

28 Diary of the invasion of France, *LP Henry VIII*, xix/2 (1544), appendix 10; White, 'Henry VIII's Irish kerne', 220.

29 Holinshed, *The historie of Irelande*, 110–11; White, 'Henry VIII's Irish kerne', 220. According to the old English chronicler, Richard Stanihurst, Gaelic soldiers regularly tied bulls to a stake, scorched the beasts with faggots causing them to roar, and thereby attracted all the cattle of the countryside which were slaughtered and used to provide the camp with beef.

30 Ellis, *Ireland in the age of the Tudors*, 156.

into submission. By 1544 the Scots had been driven directly into the arms of the French. Reginald Pole looked set to make a re-appearance, with Charles V fearing that the pope might send Pole to lead a joint French–Scottish invasion of England.[31] In contrast with circumstances that obtained in 1540 when François I was mildly concerned to appear beyond reproach in his handling of Gerald's passage through France, in 1544 he was at war with Henry VIII and prepared to use every strategy to ensure French victory.

In this context, both the Irish and English councils were disturbed in May 1544 by revived rumours of Gerald Fitzgerald's alleged involvement in continental conspiracy. The French deliberately timed their circulation of these rumours to maximise their impact in Dublin and Whitehall. Within days of the departure of the Irish troops for England, the mayor and citizens of Waterford advertised the Dublin administration that, through continental contacts, they had learned that Gerald had allegedly left Italy and 'is come into Brittany to the town of Nantes'.[32] Significantly, their source was a Frenchman, William de la Cluse, whom they deemed to be 'of an honest estimation' but who intentionally or otherwise proved little more than a purveyor of French war propaganda. He reported that by order of the French king, a navy and an army awaited Fitzgerald's arrival in Brittany with a view to staging an invasion of Ireland. As, allegedly, the plan was for the fleet to besiege Waterford, the mayor and citizenry were stirred up to fortify the city's defences.[33] Further weight was lent to this report in the testimonies of a number of men from Wexford town recently returned to Ireland from Brittany where they had been imprisoned. They reported that the French were so favourably disposed towards Fitzgerald that when they pretended that they 'willed to adhere to the same Gerald, and to be in his entertainment', they were freed and allowed to travel to Ireland. As prisoners, they were often interrogated in relation to the 'strength' of MacCarthy Reagh and to a lesser extent, that of his kinsman, MacCarthy More. Their French interrogators' interest in both lords undoubtedly stemmed from their knowledge of the political geography of Munster but may also have arisen from their acquaintance with Gerald Fitzgerald whose aunt, Eleanor, was MacCarthy Reagh's widow.

Several aspects of these rumours suggest that they amounted to little more than propaganda circulated by the French as part of their war strategy. During 1544–5 Gerald Fitzgerald was in Malta with the Knights of St John and upon his return to Italy in 1545 he took up residence at the court of Cosimo de Médici, duke of Florence, for a period of three years. There is no evidence

---

31 Scarisbrick, *Henry VIII*, 444–5; Head, 'Henry VIII's Scottish policy', 22.
32 The lord justice and council of Ireland to Henry VIII, 20 May 1544, *LP Henry VIII*, xix/1 (1544), 542; *SP Henry VIII*, iii. 501; postscript to lord justice and council of Ireland to Henry VIII, 20 May 1544, *SP Henry VIII*, iii. 503.
33 The lord justice and council of Ireland to Henry VIII, 20 May 1544, *LP Henry VIII*, xix/1 (1544), 542; *SP Henry VIII*, iii. 501.

therefore to indicate that Fitzgerald was in France prior to early 1549 at which time a young Irishman, matching his description though unnamed, was at the French court.[34] At other times it was Irish parties to Franco-Irish intrigue who propagated rumours of French invasion in a ploy to generate stronger support for their cause or to make their insurgence appear more menacing than it was in reality. However, the accounts of French schemes to launch an invasion of Ireland under Fitzgerald's leadership that circulated in 1543–6 cannot be seen as Irish propaganda. Rather it was decidedly French propaganda recounted by loyal English subjects from Waterford and Wexford who were not parties to intrigue with the French. Moreover, their reports were based on information gleaned not from Ireland but from Brittany where the Geraldine lord had been afforded refuge in 1540 and where the authorities and the wider population were apprised of his political importance in Irish and in continental Catholic circles.

In contrast with other episodes of Franco-Irish engagement, when the Irish strenuously lobbied a relatively indifferent French court, on this occasion the French were at pains to appear to the English administrations of Dublin and Whitehall as more disposed than the Irish to launching an invasion of Ireland. In this context their use of loyal English subjects as conduits for their propaganda proved highly politic and effective in stirring English anxiety at Ireland's strategic vulnerability. Lord Justice Brabazon and the Irish council treated these allegations seriously, convinced 'that the French king will, if he may by any means possible, annoy this your grace's realm'.[35] The fact that none of those interrogated provided any indication that the French invasion was planned in collusion with Irish lords based in Ireland also suggests that there was little substance to the reports. The alleged involvement of Fitzgerald in the invasion also points to the propaganda nature and intent of these rumours. In a manner reminiscent of their harnessing the cause of Richard de la Pole during the Anglo-French war in the 1520s, and not for the last time, the French seized upon Gerald Fitzgerald as a figurehead whom they could use to legitimate their intervention in Ireland and to rally Gaelic and Anglo-Irish support. Most important, they sought to exploit English uncertainty in relation to Gerald's whereabouts in designs to prey on Henry VIII's insecurities regarding a possible revival of the Geraldine interest in his peripheral kingdom.

While acknowledging that Waterford was the most obvious choice as a base for a French fleet to launch an attack on Ireland, owing to French mariners' familiarity with it as a key trading post between Brittany and Scotland, Brabazon and the council calculated that the French would instead target the MacCarthys' territory where there were several good havens suitable for a

<hr>

[34] Jean de St Mauris to Charles V, 5 Feb. 1549, *CSP Spain, 1547–9*, 336; Fitzgerald, *The earls of Kildare*, 204–5.
[35] The lord justice and council of Ireland to Henry VIII, 20 May 1544, *LP Henry VIII*, xix/1 (1544), 542; *SP Henry VIII*, iii. 501.

landing. They predicted that Gerald and the French forces would attempt to capture and garrison Cork city and port which was of particular strategic importance since it 'lieth most directly to Brittany'. They also surmised that the French intended to 'maintain Scotland' and 'to give impediment' to Henry VIII in Ireland 'by maintenance of young Gerald', and therefore urged the king to provide adequate men and munitions to secure the Irish ports and havens in anticipation of imminent attack. Owing to the comparative stability of the political climate in Ireland and the Irish servicemen's involvement in Henry's French campaign, the English government reduced expenditure on Ireland's defence.[36] Irish councillors consoled themselves in the belief that 'the Irishmen being reconciled to . . . [Henry VIII] and joining with us, we together were sufficient to resist nine or ten thousand Frenchmen'. While convinced that 'all the country would join with us against them, and all other strangers', they conceded that this would only be the case 'if young Gerald came not with them'.[37]

The councillors suspected a Geraldine confederation comprised of the MacCarthys (and specifically Eleanor, Gerald's aunt), Brian O'Connor Faly, who refused to have any dealings with the Irish council in St Leger's absence and whose wife, Lady Mary O'Connor (née Fitzgerald), had afforded her brother protection in 1536, all the Geraldines (Desmond excepted), and various others 'vehemently suspected to take his part'.[38] They were acutely conscious of the serious ramifications of such a resurgence as they estimated that the MacCarthys alone were capable of fielding 3,000 footmen.[39] They therefore made known to Henry VIII their apprehension that

> if there should come an army, either to besiege any your highness['s] cities or ports here, or invade this your realm, without further provision of men and munition than is here already, your majesty, we fear, might perchance take dishonour.[40]

They stressed the inability of the citizens of Waterford to withstand a French attack with existing supplies of munitions. In an effort to make the best of what limited resources they had at their disposal, Lord Justice Brabazon and the Irish council resolved to retain 200 galloglas in readiness at government cost. The earls of Ormond and Desmond were also charged to retain 200 soldiers each in their respective territories, at the charge of the king's subjects. While assuring Henry VIII of their vigilance in the event of Gerald's landing, the councillors pressed for additional ammunition and a navy,

---

[36] The lord justice and council of Ireland to Henry VIII, 20 May 1544, *LP Henry VIII*, xix/1 (1544), 542; *SP Henry VIII*, iii. 501, 502.
[37] Ibid.
[38] The lord justice and council of Ireland to Henry VIII, 20 May 1544, *LP Henry VIII*, xix/1 (1544), 542; *SP Henry VIII*, iii. 502.
[39] Ibid.
[40] Ibid.

emphasising that if the requisite defences were provided, and if Gerald did not return to Ireland, 'the French men, . . . we trust shall take little advantage here without displeasure at land'.[41]

By mid-June the councillors' preoccupation with the rumoured French invasion had begun to dissipate, though they felt duty-bound to advertise Henry of a fresh report that they received, also alleging that Gerald was to head a French expedition to Ireland. On this occasion it was another Englishman, the son of the lord chief justice of Ireland, Sir Gerald Aylmer, who was the source of the intelligence. Under interrogation, Aylmer's son explained that he had returned to Ireland following his release from a prison in the Breton town of Le Croisic where he and several merchants from Wexford town had been incarcerated for approximately two years. Upon his arrival, he was immediately questioned by the English authorities on suspicion of having smuggled into Ireland private letters addressed by Gerald to his secret allies. Aylmer stated that when he departed Le Croisic, it was commonly reported that François I had appointed a navy comprised of 15,000 men, which lay in waiting at Brest, to accompany Gerald Fitzgerald to Ireland. As far as he was aware the fleet was to land either in O'Donnell's country in Ulster, or alternatively in Limerick or Waterford.[42] Again, no evidence is available to indicate that there was any substance to these rumours.

In contrast with their startled reaction to similar reports from Waterford the month before, Brabazon and the council were unperturbed by this second report, dismissing it as 'not so likely in all parts to us, as we judge the same to be true'.[43] In any event, it was Scotland rather than Ireland that caused Henry VIII the greatest concern. Exasperated by Scottish intransigence, he had Edward Seymour burn and waste the Lowlands, sack Edinburgh, Leith and Cardinal Beaton's city of St Andrew's and publicise denunciations of the cardinal and of the Auld Alliance throughout Scotland.[44] In spite of the success of this brutal campaign, the Scots were more enraged than intimidated, which caused rival factions to unite in opposition to the English king during the next eighteen months. Henry was, therefore, in a vulnerable position. The campaign in France showed little sign of significant advancement and he was left to stand alone in opposition to François I while Charles V independently negotiated a peace settlement with the French king at Crépy on 18 September 1544.[45] This isolation magnified English concerns

---

[41] The lord justice and council of Ireland to Henry VIII, 20 May 1544, *LP Henry VIII*, xix/1 (1544), 542; *SP Henry VIII*, iii. 501, 502, 503.

[42] The lord justice and council of Ireland to Henry VIII, 13 June 1544, *LP Henry VIII*, xix/2 (1544), 696; *SP Henry VIII*, iii. 503.

[43] Ibid.

[44] Head, 'Henry VIII's Scottish policy', 22.

[45] Ibid.

with British security and resulted in disturbances in both Scotland and Ireland being viewed in a more serious light than had hitherto been the case.

In February 1545 councillors at Whitehall and Dublin were alarmed by the Scots' victory at Ancrum and by reports circulating in Ireland of an imminent Scottish attack.[46] Added sting to this intrigue was provided by a rumour that Gerald Fitzgerald was also expected to arrive, backed by the French who sought to capitalise on the uncertainty surrounding his movements and intentions. In contrast with the councillors' reaction to claims of Gerald's return circulated in June of the previous year, they viewed this report much more seriously on the grounds that 'the practices this last year made by the French king to diverse captains of the remote parts of this land (whereof . . . [St Leger] sent . . . [Henry VIII] knowledge from O'Donnell) makes us here the rather to believe this bruit'.[47]

Yet encouraged by O'Donnell's demonstrations of his loyalty in such situations in the recent past, St Leger remained quietly confident that he and the earl of Tyrone would continue to be 'true to his majesty' with the result that 'there shall be no great fear' of such an invasion. The deputy also drew consolation from the fact that the two lords were at odds with each other at that time: he deliberately adopted a *laissez-faire* stance in this dispute, believing it to be advantageous as

> while they two so strive, we shall be surer either of them both, or at least one of them; whereas, if they were in great amity, as they have been in times past, they might perchance, by persuasion and rewards of the French king, do some things unfitting.[48]

St Leger's calm response to the threat of invasion was evident in the modest nature of his request for defence supplies. That he asked only for one or two ships to be dispatched to patrol the Ulster coast with a view to capturing French and Scottish enemy ships testifies to his effectiveness in marshalling Gaelic and Anglo-Irish elements within the polity.[49]

In April rumours of the allegedly imminent French–Scottish invasion under the leadership of Gerald were still in circulation. Although concerned, St Leger was confident in the continued loyalty of the Ulster chiefs, and reassured Henry VIII that Ireland remained 'in the same quiet as for two or three years past'.[50] In response, Henry and the English privy council were dismissive of a rumoured invasion as evidenced by their failure to act on the

---

[46] St Leger to Wriothesley, 26 Feb. 1545, *LP Henry VIII*, xx/1 (1545), 273; *SP Henry VIII*, iii. 506. See also Nicholls, *Modern British Isles*, 92.

[47] St Leger to Wriothesley, 26 Feb. 1545, *LP Henry VIII*, xx/1 (1545), 273; *SP Henry VIII*, iii. 506.

[48] Ibid.

[49] Ibid.

[50] St Leger to Henry VIII, 14 Apr. 1545, *LP Henry VIII*, xx/1 (1545), 519; *SP Henry VIII*, iii. 515. See also Hogan, *Ireland in the European system*, 62.

deputy's modest plea for a number of ships to patrol the northern coast. St Leger was, therefore, obliged to reiterate his request that two or three ships be dispatched to police Irish havens 'for it is likely that the French king will do somewhat there considering his last year's practice with O'Donnell'. The modest catalytic impact that these rumours exerted on the Dublin administration's adoption of expedient defence measures is manifest in St Leger's pre-emptive moves to erect beacons at strategic coastal points and to order weaponry, then in low supply in Ireland. It is also reflected in his orders to the Palesmen and the residents of the cities and towns to muster troops and to be 'in a continual readiness so as . . . we shall be . . . ready for to resist his enemies' in the event of their launching an attack.[51]

A key contributory factor in St Leger's successful navigation of Irish politics during this delicate phase in international relations was his ability to adopt anticipatory measures to ensure that stable relations were maintained with the leading Anglo-Irish or Gaelic lords. In so doing he suppressed their inclination towards involvement in intrigue with England's continental enemies. This in turn yielded a welcome result in the exceedingly modest scale and negligible cost of the additional defence provisions for Ireland which is less a reflection of the perceived seriousness of the French threat and more a testimony to his effectiveness in maintaining political equilibrium in Ireland. His adroitness is especially evident in his handling of an anticipated Geraldine resurgence, with the result that by May 1545 the Dublin administration's fear of some of the key figures in the Irish league of 1537–41 regrouping had begun to recede. Tyrone proved co-operative in furnishing the government with intelligence regarding the movements of James MacDonnell, captain of the Scots, who was suspected of conspiring to join forces with the French off the northern coast of Ireland. O'Neill assured St Leger and the councillors that it was MacDonnell's intention to submit to Henry.[52] While acknowledging that 'in times passed, [Brian O'Connor Faly] hath much strayed from the king[']s obedience', the lord deputy was heartened by the apparently reformed behaviour of the Geraldine supporter who during 'three or four years past . . . hath kept so honest peace to his graces['s] subjects, as we have good hope of his continuance'.[53] In an effort to maintain good relations with O'Connor, St Leger asked that Henry VIII respond favourably to the chief's petition for permission to hold his land and for advancement to the rank of viscount, though a deterioration in O'Connor's

---

[51] Ibid. See also St Leger and council of Ireland to the privy council, 6 May 1545, *LP Henry VIII*, xx/1 (1545), 665; *SP Henry VIII*, iii. 517–18.

[52] St Leger and council of Ireland to the privy council, 6 May 1545, *LP Henry VIII*, xx/1 (1545), 665; *SP Henry VIII*, iii. 518.

[53] St Leger and council of Ireland to the privy council, 6 May 1545, *LP Henry VIII*, xx/1 (1545), 665; *SP Henry VIII*, iii. 519.

relations with St Leger's successor later in the 1540s led to his son's involvement in serious negotiations to orchestrate a French invasion.[54]

The last figure identified for neutralisation in case of a French–Scottish campaign led by Gerald, was his aunt, Eleanor O'Donnell. On 4 May 1545 she wrote to Henry VIII, requesting a pardon on her own behalf. During the previous two years, she had continually lobbied for a royal pardon through the agency of the lord deputy and Irish council who refused to represent her case to the king because she insisted on residing beyond the Pale in the MacCarthys' territory. By May she had been granted a safe conduct to stay within the Pale from where she interceded with the king to grant her suit so that she might then 'at least avoid the often suspect causeless conceived against . . . [her] by continual demoring (residing) in the extreme confines of this . . . land'.[55] St Leger explained to Henry that he had granted Lady Eleanor a safe conduct 'in respect of the time, to allure her from any practice in the south parts, where great bruit is of the arrival of the French men'. Thus, the threat of French collusion with her nephew exerted a direct, expeditious conciliatory influence over the deputy's otherwise protracted handling of Eleanor's suit.[56]

The lord deputy's view of Eleanor had changed dramatically: whereas before he suspected her as 'a practicer and procurer of dissensions and wars', now he dismissed her as 'but a woman' who could be pardoned by the Irish council were it not for her Kildare parentage. In order that 'she may repose herself, and so be put out of fear and thereby have occasion to relinquish her old fantasies', the council recommended that she be granted the royal pardon that she requested.[57] Significantly, in seeking such a pardon, Eleanor was publicly resigned to the fact that this round of Geraldine intrigue was either groundless or doomed to failure, a stance that reassured the Irish council. By the end of May 1545, therefore, Gerald Fitzgerald's key potential allies all appeared to have been appeased.

None the less, St Leger was by no means complacent. On his own initiative he had taken steps to reinforce Irish defences and continually pressed for the dispatch of more ships to police the activities of the French, Bretons and Scots who 'do much hurt here upon the sea coasts'. English apprehension concerning Gerald's reappearance as leader of a Franco-Scottish fleet, backed by his extended kin network, had faded by May 1545. Instead, it was French designs on Ireland and Scotland and the attendant threat to Ireland's security

---

54 Ibid.
55 Lady Eleanor Fitzgerald to Henry VIII, 4 May 1545, *LP Henry VIII*, xx/1 (1545), 653; *SP Henry VIII*, iii. 516.
56 St Leger and council of Ireland to the privy council, 6 May 1545, *LP Henry VIII*, xx/1 (1545), 665; *SP Henry VIII*, iii. 517–20.
57 Ibid. On 11 August 1545 St Leger notified William Paget that a bill was assigned, granting a royal pardon to Lady Eleanor Fitzgerald: St Leger to Paget, *LP Henry VIII*, xx/2 (1545), 98.

that preoccupied St Leger and the council from that point onwards. On 11 May they alerted the English privy council to Ireland's vulnerability to French attack owing to the lack of adequate defence forces, particularly in Cork and Kinsale.[58] The councillors complained 'that the retinue here being but 500 men . . . is little enough to have vigilant eye to . . . the English Pale' and even there, they warned, there was a 'likelihood that French men would attempt to do harm'.[59]

Since virtually all appeals for reinforcements failed to elicit a response from the English privy council, responsibility for the defence of Irish ports from French and Scottish raids fell to individual English captains such as John Hill and William Logan. They engaged in *ad hoc* patrols that proved entirely ineffectual as Bretons continued to trade with Ireland despite their official exclusion during the war.[60] In summer 1545, while England was gripped by a French invasion scare, Henry VIII again demonstrated his confidence in Ireland's peaceable state when he resolved to recruit a further 2,000 Irish kerne to invade Scotland in September. This mustering of kerne held the added appeal of clearing the country of 'the most wild and savage sort of them there, whose absence should rather do good than harm'.[61] By November the troops were assembled and thereafter dispatched to Dumbarton, though developments in Scotland resulted in their being immediately disbanded.

In 1546, reviewing his government strategy during the Anglo-French war, St Leger justified his refusal to pursue campaigns against the Gaelic Irish during that period on the grounds that he believed that he and the army should 'still reside about Dublin for resistance of the French men'.[62] During his term as lord deputy, the threat of French invasion impinged directly upon St Leger's domestic policy or at least the pace at which that policy was implemented. Concern at the prospect of invasion spurred him to take anticipatory steps to retain the goodwill of the Irish nobility, to keep former Geraldine supporters in check and to marshal what few resources he could to fortify the country's inadequate defences. The emergence of a comparatively stable political and economic climate in Ireland was assisted by the removal of the more fractious elements among the Gaelic kerne to France and Scotland. Without Anglo-Irish or Gaelic allies, the French could achieve nothing in Ireland. Hence, while the lord deputy's response to the rumoured invasion was particularly animated in May 1544 and in February of the following year,

---

[58] St Leger and council of Ireland to the privy council, 11 May 1545, *SP Henry VIII*, iii. 521–2.
[59] Ibid.
[60] St Leger to the privy council, 27 July 1545, *LP Henry VIII*, xx/1 (1545), 1287; St Leger to the privy council, 3 Aug. 1545, *LP Henry VIII*, xx/2 (1545), 29; St Leger and council of Ireland to Henry VIII, 12 Aug. 1545, *SP Henry VIII*, iii. 530.
[61] Quoted in Ellis, *Ireland in the age of the Tudors*, 156.
[62] 'An answere to suche notes . . . against the kinges majesties deputies' (undated, 1546), *SP Henry VIII*, iii. 571.

the French threat exerted no significant impact on the English privy council's adoption of defence measures in respect of Ireland.

The English were anxious to end the war with France from September 1545 though it was not until March of the following year that Henry VIII consented to talks that dragged on into June when a peace treaty was signed. According to the terms of this agreement, Henry undertook not to declare war on the Scots unless the latter broke the peace. The English also promised to return Boulogne to France within eight years and upon receipt of payment of 2,000,000 crowns. While the treaty ostensibly restored amicable relations between François and Henry, according to J. J. Scarisbrick, 'behind the screen of gallantry stood a good deal of well-judged suspicion' and possession of Boulogne remained a highly contentious issue.[63] However, that veneer of peace survived until after Henry's death on 27 January and that of François on 31 March 1547. Thereafter, increased strain on Anglo-Scottish relations, on St Leger's dealings with the Irish council and on the Dublin administration's handling of Gaelic lords, especially Brian O'Connor Faly, combined with political instability in England, St Leger's recall in 1548 and a revival of the Auld Alliance to generate a particularly dangerous international situation in which, for the first and only time in the sixteenth century, a French king genuinely looked set to stage a military intervention in Ireland.

II

Apart from direct political contacts between Irish lords and the French court, and the French encounter with the Irish at Boulogne in 1544–6, simultaneous advances in diplomatic relations between France and England, from the late 1530s onwards in particular, contributed significantly if indirectly to the development of broader Franco-Irish relations. While maritime contacts remained a steady source of intelligence throughout this period, the increased centralisation and bureaucratisation of government administrations in Ireland, England and France had a significant effect in advancing relations between France and Ireland. As the sphere of effective influence of the Dublin administration stretched deeper into Gaelic areas during the 1540s, a correspondingly more informed acquaintance with the personalities and the dynamics governing Gaelic politics became manifest in the correspondence of the French ambassadors to the court of Henry VIII.

During his term as ambassador to England, Louis de Perreau, sieur de Castillon (1537–9), displayed little interest in Irish affairs and only referred to Ireland when developments there had ramifications for French relations with England.[64] Beyond passing allusions to Ireland, there is little to indicate

---

[63] Scarisbrick, *Henry VIII*, 458–64, 464; Palmer, *Problem of Ireland*, 64.
[64] For a somewhat dated account of the sieur de Castillon's career see le marquis de la Jonquière, 'Une Ambassade en Angleterre au XVIe siècle: M. de Castillon à la cour d'Henri

any real understanding on the part of the French ambassador of the nature of Irish affairs in their own right.[65] Following the appointment of Charles de Marillac as ambassador to England in April 1539, the French court's acquaintance with Irish politics was advanced significantly.[66] Described by Potter as 'one of the most practised French ambassadors of the period in the arts of espionage and diplomatic intrigue', Marillac was an astute observer of current affairs, including those of Ireland.[67] Formerly a lawyer at the *parlement* of Paris, an intermediary ambassador to Constantinople and then a councillor of the *parlement*, Marillac displayed considerable incisiveness in his statements concerning Ireland.[68] In 1540, while Gerald Fitzgerald sought refuge in France, Marillac briefed the French constable, Anne de Montmorency, on the English government's defence measures for Ireland and reported details of the naval preparations by Scots suspected of intending to invade Ireland.[69] In June 1540 he closely observed Henry VIII's and the English privy council's treatment of Fitzgerald's uncle, Lord Leonard Grey, and recounted to the constable details of how Henry had captured Grey's Geraldine relatives in Ireland and brought them to London where they were executed.[70] While he was attuned to Gerald's movements during his exile on the continent, Marillac was also apprised of the agitated state of a handful of Irish lords who had been admitted to the Irish parliament but who subsequently became 'inobéissants et peu à peu se sont après revoltés d'avantage'.[71] In 1542 the ambassador exhibited the same confidence regarding the success of English policy in Ireland as characterised communications from Dublin officials at this time. François I was made aware of the monumental constitutional importance of the act passed in the 1541 parliament in which Henry VIII was named king and head of the Church of Ireland.[72]

Marillac recognised the important ramifications of the early stages of the implementation of the surrender and regrant programme, and in his reportage of its progress deepened François's knowledge of Ireland's political potentates and potential allies. In July 1542 François was apprised that the thirteenth earl of Desmond, 'qui a longtemps faict la guerre à ce roy', had submitted to

VIII', *Revue des Deux Mondes* xcviii (mars 1890), 123–58. See also Fleury Vindry, *Les Ambassadeurs français permanents au XVIe siècle*, Paris 1903, 32.

[65] De Castillon to de Montmorency, 2 fév. 1538, AE, CP Angleterre, iii, ambassade de M. de Castillon, 72v; *Correspondance politique de MM de Castillon et de Marillac*, 22.

[66] See Vindry, *Les Ambassadeurs français*, 33, and Pierre de Vassière, *Charles de Marillac, ambassadeur et homme politique sous les règnes de François Ier, Henry II et François II, 1510–60*, Geneva 1971.

[67] Potter, 'Diplomacy in the mid-sixteenth century', 329.

[68] Vindry, *Les Ambassadeurs français*, 33; de Vassière, *Charles de Marillac*, 9.

[69] De Marillac to de Montmorency, 24 av., 21 mai 1540, *Correspondance politique de MM de Castillon et de Marillac*, 180, 186.

[70] De Marillac to François I, 23 juin 1540, 30 juin 1541, ibid. 196, 318–19.

[71] Ibid. 319.

[72] De Marillac to François I, 5 fév. 1542, ibid. 386.

Henry VIII as sovereign of Ireland and three months later he learned of Con O'Neill's submission:

> le plus grand et plus bel seigneur et capitaine, qui toute sa vie fait guerre aux anglois, qu'on appelle le Grand O'Neill, depuis trois ou quatre jours s'est venu rendre à ce roy, lui faisant hommage et serment de le servir et lui promettant au surplus, une grand force contre ses ennemis.[73]

Marillac also testified to the unprecedented loyalty shown Henry by the Gaelic Irish, emphasising the readiness of 'un grand nombre de sauvages' in Ulster to assist the English in defending the northern coastline from attack by the Scots, and the absence of a Gaelic threat to the Dublin administration.[74] His successor, Odet de Selve, who served between 1546 and 1549, further extended the breadth of French acquaintance with the Dublin administration's policies and the dynamics governing Gaelic politics.[75]

From the early 1540s the correspondence of French ambassadors based in England and Scotland became an increasingly important channel whereby the French king indirectly garnered 'reliable' (in the sense of officially reported) information concerning the country's most powerful Gaelic lords, their military capabilities, their grievances and details of government strategies for dealing with them. As such, it became a crucial conduit by which the French could gauge the likelihood of a successful outcome to a potential military intervention. The importance of these diplomats was especially magnified in the 1550s when Antoine de Noailles and Henri Clutin d'Oisel, ambassadors to England and Scotland respectively, used their positions to furnish the French court with regular and detailed reports on domestic Irish politics that in turn fuelled French–Irish intrigue.

III

During the period 1522–47, the French were brought into unprecedented direct contact with Irish dissidents and Gaelic soldiers. While successive rounds of serious intrigue failed to bring about a French invasion of Ireland, the threat of French intervention exerted a mild catalytic effect on the 'policy' of the lord deputy in respect of Ireland's defence in the 1520s and 1540s. Although Henry VIII and the English privy council blustered about the menace posed by the French and the Scots, in the final analysis their parsimony outweighed their concern and St Leger's track record in capably handling the Irish situation allowed them to ignore his calls for reinforce-

[73] De Marillac to François I, 2 juill., 19 sept. 1542, ibid. 429, 464.
[74] Ibid.
[75] See *Correspondance politique de Odet de Selve, ambassadeur de France en Angleterre (1546–9)*, ed. Germain Lefèvre-Pontalis, Paris 1888, 41–2, 50, 61, 96, 145, 146, 148, 151–2, 248, 261.

ments that were so modest as to be self-defeating. Apart from a handful of ships dispatched to patrol the Irish coastline, ultimately both Lord Deputy Ormond in the 1520s and Lord Deputy Anthony St Leger in the 1540s were left to their own devices in marshalling what few resources they had at their disposal in an effort to provide some form of expedient defence measures.

During the first half of the sixteenth century, domestic Irish politics were drawn into the sphere of British and western European politics and diplomacy, and changes in both dictated the direction and the outcome of Franco-Irish intrigue. In the process, the French perceived the locus of power within Ireland gravitating from Desmond's patrimony in the south-west to the territories of Manus O'Donnell and Con O'Neill in Ulster by the late 1530s. This in turn dictated their targeting the northern chiefs in negotiations for mounting a French invasion in the 1540s. As political relations between the Irish and the French advanced in the early 1540s, increasingly Scottish–Irish collaboration was regarded as the most viable route for a French descent on Ireland.

An enduring by-product of the episodic engagement between French and Irish in the 1520s and early to mid-1540s was the increased mutual awareness of the Irish and French ruling elites whose acquaintance with the key personalities and fundamental dynamics governing political affairs in each others' countries was deepened in a significant way. Slowly French appreciation of the dynamics governing Irish domestic politics grew more sophisticated (though this should not be exaggerated), particularly in the 1540s, when they demonstrated a grasp of the importance of Gerald Fitzgerald and Catholicism as key causes guaranteed to whip up Irish support for French designs on Ireland. It was also during the 1540s that figures such as Manus O'Donnell in Tyrconnell, Con O'Neill in Tyrone, the MacDonnells in Scotland and Ireland, Archibald Campbell, fifth earl of Argyll and Marie de Guise, James V's widow, in Scotland, forged a network of overlapping contacts connecting Ulster, Scotland and France. While the rumoured French invasion of Ireland, headed by Gerald Fitzgerald, failed to materialise in the 1540s, these individuals emerged as the key players in the century's most serious episode in Franco-Irish-Scottish triangular intrigue during the winter of 1549–50.

4

The French Diplomatic Mission to Ulster and its Aftermath, 1548–1551

The establishment of garrisons beyond the Pale in Ireland during the late 1540s initiated a process of piecemeal conquest which antagonised displaced Gaelic lords, drove them to seek foreign intervention and created strategic threats to the British polity where none had hitherto existed.[1] Throughout the period from the late 1540s to the mid-1560s, Gaelic dissidents became embroiled with the French, the Scots and disaffected elements in England in intrigue which involved varying degrees of collaboration and which aimed at undermining the Tudor *régime*. For the first time the Gaelic lords' projection of the Irish cause in quasi-religious terms impacted in a real sense on the consciousness of France's leading statesmen.[2] The highpoint of this convergence of interests occurred in the winter of 1549–50 when Henri II came closest to staging an invasion of Ireland via Scotland.

This episode took place at a critical phase in relations between France and the three kingdoms of the British Isles that revolved around two highly contentious issues – the dispute between France and England concerning the latter's determined hold on its few French possessions, and their conflicting interests in Scotland. Henri II's ascension to the French throne in 1547 and the concomitant ascendancy of the Guises, their joint support for Marie de Guise in Scotland, the vulnerability of the minority *régime* in England, the disturbed state of the Gaelic polity and strained relations between France and England in the late 1540s and early 1550s all augured well for Irish prospects of securing French intervention.

Apart from representing a marked advance in political relations between the Irish and French, the negotiations conducted between two leading French officials and Con O'Neill and several other notables from Ulster in the winter of 1549–50 have wider political significance in two respects. First, in the mid-sixteenth century French foreign policy in general was shaped by fear of Habsburg encirclement. This caused Henri II and the Guises to pursue a British policy whereby they lent considerable military and financial support

---

1   Morgan, 'British policies before the British state', 76.
2   See Potter, 'French intrigue', 159. Potter's work serves as a valuable revision of Hogan's, *Ireland in the European system*, chs v, vi, which contain several unsustainable extrapolations and inaccuracies. See also Jane Dawson, 'Anglo-Scottish Protestant culture and integration in sixteenth-century Britain', in Ellis and Barber, *Conquest and union*, 89–91.

to Marie de Guise's *régime* in order to apply pressure on the Tudors in peripheral quarters of the British Isles. To that end the French sporadically encouraged insurgency in England, Ireland or Scotland, secretly or otherwise. The 1549–50 negotiations therefore represented a serious attempt on the part of the French to move towards encircling England by forging alliances between dissidents from Scotland and Ireland. Second, by exposing the strategic vulnerability of Ireland and of the wider British polity, this episode lent urgency to the English administration's intensifying search for a British policy with which it might counter French designs.

I

The initial pretext for Irish involvement with the French in the late 1540s was the insurrection of the midland Gaelic septs of O'More and O'Connor who had a truculent relationship with the Dublin administration in the aftermath of the Kildare rebellion and prior to agreeing terms for peace with Sir Anthony St Leger in the early 1540s. The uprising stemmed largely from an essentially localised episode in an ongoing political power struggle between supporters of the two most influential dynasties in Ireland, the Ormonds and the Kildares. The death of James, tenth earl of Ormond, in October 1546 precipitated a crisis and left a major power vacuum in Irish dynastic politics almost comparable to that which had followed the removal of the Kildares a decade before. Ormond's lands and claims to lordship in north Munster and Leinster were in jeopardy as he was succeeded by a fifteen-year-old heir who was to be kept as a ward of court in England. The earl's Geraldine opponents in Leinster immediately set about capitalising on the Ormond dynasty's vulnerability. Kildare supporters re-emerged among the O'Mores, the O'Tooles, the O'Byrnes and, particularly among the Fitzgerald's strongest Gaelic allies, the O'Connors, who had been engaged in sporadic war with the Butlers throughout the mid-1540s.[3]

In the summer of 1548 St Leger's successor, Sir Edward Bellingham, led a hosting into O'More's territory and established a garrison at Fort Protector. Cahir O'Connor rose in rebellion soon after, and before the end of the year disturbances extended from Kildare through Leix and Offaly, westwards to the Shannon and to the districts of Nenagh and Athlone. By spring 1549 the O'Mores and the O'Connors had submitted and their lands were confiscated; Cahir O'Connor was executed for treason; Brian O'Connor Faly was imprisoned in London, and the Dublin government faced a vengeful Irishry, led by

[3] Brady, *Chief governors*, 48–9, 56–7 n. 36; Ellis, *Ireland in the age of the Tudors*, 266; Lennon, *Sixteenth-century Ireland*, 165–6; D. G. White, 'The reign of Edward VI in Ireland: some political, social and economic aspects', *IHS* xiv (Mar. 1965), 199–203; Potter, 'French intrigue in Ireland', 161; Palmer, *Problem of Ireland*, 72.

Brian's son, Cormac, who in turn sought French aid through their emissary, George Paris.[4]

Following the midlands revolt, George Paris, a Westmeath gentleman, became the chief representative of the Irish in negotiations at the French and Scottish courts and he continued to serve as 'a common post between the wild Irish and the French' in his capacity as O'Connor's envoy until 1560. Paris sought to secure French intervention in support of all Gaelic lords opposed to the crown. In the immediate term this necessitated involving the Ulster lords, and specifically Con O'Neill, within his scheme if plans for an invasion were to have any chance of success.[5] As this study shows, Paris was, in many respects, ill-suited to his role as envoy and negotiator and this may be seen as a contributory factor in the failure of Franco-Irish talks to bring about a French invasion of Ireland in the mid-sixteenth century. He was considered untrustworthy and capable of duplicity, an unscrupulous opportunist predominantly motivated by self-interest. His diplomatic capabilities were not highly rated, the English ambassador to France, Sir John Mason, dismissing him as ill suited to diplomatic affairs, 'a man of cantakered malice . . . and of light behaviour' and in 1551, impatient at Paris's failure to secure French aid for his cause, Cormac O'Connor Faly travelled to the French court to present his case in person.[6] In the early 1550s it also emerged that Paris's duplicity as envoy had caused 'great hurt of the Irish princes' whose interests he claimed to represent.[7] However, in 1548 and 1549, Paris played a pivotal role in maintaining the momentum of ongoing negotiations between the French and Scottish courts that preceded the French diplomatic mission to Ulster in October 1549. He also accompanied the two envoys on their visit.[8]

While the midlands revolt in 1548 did not present a threat to the Dublin administration of comparable magnitude to that posed by the league in 1539–40, fears of O'Connor's collusion with the French and anxiety at what was perceived as a revived 'Geraldine adventure' caused English privy councillors to question the viability of Sir Anthony St Leger's conciliatory policy in governing Ireland. The delicacy of international political relations, the

---

4   Brady, *Chief governors*, 57; Ellis, *Ireland in the age of the Tudors*, 266; Lennon, *Sixteenth-century Ireland*, 165–6; White, 'The reign of Edward VI in Ireland', 199–203; Potter, 'French intrigue', 161; Palmer, *Problem of Ireland*, 72.
5   Sir John Mason to the privy council, 14 June 1550, PRO, SP 68/9a/17; Patrick Fraser Tytler, *History of Scotland*, 6 vols, Edinburgh 1828–37, i. 292. See also Potter, 'French intrigue', 169.
6   Mason to the privy council, 18 Apr. 1551, SP 68/9a/291. Given the very privileged social background of the majority of the diplomats representing the English and French courts, it is hardly surprising that Mason had little regard for Paris who was of comparatively humble origins.
7   Memoir, 6 Oct. 1552, CSP Spain, 1550–2, 587.
8   Jacques Melvil, *The memoires of Sir James Melvil of Hal Hill: containing an important account of the most remarkable affairs of state . . .*, ed. George Scott, London 1683 edn, 8–9 (account of diplomatic mission to Ireland), and *Mémoires historiques . . .*, ed. George Scott, 2 vols, London 1694, i. 30, 33; Potter, 'French intrigue', 165.

vulnerability of the protectorate administration in England, and the increasingly antagonistic relations between the English and Scottish courts at that precise time left the English councillors acutely sensitised to the danger of such insurgence to British security, regardless of motives, and caused them to insist on decisive suppression of any disturbance.

Both François I and Henri II were informed of the midlands conflict in Ireland in the late 1540s by their ambassadors to the English court.[9] They were also aware of the impenetrable nature of Irish domestic politics that posed an insurmountable obstacle to successive attempts at negotiating effective foreign intervention in the sixteenth century.[10] However, the French diplomatic initiative in Ulster in winter 1549–50 demonstrated that when continental and Scottish circumstances were favourable, the French were prepared to pursue their interest in Ireland by endeavouring to reach terms with the Ulster lords without fully grasping the intricacies of Gaelic politics. Odet de Selve, the French ambassador to the English court, had a very superfical understanding of Gaelic politics, but none the less did grasp one essential feature of its dynamics. In repeating rumours that Gerald Fitzgerald was one of the principal architects of the Gaelic lords' rebellion in his report to the French king, Selve echoed the English government's anxiety regarding the Geraldine dimension to the disturbances. In so doing he confirmed French convictions regarding Fitzgerald's pivotal influence and importance in domestic Irish politics and his indispensability to any designs for French intervention in Ireland.[11]

The propaganda generated around the Geraldine dimension to the insurrection was deliberately used as bait to entice the French monarch to consider extending his Scottish campaign into Ireland in 1549–50 in response to the solicitations of O'Connor's envoy, George Paris. By ostensibly taking up the banner of the Geraldine cause, Paris aimed to muster more widespread support throughout Ireland for the defeated Gaelic septs of the midlands and adopted a rallying cause that he badly needed in order to elevate a localised dispute in the midlands to the level of a countrywide campaign of resistance to the Tudor *régime* that might secure the backing of the French crown. In casting the insurrection in the style of a 'Geraldine adventure', Paris also provided Henri II with a legitimate reason for potential military intervention in defence of Fitzgerald and his victimised allies in Ireland.

As already indicated, both the English and the French appreciated the indispensability of the Geraldine heir to the success of a French invasion of

9 Odet de Selve to the admiral of France, 12 oct., 4 nov. 1546, *Correspondance politique de Odet de Selve*, 41–2, 50; de Selve to François Ier, 25 nov. 1546, 31 jan., 23 mai 1547, ibid. 61, 96, 145; de Selve to the constable of France, 23 mai 1547, ibid. 146; de Selve to de Vieilleville, 29 mai 1547, ibid. 148.

10 Potter, 'French intrigue', 160, 180.

11 De Selve to the constable of France, 16 juin, 5 déc. 1547, 28 mars 1548, *Correspondance politique de Odet de Selve*, 151–2, 248, 261.

Ireland and the French had, on previous occasions, deliberately magnified English insecurities by propagating intrigue centred on Gerald's rumoured return. In the years 1547–9, Selve, the papal nuncios to France and Henri Clutin d'Oisel, the astute French ambassador to Scotland heavily implicated in Franco-Scottish-Irish triangular intrigue, testified to the acknowledged *gravitas* of the Geraldine heir and to the desirability of having him as an ally in the event of a French assault on Ireland. Meanwhile, by November 1548 the efforts of George Paris, who had been actively engaged in substantive negotiations at the French and Scottish courts, seemed to pay off as the French court was widely believed to have been favourably disposed to the overtures of Irish political dissidents.[12]

Henri II's accession to the throne and the attendant rise of the Guise faction to dominance at court augured well for Paris and his associates being afforded more than the usual platitudes at the French court. Militantly Catholic, the Guise dynasty was a cadet branch of the ducal house of Lorraine and made their careers in the French army and in the Church. Though Claude, first duc de Guise and duc d'Aumale, and his brother, Jean, first cardinal of Lorraine, died in 1550, the next generation enhanced the standing of the dynasty. By 1559 Claude's eldest son and the head of the family, François, duc de Guise (d. 1563), was acknowledged as France's ablest military commander as a result of his achievements leading the French army to victory against the imperial forces in Metz and regaining Calais from English occupation. His brother, Charles, the cardinal of Lorraine (d. 1574), was held in high esteem in Rome and led the French delegation to the plenary session of the Council of Trent. Both sat on the king's council. Their sister, Marie (d. 1560), the widow of James V of Scotland, governed Scotland during the minority of her daughter Mary Stuart, and their brothers, Claude (d. 1573), marquis de Mayenne and duc d'Aumale, Louis, cardinal of Guise, and René, marquis d'Elboeuf, supported the interests of their two elder brothers. This dynastic solidarity was the main reason for the rise of these French grandees and it proved fundamental to French designs on Scotland, and by extension Ireland, in the mid-sixteenth century.[13] By the early 1550s, although the constable, Anne de Montmorency, was believed to have had 'the outward administration of all thing', in reality 'the credit of the house of Guise in this court passeth all others'.[14]

The dominance of the Guise faction at the French court helped stiffen Henri II's resolve actively to support their sister, Marie de Guise, in governing Scotland and in withstanding English attack, particularly from 1548 onwards. This resulted in the French being in the unprecedented position of being both interested in and logistically capable of undertaking a military operation

---

[12] Lord Chancellor Alen to Paget, 21 Nov. 1548, PRO, SP 61/1/130; Jean de St Mauris to Charles V, 5 Feb. 1549, CSP *Spain, 1547–9*, 336.

[13] Garrisson, *Sixteenth-century France*, 275.

[14] Mason to the council, 23 Feb. 1551, CSP *Foreign 1547–53*, pp. xii–xiii, 65–6.

in Ireland.[15] The prospect of a marriage alliance between the future Mary Queen of Scots and the dauphin provided Henri with a legitimate rationale for his intervention in Scottish affairs.[16] Under pressure from the queen dowager and the Guise faction at the Scottish court, Henri launched a French military campaign in Scotland in 1548, in fulfilment of his obligation to protect that realm and the Catholic faith.[17] Henri was not daunted by the inconclusive outcome of the 1548 Scottish campaign. Events in Scotland in the following year provided the French with the necessary impetus seriously to consider an assault on Ireland. At a time when the English protector's authority was particularly vulnerable, George Paris's reports of a groundswell of discontent in Gaelic areas were especially opportune in encouraging French designs on Ireland.

Prior to the summer of 1549 George Paris, d'Oisel, the French ambassador to Scotland, and Archibald Campbell, fifth earl of Argyll, the ringleaders in triangular Franco-Scottish-Irish intrigue, held out hopes for launching a French military expedition to Ireland led by Gerald Fitzgerald as a figurehead. Beginning in December 1547 there were reports of Gerald Fitzgerald's having arrived in Scotland, accompanied by French vessels and companies of French officers. However, from early 1548, both the French and English competed for Fitzgerald's assurances of his future loyalty and until June 1549, when Gerald finally agreed terms with the English king, Irish dissidents capitalised on the uncertainty surrounding his whereabouts and intentions by circulating wildly fantastic reports alleging his supposed involvement in disturbances in Ireland as the French had done in the mid-1540s. Early in 1548 the English council took the first in a series of steps to neutralise Fitzgerald by passing a resolution to have him admitted to the king's favour.[18] In June Gerald was said to have been at the French court planning an insurrection in Ireland giving rise to a wave of rumours of his imminent return to Ireland via Scotland.[19]

Between November 1548 and early January of the following year, unsubstantiated reports that Henri II intended to dispatch Gerald to Ireland, backed by a French army, that Fitzgerald was in Dumbarton, that he was about to marry the young queen of Scots, and that he would have the support of the French in an effort to assert a claim to the crowns of both kingdoms

---

[15] Baudouin-Matuszek, 'Les Expéditions françaises', 340, 349–50; Henry Lemonnier, *Histoire de la France et de la Renaissance, 1492–1598*, Switzerland 1983 edn, 155. For discussions of the Guise ascendancy see Constant, *Les Guise*, and Carroll, *Noble power*.

[16] Baudouin-Matuszek, 'Les Expéditions françaises', 340, 349–50; Bonner, 'First phase'.

[17] Badouin-Matuszek, 'Les Expéditions françaises', 357; Bonner, 'First phase'.

[18] Hogan, *Ireland in the European system*, 59–61.

[19] See *Correspondance des nonces en France: Dandino, Della Torre et Trivultio (1546–51) avec des documents relatifs à la rupture des relations diplomatiques 1551–2*, ed. Jean Lestocquoy, Paris 1966, nos 175, 184, 188, 194.

sparked anxiety both in Dublin and Whitehall.[20] The Irish lord chancellor, Sir John Alen, was fearful lest the French should land at and fortify Skerries, a traditional trading port between Brittany and Scotland, and was unnerved by the arrival in Ireland of James Delahide, a close associate of Gerald's, whom he suspected of collusion with the earl of Desmond. Alen's suspicion of O'More and O'Connor as conspiring with the French stirred him to caution Somerset against restoring either lord to his lands.[21] While dismissive of their more fantastic claims, the English privy council also took a serious view of such reports of French designs on Ireland. In January 1549 Bellingham was warned to be alert to the duplicity of French merchants who 'under colour of merchandise' might be operating 'to the danger of any part of Ireland'.[22]

At the French court, too, ominous advances in negotiations with the Irish were manifest. In early February 1549 the imperial ambassador, St Mauris, notified Charles V that

> There is a young gentleman, son of one of the great Irish lords who lost their heads, in the nuncio's household here. The pope and the king [Henri II] give him a good allowance. The king hopes to set something afoot among his friends and relations that will keep the English busy.[23]

The young man in question was Gerald Fitzgerald. Now in his mid-twenties, he was anxious to return to Ireland to assume his hereditary titles and lands. While he was at court, Nicholas Wotton, the English ambassador, and Henri II vied to win his allegiance.[24] Wotton believed that Gerald was genuinely anxious to return to Ireland and that he sought to align himself with the English side by supplying the ambassador with intelligence concerning planned dispatches of French aid to Scotland.

In early April, however, the Irishman's gravitation towards the English crown in response to the ambassador's enticement seemed threatened as Henri II was said to have been pressing him strongly to lead either a rising with the king's assistance in Ireland or an expedition to Scotland.[25] Wotton offered Gerald a host of concessions including a free pardon, an assurance of a safe return to Ireland, a grant of a competence pending the restoration of his ancestral property and a guarantee that Somerset and the privy councillors would support him in his suit for restitution of his title and lands. Still hopeful of winning Fitzgerald's support, Henri II countered Wotton's induce-ments by sending a gentleman named Breton 'to exhort the young Irishman

[20] Privy council to Lord Deputy Sir Edward Bellingham, 6 Jan. 1549, SP 61/2/330; Wilson, *Beginnings of modern Ireland*, 308.
[21] Alen to Paget, 21 Nov. 1548, SP 61/1/130.
[22] Privy council to Bellingham, 6 Jan. 1549, SP 61/2/330.
[23] Jean de St Mauris to Charles V, 5 Feb. 1549, *CSP Spain, 1547–9*, 336.
[24] Dr Nicholas Wotton to the duke of Somerset, 23 Feb. 1549, *CSP Foreign, 1547–53*, 28.
[25] De St Mauris to Charles V, 5 Apr. 1549, *CSP Spain, 1547–9*, 362–3.

not to yield', impressing upon him that his life was in jeopardy whilst also assuring him that he should be safe and honourably treated if he consented to serve France.[26]

II

At this point Henri II was clearly affording serious consideration to under-taking a French invasion of Ireland. Breton was dispatched to Ireland 'to find out if there are any grounds for inciting the people to rise' through discussions with specific Irish lords whom he presented with gifts from Henri II. Upon his return to the French court Breton reported that he had 'found matters fairly well disposed for a future revolt, if the said Irish gentleman [Fitzgerald] could be induced to join it, for he is among the first of the land'.[27] Meanwhile, d'Oisel was in the throes of devising a strategic plan for a French attack on Ireland and Gerald Fitzgerald's involvement was identified as a vital linchpin in that design.[28] However, it was not the French who first tabled a strategy for staging such an attack. Rather it was the fifth earl of Argyll, who in February 1549 suggested to Beccarie de Pavie, baron de Fourquevaux, a commander of the French army deployed in the Scottish campaign of 1548, that the French should send aid to Irish dissidents.[29] Argyll urged Fourquevaux to consider subsidising his campaign aimed at inciting the Ulster chiefs to rebel along with the Gaelic septs of western Scotland. James MacDonnell, lord of the Isles, was also a crucial figure in facilitating plans for a French descent in Ulster. It was he who would organise the conveyance of the French diplomats to and from Lough Foyle for their mission in the winter of 1549–50.[30]

Argyll's proposal immediately won d'Oisel's approval. Still hopeful of securing Fitzgerald's involvement, the ambassador suggested harnessing the Geraldine cause as a justification for Henri II's invasion that aimed to split the English defence forces in Ireland. D'Oisel proposed launching a two-pronged attack on the island, with Gerald Fitzgerald leading the French army in attacking Waterford while Argyll simultaneously invaded Ulster with the co-operation of the province's Gaelic septs. The ambassador drew up detailed specifications for the Irish participants in the planned campaign.[31] Meanwhile, apparently encouraged at the prospect of French and Scottish intervention in Ireland, in late March 1549 Robert Wauchop, the Scottish claimant to the archbishopric of Armagh, and close ally of Cardinal Farnese

[26] Ibid.
[27] Ibid.
[28] Ibid.
[29] *Mission de Beccarie de Pavie, baron de Fourquevaux, en Ecosse, 1549*, ed. Gladys Dickinson, Oxford 1949, 30.
[30] See Melvil, *Mémoires historiques*, i. 34.
[31] *Mission de Beccarie de Pavie*, 32–3.

and of the Jesuits, left Rome for the French court where he arrived in May before proceeding to Scotland during the summer.[32] Wauchop was a very influential figure in continental ecclesiastical circles, having served as papal representative at the Diets of Worms, Ratisbon and Spiers. A close confidant of George Paris, he was also heavily implicated in the continental intrigues of the Guises and Cardinal Reginald Pole who aimed to unite France, Scotland and Ireland in a confederacy that would undermine the Protestant Tudor *régime*.[33] Wauchop's arrival in Scotland in the summer of 1549 indicated that plans for a French invasion of Ireland were gaining pace. During the following months he became a central figure in the negotiations preceding the French diplomatic mission to Ulster in the winter of 1549–50, and he accompanied the two envoys for the duration of their visit.[34]

Around the time of the recapture of Haddington fort by the Scots in September 1549, Marie de Guise also made known her support for French intervention in Ireland, suggesting to her brothers at the French court that they ought to further their interest in the Irish cause.[35] Unfortunately for d'Oisel, Argyll, Paris and the other parties hoping for French intervention in Ireland, by the end of June Gerald Fitzgerald ended months of speculation when he aligned himself with the English crown and accepted a payment of 250 French crowns by order of the protector, the duke of Somerset.[36] Apparently Cardinal Pole influenced Gerald's ultimate decision as he had recommended that Fitzgerald should return to Ireland provided he received assurances of just treatment in advance.[37]

Deprived of the opportunity to use support for the Geraldine cause as a plausible excuse for French intervention in Irish affairs or even for political propaganda, d'Oisel's need for another pretext was now particularly pressing

[32] Benignus Millett, 'The pastoral zeal of Robert Wauchope', *Seanchas Ardmhaca* ii (1956), 55.

[33] For evidence of his intrigue with the Scots and the French see Simon Renard to Charles V, 17 Sept. 1550, *CSP Spain, 1550–2*, 176; Tytler, *History of Scotland*, vi. 437. See also Hogan, *Ireland in the European system*, 100–2, 104–7, 143, 148–9, 154. For his contacts with Rome see *Correspondance des nonces en France: Dandino*, no. 194. In March 1549 he returned to Ireland: ibid. See Henri II to Marie de Guise, 11 mai 1549, *Miscellany of the Maitland Club*, Edinburgh 1837, I/2, 220. For more specialised studies of Wauchop's career see John Durkin, 'Robert Wauchop', *Innes Review* i (1950), 48–65; Millett, 'Pastoral zeal', 32–6; Roland Francisque Michel, *Les Écossais en France: les français en Écosse*, 2 vols, London 1862, i. 475–6.

[34] George Dowdall to Alen and council, 22 Mar. 1550, SP 61/2/116; Brabazon to Alen and council, 26 Mar. 1550, SP 61/2/118–19 (see enclosures); Melvil, *Mémoires historiques*, i. 33. See also Tytler, *History of Scotland*, iv. 437.

[35] Marie de Guise, letter, BN, MS Fr. 20457, fo. 265; Baudouin-Matuszek, 'Un Ambassadeur en Écosse', 100, and 'Les Expéditions françaises', 372 n. 1; Gordon Donaldson, *Scotland: James V to James VII*, Edinburgh 1971, 79; Bonner, 'First phase'.

[36] William Dansell to Sir Thomas Smith, 27 June 1549, *CSP Foreign, 1547–53*, 39. See also Carey, *Surviving the Tudors*, 53.

[37] De St Mauris to Charles V, 5 Apr. 1549, *CSP Spain, 1547–9*, 362–3.

and he promptly found a substitute. Just as Henri II had used his defence of Catholicism in Scotland as an element of his justification for intervention in Scottish affairs, so the ambassador sought to adopt and publicise a similar rationale for extending that intervention into Ireland in 1549. That he did so is hardly surprising given the reliance of the French upon Wauchop as an intermediary, and also in light of their acquaintance with Gaelic lords such as O'Neill and O'Donnell whose well-known sense of religious grievance could be harnessed as a pretext for intervention. D'Oisel claimed that Henri II was entitled to intervene in Ireland in order to uphold the Catholic faith as both Henry VIII and Edward VI were in contravention of the papal bull, *Laudabiliter,* whereby Pope Adrian IV had originally entrusted the lordship of Ireland to the English crown on condition that it defended the rights and privileges of the Catholic Church.[38] D'Oisel proved shrewd, well-informed and highly circumspect in his role as one of the principal architects of a strategy for extending the French campaign to Ireland. His grasp of the potential for using the Geraldine cause and the defence of Catholicism to rally widespread support in Ireland and to legitimate the envisaged French invasion, combined with his well-founded if extremely general knowledge of the limited military capabilities of the Irish, were of pivotal importance in determining first the formulation, and later the abandonment, of the French crown's designs on Ireland.

The explanation for the timing of the diplomatic mission in the winter of 1549–50 is obvious. France was again at war with England. Dalliance with Gaelic chiefs on the part of the French was therefore at best a strategy to extend the Scottish military campaign to Ireland, and at the very least a scare tactic devised to exert further pressure upon the already vulnerable minority administration in England. The latter had already withstood a conspiracy directed against Somerset by his brother, Admiral Thomas Seymour, followed by popular uprisings in central and western England and, finally, insurrection in Ireland.[39] Relations between France and England had been uneasy since England's capture of Boulogne. Despite the signing of the compromise treaty in June 1546, France had failed to come to terms with England. Henri II had sought to counter England's apparent triumph in Scotland by intervention that, although tentative at the outset, none the less inexorably drew the French into overt confrontation with English forces. French foreign policy was therefore focused upon the recapture of Boulogne and the elimination of the English threat to Scotland through Henri II's adoption of a protectorate role with respect to that kingdom and the establishment of a *régime* there that would ensure harmony between Scotland's diplomatic position and that of France.

Henri II was aware that the recovery of Boulogne would involve England's

38 *Mission de Beccarie de Pavie,* 32.
39 Baudouin-Matuszek, 'Les Expéditions françaises', 364.

being drawn into co-operation with France or, at least, a position of neutrality which would in turn enable him to devote his energies to imminent renewed hostilities with Charles V.[40] In Scotland there had been undeclared war between the joint French-Scottish forces and the English army since June 1548. However, fighting was erratic and neither side was anxious to see the Scottish campaign escalate into a full-scale war. France's circumspect dealings with England were determined by the uncertainty regarding the emperor's intentions following his victory over the forces of the Schmalkaldic League at Mühlberg. By early summer 1549 French diplomats were convinced that the emperor was not prepared to support the English side and that he was therefore giving Henri II free rein to press his challenge against England on the issues of Boulogne and Scotland. It was this opportune opening in continental politics that determined the timing of the French attack which was heralded by the dispatch of heavy military reinforcements to Scotland under the command of Paul de Termes in May.[41]

In August Henri declared war on England and led the invasion of Boulogne. However, the English faced considerable domestic problems, the French were unable to make any inroads into the fortifications of Boulogne itself and neither side seemed confident of the outcome of the campaign.[42] By September negotiations were about to begin on the frontier but were disrupted by Somerset's fall and throughout the following months contact was maintained between both courts. In early November Anglo-French relations reached their nadir when talks that had been in progress near Boulogne petered out due to a lack of trust on both sides.[43] By October 1549 the time was ripe for the French to undertake a reconnaissance of the feasibility of an invasion of Ireland and a ship carrying two French diplomats, Jean de Monluc, bishop of Valence, and the baron de Fourquevaux, accompanied by George Paris and a young Scot named James Melville, sailed from Scotland via Sand Island near Kintyre for Ulster.[44] After a perilous crossing, they managed to dock in Lough Foyle and found lodgings in the homes of O'Doherty and his son-in-law and later in the residence of the Catholic claimant to the bishopric of Derry.[45]

---

[40] Ibid. 361; Garrisson, *Sixteenth-century France*, 164; Potter, *History of France*, 273.

[41] D. L. Potter, 'The Treaty of Boulogne and European diplomacy, 1549–50', *BIHR* lv (1982), 52–3.

[42] For accounts of Franco-English relations at this point see Potter, 'Diplomacy in the mid-sixteenth century'; *Relations entre la France et l'Allemagne au milieu du XVIe siècle, d'après des documents inédits*, ed. Jean-Daniel Pariset, Strassburg 1981, 105, and 'La France et les princes allemandes: documents et commentaires, 1545–57', *Francia* x (1982), 229; Potter, 'Treaty of Boulogne', 50–5; 'Documents concerning the negotiation of the Anglo-French treaty of March 1550', ed. D. L. Potter, *Camden Miscellany XXVIII* (Camden 4th ser. xxix, 1984), 58–180; Potter, *History of France*, 273.

[43] Potter, 'Treaty of Boulogne', 57.

[44] See *DNB* xxxvii (1894), 240–1.

[45] Melvil, *Mémoires historiques*, i. 30–2; Hogan, *Ireland in the European system*, 111.

The credentials of the two diplomats underscore the seriousness with which the French then contemplated intervention in Ireland. Monluc had, by this time, a reputation as an able and experienced negotiator. He had been engaged as *attaché* to Rome, as envoy to the Levant and Venice and as ambassador to Constantinople prior to being posted to Scotland in January 1549 with responsibility for matters concerning French involvement there. He had experience in Scottish and English affairs, having been involved in negotiations with England in 1546.[46] Fourquevaux, too, had a distinguished reputation as a military commander, having served at Pavia, Fossano and Piedmont in the 1520s and 1530s, and at Toulouse and Guyenne in the 1540s before being appointed a commander of the expedition to Scotland in 1548.[47]

In addition to the general instructions for their mission, each diplomat had a distinct brief. According to Melville, Monluc had been instructed to investigate whether there was any substance behind offers made by O'Neill, O'Doherty, O'Donnell and his son, Calvagh, to cast off the yoke of England and submit to the king of France on condition that Henri II would help them by supplying 2,000 infantry, 200 horses and four cannons, and that he would obtain a grant of Ireland from the pope.[48] While Fourquevaux likewise viewed the purpose of the diplomatic mission as being to negotiate with the Irish lords, to summon them to be loyal to Henri II and to declare themselves opponents of all who were enemies of the French king, his main object was to conduct a detailed reconnaissance of the military capacity and resources of the Gaelic lords with whom they were negotiating with a view to ascertaining the feasibility of French military intervention.[49]

Monluc led the negotiations with Con O'Neill and his allies including

O'Doherty's tower house was constructed in compliance with the prevailing continental architectural fashion and formed part of a whole series of tower houses along the western seacoast constructed by merchants and small sea-going lords such as the O'Driscolls, O'Mahonys, O'Sullivans, MacNamaras, O'Flahertys, O'Malleys and O'Donnells. See Caoimhín Ó Danachair, 'Irish tower houses and their regional distribution', *Béaloideas* xlv–xlvii (1977–9), 161.

[46] For surveys of Monluc's career see *Biographie universelle (Michaud)*, xxix (n.d.), 164–5; *Dictionnaire général de biographie et de l'histoire*, ii, Copenhagen 1873, 1841; Vindry, *Les Ambassadeurs français*, 34; *Correspondance politique de M. de Lanssac (Louis de Saint-Gelais) 1548–57*, ed. C. Sauzé de l'Houmeau, Poitiers 1904, 208–9; *Nouvelle Biographie générale depuis les temps les plus reculés jusqu'à 1850–60*, comp. Firmin Didot, Paris 1963– , xxxv–xxxvi (1968), 323–6.

[47] See *Biographie universelle (Michaud)*, xiv (1856), 557; Vindry, *Les Ambassadeurs français*, 41–2. For his involvement in the Scottish campaign in early 1549 see Baudouin-Matuszek, 'Les Expéditions', 363 n. 1 and ff. Fourquevaux also published on the subject of war tactics: *Instructions sur le faict de la guerre of Raymond de Beccarie de Pavie sieur de Fourquevaux*, ed. Gladys Dickinson, London 1954.

[48] Melvil, *Mémoires historiques*, i. 29–30.

[49] See the preface to letter from Manus O'Donnell to Henri II, 23 Feb. 1550, BN, MS Fr. 10751, 7–8; *Mission de Beccarie de Pavie*, 32–3; Vindry, *Les Ambassadeurs français*, 36. For a detailed discussion of his service in Scotland see Baudouin-Matuszek, 'Un Ambassadeur en Écosse'.

Plate 1 Jean de Monluc, c. 1508–1579, bishop of Valence

Robert Wauchop and listened to their proposals.[50] Significantly, Manus
O'Donnell avoided meeting the French officials, though he was advertised of
their arrival. In spite of George Paris's connection with the O'Connor sept,
the French envoys limited their negotiations to the country's strongest Gaelic
magnates who had close Scottish connections that would be vital in
extending the Scottish campaign to Ireland via Ulster. Following the
conclusion of talks, James MacDonnell's brother, Angus, took the party
(excepting Wauchop who stayed in Ulster) back to Kintyre where they were
received by James upon their arrival in January 1550.[51] Having reported to
Marie de Guise at Stirling, both diplomats departed for France in early

---

[50] *Memoirs of Sir James Melvil*, 8–9; Melvil, *Mémoires historiques*, i. 29–34.
[51] Melvil, *Mémoires historiques*, i. 33–4; Millett, 'Pastoral zeal', 56.

March.[52] Monluc's report has not survived but Fourquevaux was greatly disappointed by his findings, concluding that the Irish were a 'peuple barbare et sans raison'.[53]

No sooner had the diplomats left Scotland on their reconnaissance trip to Ulster than French interest in Ireland began to wane dramatically. Even prior to their departure Henri II had expressed doubts about George Paris's trustworthiness and sought Con O'Neill's assurances in the matter.[54] During the months of November and December Marie de Guise repeatedly voiced her disapproval of the cost of the ailing Scottish campaign.[55] Throughout the winter French troops continued to be withdrawn from Scotland and at the time of the return of Monluc and Fourquevaux to Stirling in January 1550, Marie de Guise appears to have become generally despondent, expressing surprise at the diplomats' having returned at all.[56] Nevertheless, she had not entirely lost interest in pursuing designs on Ireland: in December an unnamed gentleman from Ireland who had arrived in Stirling from France was granted a payment from the treasury.[57] Unfortunately for such Irish dissidents, the waning French and Scottish commitment to the exorbitantly expensive and unpopular Scottish campaign coincided with the Florentine merchant Guidotti's submission in early November of two schemes to Henri II suggesting possible avenues for a solution to his predicament.[58] This renewed initiative was aimed at securing peace between England and France regarding Boulogne and resulted in the relegation of the Scottish question. French designs on Ireland were immediately dropped, at least in the short term, as both sides pushed ahead with the negotiating proceedings in an effort to maximise and sustain the rejuvenated diplomatic momentum. Scotland's pivotal importance as the channel by which a French invasion of Ireland would most likely be staged thus emerged when Marie de Guise and Henri II's

---

[52] Melvil, *Mémoires historiques*, i. 35; Marie de Guise to the duc d'Aumale, 10 jan. 1550, *Relations politiques de la France et de l'Éspagne avec l'Écosse au XVIe siècle, I: Correspondances françaises, 1515–60*. ed. Alexandre Teulet, new edn, Paris 1862, 214. For their return to France see Marie de Guise to the duc d'Aumale and the cardinal de Guise, 12 Mar. 1550, BN, MS Fr. 20457, 239: 'et porce que ledict Sr de Monluc sen retourne par dela, lequel scaura amplement rendre compte de leur voyaige'. See also Potter, 'French intrigue', 168 n. 46.
[53] Quoted in Potter, 'French intrigue', 165.
[54] Copy of a letter of Henri II of France to Con Bacagh O'Neill, earl of Tyrone, 11 oct. 1549, BL, MS Stowe 154 (extract) (NLI microfilm, n. 1924, p. 1458).
[55] Marie de Guise to the duc d'Aumale and the cardinal of Guise, 12 nov. 1549, *Relations politiques de la France*, i. 205; Marie de Guise to the cardinal of Guise, 29 nov. 1549, ibid.; Badouin-Matuszek, 'Les Expéditions françaises', 368; Bonner, 'First phase'.
[56] Marie de Guise to the duc d'Aumale, 10 jan. 1550, *Relations politiques de la France*, i. 214.
[57] *Accounts of the lord high treasurer of Scotland, IX: 1546–51*, ed. Sir James Balfour Paul, 361.
[58] Potter, 'Treaty of Boulogne', 57–8; Baudouin-Matuszek, 'Les Expéditions françaises', 366.

relaxation of their commitment to continuing their campaign in Scotland automatically dictated the abortive outcome of the mission to Ulster.[59]

Meanwhile, the English privy council took the prospect of French intervention in Ireland seriously: in January 1550 sixteen vessels were posted in three havens in Ireland to guard against a French landing.[60] Soon after, James Croft was appointed lord deputy and was charged with strengthening the fortification of Irish havens. By mid-January, days after Monluc and Fourquevaux had reported on their findings in Ireland to Marie de Guise at Stirling, French and English commissioners were appointed to commence negotiating a peace settlement.[61] In February the talks came to a sharp halt when, at the first meeting, the French rejected England's maximum concessions but the final details of the hand-over of Boulogne were eventually thrashed out by 1 March when Henri II gave his broad assent to the English proposals.[62] The duc de Guise frankly welcomed the peace as a great relief to the French treasury. Thus a key exponent of French intervention in Scottish affairs, perhaps the most crucial figure buoying up Scottish and Irish hopes of securing French intervention in Ireland, exhibited his fading interest in maintaining such close and expensive ties with Scotland.[63] The two negotiating teams wrangled over issues concerning military occupation in Scotland but agreed to tackle them afresh after the signing of the accord. By 14 March both sides had come to a final agreement and on 24 March the treaty was concluded at the fort of Oultreau, with shows of cordiality that concealed the lingering sense of dissatisfaction felt at both the English and the French courts.[64]

It was not until the last stages of the Anglo-French negotiations in early March that the Ulster lords concluded that events no longer lent themselves to the prospect of French intervention in Ireland. In mid-February, when the French negotiators were strenuously opposing consecutive sets of proposals tabled by their English counterparts, Manus O'Donnell evidently believed that the proposed French invasion was still a possibility, however remote. In a letter to Henri II, dated 23 February and designed to sustain the momentum of the negotiations conducted during the previous three months, O'Donnell sought to address what appears to have been the most problematic issue that emerged in the course of the talks, that of Gaelic disunity. Clearly compromised in this respect by his own failure to join Con O'Neill and other Ulster lords in meeting the French delegates, O'Donnell was at pains to excuse his surreptitious avoidance of Monluc and Fourquevaux, to assure the king of his

---

[59] Baudouin-Matuszek, 'Les Expéditions françaises', 368–9.

[60] Palmer, *Problem of Ireland*, 69–70.

[61] Ibid. 69–70; Potter, 'Treaty of Boulogne', 58.

[62] Potter, 'Treaty of Boulogne', 59–62.

[63] Ibid. 62.

[64] Pariset, 'Relations entre la France et l'Allemagne', 105; 'Documents concerning the Anglo-French treaty', 60; Potter, 'Treaty of Boulogne', 273.

loyalty and that of the other Irish lords and to insist that the French crown should honour the rights of all Irish lords and Catholic clergy. He admitted that although he had not met the two envoys, he had received letters addressed to him by Henri II. He made hollow claims of having been deeply concerned for the safety of the French diplomats during their sojourn in Ulster, and commended them for their wisdom in not visiting him as this would have attracted the attention of the English, 'nos ennemis', who would have gathered their forces to resist a French army.[65] So concerned was he for the safety of the delegates that he requested a close friend named du Bosc, who liaised with the party on his behalf, to urge them to return to Scotland.[66] He claimed to have instructed du Bosc, Monluc and Fourquevaux, to explain his stance and that of Con O'Neill, to Henri II, and assured the French king of the loyal service and obedience of all the lords of Ireland and their succes-sors, declaring that any monarch who was king of France was also king of Ireland.[67] O'Donnell reiterated that there was none among the other Irish lords who did not wish to be obedient to the French crown, thanks to the efforts of George Paris, who was by that time clearly receiving his directives mainly from the Ulster lords, and guaranteed that any opposition to French intervention would be suppressed.[68]

Given that O'Donnell was appealing for French aid and very overtly endeavouring to counter what he evidently expected to be the diplomats' assessment of the Irish as unsuitable allies owing to their being so divisive, his portrayal of harmony and unanimity amongst the Irishry was only to be expected. His correspondence provides important evidence not only of the problematic issues that emerged in the negotiations but also of the highly conditional nature of the tentative proposals and undertakings tabled by both the French and the Irish during the talks. The evidence of the French king's attempts to entice Fitzgerald to lead an expedition to Ireland or Scotland combined with O'Donnell's outline of terms to be honoured as a condition for submission to French sovereignty, belies the assumption that Ireland was a mere pawn in European politics. While it may well have been viewed as such by continental rulers, the Irish lords, like the tenth earl of Desmond in 1522–3, equally had an agenda that they sought to realise by manipulating their continental co-conspirators. O'Donnell referred to his Gaelic peers' having already discussed their terms for submission with Monluc and Fourquevaux. He was anxious that Henri II should not renege on the diplo-mats' undertakings since O'Donnell himself, and the other lords, had prom-ised all the lords of Ireland that the French king would treat them in a benign, humane and Christian manner. He emphasised that Gaelic co-operation with the French was contingent upon Henri's providing them with assurances

[65] Manus O'Donnell to Henri II, 23 Feb. 1550, BN, MS Fr. 10751, 8–9.
[66] Ibid.
[67] Ibid. 9–10.
[68] Ibid.

that he would not deprive them of their rights and liberties as nobles and that he would maintain the privileges and franchises of the Catholic clergy and of their churches.

Manus signed himself 'votre très fidèle serviteur O Donnell'. Yet as in the case of his implication in the escape of Gerald Fitzgerald to Brittany in March 1540, he again showed his decidedly Machiavellian, chameleon character in his efforts to absolve himself from allegations of treasonous conspiracy in order to ensure self-preservation. Within a fortnight of writing to Henri II, as peace between France and England seemed imminent, he wrote to the lord deputy and council in Dublin, in an obviously agitated state, in what was clearly a damage limitation exercise. In contrast with Con O'Neill and other Gaelic parties to the intrigue, who were called to account for their involvement with the two French diplomats, O'Donnell resolved to disarm the Dublin government by taking the preemptive step of exonerating himself from accusations of involvement in the intrigue and, in the process, pinpointed the protagonists in that conspiracy.[69] He implicated Bishop Robert Wauchop who had been 'in other places and countries before he came to my country' where he was said to have been unwelcome unless the deputy and council instructed O'Donnell to treat him otherwise.[70] O'Donnell informed the council that he was in Donegal when two French lords arrived at Lough Foyle from Scotland and that the envoys dispatched du Bosc to address him.[71] In blatant contradiction of his assurance to Henri II that he had received the French king's letters from du Bosc, O'Donnell insisted that Henri had sent him no letters since the French envoys knew that he had forwarded previous communications that he had received from France to the council.[72]

In a further effort to ingratiate himself with the suspicious Dublin council, O'Donnell created the impression of providing insider intelligence regarding French designs. He declared that the French aimed to secure as many allies as possible in Ireland against the English and that they were determined 'to do a great deed if they can' before Whitsuntide. But the transparency of O'Donnell's duplicity was evident as these vague pronouncements merely amounted to a sop to the government. In a strongly defensive response to the allegation of his implication with the Scots, he asserted that it could not be proven that he had ever drawn Scots into Ulster.[73]

O'Donnell's co-operative attitude did not come without a price, however. In return for volunteering intelligence that was accompanied by characteris-

---

[69] Ibid; O'Donnell to the lord deputy and council, 4 Mar. 1550, SP 61/2/120–1 (enclosure).
[70] O'Donnell to the lord deputy and council, 4 Mar. 1550, SP 61/2/120–1 (enclosure).
[71] Ibid.
[72] O'Donnell to Henri II, 23 Feb. 1550, BN, MS Fr. 10751, p. 8; O'Donnell to the lord deputy and council, 4 Mar. 1550, SP 61/2/120–1 (enclosure).
[73] O'Donnell to the lord deputy and council, 4 Mar. 1550, SP 61/2/120–1 (enclosure).

tically arrogant reminders to the Dublin council that 'you do know your self you have not deserved of me as yet to be so good towards you', he sought the help of the council against his son, Calvagh, who had been involved in the negotiations with the two diplomats and who had arrested Manus's other son, Hugh.[74] Thus, like the tenth earl of Desmond in 1523, O'Donnell engaged in a complete *volte-face* in the early months of 1550, proving the persistent pre-eminence and obstructive influence of dynastic and provincial interests over efforts to foster a broad-based allegiance to a 'national' cause in the Gaelic polity.

Con O'Neill, who was in a far more compromised position than O'Donnell by virtue of his having met the French diplomats, also realised the futility of clinging to expectations of French intervention at this time. In response to threats and inducements by George Dowdall, archbishop of Armagh, he consented to hand over his correspondence with George Paris and with Henri II which proved significantly more informative and reliable than the intelligence proffered by O'Donnell.[75] Tyrone informed the archbishop that Robert Wauchop had recently come to Ulster, accompanied by certain French noblemen who brought him letters from the French king, and identified James MacDonnell and his brother, Angus, as having been involved in arranging the delegates' visit.[76] The lord chancellor and council warned O'Neill that these French emissaries were seeking an opportunity to invade Ulster and intended to dupe him and his allies into believing that they only intended to attack Englishmen, whereas in reality they aimed to subject all Ireland to their tyrannical control.[77]

By the third week of March Irish councillors had in their possession vital documentation from the protagonists in the intrigue, and for the first time they were in a position to assess the seriousness of the threat posed. Throughout March the activities of Wauchop, a 'very shrewd spy . . . and a great brewer of wars' in the territories of the O'Neills and the O'Donnells in Ulster, ongoing reports of a French invasion, the 'halt and strange' demeanour of the Gaelic lords and the Palesmen's dismay at the prospect of such an invasion, gave the councillors cause for serious concern. The justiciar, Sir William Brabazon, was especially preoccupied with preventing Brian O'Connor Faly from becoming involved with the French. He insisted that the Gaelic lord should be detained in England, particularly as Paris was known to be colluding with O'Connor's son, Cormac, in ongoing serious efforts to entice the French and Scottish to invade Ireland.[78] English optimism and

---

[74] Ibid. See Ó Cléirigh, *Beatha Aodha Ruaidh Uí Domhnaill*, p. xxviii.
[75] Irish council to the privy council, 20 May 1551, SP 61/3/130.
[76] Con Bacagh O'Neill, earl of Tyrone, to George Dowdall, 7 Mar. 1550, SP 61/2/122 (enclosure).
[77] Alen and council to Con Bacagh O'Neill, 17 Mar. 1550, ibid.
[78] Dowdall to Alen and the Irish council, 22 Mar. 1550, SP 61/2/116; Brabazon and the

confidence, fostered by the apparent success of Sir Anthony St Leger's reform initiatives of the early 1540s and by the show of Gaelic support for Henry VIII at Boulogne in 1544–6, soon gave way to renewed mistrust of the Gaelic lords, including Con O'Neill, with whom St Leger had negotiated surrender and regrant agreements.[79]

Archbishop Dowdall's response to discovery of the details of the negotiations held in Tyrconnell was rapid and decisive. His confiscation of correspondence and his isolation of Con O'Neill from further contact with the French court effectively crushed the prospect of an invasion in the foreseeable future. In publicising their denunciations of the French diplomatic mission and those implicated with the two ambassadors, O'Donnell and O'Neill were merely acknowledging a virtual *fait accompli*: in early March it was reported in continental diplomatic circles that 'the insurrection in Ireland is quelled'.[80]

The French invasion failed to materialise for a combination of reasons. First, while negotiations were held in Ulster in the winter months of 1549–50, they only resulted in conditional proposals presented by both sides. These were never formulated into a treaty such as that signed by the tenth earl of Desmond and François I in 1523. O'Donnell's letter to Henri II explicitly stresses the highly conditional, exploratory and tentative nature of the negotiations. Second, on this, as on several other occasions, the Gaelic figures who spearheaded the discussions with the French encountered the long-standing problems associated with uniting the various Gaelic lords and their septs and bringing the Scots within the orbit of their plans. In his plea for assistance, O'Donnell naturally tried to gloss over this stumbling-block to orchestrating a French invasion. Yet at least part of the failure to bring about such intervention stemmed from the inability of the Irish leaders to convince the French of their capacity or real intention to forge a broad-based alliance and field an army with which the French could then join forces. Moreover, James MacDonnell's efforts to capitalise on Manus O'Donnell's feud with his own son, Calvagh, by switching his allegiance between them, while at the same time striving to establish his own foothold in Ulster, complicated the political geography and factional alliances of the province and increased existing endemic instability.[81] The inability of the Scots and the French to exploit optimally the Geraldine cause as a rallying call to unite the various factions, and their failure to rouse support for their intervention under the

---

Irish council to the privy council, 26 Mar. 1550, SP 61/2/118–19; Millett, 'Pastoral zeal', 56.

[79] Brabazon and the Irish council to the privy council, 26 Mar. 1550, SP 61/2/118–19.

[80] François Van der Delft to Charles V, 8 Mar. 1550, *CSP Spain, 1550–2*, 44.

[81] MacDonnell again intervened in a dispute between Manus O'Donnell and his son, Calvagh, in 1555: Micheál MacCraith, 'The Gaelic reaction to the Reformation', in Ellis and Barber, *Conquest and union*, 140–1.

guise of religious protectionism as a compensatory measure, also contributed to the failed outcome of the plan.

Third, while Henri II is said to have been pleased by Monluc's report, and Marie de Guise claimed that both Monluc and Fourquevaux had achieved their objectives in visiting Ireland, the Irish demands for military aid in return for conditional and minimal commitments dampened French enthusiasm for extending a military campaign which was already absorbing an exorbitant amount of money both in Scotland and at home in France.[82] Moreover, O'Neill's surrender of his correspondence relating to the planned French campaign to Dowdall and the Irish council, combined with O'Donnell's overtures, not only indicated their resignation to the futility of plans for an invasion, it also constituted a major set-back to the realisation of any designs to launch a similar attack in the future. Instead of viewing French treatment of the Irish purely in terms of callous compliance with the rapidly changing dictates of continental diplomacy, considerable responsibility for the failed outcome of plans for French intervention must be assigned to the inability of the Irish to present a sufficiently united and convincing front as dependable allies.

III

By the end of March 1550 Henri II had signed the peace treaty of Boulogne with England which left him free to pursue his main objective, the long-deferred offensive against Charles V.[83] Having struggled to secure England's neutrality, he was not prepared to jeopardise the progress of his anti-imperial designs by persisting with the discovered negotiations between his ambassadors and Gaelic lords whose principal representatives had by then abandoned the entire effort as an embarrassment that threatened to upset their relations with the English crown. The death of Marie de Guise's father, Claude, duc d'Aumale and first duc de Guise, on 12 April 1550 at Joinville, dealt a further decisive blow to fading Irish hopes for French assistance. However, during the following two years, a handful of 'diehards' involved in the 1549–50 negotiations, notably George Paris, Cormac O'Connor, MacWilliam Burke of Mayo and Robert Wauchop, struggled to revive the flagging momentum of the Franco-Irish talks.

Between March 1550 and the summer of the following year Henri capital-

---

82 Marie de Guise to the duc d'Aumale, 10 jan. 1550, *Relations politiques de la France*, i. 214; *Papiers d'état, pièces et documents inédits ou peu connus relatifs à l'histoire de l'Écosse au XVIe siècle*, ed. Alexandre Teulet, 3 vols, Paris 1852–60, i. 716–19; Baudouin-Matuszek, 'Les Expéditions françaises', 361–9.

83 See Spooner, 'The Habsburg–Valois struggle', 356–7; Knecht, *French Renaissance monarchy*, 44–5; Garrisson, *Sixteenth-century France*, 164–5; Potter, *History of France*, 272–3.

ised on the uncertainty about his dealings with the Irish in order to balance optimally his relations with England. He did so with a view to manoeuvring into a position from which he could throw his support behind the German Protestant princes in opposition to Charles V. Irish representations at the French and Scottish courts gained significant momentum in the early months of 1551 but thereafter petered out and ended in 1552 when Paris and his consorts finally accepted as categorical the French refusal to be party to their plans. Crucially, for the remainder of his reign (until 1559) simmering dissatisfaction between France and England concerning French intervention in Scotland fuelled several less serious episodes of Franco-Irish intrigue as Henri retained an active interest in Scotland, and Marie de Guise and Henri d'Oisel maintained their contacts with Gaelic Ireland's potentates.[84]

In the immediate aftermath of the signing of the Treaty of Boulogne, the axis of Franco-Irish intrigue again centred on the Scottish and French courts, causing Sir William Brabazon to suspect all those resorting to Scotland of involvement in subversive scheming.[85] Reaction to the signing of the treaty was swift in Scotland and in France. In May one of a group of Irish exiles resident in Scotland, thought to be MacWilliam Burke of Mayo, a close associate of Paris and a leading member of Connaught's most powerful clan, wrote to Henri, urging him to have Ireland included in the terms of the Treaty of Boulogne. He did so in the hope that the Gaelic lords might have their lands restored, claiming that, as it stood, the treaty had left Ireland prey to English 'molestation'.[86] MacWilliam Burke was by no means acquiescent in the termination of the round of negotiations held in winter of 1549–50 and George Paris was promptly dispatched to the French court in an effort to continue talks with the French king.[87]

Meanwhile Henri II and Constable Anne de Montmorency rapidly moved to adopt a definite public stand on abandoning French designs on Ireland. At the end of March Henri II charged de Fumel, now French ambassador to Scotland, to instruct the two diplomats, Monluc and Fourquevaux, to end their dealings with the Irish lords. Montmorency reinforced the king's directives, impressing upon Fourquevaux that there was no further need to pursue

---

84 Potter, 'Treaty of Boulogne', 63.
85 See Irish council to the privy council, 26 Mar. 1550, SP 61/2/118; *Accounts of the lord high treasurer of Scotland*, ix. 361; x. 229, 237, 239, 270–1 (grants of payments to Irishmen in Scotland). See also *Scottish correspondence of Mary of Guise, including some three hundred letters from 20 February to 15 May 1560*, ed. Annie Cameron, Edinburgh 1927, 319; Potter, 'French intrigue', 170.
86 Potter, 'French intrigue', 170.
87 Mason to the privy council, 14 June 1550, *CSP Foreign, 1547–53*, 48; Patrick Fraser Tytler, *England under the reigns of Edward VI and Mary, with the contemporary history of Europe, illustrated in a series of original letters never before printed*, 2 vols, London 1839, i. 291–3.

negotiations with the Irish.[88] In diplomatic circles the king's forbidding stance was said to have ensured that Paris and his consorts made no progress.[89] However, the suspicions of Sir John Mason, the English ambassador to France, were aroused. One of the ablest diplomats in the service of the English crown, with an effective spy network at the French court which kept him very well informed, Mason was an alarmist who was inordinately sensitive to any signs of French conspiracy involving Ireland and who harboured a deep-seated contempt for the Irish.[90] Although unable to pinpoint any overtly incriminating evidence of Henri's complicity with the Irish dissidents, by June he complained that the king afforded continued hospitality to the Irish at court and reported that George Paris was negotiating with both the king and the Guise faction.[91] Mason, like several others, believed that Paris was implicated in these ongoing efforts to secure French intervention in Ireland for personal ends, his desire for revenge for the execution of his father or brother causing him 'to seek all the mean[s] he can to annoy the king [Edward VI] and the realm'. The ambassador's suspicions of Henri were further stirred by his discovery that a Breton named de Botte had been sent from the French court to Ireland at Easter.[92]

Mason put it to Henri II that Edward VI had heard from several sources in Ireland 'that there are yet practices continued between . . . [Henri II] and the Irish'. He let the French king know that he was aware that de Botte had been despatched to Ireland and that Paris was being entertained at court. He reminded Henri that Edward VI expected that he would not 'by any means animate them [the Irish] to forget their duties of obedience' and that he would dissuade them through constant reiteration of the amicable nature of relations between the monarchs.[93] Mason also urged the French king to advise the Irish to remember their allegiance to the English crown and emphasised that in the event of their refusal to do so, Edward would expect Henri's co-operation in chastising them.[94]

In response to Mason's allegations, Henri admitted that during the war with England he did his utmost 'to annoy his enemy' and part of his strategy involved undertaking a 'practice with the Irish'. He defended his stance by insisting that as soon as the Treaty of Boulogne had been signed, he had broken off contacts with the Irish and withdrew those officials whom he had despatched to Ireland to negotiate with the Gaelic lords. Since then, he

---

[88] Gladys Dickinson, 'Instructions to the French ambassador, 30 March 1550', SHR xxvi (1947), 154–67. See also Potter, 'French intrigue', 170.

[89] Jehan Scheyfve to Charles V, 6 June 1550, CSP Spain, 1550–2, 97.

[90] Mason to the privy council, 29 June 1550, CSP Foreign, 1547–53, 49; Tytler, England under Edward VI and Mary, i. 299.

[91] Mason to the privy council, 14 June 1550, CSP Foreign, 1547–53, 48; Tytler, England under Edward VI and Mary, i. 291–4.

[92] Ibid.

[93] Ibid.

[94] Ibid.

declared, he had never afforded the Irish any hearing. Henri admitted that he had recently received messages from Irish correspondents but explained that his replies had given them little grounds for expectations of support from France.[95] He assured Edward VI that neither in this nor in any other matter could he be found in contravention of the terms of the peace treaty. Nevertheless, Mason remained unconvinced of the sincerity of Henri's protestations, wryly remarking 'yet am I well assured that . . . Paris was on Monday last at the court, being appointed that day to have audience'.[96]

Later in June Mason was unsettled by the recent arrival of additional Irishmen at the French court bearing another batch of letters from MacWilliam Burke and others who boasted that the nobility of Ireland were conspiring to overthrow English rule.[97] The Irish delegation justified their defiant stance to the French on the grounds that the inevitable alternative was dispossession as had occurred in the case of the O'More and O'Connor clans in the late 1540s. Montmorency's response to Mason's reiteration of allegations of French complicity with Irish dissidents was consistent with that proffered by Henri II. He too acknowledged that, in the past, Irishmen had indeed sought French support, but emphatically declared that their recent requests had been directly refused and that they had been instructed to 'keep themselves quiet and acknowledge their obedience' to Edward VI. He explained to Mason that Paris's embarrassingly prolonged stay at court resulted from his ill health, and assured the ambassador that were it not for his poorly state, he would have been sent away 'with such answer as . . . he would not gladly return with any such commission'. Mason's reluctance to accept this explanation was increased when he learned that within the previous two days, Paris had received a visit from Monluc, the envoy who visited Ireland in 1549–50, who presented him with fifty crowns 'to help him in his sickness'.[98] In short, during the summer months of 1550, in spite of the ostensibly amicable relations between the French and English kings, there was 'much talk of Ireland' at the French court which caused the English privy council to suspect Henri II of continuing to lend tacit, if covert, support to the Irish.

By September the focus of Irish efforts to secure foreign aid had again shifted to Scotland where there was 'trouble brewing over the Irish refugees' as Robert Wauchop and others whipped up opposition to Edward VI with a view to handing Ireland over to Henri who allegedly pledged them his encouragement and protection.[99] English councillors' anxieties were heightened by Mason's report in October which intimated that since the arrival at

---

[95] Ibid.
[96] Ibid.
[97] Mason to the privy council, 29 June 1550, SP 68/9a/23–4; Tytler, *England under Edward VI and Mary*, i. 301–2.
[98] Ibid.
[99] Renard to Charles V, 17 Sept. 1550, *CSP Spain, 1550–2*, 176.

the French court of several Scots, especially Thomas Erskine, the Scottish ambassador, the lower ranking courtiers had been convinced that 'Ireland is their's whenever the king [Henri II] shall give them a signal'.[100] Furthermore, the Scots at court displayed a particularly keen interest in de Botte's report on his reconnaissance mission to Ireland from which he had just returned. Significantly, de Botte declared that the greater part of Ireland was subject not to the Ulster lords but rather to the earl of Desmond whose kinsman, Gerald Fitzgerald, had likewise been perceived by François I as the most powerful lord in Ireland.

In September 1550 Marie de Guise travelled to France where she spent a year in the company of her brothers whose advice she sought on her plans to oust the earl of Arran from the Scottish regency and more generally in respect of her governance of Scotland.[101] Her presence in their company in France was to prove very significant in the playing out of French–Irish intrigue during the ensuing eight months, not least as it enhanced the Irish emissaries' opportunities for gaining access to the Guises and facilitated their directing all their energies towards the French court. By December Mason was clearly weary of their relentless solicitations and connivance which he had 'every day in his dish' and burdened by suspicion that the Irish were set to transfer their allegiance to the French sovereign.[102] By this stage MacWilliam Burke appears to have returned to Ireland, followed by George Paris who brought with him replies to the letters from MacWilliam Burke and others that he had presented at the French court. Paris departed the court at Blois 'with a good reward' and in a very optimistic mood, informing his friends that 'he doubteth not to see the French king shortly to bear the crown of Ireland' and that he hoped 'to bring jolly news' when he would return at the end of Lent. Obviously incensed by Paris's flagrant publicising of his alleged success in securing French backing, Mason complained of having to endure this brag every day at the French court.[103]

After Paris's departure, his accomplices obstinately persevered in the hope of securing Henri's support. Early in January 1551 three Irishmen were at the French court where they were said to have been engaged in sustained efforts to induce the king to accept the crown of Ireland and to annex it to 'his' Scottish kingdom. Simon Renard, the imperial ambassador to France, was doubtful about the prospect of a favourable response to their appeal, astutely remarking that 'from what I hear it appears that the king [Henri II] will put them off and meanwhile temporise with the English until he can feel more sure of . . . [Charles V]'.[104] As the events of the following months were to demonstrate, Renard's analysis was entirely accurate. Henri II was indeed

---

100 Mason to the privy council, 19 Oct. 1550, *CSP Foreign, 1547–53*, 58.
101 Francisque Michel, *Les Écossais en France*, i. 471–7.
102 Mason to the privy council, 4 Dec. 1550, SP 68/9a/182.
103 Ibid.
104 Renard to Charles V, 5 Jan. 1551, *CSP Spain, 1550–2*, 197.

'nursing his designs' against the English for the recovery of their possessions in France. While post-treaty negotiations were in progress between the English and the French regarding delineation of boundaries near Calais and Ardres, the French were said to have been storing opportunities for breaking off the talks, being ready to take advantage of the discord caused by what Renard termed 'religious differences' in England.[105]

In Ireland, the lord deputy, Sir Anthony St Leger (reappointed in August 1550), proved equally astute in his highly circumspect assessment of the threat posed by the Irish at the French court. He discounted reports in January 1551 that the French were intending to annex Ireland, instead believing that they were concentrating on distracting the English whilst supporting Scotland.[106] Throughout the spring, as George Paris and his consorts grew more optimistic at the prospect of securing French aid than they had been since the previous summer, rumours in English government circles were rife that amongst other things, Henri II was behind Con O'Neill's stirring of disturbances in Ulster, that he was endeavouring to incite the Scots to declare war on England in order to facilitate his attack on Ireland and that the pope had transferred to the French king all the papacy's rights to the kingdom of Ireland.[107]

The French were said to have believed that they had been presented with an unprecedented opportunity to take advantage of Edward VI's minority and, as they perceived it, the protector's fear of the populace. The English were aware of the 'good understanding' between Henri II and the Irish and it was believed that the latter, backed by the French, were set to declare war unless Henri was restrained from involvement by his fear of Charles V.[108] In mid-March Mason's suspicions were further aroused by reports that the French master of the ordnance had shipped ordnance and ammunition from Brest to Scotland under the charge of a Scottish gentleman. The ambassador believed that the supplies were in fact intended for Ireland.[109] Not surprisingly, St Leger grew apprehensive on hearing reports regarding the loss of eight or ten French ships that were *en route* to Scotland.[110]

April brought an intensification of Irish intrigue at the French court. Paris and his associates grew desperate as their window of opportunity to convince the French to intervene in Ireland before the French government's preparations to launch their anti-imperial campaign came to a head in the summer was rapidly closing. By 18 April Paris was back at the court, now located at Amboise. This time he was accompanied by his close ally, Cormac O'Connor. Clearly frustrated by, and probably suspicious of, Paris's protracted and appar-

105 Ibid.
106 Potter, 'French intrigue', 175–6.
107 Scheyfve to Charles V, 1 Mar. 1551, *CSP Spain, 1550–2*, 227.
108 Renard to Charles V, 9 Mar. 1551, ibid. 243–4.
109 Mason to the privy council, 18 Mar. 1551, *CSP Foreign, 1547–53*, 79.
110 Lord Deputy St Leger to Sir William Cecil, 23 Mar. 1551, *CSP Ireland, 1509–73*, 112.

ently futile negotiations, though still hopeful of some prospect of French assistance, O'Connor made his personal appearance at the court in a strategic move aimed at lending a necessary impetus to the talks at a critical juncture. Presenting himself as the eldest of nine brothers and the son of the Gaelic lord, Brian O'Connor Faly, whose insurrection and subsequent imprisonment in London was already well known to Henri II, Cormac applied moral pressure on the king, emphasising that it was his messengers who had been responsible for the recent disturbances in Ireland (an opinion also expressed by Sir John Mason).[111] On that basis O'Connor requested troops from the French constable.[112] As an enticement to Henri, both O'Connor and Paris pointed to the potential for extending the Irish campaign to a British level, providing the king with what could only be regarded as extremely dubious assurances that in the event of his sending aid to the Irish, Welsh dissidents would join forces with them.[113] O'Connor's direct intervention was important for sustaining Irish efforts to foster interest in intervention in Irish affairs at both the French and Scottish courts: if indeed Paris had been motivated solely by self-interest, the same was not true of O'Connor. While the latter certainly capitalized on his lineage to win French support for restitution of his dynastic inheritance, he also used it to prove his credentials as a representative of all Gaelic dissidents who had likewise been denied rightful possession of their lands. As Cormac became more deeply and directly involved in pressing the case for French intervention in 1551 and early 1552, he gained the respect of Marie de Guise and of Henri Clutin d'Oisel in particular. He also steadily won the confidence of the Gaelic lords engaged in simultaneous efforts to secure French and Scottish backing who grew mistrustful of Paris whom they rightly suspected of inadequately representing their interests.[114]

However, O'Connor's overtures also fell on deaf ears. While he and Paris were well received by both the French king and Montmorency, and although they had supposedly been in contact with the papal nuncio, both were promptly instructed not to seek aid from the French court in the future. O'Connor had been dissuaded by 'fair words'. He and Paris were told to remain in their lodgings, and were charged not to resort to the court until they were sent for. Yet even that did not allay Mason's suspicions. He surmised that this decision had been taken in order to facilitate the Irishmen's being secretly dispatched away from the court or alternatively as a ploy to conceal their reception at court which was regarded as wholly inappropriate given that the true purpose of their mission was common knowledge.[115]

By the end of April the coterie of continental diplomats in London were

---

[111] Mason to the privy council, 18 Apr. 1551, CSP Foreign, 1547–53, 89.
[112] The number requested is sometimes said to be 5,000 and on other occasions 1,000.
[113] Mason to the privy council, 18 Apr. 1551, CSP Foreign, 1547–53, 89.
[114] Mémoire, 6 oct. 1552, CSP Spain, 1550–2, 587–8.
[115] Mason to the privy council, 18 Apr. 1551, CSP Foreign, 1547–53, 89.

interpreting Henri's refusal to help the Irish as a demonstration of his wish not to jeopardise the anticipated marriage proposal (between Henri II's eldest daughter and Edward VI) and not to anger the English.[116] Any glimmer of hope which the Irish may have held out for an attempted revival of the Geraldine cause was decisively quenched by the end of the month when Gerald Fitzgerald took a further step in his rehabilitation by accepting the offer of part of his dynasty's confiscated estates.[117]

Meanwhile, English anxieties were stirred by reports (which ultimately proved incorrect) alleging that Robert Wauchop, a pivotal figure in the 1549–50 intrigue, was preparing to return to Ireland after Easter. If indeed he had intended travelling to Ireland, his plans changed following his elevation to the position of apostolic nuncio to Ireland. He then engaged Ignatius Loyola in unsuccessful negotiations with a view to members of the Society of Jesus leading a mission in Ireland.[118] Help was forthcoming, however, from the French: Henri II provided Wauchop with 'a certain reward and letters of recommendation' addressed to the bishop of Mirepoix, who was in Rome at that time. The French bishop was instructed by the king to assist Wauchop and his associates in advancing their cause and to provide them with accom- modation during their sojourn in Rome. However, Mason dismissed Wauchop's intrigue, surmising that it 'shall take the same effect as have other malicious practices which have hereto been meant against England from that See'. In the event, Wauchop does not appear to have returned to Ireland and died in Paris later that year.[119]

Following Henri II's decisive refusal to assist the Irish in April, Marie de Guise and François de Vendôme, *vidame* de Chartres, were believed to be the only likely sources of assistance to the Irish party at the French court.[120] Although the *vidame* personally offered to take Ireland with a very small force, even before the Irish had departed the French court (then at Tours), the mood of the courtiers had turned against them. Several courtiers ridiculed and scorned the young French aristocrat for his presumption and naivety, with the result that even the alarmist Mason was more relaxed about the threat posed by the Irish dissidents.[121] Meanwhile, the governments in England and Ireland were far from complacent. The English privy council was acutely sensitive to the potential ramifications of this continental intrigue for the defence of the island, particularly since George Paris was once

---

116 Renard to Charles V, 28 Apr. 1551, CSP Spain, 1550–2, 286.
117 Ibid.
118 Millett, 'Pastoral zeal', 57.
119 Peter Vannes to the privy council, 5 Apr. 1551, CSP Foreign, 1547–53, 82; Mason to the privy council, 19 May 1551, ibid. 108; Tytler, History of Scotland, vi. 441. See also Millett, 'Pastoral zeal', 58.
120 Mason to the privy council, 10 May 1551, CSP Foreign, 1547–53, 103.
121 Ibid. Scheyfve stated in November 1550 that the English trusted M. le vidame too much and that he had taken advantage of them, especially those who were constantly in his company: Scheyfve to the queen dowager, 4 Nov. 1550, CSP Spain, 1550–2, 186.

again back in Ireland, on this occasion conducting negotiations with MacCarthy More.[122] Consequently Sir James Croft was dispatched to fortify the Irish havens and a fleet was sent to guard the south coast of Ireland.[123]

By mid-May the French, moving inexorably towards confrontation with Charles V, were acutely aware of their need to retain English 'neutrality' as a precondition for launching this campaign. Any form of military intervention in Ireland would draw England into the imminent war on the side of Charles. Having committed France to the anti-imperial campaign, the time for procrastination was over: Henri II had no option but to issue a blanket refusal to receive or assist Irish rebels on any future occasion. In contrast to their response to a similar declaration in March of the previous year, this more emphatic refusal was interpreted and reluctantly accepted as unequivocal by Paris, O'Connor and their associates. Thereafter, Franco-Irish negotiations were dramatically scaled down, though less focused intrigue, at both the French and Scottish courts, continued for several years thereafter.

Henri's dalliance with the Irish envoys, which spanned the period June 1550–May 1551, can only be explained in terms of the redirection of French foreign policy that occurred between the signing of the Treaty of Boulogne and the severing of diplomatic relations with Charles V in May 1551. In spite of his having signed the peace agreement, and notwithstanding his declarations of amicable intentions towards Edward VI in the months that followed, Henri deliberately aimed to irritate the English by clandestine, indirect means.[124] Whether or not he seriously contemplated establishing his hegemony over the British Isles, Henri used his contacts with the Irish deliberately to stir English anxiety at his harbouring such an ambition. It suited him to divert English attention from continental politics by entertaining the Irish at court whilst falling short of supplying them with men or ammunitions that would result in English recriminations and cost to the French exchequer. With the English on the defensive, the French would be able to pursue their anti-imperial campaign. Until such time as he was in a position to go to war against Charles, it worked to Henri's advantage to allow the notion that he had designs on Ireland to gain currency as this enabled him to confuse both the English and Charles V *vis-à-vis* French intentions to mount an offensive against the emperor in support of the German Protestant princes.

It is therefore highly unlikely that the French had any real interest in invading Ireland at this time. Rather, insubstantial intrigue with the Irish served as a convenient smokescreen that Henri II used to full effect while he weighed up his options with respect to England and Charles V. Henri and Montmorency publicly and officially proclaimed their honourable conduct in their dealings with Edward VI. In private, Henri at best tolerated the Irish,

---

122 Potter, 'French intrigue in Ireland', 174.
123 Instructions by the king to Sir James Croft, May 1551, SP 61/3/32. Croft took up office as lord deputy on 1 June 1551.
124 Potter, 'French intrigue', 174–5, 175 n. 76.

allowing them to stay at his court and giving them a hearing, and at worst secretly conspired to assist them in overthrowing English rule in Ireland. By late 1550 it was clear to the French king that his priority should be to press ahead with supporting the German Protestant princes against Charles V, and by the following May the French had taken decisive steps in that direction. In those circumstances, compromising Irish appeals for French assistance were strictly prohibited.

For the duration of this episode of intrigue, from 1550 to 1551, the Irish, particularly George Paris, inevitably played up the level of progress achieved in their negotiations at both the French and Scottish courts, publicising even the slightest sign of interest from the king as evidence of a promise of support for their cause. Despite their scepticism regarding Irish claims, diplomats at the French court, most especially Mason, could not help but be alarmed by the all too apparent 'evidence' that the Irish publicly enjoyed the French king's favour. The discovery of inconsistencies in the king's declarations, and in his treatment of the Irish, further complicated their interpretation of his motives and actions that at once fuelled English anxiety and Irish hopes.

This tail to the round of intense intrigue in 1550–1 came to nothing. As had been the case in the winter of 1549–50, it was the wrong time for the French to pursue a campaign in Ireland. Throughout 1549–50 the German Protestant princes had been engaged in efforts to settle the outstanding dispute between France and England as a prelude to a new French intervention in Germany. By February 1551 French negotiations with the German princes, aimed at a renewal of the long-anticipated anti-imperial campaign, were already advanced.[125] Mindful of the possible ramifications of any destabilisation of their relations with England in the lead-up to this important campaign, the French were therefore intent upon publicly preserving their good relations with the English at that time. In May 1551 the Treaty of Torgau created a new alliance of princes and Henri II proposed taking over Metz, Toul and Verdun as 'imperial vicar'. By July diplomatic relations with the emperor had been broken off and Irish hopes were once again dashed.[126]

IV

In the immediate aftermath of Henri II's second and categorical refusal to intervene in Ireland, there was no evidence of any further grounds for suspecting that the king was involved with Irish dissidents. In what amounted to a damage limitation exercise, those Irish who had been

[125] Pariset, 'Relations entre la France et l'Allemagne', and 'La France et les princes allemands'.
[126] Potter, *History of France*, 274.

conducting negotiations with the French reached terms with the English crown. With the exception of a few individuals outside Ireland, on whose behalf the French king promised to intercede to obtain their pardon, all parties to the intrigue, including, significantly, MacCarthy More, were said to have laid down their arms.[127]

The English government was heartened by Henri II's consistent rejection of both Irish and English dissidents' solicitations for aid, and this in spite of his allegedly having damaged his reputation by leaving the Irish unaided.[128] Yet they were suspicious of the duc de Guise, the duc d'Aumale and the cardinal of Lorraine, all of whom, 'partly at her egging, and partly upon an ambitious desire to make their house great', had been 'no hindrance' to Marie de Guise's 'malicious designs' to subvert the Tudor *régime*.[129] However, early in 1552 she too made a gesture to peace by delivering to the English a Scotsman who had tried to have Henri created lord of Ireland. By that time George Paris was back in Scotland.[130] By the end of February, however, Henri II's supposed unflinching adherence to his policy of ignoring the petitions of Irish dissidents came under the suspicious eye of Sir William Pickering, Mason's successor. He admitted to having 'an inkling that the French king hath a practice in hand in Ireland' owing to Henri's show of hospitality and donation of money to Bernard O'Higgin, bishop of Elphin, and his companion, a friar named Thady, during their stay at court. In the event, however, nothing came of their sojourn.[131]

Clearly the individuals most at risk following Henri's pronouncement were George Paris and Cormac O'Connor. Soon after their dismissal from the French court in May 1551, Paris's role in the negotiations was called into question, bringing to light the factionalism, duplicity and predominance of self-interest that evidently marred the conduct of Franco-Irish talks and ultimately contributed to their failure. From France he and Cormac O'Connor travelled to Scotland in compliance with Henri II's orders and delivered letters from the king addressed to the queen dowager. Paris subsequently made the crossing to Ireland where he had contacts with MacCarthy More before returning to the Scottish court.[132] While in Scotland Paris resumed his primary role as envoy for the O'Connor sept, becoming involved in plans to

---

[127] Renard to Charles V, 12 May 1551, CSP Spain, 1550–2, 293; Croft to the privy council, 28 July 1551, CSP Ireland, 1509–73, 115.

[128] Renard to Charles V, 10 July 1551, CSP Spain, 1550–2, 328.

[129] Mason to the privy council, 23 Feb. 1551, CSP Foreign, 1547–53, 75.

[130] Scheyfve, advices, 18 Jan. 1552, CSP Spain, 1550–2, 445; privy council to Croft, 23 Feb. 1552, CSP Ireland, 1509–73, 123.

[131] Sir William Pickering to the privy council, 25 Feb. 1552, BL, MS Harleian 1582, fo. 2r, quoted in Potter, 'French intrigue', 176–7; F. X. Martin, 'Confusion abounding: Bernard O'Higgins, O.S.A., bishop of Elphin, 1542–61', in Cosgrove and McCartney, Studies in Irish history, 65.

[132] The queen dowager to the emperor, 11 Nov. 1552, CSP Spain, 1550–2, 585–8; memoir, 6 Oct. 1552, ibid. 587; Hogan, Ireland in the European system, 159.

secure the release of Cormac O'Connor's father, Brian O'Connor Faly, who had been imprisoned in the Tower of London since 1548.

Now Paris was discovered as a traitor to the French king and 'faithless' towards the Irish lords whom he claimed to represent.[133] Convinced that there was no hope of securing French aid for a campaign in Ireland, self-preservation spurred Paris to sue for a pardon from Edward VI in return for handing over the intelligence which he had in his possession. He managed to elicit a pardon and letters remissive of all offences that he had committed from the king and made further provision for his personal protection by obtaining a safe conduct and a passport to proceed to England.[134]

Not surprisingly, Marie de Guise and d'Oisel were seriously concerned at Paris's defection. They were especially alarmed by reports that he intended taking with him all those letters written by Henri II to the Irish lords and also those written by the Irish to the French king, all of which Paris still had in his personal possession. Fortunately for them, d'Oisel discovered Paris's 'malicious intention' on 4 October 1551, and immediately seized all the papers in his possession, in the name of the Scottish regent, the duc de Châtellerault.[135] Among them he found incriminating letters and scripts which showed that Paris had practised duplicity 'to the great hurt of the Irish princes' and provided the English government with categorical proof of French involvement with Irish dissidents.[136] The suspicions of both Henri II and Mason that Paris was a completely unscrupulous opportunist were therefore vindicated. In his defence, however, following his abandonment by both the French king and the Scottish regent, the Irish agent can hardly be condemned for suing for the best terms to ensure his own protection.[137]

D'Oisel justified his confiscation of the letters on the grounds that if the English had gained possession of them, they would have been used to seize the property of those Irish lords who were implicated or, alternatively, to execute them.[138] Paris's duplicity was therefore exposed and his credibility plummeted. The queen dowager and the French ambassador concluded that his protestations of devotion to Henri II, and his proclaimed zeal for the welfare and freedom of Ireland were entirely false. They were gratified that he had been imprisoned in Falkland Castle in Scotland on charges that the English government could not question.[139] While he was in prison, in April 1552, another pardon was issued to Paris by Edward VI, though it proved of

---

133 Memoir, 6 Oct. 1552, CSP Spain, 1550–2, 587.
134 Ibid. The English privy council granted Paris a pardon and a promise of restitution of his lands forfeited in Ireland on 25 October 1552: privy council to George Paris, 25 Oct. 1552, CSP Ireland, 1509–73, 128; memoir, 6 Oct. 1552, CSP Spain, 1550–2, 587.
135 Memoir, 6 Oct. 1552, CSP Spain, 1550–2, 587. Marie de Guise replaced Châtellerault as regent in 1554.
136 Ibid.
137 Ibid. See also Mason to the privy council, 18 Apr. 1551, SP 68/9a/291.
138 Memoir, 6 Oct. 1552, CSP Spain, 1550–2, 587.
139 Ibid.

little worth to him, and in March of the following year, the English made a further attempt to secure his release. At an unknown date he was released.[140]

Having also visited Ireland briefly following his departure from the Scottish court, Cormac O'Connor returned to Scotland with letters from Irish lords addressed to the queen dowager in which they indicated their mistrust of Paris as their envoy.[141] Suspecting that Paris was about to surrender his intelligence to the English, O'Connor reported him to Marie de Guise. D'Oisel held O'Connor in high esteem as 'a man of zeal, integrity and devotion, as the Irish lords well know', an 'homme de service veritable', more honest than Paris, though this deference might be explained in terms of O'Connor's standing as a Gaelic lord as opposed to Paris, a humble, dispossessed gentleman. Banished from Ireland, with his father in prison and his property confiscated, Cormac interceded with Henri II to assist him in order that he might 'live like a gentleman until times shall improve'.[142]

In October 1549 the prospect of a French invasion of Ireland appeared more real that it had done previously or would do again in the sixteenth century. For a very brief interval, Henri II, Marie de Guise, her brothers, the duc de Guise and the duc d'Aumale, along with Henri Clutin d'Oisel, the earl of Argyll, Robert Wauchop, Con O'Neill, Manus O'Donnell, O'Doherty, James MacDonnell and his brother, Angus, were willing to give serious consideration to the feasibility of such an expedition, and the Irish council genuinely feared that their plans might materialise. However, that opportunity quickly passed as waning French interest in both Scotland and Ireland, the divisiveness of the Gaelic Irish and of their representatives, improved Anglo-French relations and the discovery of the conspiracy by the Irish council effectively sabotaged all plans for an invasion. While Paris, O'Connor and others persisted in attempts to revive negotiations with the French crown following the signing of the Treaty of Boulogne, by May 1551 they had abandoned all hope for French assistance and instead devoted their energies to pursuing their personal and dynastic agendas in the wake of the failure of another significant episode in Franco-Irish intrigue.

---

[140] CPR Ireland, Hen. VIII–Eliz., iv. 335, 13 Apr. 1552; Acts of the privy council of England, new ser., 46 vols, London 1890–1964, iv. 12, 138, 151; Potter, 'French intrigue', 179.
[141] Memoir, 6 Oct. 1552, CSP Spain, 1550–2, 587–8.
[142] Ibid.

5

French Conspiracy at Rival Courts and Shane O'Neill's Triangular Intrigue, 1553–1567

> Not so much for the care I have for Ireland, which I have often wished to be sunk in the sea, as for that the French should set foot therein, they should not only have entry to Scotland . . . but also by the commodity of the havens *here* [Ireland] and in Calais . . . whereby would endure such a ruin to England I am afeared to think on: The opinion of the earl of Sussex, touching reformation of Ireland, 11 Sept. 1560, *Carew* MSS, 302.

Although Franco-Irish intrigue during the period 1553–67 never reached the intensity or the seriousness that it had in the winter of 1549–50, a level of engagement between the French and Scottish courts and Irish dissidents persisted throughout the following two decades and quickened significantly in three distinct phases. The first serious engagement in the autumn and winter of 1553 centred on a plot to stage an uprising in Ireland to coincide with Sir Thomas Wyatt's rebellion in England. The crucial parties to this intrigue were Antoine de Noailles and Henri Clutin d'Oisel, ambassadors to England and Scotland respectively, along with Marie de Guise, the ring-leaders of the Wyatt rebellion and probably Henri II. The second though much less consequential episode occurred in spring 1557, on the eve of the outbreak of war between France and England, when an Irishman named Power sought to capitalise on the tensions between the two monarchs by presenting Henri II with a proposal for a French invasion of Ireland. The third and to date most protracted phase of Franco-Irish intrigue began when Mary I declared war on France in 1557 and continued with varying degrees of intensity and gravity until Shane O'Neill's death in June 1567. In essence this intrigue centred upon lofty allegations of Gerald Fitzgerald's involvement in plans to stage a Franco-Scottish invasion of Ireland and on more general reports of an international Catholic conspiracy headed by the Guise dynasty to undermine the Tudor *régime*. In particular, French backing for Mary Stuart's return to Scotland in summer 1561, for the earl of Argyll's withdrawal of his initial support of the English in 1565 and for Shane O'Neill's increased opposition to the crown all boded ill for the security of the entire British polity. However, Shane O'Neill's collusion with Fitzgerald, Charles IX, the cardinals of Lorraine and of Guise, Mary Queen of Scots and disaffected Scots including Argyll was by far the most dangerous dimension to all of this intrigue. O'Neill's connivance reached its climax between 1565 and the summer of 1567, coming to an abrupt and decisive end with his assassination in the month of June.

Following two years of inactivity, domestic instability in England in 1553 initiated a phase of Franco-Irish intrigue in which the Irish, the Scots and English were used by their more powerful European partners purely as pawns in the Habsburg–Valois struggle which dominated European politics in the first half of the sixteenth century.[1] During Mary I's reign (1553–8), the French ambassador and the queen dowager of Scotland, and later Henri II, were implicated in plots to undermine the Marian *régime*, lending support to insurgence in Ireland as part of a broader policy of supporting popular opposition throughout the realm to the Tudor–Habsburg marriage. While in 1549–50 the French displayed commitment to negotiating terms with their Irish counterparts, their interest in Ireland thereafter centred on their hope that disturbances could be maintained purely for their nuisance value to the English queen and her council. Until the declaration of war between England and France in June 1557, this was to remain the constant feature of French relations with Ireland and *vice versa*. Insofar as the French had a policy in respect of Ireland it was but one element of their British policy, the goal of which was to prevent England's absorption within the Habsburg dominion. It is in this context that relations between Ireland and France are presently examined.

I

The first significant episode in Franco-Irish intrigue during the Marian reign occurred in the autumn and winter of 1553–4 by which time England had become the epicentre of European diplomacy as the outcome to Habsburg–Valois feuding hinged on the new queen's choice of a husband. If Charles V could establish his son, Philip, on the English throne, he could secure the sea routes between the Netherlands and Spain, and the Netherlands would be spared from falling into the hands of Henri II as the provinces seemed set to do at that time. Having annexed England, the way would be opened for achieving Habsburg encirclement of France.[2] Conversely, if Henri could derail the emperor's scheme by cultivating popular opposition to the Spanish match in England, French influence in Scotland could be strengthened, the French army could be protected against any surprise attack from Calais and the latter might be regained by the French either through intrigue or by treaty.[3]

---

[1] See Dawson, 'Anglo-Scottish Protestant culture', 90.
[2] Harbison, 'French intrigue', 533–4.
[3] Renard to Charles V, 6 Nov. 1553, CSP *Spain*, *1553*, 338; Harbison, 'French intrigue', 533–4.

This round of Franco-Irish intrigue differed from previous engagements as it constituted a peripheral dimension to a serious domestic conspiracy hatched in England by English malcontents, headed by Sir Thomas Wyatt, to oppose Mary's marriage with Philip of Spain. It was also different in that whereas Paris, O'Connor, MacWilliam Burke, O'Neill, O'Doherty and O'Donnell had actively sought French intervention in Ireland, on this occasion it was the French ambassador, Antoine de Noailles, along with Marie de Guise, Henri Clutin d'Oisel, possibly Henri II, and a coterie of English conspirators who spearheaded plans for insurgence, deliberately fanning the flames of discontent among disaffected Gaelic elements as part of their strategy to elevate an essentially English conspiracy to the level of a British security crisis.

In his capacity as self-appointed leader of 'her Majesty's Opposition', Antoine de Noailles was a vital conduit for all intrigue, including Franco-Irish intrigue, which he encouraged and harnessed as one of several strategies aimed at cultivating disturbances throughout the British Isles in order to prevent England's absorption within the Habsburg orbit. De Noailles was the consummate professional diplomat, a master of diplomatic dexterity, an excellent strategist and keen observer, approachable and generally shrewd in concealing his implication in surreptitious plots and, most important, an official who was motivated by an innate and inarticulate loyalty to Henri II.[4]

By early September he had already begun to organise a parliamentary and popular opposition to the Spanish match while he and Marie de Guise were almost certainly involved in plans to undermine the Marian *régime* by stirring trouble in Ireland. Soon Henri II was 'compromised' by *faux pas* committed by both in respect of their collusion with Irish dissidents. In September 1553 news broke of plans for an imminent French attack on Ireland, causing the 'wild Irish' to be even more agitated than usual. De Noailles and Marie de Guise were suspected of involvement, though Henri appeared not to have been directly implicated, or if he was, his involvement was successfully concealed by de Noailles.[5] While he dabbled in plotting with English and Gaelic malcontents, de Noailles, on Henri's instructions, assured the queen of his master's wish to 'vivre en toute sincérité, d'amitié et fraternité' with her. Henri was, he declared, determined not to become involved with Irish rebels in spite of the many offers that de Noailles had received from such parties and contrary to the numerous damaging allegations made by imperial ambassadors.[6] However, given his unwavering loyalty to the French king, it may

4 Harbison, 'French intrigue', 534.
5 The [imperial] ambassadors in England to Charles V, 30 Sept. 1553, *CSP Spain, 1553*, 261.
6 Henri II to M. de Noailles, 14 nov. 1553, AE, CP Angleterre, correspondance d'Antoine, François et Gilles de Noailles, ix. 170; [imperial] ambassadors in England to Charles V, 30 Sept. 1553, *CSP Spain, 1553*, 261; Renard to Charles V, 4, 6 Nov. 1553, ibid. 335, 338; Henri II to de Noailles, 14 nov. 1553, correspondance de Antoine, François et Gilles de Noailles. ix. 170; Harbison, 'French intrigue', 547.

Plate 2 Antoine de Noailles, 1504–1585,
French ambassador to England

reasonably be assumed that in trifling with Gaelic dissidents, de Noailles was
not acting without Henri's passive support at very least, though it is difficult
to distinguish between diplomatic dexterity and duplicity in interpreting the
correspondence between the king and his ambassador.[7]

In late autumn and early winter 1553 Henri apparently believed that as
long as there was no concrete proof of Mary's intention to marry Philip II, his
best strategy was, in E. H. Harbison's words, 'to persuade and flatter [rather]
than to threaten and intrigue'.[8] Henri's main concern was to avoid any inci-
dent that might cause Mary to ally with his Spanish opponent, thereby
leaving him faced with the threat of Habsburg encirclement.[9] Intent upon

7 Harbison, 'French intrigue', 534.
8 Idem, *Rival ambassadors*, 94.
9 Ibid.

112

being seen to be beyond suspicion of involvement with Gaelic dissidents, he warned Noailles to 'fermer du tout les oreilles à tous ces gens passionnés qui vous mettez parties . . . et font de ouvertures au dommage de ladite reine [Mary I] pour se retirer en mon service'.[10]

None the less, de Noailles intensified his involvement in various intrigues. While mainly implicated at a distance with English dissidents, he keenly observed developments in Ireland, watching for an opportunity for the French to harness disturbances in that kingdom as a dimension of British intrigue aimed at influencing Mary's decision regarding her marriage alliance. In mid-October he expectantly alerted Marie de Guise to the particularly weakened state of the English government's control in Ireland and pressed the queen dowager to send trusty persons to fan the flames of discontent there.[11] He also engaged in talks with the ringleaders of the Wyatt conspiracy, namely, Sir James Croft (former lord deputy of Ireland, April 1551–December 1552), Sir William Pickering, Rogers and possibly Carew, who planned simultaneous uprisings in England and Ireland in opposition to Mary's marriage to Philip of Spain.[12] Croft sought the French king's assistance for an insurrection in England and Ireland on the grounds of his supposed ability to 'susciter infinis troubles en Angleterre et Irlande'.[13] In an obvious move to exculpate himself from allegations of complicity in this intrigue, and in order to exonerate himself from the suspicion which their resort to him undoubtedly aroused at the English court, de Noailles assured the king that he had received the propositions of these English noblemen 'fort froidement'. He did so, ostensibly assured that Henri did not wish to learn of any conduct on his ambassador's part that would cause Mary's displeasure.[14]

However, de Noailles failed to evade the censorious eye of Simon Renard, the imperial ambassador to the English court, who suspected the French of lending support to the insurgents in Ireland.[15] Unnerved by the extent of Renard's discoveries, de Noailles briefed Henri II on a number of potentially incriminating though unsubstantiated reports then circulating at the English court. These alleged that French troops had been dispatched to Ireland, that the French were being blamed for inciting all disturbances in the country and that François de Lorraine and sixty gentlemen were in Ireland devising plans

---

[10] Henri II to Antoine de Noailles, 9 oct. 1553, dépêches et mémoires de MM de Noailles, xii. 181.

[11] De Noailles to the queen of Scotland, 14 oct. 1553, ibid. xii. 153; Potter, 'French intrigue', 177.

[12] De Noailles to Henri II, 17 oct. 1553, dépêches et mémoires de MM de Noailles, xii. 161; Henri II to de Noailles, 30 déc. 1553, correspondance de Antoine, François et Gilles de Noailles, ix. 199–200. See also Harbison, 'French intrigue', 536, 548; Nicholls, *Modern British Isles*, 148–51.

[13] De Noailles to Henri II, 17 oct. 1553, dépêches et mémoires de MM de Noailles, xii. 161.

[14] Ibid.

[15] Renard to Charles V, 6 Nov. 1553, *CSP Spain, 1553*, 338.

for an insurrection.[16] While de Noailles dismissed these reports as the work of 'un mistère joué de l'invention', Henri II took a very serious view of their potential to exert a strain on his relations with Mary who remained suspicious of French involvement in disturbances in Ireland.[17]

Henri's efforts to prevent Mary's marriage to Philip of Spain were negated by the queen's decision in November to reject the substance of the parliamentary petition not to marry outside the realm. While he continued to present the appearance of an ally, his implication in conspiracy against the queen gradually came to light. In late November it was reported in London that Henri was lending covert support to the Scots for their attack on the English borders and Ireland.[18] By then de Noailles and Marie de Guise regularly swapped intelligence reports concerning disturbances in Ireland and the ambassador's involvement in triangular intrigue between English, Scottish and Irish malcontents came close to being exposed. On 24 November Mary I challenged de Noailles in relation to Henri II's rumoured involvement in seditious practices in Ireland and identified the Scots and particularly the Gaelic highlanders as key participants.[19] In spite of the fact that early in December the queen dowager was obviously feeling the glare of English suspicion on her trifling with Gaelic dissidents, she persistently colluded with de Noailles in inciting disturbances in Ireland, assuring him that 'je vous en advertirai incontinent, vous priant aussi faire le semblable'.[20]

Meanwhile, Simon Renard's representation of Henri II's position as duplicitous and his suspicion of de Noailles seemed increasingly justified.[21] In early December there was a growing sense of unrest in northern England among dissidents who were allegedly hopeful of 'having aid and support from Scotland through the king of France'.[22] By the end of 1553 the Irish dimension had become entirely peripheral to the Wyatt conspiracy. Henri backed de Noailles in his intrigue, assuring Sir James Croft of his (Henri's) willingness to assist him when he would stage the rising.[23] In the event, however, no French aid was forthcoming to back the planned uprisings in England and Ireland and Wyatt's challenge to the Marian *régime* collapsed in January of the following year. Mary and Renard took immediate steps to

---

16 De Noailles to Henri II, 4 nov. 1553, dépêches et mémoires de MM de Noailles, xii. 171–2.
17 Henri II to de Noailles, 14 nov. 1553, correspondance de Antoine, François et Gilles de Noailles, ix. 170; de Noailles to Henri II, 17 nov. 1553, dépêches et mémoires de MM de Noailles, xii. 189.
18 Renard to Charles V, 20 Nov. 1553, *CSP Spain, 1553*, 371.
19 De Noailles to Marie de Guise, 24 nov. 1553, dépêches et mémoires de MM de Noailles, xii. 191.
20 Marie de Guise to de Noailles, 7 déc. 1553, ibid. 221–2.
21 Renard to Charles V, 29 Nov. 1553, *CSP Spain, 1553*, 400–1.
22 Quoted in Harbison, 'French intrigue', 550.
23 Henri II to de Noailles, 30 déc. 1553, correspondance de Antoine, François et Gilles de Noailles, ix. 199–200.

render de Noailles incapable of inciting further sedition. His intelligence network was demobilised: his couriers were delayed, his agents imprisoned, his informers frightened and visitors to his house were chastised.[24] By the end of April 1554 de Noailles complained of being treated as a prisoner rather than an ambassador. Consequently his knowledge of all current developments was severely restricted and his acquaintance with Irish affairs and contact with Irish dissidents temporarily suspended. From January 1554, until his recall to France in June 1557, although he was involved in the Dudley conspiracy in March 1556, de Noailles played no comparable part in intrigue with disaffected Irish lords; instead his role was confined to mere observation of disturbances in Ireland.[25]

While Antoine de Noailles's youngest brother, Gilles, who served as agent to England until 6 November and his other brother, François, appointed ambassador to England on 6 November 1557, closely observed Irish affairs and Sussex's Scottish campaign, neither became implicated in intrigue centred on Ireland to the extent that their elder brother had done in 1553.[26] None the less, after Antoine's recall, his close friend, d'Oisel, by then lieutenant-general of Scotland, continued to avail himself of every opportunity to exploit the weakness of the Tudor *régime*, and even carried out a feasibility study for launching an attack on Ireland via the west coast of Scotland in 1559. In the event, however, d'Oisel's schemes came to nothing.[27]

In spring 1557, when England and France were on the eve of the outbreak of war, an Irishman named Power whose property (including two strong castles in the northern march lands) and 20,000 pounds sterling had been confiscated by Queen Mary 'sous l'ombre de la religion' endeavoured to revive Franco-Irish intrigue by engaging the attention of ambassador de Noailles at the English court. Power presented de Noailles with a strategic plan designed to launch a joint French-Irish attack on England when the latter would be at war with France.[28] However, his proposal was a non-starter, and in any case it was not French involvement with disaffected Irish lords that ultimately triggered Mary's declaration of war with France. In April the

[24] Harbison, 'French intrigue', 536.
[25] De Noailles to constable de Montmorency, 4 mai 1554, dépêches et mémoires de MM de Noailles, xii. 402–7; *Ambassades de MM de Noailles en Angleterre*, ed. René Aubert de Vertot, 5 vols, Paris 1763, iii. 190; de Noailles to de Montmorency, 25 fév. 1555, dépêches et mémoires de MM de Noailles, xii. 926–7; *Ambassades de MM de Noailles*, iv. 306; M. de Noailles to Henri II, 9 av. 1555, dépêches et mémoires de MM de Noailles, xii. 942–3; *Ambassades de MM de Noailles*, v. 331. See also Nicholls, *Modern British Isles*, 156.
[26] Harbison, 'French intrigue', 533 n. 1.
[27] M. de Villeparisis (Henri Clutin d'Oisel) to de Noailles, 30 juin 1559, dépêches et mémoires de MM de Noailles, xiii. 511. See also Vindry, *Les Ambassadeurs français*, 37–8; Harbison, 'French intrigue', 533 n. 1; Baudouin-Matuszek, 'Les Expéditions françaises', 372 nn. 1, 2, and 'Un Ambassadeur en Écosse', 99.
[28] 'Instructions au sieur de la Cassaigne allant devers le roy', 10 av. 1557, dépêches et mémoires de MM de Noailles, xii. 356.

queen was faced with yet another conspiracy when the Protestant exile Thomas Stafford 'invaded' England with two ships and a few dozen men. As Henri II was suspected of complicity with Stafford, Mary had little option but to declare war on France on 4 June.[29]

II

During the course of the Anglo-French war (June 1557–April 1559), the prospect of French and Scottish intervention in Ireland aimed at undermining the Marian and Elizabethan *régimes* greatly exercised the attention of the English administrations in Whitehall and Dublin. In particular, concern was focused on the suspected involvement of Gerald Fitzgerald, the now restored eleventh earl of Kildare, with the French, and on the redoubtable George Paris's release from imprisonment in Scotland and his reappearance as an agent at the French court. The loss of Calais in January 1558, followed by the marriage between Mary Queen of Scots and the dauphin in April of that year, transformed Whitehall's prioritisation of its relations with Scotland and lent urgency to its need to formulate a 'British' defence strategy. As a direct result of these two developments, to use Jane Dawson's analogy, the old postern gate through which the Scots could have created diversions as they had done in the past now served as a front door through which the French could mount a full-scale attack on England. Throughout 1558 English privy councillors feared that the French would invade Scotland and would use Elizabeth's accession as justification for the invasion of England. Their anxieties were compounded by fears regarding Irish defence, in particular the potential for the French to exploit the unguarded stretch of sea between Scotland and Ulster, which was of great strategic importance since Antrim lay beyond the sphere of control of the Dublin administration and in the hands of the MacDonnells, the southern branch of the Scottish clan of Donald, rulers of Kintyre. The English feared that the French might win the support of the MacDonnells and the Gaelic lords of Ulster as they had unsuccessfully sought to do in 1550. Once they had occupied Ireland, the French could then either mount a naval blockade or use Ireland as a base for launching an attack on the undefended western coast of England. Thus Scotland became a security priority as a frontier for a possible French invasion and Ireland, the lateral outpost. Both fronts were earmarked as strategic liabilities to the English administrations in Whitehall and Dublin.[30]

In the wake of the French recovery of Calais under the command of François de Guise in January 1558, rumours of a French invasion of Ireland increased the Irish council's preoccupation with the island's defence and

---

[29] Palmer, *Problem of Ireland*, 75; Nicholls, *Modern British Isles*, 159.
[30] Dawson, 'William Cecil', 201–2.

Gerald Fitzgerald became the object of intense suspicion.[31] Between 1556 and 1560 Lord Lieutenant Radcliffe, earl of Sussex, strove to check Geraldine interests, convinced that Fitzgerald was constantly engaged in intrigue to undermine his viceroyalty. In 1558 he believed that the earl was at the centre of a conspiracy to stage a French invasion of Ireland and to overthrow English rule in the country altogether. He was angered by assertions that Fitzgerald was 'a true French man, and the chief doer with the Scots and French men'.[32] Throughout 1558 and 1559 Sussex's fears of a Geraldine conspiracy continued to be fuelled by reports circulated by English agents in Scotland, France and Spain.[33] In another worrying development, George Paris reappeared in 1558 as an agent at the French and Scottish courts.[34] However, in the final analysis, all of this speculation amounted to little more than scaremongering aimed at pressurising the English monarch on both Irish and Scottish fronts while she was at war with the French.

In spite of the signing of the treaty between France and England at Câteau Cambrésis in April 1559, and notwithstanding the failure of the rumoured French attack on Ireland to materialise, English apprehension concerning foreign intervention was not allayed. On the contrary, some Englishmen believed that the treaty had only served to strengthen French powers of intimidation since they now appeared to be 'bestriding the [English] realm, having one foot in Calais, the other in Scotland'.[35] Henri II's accidental death in July 1559, and the accession of his son, François II, to the throne, prompted fundamental changes in the Scottish polity that disturbed the new queen, Elizabeth I, and her councillors and also appeared conducive to a revival of French interest in staging an invasion of Ireland. The dauphin's accession made Mary Stuart the queen of France, and her uncles, the duc de Guise and the cardinal of Lorraine, acquired even greater influence at the French court when Anne de Montmorency was replaced by Guise as *grand maître de la maison du roi* which gave him authority over all courtiers.[36] The Guises favoured the rapid extension of French power in Scotland and actively supported their sister and regent, Marie de Guise. The revival of involvement of the Guise faction in Scottish affairs in the mid to late 1550s restored the indispensable dynamic for French engagement in intrigue with the lords of Ireland that existed almost a decade before.

In the early stages of her reign, Elizabeth I's main sources of anxiety were Scotland, where she feared a renewed intervention by the militantly Catholic Guise dynasty, and Ulster, where Shane O'Neill displayed increasingly

31 Garrisson, *Sixteenth-century France*, 168; Nicholls, *Modern British Isles*, 159–60.
32 Hugh Curwen, archbishop of Dublin and chancellor, to Thomas Radcliffe, earl of Sussex, 26 Feb. 1558, PRO, SP 62/2/13.
33 Brady, 'Shane O'Neill', 18.
34 Queen Mary to Lord Deputy Radcliffe, 2 June 1558, SP 62/2/48 (1).
35 Palmer, *Problem of Ireland*, 77.
36 *Biographie universelle (Michaud)*, xviii (1857), 224; Constant, *Les Guise*, 38.

worrying potential for collaboration with the Scots. Once again the Scottish regent, Marie de Guise, drew on her brothers' assistance as she struggled to overcome stiff opposition to the new policies through which she sought to assert her control over Scotland and to the appointment of an increasing number of French officials, government advisors and military officers.[37]

Throughout 1559–60, while Sir William Cecil worked to bring about an agreement that would legislate for the establishment of a Scottish adminis-tration free of French influence and favourably disposed towards England, French intervention in Ireland remained a constant if distant possibility in the minds of Irish councillors.[38] In summer 1559 both d'Oisel and François II deliberated over propositions presented to them by Irish dissidents, some of whom had had previous contact with Charles, cardinal of Lorraine.[39] Mean-while, unfounded rumours circulated in England alleging that François II had declared himself king of France, England and Ireland and that he was making great preparations in Normandy and Brittany to send forces to Scotland.[40]

That there were good grounds for English suspicion of Irish intrigue with the French during the summer and autumn months of 1559 is intimated by Alvaro de la Quadra, bishop of Aquila. He believed it altogether possible 'that finding themselves so sorely pressed about religion they [the Irish] may have appealed to France, as I have heard some of these Frenchmen speak of them with great regard'.[41] It was in October that François II was alerted to the growing threat posed by Shane O'Neill, 'le Grand O Néal le premier dudit royaume', who was instrumental in causing the disturbances in Ireland.[42] Meanwhile, Cecil remained acutely aware of the wider British dimension to the French threat, fearing that they 'intend to attempt this practice [not only] against Scotland, but against Ireland and England also'.[43] Throughout the winter months of 1559–60 he worked to convince Elizabeth to dispatch aid to the Scottish rebels, led by the Lords of the Congregation; the agreement with the Scots which provided for the deployment of these forces was forma-lised in the Treaty of Berwick, signed in February 1560. Cecil thereby master-minded an accord on the strength of which he could demand Scottish

[37] Dawson, 'William Cecil', 204.

[38] Idem, 'Two kingdoms or three?', 118, and 'William Cecil'; Palmer, *Problem of Ireland*, 78–80.

[39] Clutin d'Oisel to de Noailles, 30 juin 1559, dépêches et mémoires de MM de Noailles, xiii. 511; François II to de Noailles, 18 août 1559, ibid. xiii. 582.

[40] De Noailles to François II, 29 juill. 1559, xiii. ibid. 551; de Noailles to cardinal de Lorraine, [29 juill. 1559], ibid. xiii. 551, 554; de Noailles to M. de Limoges, 6 juill. 1559, ibid. xiv. 35.

[41] Bishop of Aquila to Philip II, 5 Oct. 1559, *CSP Spain, 1558–67*, 96, 105. At this time the Spanish court too became the target for Irish solicitations for aid but to no avail. See also J. J. Silke, *Ireland and Europe, 1559–1607*, Dundalk 1966, 5.

[42] De Noailles to François II, 6 oct. 1559, dépêches et mémoires de MM de Noailles, xiii. 631.

[43] Cecil to Sir Ralph Sadler and Sir James Croft, 12 Nov. 1559, *CSP Foreign, 1559–60*, 105.

assistance in the subjugation of Ireland. The agreement also stipulated that the earl of Argyll would employ his forces to subject Ulster to Elizabeth's authority with the co-operation of the lord deputy.[44]

Argyll was grateful to the English for their assistance in expelling the French and establishing Protestantism, and was in a unique position to reciprocate English aid since he dominated western Scotland and could readily intervene in Ulster with his mercenary forces by virtue of his proximity and his knowledge of the province.[45] Although these developments appeared to augur well for withstanding a French attack on Ireland, the Irish council remained anxious about British security. Their unease was fuelled in the spring of 1560 by rumours of French assistance for Donald O'Brien, rival to Connor O'Brien, third earl of Thomond, and by other dissidents returning from France. The manifestly truculent attitude displayed by the earls of Kildare and Desmond, the contacts between O'Brien, the two Geraldine earls and Shane O'Neill, and Brian O'Connor Faly's escape from prison gave further cause for concern.[46] It was indeed fears of a Geraldine conspiracy, backed by the French and fanned by Sussex's propaganda, that hardened Elizabeth's attitude toward O'Neill. The queen's overriding concern was the 'inevitable danger to England if the French are permitted to subdue Scotland by force or by practice'.[47] She was insistent that Ulster be 'reduced to the obedience of England so that the force here may be better employed to the defence of the realm against the French who will provide an enemy to both'.[48] Elizabeth charged Norfolk with formulating a strategy for the subjugation of Ireland which would facilitate the re-deployment of English troops to serve in Scotland against the French.[49]

Still smarting after the loss of Calais to the army of Lieutenant-General François de Guise, the queen suspected the Guises of being prime movers behind all of the Catholic plots throughout the British Isles aimed at undermining her *régime*. On 24 March she issued a proclamation for maintaining peace with Scotland and France in which she provocatively accused the Guise faction of 'intermeddling' in a manner that threatened the kingdoms of Ireland and England. She alleged that the Guises had no means of achieving their own advancement other than through the aggrandisement of their niece, Mary Queen of Scots. Furthermore, she complained that they had 'injurieusement et insolemment' conspired in public, even in peacetime, to attribute the arms and titles of the kingdoms of England and Ireland to their niece, as well as directing many other serious reproaches at her as queen of

---

44 Dawson, 'Two kingdoms or three?', 119.
45 Ibid. 120; Palmer, *Problem of Ireland*, 79; MacCraith, 'Gaelic reaction', 141.
46 Ellis, *Ireland in the age of the Tudors*, 276; Dawson, 'William Cecil', 202.
47 Elizabeth I to the duke of Norfolk, 15 Feb. 1560, *CSP Foreign, 1559–60*, 362.
48 Ibid.
49 Elizabeth I to Norfolk, 15 Feb. 1560, HMC, *Salisbury MSS*, i. 181.

England.[50] In Ireland Lord Justice Sir William Fitzwilliam was clearly unsettled in March 1560 by news that the earl of Kildare and the fourteenth earl
Desmond had been engaged in conspiracy while they were at Limerick late
the previous year, and by subsequent rumours of an imminent invasion by
France and Spain that added to the widespread expectation of an insurrection
in Ireland.[51] The Irish, he noted, 'watch[ed] the enterprise of Scotland',
demonstrating that they too were attuned to the wider British dimension to
French designs.[52]

III

During the early 1560s the locus for the most serious threat to British security
shifted from Scotland to Ulster as Shane O'Neill engaged in intrigue with the
Scots, and to a lesser extent the French, stirring fears of another Catholic
conspiracy against Elizabeth. In the summer of 1560 decisive changes
occurred in the Scottish polity that weakened the bonds of the Auld Alliance
(by then fatally associated with Catholicism and viewed as a challenge to
Scottish sovereignty) and appeared to strengthen the English position in the
face of the French threat.[53] In June 1560 Marie de Guise died. The following
month the Treaty of Edinburgh brought the Scottish civil war to a close and
legislated for the expulsion of most of the French troops from Scotland, a
diminution of French influence in government and, critically, the establishment of the Reformed religion in Scotland. French and Scottish opponents of
Elizabeth were thus deprived of a haven from which to conduct their
intrigues. Although Mary Stuart returned to Scotland in August, French
presence and influence there was effectively eradicated by the departure of all
remaining French troops, and by the tacit recognition by both Mary and the
French faction of the reality that in the immediate future, the Lords of the
Congregation would govern in Edinburgh. Also in August Catholicism was
dealt a fatal blow by the abolition of papal jurisdiction and the mass, which
served to strengthen the Scots' ties with their English Protestant brethren.
Cecil had demonstrated an unprecedented awareness of Scottish sensibilities
in conducting the negotiations and in the assistance that the English
provided for the Scots. Both helped engender a cautious Scottish confidence
in Elizabeth and her council. The result was a considerable strengthening of

---

[50] Proclamation de la paix, 24 mars 1560, dépêches et mémoires de MM de Noailles, xiv. 1;
Tudor royal proclamations, ed. P. L. Hughes and J. F. Larkin, 3 vols, New Haven 1969, ii. 142.
See also Malcolm Thorp, 'Catholic conspiracy in early Elizabethan foreign policy',
Sixteenth Century Journal xv (1984), 431–48.
[51] Lord Justice Sir William Fitzwilliam to Cecil, 15 Mar. 1560, SP 63/2/9; Fitzwilliam to
Cecil, 20 Apr. 1560, SP 63/2/27.
[52] Ibid.
[53] Dawson, 'Anglo-Scottish Protestant culture', 90.

the English queen's position in the short term, and the establishment of the fragile foundations for the Union of the English and Scottish crowns in 1603.[54]

Meanwhile, domestic affairs in France also contributed to a diminution in French intervention in Scotland and by extension, Ireland. The death of Henri II in July 1559 and of his son, François II, in December 1560, brought a decisive shift in the political fortunes of the Guise faction. Deprived of vital royal support, they lost their position of supreme authority at the French court, though they remained a potent force. François's death unleashed bitter hostilities between the Bourbon and Guise factions that erupted in the first of the wars of religion in 1562 which effectively neutralised French foreign policy for a generation.[55] It also resulted in Catherine de Médicis's appointment as regent for her son, Charles IX, a further development that worked to the detriment of the Guises. While Catherine was astute enough to be circumspect in her dealings with the Guises, both Charles and his brother, the future Henri III, despised them. Catherine displayed no interest in continuing Henri II's or François II's policy of actively supporting the Guise faction in Scotland. Instead she encouraged François's young wife, Mary, to return to Scotland.[56]

In spite of these ominous developments at the French court, throughout the winter of 1560–1 the Irish were reported as being in direct negotiations with the French. However, there is no substantive evidence for this assertion. None the less, the presence of the papal nuncio to France at the abbey of Redon in Brittany, held by Cardinal Salviati, where he was concealed until his passage to Ireland could be arranged in early December 1560, prompted understandable concern. So too did the reports of Bishop Quadra of Spain that these senior clerics 'have listened to Irish appeals in France', though there is no record of the nuncio having subsequently visited Ireland.[57]

IV

Meanwhile, Elizabeth's intervention in Ulster was proving tortuous. In May 1560 the decision was taken to tackle the problem of Ulster by isolating O'Neill and commencing negotiations with the earl of Argyll and some of the MacDonnells 'not because the Scots were preferable to Shane in principle, but because Shane was a tool of Kildare, and Kildare's ambitions augured

---

54 Alan G. R. Smith, *The emergence of a nation state: the Commonwealth of England, 1529–1660*, Essex 1984, 101; Dawson, 'William Cecil', 209–10, and 'Two kingdoms or three?', 124; Ellis, 'Tudor state formation', 59; Dawson, 'Anglo-Scottish Protestant culture', 89–91; MacCraith, 'Gaelic reaction', 140–1; Brady, 'Shane O'Neill', 25.
55 Constant, *Les Guise*, 45–6.
56 Ibid. 79.
57 Quadra to Philip II, 23 July 1561, *CSP Spain, 1558–67*, 210.

worse for the future of English government in Ireland than any short-term concessions to the Scots'.[58] Again, Cecil accepted Argyll's proposition to deploy his mercenary forces in support of the crown in Ulster. Initially, the prospects for a successful implementation of this novel policy seemed promising. Shane's connections with the Scots served as a complication which delayed the enactment of Elizabeth's decision on how he ought to be handled: at this point Argyll undertook to separate James MacDonnell and his followers from the other leading families of the Isles, and from Shane O'Neill.[59] By a bond of manrent made between Argyll and James MacDonnell of Dunyveg and the Glens, James pledged that he would resist any invasion of French men in Ireland. In late August Argyll refused to respond to O'Neill's overtures.[60] Another encouraging development from the English perspective was George Paris's defection from the service of Marie de Guise immediately prior to her death.[61]

In spite of these favourable occurrences, Sussex remained anxious about the threat posed by the French and especially after 1559 by Shane O'Neill's growing dependence upon the earl of Kildare.[62] In September 1560 the lord lieutenant suspected Kildare of becoming a focal point for Gaelic conspirators, regarding him as 'the likeliest and most dangerous instrument to allure foreign aid'.[63] He echoed Elizabeth's and Cecil's frequent reiterations of their preoccupation with the wider British dimension to the threat posed by Ireland in admitting that his fears stemmed

> not so much for the care I have for Ireland, which I have often wished to be sunk in the sea, as for that the French should set foot therein, they should not only have entry to Scotland . . . but also by the commodity of the havens here and in Calais . . . whereby would ensure such a ruin to England I am afeared to think on.[64]

The threat of French intervention in Irish affairs in the winter of 1560 acted as a catalyst in galvanising the Scottish loyalist party, the English privy council and the Irish council to adopt a defence strategy designed to encompass the three kingdoms.[65]

[58] Brady, 'Shane O'Neill', 18.
[59] Ibid. 16.
[60] Thomas Randolph to Cecil, 25 Aug. 1560, CSP Scotland, 1547–63, 469; Jenny Wormald, Lords and men, Edinburgh 1985, 185.
[61] Potter, 'French intrigue', 179. Thereafter, for several years, Paris remained an unsatisfied petitioner at the Elizabethan court, being described as 'a poor old gentleman' in 1566.
[62] Palmer, Problem of Ireland, 80; Brady, 'Shane O'Neill', 17.
[63] 'The opinion of the earl of Sussex touching reformation of Ireland', 11 Sept. 1560, Carew MSS, 1515–74, 302.
[64] Ibid. Gaspard de Coligny believed that Elizabeth was planning to annex both Scotland and Ireland to her state: Coligny to the constable, 1 mars 1559, Négociations, lettres et pièces diverses relatives au règne de François II, ed. Louis Paris, Paris 1841, 319.
[65] Sir Nicholas Throckmorton to Cecil, 29 Nov. 1560, CSP Foreign, 1560–1, 413; lords of Scotland to the privy council of England, 7 Dec. 1560, ibid. 435.

Meanwhile English procrastination in deploying Argyll's forces in a campaign to conquer Ulster worked to the advantage of Shane O'Neill. By February 1561 he was preparing to attack the Pale.[66] The catalytic impact of the ongoing reports of an imminent French invasion in shaping English policy is manifest in Elizabeth's order, issued on 25 April, to Sir Henry Sidney, lord president of Wales, to levy 200 men in Wales for service in Ireland.[67] While 'odious rumors from France, Scotland, and Spain' continued to circulate in Ireland, Lord Justice William Fitzwilliam's desperate efforts to tackle dissension in Ulster were dealt a blow by a change in James MacDonnell's allegiances. MacDonnell, who had promised Argyll that he would reject French advances, was now said to be corresponding with the French and had declared Mary Queen of Scots the rightful heir to the English throne.[68]

However, the lord lieutenant's disastrous campaign against O'Neill in July 1561 made the resumption of talks with Shane inevitable and, by autumn, Kildare was authorised to recommence negotiations with O'Neill with a view to arranging an embassy to the Elizabethan court.[69] By that stage both the French and Spanish courts were well informed of Shane O'Neill's potency, and monitored his mounting challenge to the Dublin administration.[70] Councillors in Whitehall and Dublin were disturbed at the increasingly widespread perception on the continent of O'Neill as a potential instrument in French, Scottish or Spanish intrigue, which Shane himself was quick to capitalise on to advance his position.

France was plunged into eight years of civil war shortly after the death of François II in 1560. Yet Irish solicitations for French intervention continued, their authors buoyed up by Shane O'Neill's promising record of defiance, and by Guise support for Mary Stuart's defence of Catholicism in Scotland and for essays at undermining Elizabeth I's authority. Cecil feared English papists' involvement with their continental counterparts in inciting disturbances in England or Ireland and warned that 'whosoever thinks that relenting in religion will assuage the aspirations of the Guisans [sic] are deceived'.[71] In reality, the French regent, Catherine de Médicis, had no interest in supporting the plans of her widowed daughter-in-law. However, this was of little consolation to the English queen and her councils since it was the Guise faction that was perceived as the real powerbroker at the French court.[72] Shane O'Neill shared that viewpoint. With the ascendancy of the Guises in France, and strong associations between Ulster and Scottish Gaelic factions, the French

66 Fitzwilliam to Cecil, 8 Feb. 1561, SP 63/3/25.
67 Elizabeth I to Sir Henry Sidney, 25 Apr. 1561, *CSP Domestic, 1547–80*, 175.
68 Captain Pers, constable of Carrickfergus, to Fitzwilliam, 28 Apr. 1561, SP 63/3/64 (1) (enclosure); Fitzwilliam to Cecil, 30 May 1561, SP 63/3/84.
69 Brady, 'Shane O'Neill', 18.
70 Quadra to the cardinal of Granville, 3 Apr. 1562, *CSP Spain, 1558–67*, 235.
71 Quoted in Palmer, *Problem of Ireland*, 82.
72 G. D. Ramsay, 'The foreign policy of Elizabeth I', in Christopher Haigh (ed.). *The reign of Elizabeth I*, London 1984, 149.

regent's indifference was a secondary consideration in the broader scheme of events.

Throughout 1561 Argyll confirmed his interest in keeping plans for his proposed intervention in Ulster alive by furnishing Cecil with regular reports on Shane's requests for Scottish and French military aid. Early in 1562, while Shane was at the English court, the time seemed ripe to respond to Argyll's latest overtures. Cecil resolved to adopt a harder line with O'Neill to embarrass his court rival, Lord Robert Dudley, and his ambitious Irish client, the earl of Kildare, while preserving his endangered Scottish links and maintaining Argyll's interest in intervening in Ulster. In the event, however, the talks with O'Neill broke down. In the short term this proved advantageous for several of the parties involved: 'Kildare had been thwarted, Dudley forestalled, and Argyll reassured; Cecil had been granted an opportunity to re-inject some confidence into his flagging Scottish alliance, and Sussex a chance to make one more effort against O'Neill'.[73] In the longer term, however, the political cost was very significant. Shane returned to Ireland and prepared for war, while Cecil's hopes of sustaining Anglo-Scottish collaboration in Ulster collapsed as Argyll broke faith with him, suspended contact with Whitehall and began to explore an alternative alliance with O'Neill.[74]

Throughout 1562–3 there was intense suspicion in both England and at the imperial court that the Guises were actively engaged in an international conspiracy to stir up trouble in Ireland.[75] Reports from officials based in France and Scotland pointed to Ireland's crucial role in that conspiracy.[76] In June Henry Middlemore, then in France, alerted Cecil to the possibility of a rebellion in Scotland and Ireland as French informants had confidently told him that 'their instruments are working'.[77] Meanwhile Irish bishops were said to have been received hospitably at the French court before returning to Ireland.[78] Apart from the concern aroused by rumours of French intervention in Ireland, English efforts to subjugate Ulster were, Sussex conceded, severely retarded. He warned Cecil that the success of the Guise faction and of the papists was likely to lead to a renewal of French claims to the Scottish title, and was unsettled by the brazen manner in which the Irish openly practised Catholicism.[79] Both Irish and Scottish dissidents preyed on English insecurities in relation to a supposed Guise conspiracy against Elizabeth at a time when the grandees were spearheading a defence of Catholicism in the first of the French wars of religion (1562–3). In reality, however, the Guises's in-

73 Brady, 'Shane O'Neill', 27.
74 Ibid.
75 Throckmorton to Elizabeth I, 15 Oct. 1562, CSP Foreign 1562, 369; Christopher Mundt to Cecil, 28 Dec. 1563, HMC, Salisbury MSS, i. 286.
76 Palmer, Problem of Ireland, 83.
77 Henry Middlemore to Cecil, 17 June 1563, CSP Foreign 1563, 419.
78 'Occurrences in France', 28 Dec. 1563, ibid. 647.
79 Radcliffe to Cecil, 22 July 1562, SP 63/6/57.

volvement in the French wars necessarily diminished their chances of under-taking a venture in Ireland in those years. They suffered a serious setback in the assassination of their leader, the duc de Guise, in 1563. Without his brother's collaboration, and unable to rely on François's son Henri, who was still a minor at the time of his father's death, the cardinal of Lorraine's ability to exercise the dynasty's military might was severely curtailed in the mid-1560s.[80]

In 1562 and the early months of the following year, Sussex regarded the threat of French intervention in Ireland as a further complication in the Irish council's handling of Shane O'Neill. Apprehension grew at what appeared to be the increasingly likely prospect of an imminent French invasion of England; Ireland's role as a springboard for such an attack was never discounted by the Irish council.[81] The threat to English security from Scot-land and Ireland continued to escalate. By 1564 Shane was growing restless, mistrustful of the government's delay in ratifying the terms of the treaty that he had negotiated with Sir Thomas Cusack at Drumcree the previous September. The protracted stalemate which followed forced O'Neill to take action against the Scots in Ulster in summer 1564.[82] By 1565 he had caused widespread destruction and disturbance in Ulster and Leinster and had become the Dublin administration's priority in Ireland. Early that year James MacDonnell returned to Ulster with a large Scots mercenary force but Shane defeated him at Glenshesk in May, took James and his brother, Sorley Boy, captive, and incurred the implacable enmity of the Scots.[83] Sussex was effec-tively losing control and O'Neill seemed beyond restraint.

Following the marriage of Mary Queen of Scots to Lord Darnley in July 1565, the breakdown in relations between Whitehall and Edinburgh became a source of additional pressure, driving Argyll's close friend, the Protestant Lord James Stewart, earl of Moray, to lead a rebellion in opposition to the feared Catholic revival. Argyll sought the support of the Irish councillors for Moray's cause, even promising Archbishop Adam Loftus 4,000 troops to serve in Ireland at his own expense in return for the requested support for his ally.[84] However, Elizabeth's public rebuke to Moray for staging a rebellion drove Argyll to adopt a stance of overt hostility to the English crown and to

---

[80] Constant, *Les Guise*, 51; Nicholls, *Modern British Isles*, 193.
[81] Lord Lieutenant Radcliffe to Cecil, 20 May 1563, SP 63/8/46, 46(1); Fitzwilliam to Cecil, 28 May 1562, SP 63/6/14; 'Reasons for peace with France', Mar. 1564, SP 70/69/49; Palmer, *Problem of Ireland*, 83. The English privy council's problems were compounded by reports of manifestations of Spanish interest in Irish affairs. See Quadra to Philip II, 7 Feb. 1563, *CSP Spain, 1558–67*, 298, for evidence of contact between O'Neill and the bishop in London; Palmer, *Problem of Ireland*, 83.
[82] Ciaran Brady, *Shane O'Neill*, Dundalk 1996, 51–5.
[83] Ibid. 56–7; Palmer, *Problem of Ireland*, 84; Grenfell Morton, *Elizabethan Ireland*, London 1971, 26–33; Dawson, 'Two kingdoms or three?', 125; Ellis, *Ireland in the age of the Tudors*, 290–91; Lennon, *Sixteenth-century Ireland*, 267–74; Brady, *Chief governors*, 120.
[84] Nicholls, *Modern British Isles*, 98, 106–10.

withdraw definitively his support for the English campaign in Ulster.[85] As a consequence the Scots-Irish alliance was again rekindled under the direction of two strong leaders, thereby disabling Cecil's British strategy.

Having subordinated the O'Donnells and MacDonnells, his two principal opponents in Ulster, O'Neill moved to capitalise on his reputation outside Ireland by endeavouring to forge alliances with Argyll, the Guises and Charles IX of France.[86] In autumn 1565 he was suspected of having reached an agreement with Argyll.[87] In contrast with the situation which obtained in spring 1550, when the Irish side was divided and O'Donnell feared the discovery of his involvement with the French, Shane O'Neill was brash and confirmed in his dealings with the French. Throughout the autumn and winter of 1565, while Sir Henry Sidney, Dudley (now earl of Leicester) and even the earl of Kildare worked assiduously to persuade Elizabeth to sanction all-out war against Shane, the French court was briefed on the successes of O'Neill's campaign.[88] The Scottish queen's involvement with the Irish heralded a realignment of factions similar to that obtaining in 1549 as she dispatched two 'gentilshommes du pays des sauvages d'Écosse', who were versed in Gaelic, to conduct negotiations with O'Neill.[89] Throughout the remainder of 1565 the French ambassador to Scotland, Paul de Foix, apprised Charles IX of O'Neill's progress.[90]

By early summer of the following year O'Neill's contacts with Argyll, Mary Queen of Scots, Charles IX and the Guise faction had gained pace, though they were purely speculative gambits.[91] Ciaran Brady has suggested that there are grounds for suspicion that in each case the letters were designed for interception by English intelligence agents in a deliberate ploy to demonstrate just how serious O'Neill was in preparing for the imminent war.[92] There is no evidence to indicate with certainty that either the French king or the cardinals of Lorraine and Guise ever received O'Neill's communications. On 25 April Shane wrote to Charles IX requesting that 5,000 or 6,000 well-armed French troops be dispatched immediately to assist him in his expulsion of the English from Ireland. He pledged that he and his successors would be humble subjects of the French crown and requested that Charles write to Mary Queen of Scots in favour of the Irish lords.[93] On the same day Shane also wrote to the cardinal of Lorraine, the most powerful member of the dynasty at that

---

[85] MacCraith, 'Gaelic reaction', 141.

[86] Dawson, 'Two kingdoms or three?', 125.

[87] Randolph to Cecil, 13 Oct. 1565, *CSP Foreign, 1564–5*, 490; Brady, *Shane O'Neill*, 57.

[88] Paul de Foix to Catherine de Médicis, 29 sept. 1565, *Relations politiques de la France*, ii. 235; de Foix to Charles IX, 11 oct. 1565, ibid. ii. 239; Brady, *Shane O'Neill*, 58–9.

[89] De Foix to Catherine de Médicis, 29 sept. 1565, *Relations politiques de la France*, ii. 235.

[90] De Foix to Charles IX, 11 oct. 1565, ibid. ii. 239–40.

[91] Brady, *Shane O'Neill*, 60.

[92] Ibid.

[93] Shane O'Neill to Charles IX, 25 Apr. 1566, SP 63/17/94.

time. He explained that he had already written to Charles IX seeking armed troops, and asked that the cardinal use his influence to persuade the French king to send the required aid as a demonstration of support for his effort to defend Catholicism.[94]

However, O'Neill's solicitations to the French court yielded no return, and it was Mary Queen of Scots who instead appeared the most promising source of assistance, with Argyll at hand to serve as intermediary.[95] Shane took the initiative in reopening negotiations with the Scottish earl who in turn represented the Ulster chief's cause at the Scottish court. By summer 1566 it appears as though, thanks to Argyll's efforts, Mary had resolved to back O'Neill, and Arygll's redshank mercenary soldiers would soon be sent to Ulster to bolster Shane's campaign against the English.[96] In May Shane's envoys were said to have been engaged in talks with Queen Mary, leading Elizabeth I to suspect that 'the earl of Argyll pretends some diminution of his former good will towards her service, especially in matters of Ireland'.[97] The following month Mary Queen of Scots was allegedly aiming to 'stir up war in Ireland to keep England occupied and then march her army into England and proclaim herself queen'.[98] By that stage, Sidney was as beset with difficulty in tackling the problem of Shane O'Neill as Sussex had ever been. Exasperated by the indefatigable defiance of O'Neill whom he described as destined to become 'a tyrant over all Ireland', Sidney ominously warned that should Elizabeth fail to supply the requisite military and financial support, she would lose Ireland just as her predecessor had lost Calais.[99]

Throughout the summer and autumn of 1566 Shane continued to direct written appeals for assistance to the French court, proving the indispensability of the Scottish element to his scheme.[100] In February 1567 he again sought the backing of the cardinals of Lorraine and Guise, asking them to use their influence to convince Charles IX to send an army in support of his campaign in order that he might restore and defend the Catholic faith.[101] In March he invited Cormac O'Connor, a key protagonist in the 1550–1 episode of intrigue, to return to Ireland 'to help . . . win this country'.[102] But

---

94   Shane O'Neill to the cardinal of Lorraine, 25 Apr. 1566, SP 63/17/95.
95   Dawson, 'Two kingdoms or three?', 125. For an insight into the issues which preoccupied the cardinal of Lorraine on the two occasions on which Shane O'Neill sought his assistance see *Lettres du Cardinal Charles de Lorraine (1525–1574)*, ed. Daniel Cuisiat, Geneva 1998.
96   Instructions to Henry Killigrew, special ambassador to Mary Queen of Scots, 13–15 June 1566, PRO, SP 52/12/150–6; Randolph to Cecil, 14 June 1566, *CSP Scotland, 1563–9*, 285–6; Dawson, 'Two kingdoms or three?', 125.
97   Elizabeth I to Randolph, 23 May 1566, *CSP Foreign 1566–8*, 72.
98   Christopher Rokeby to Cecil, June 1566, HMC, *Salisbury MSS*, i. 338.
99   Sidney to Cecil, 3 June 1566, SP 63/18/1.
100 Guzman de Silva to Philip II, 6 Apr., 18 May, 27 July, 6, 14 Sept. 1566, *CSP Spain, 1558–67*, 539, 550, 569, 578, 580.
101 Shane O'Neill to the cardinals of Lorraine and Guise, 1 Feb. 1567, SP 63/20/53.
102 Shane O'Neill to Cormac O'Connor, 20 Mar. 1567, SP 63/20/108.

neither French nor Scottish aid was immediately forthcoming, and O'Neill's efforts to transcend factional divisions within Ulster ultimately led to his assassination at a dinner brawl at the residence of the MacDonnells of Antrim in June 1567.[103] As a result, all hope of staging a successful French invasion of Ireland faded and the Elizabethan *régime* survived another round of menacing but ultimately futile international intrigue.

V

The history of Franco-Irish political relations in the period from the late 1540s to the late 1560s may be interpreted as amounting to little more than a succession of failed episodes of intrigue, of varying degrees of intensity and importance, in which the French used Irish dissidents as dupes in their effort to undermine the Edwardian, Marian and Elizabethan *régimes*. During this era all Franco-Irish intrigue was understood by the parties involved to represent only one element within grander British strategies aimed at achieving that goal. Without exception, plans for staging a French invasion of Ireland were inextricably intertwined with, and ultimately decided by, politics in Scotland. Ironically, while Gaelic lords such as Shane O'Neill believed Scotland was the most likely conduit for French aid to Ireland, the fact that they were at the mercy of the Scots and of the French in Scotland as intermediaries invariably proved detrimental to a successful outcome to all of their designs. Throughout this period, much Franco-Irish intrigue consisted of groundless rumours and speculations. Such deliberate manipulation of English insecurities was in the main based on the at best tacit interest displayed by successive French kings, by Marie de Guise and Mary Queen of Scots, and by their kinsmen, the Guises. The intrigue of the 1550s and 1560s never reached the advanced stage that the negotiations held in Ulster in the winter of 1549–50 had done, as notwithstanding the fact that Shane O'Neill posed a serious threat to British security in his own right, neither Charles IX nor the Guises appear to have even responded to his written requests.

The fundamental preconditions for these episodes of Franco-Irish intrigue remained constant throughout this twenty-year period. These included the ascendancy of the Guise faction at the French court, along with concerted French and specifically Guise commitment to the furtherance of French and Scottish Catholic interests in opposition to the English crown. The active support of Marie de Guise, and later Mary Queen of Scots, was also essential. Strong military leadership, such as that provided by Shane O'Neill, the suppression of factionalism among Gaelic dissidents, especially in Ulster, consensus between Ulster and Scottish Gaelic lords in opposition to the

---

[103] Morton, *Elizabethan Ireland*, 33; Ellis, *Ireland in the age of the Tudors*, 291; Lennon, *Sixteenth-century Ireland*, 274; Brady, *Chief governors*, 124–5.

Dublin government, and strained if not hostile relations between the French and English crowns were also essential preconditions for any prospect of a concrete outcome to French intrigue focused on Ireland. While several of these elements in a complex web of contingent circumstances in all four kingdoms occasionally coincided to create conditions that were highly conducive to bringing about the much rumoured French invasion of Ireland (notably in winter 1549–50 and in 1566), at no stage did all the vital determinants coincide: hence the failed outcome to successive waves of solicitations, conspiratorial plots and even substantive negotiations.

These episodes of intrigue were not, however, entirely without political repercussions and can be seen to have exerted a demonstrable influence on English domestic and foreign policy. As Steven Ellis, Jane Dawson and William Palmer have shown, the prospect of combined French–Scottish intervention in Ulster had a significant catalytic impact on both the Westminster and Dublin administrations by alerting them to Ireland's strategic vulnerability, particularly as it magnified the already alarming domestic threat posed by Shane O'Neill. Nevertheless, the parsimonious Tudors continually checked expenditure on defending and subjugating Ireland, in spite of the security risks involved. While many of the English privy council's reactionary steps were undeniably expedient and intermittent, the British scale of the French threat heightened the English councillors' consciousness of the need to respond in similar terms by formulating a British defence policy such as William Cecil sought to do in 1559–60.[104]

By virtue of their involvement in such protracted intrigue, the Irish acquired an unprecedented amount of experience in interpreting the shifting dynamics and contingencies of international politics. One particularly salient lesson arising from that experience was a realisation on the part of the Irish of the immensely convoluted and precarious contingencies that bedevilled all efforts to extend a French campaign into Ulster from Scotland. In addition, the Irish became versed in the protocol governing the conduct of international diplomacy that would otherwise have been denied them since Ireland had no structured diplomatic relationship with France or Scotland. Emissaries to the French and Scottish courts, notably George Paris, Cormac O'Connor and MacWilliam Burke, acquired skills in the formulation of statements of Irish grievances for presentation at court. They became proficient in effective networking in court circles, in the accurate and safe conveyance of intelligence, in the manipulation of rumour and intrigue in diplomatic circles to enhance their designs, and gained valuable experience in the practice of diplomatic dexterity and duplicity. In spite of the failed outcome to their appeals for French aid, the Irish learned valuable lessons in diplomacy and

---

104 Ellis, *Ireland in the age of the Tudors*, 276; Dawson, 'Two kingdoms or three?', and 'William Cecil'; Palmer, *Problem of Ireland*, 84–6.

intrigue that stood them in good stead, particularly in their engagement with the court of Philip II of Spain in the 1580s and 1590s.

A valuable by-product of this political contact was the vast expansion of the French court's acquaintance with a broadening spectrum of Ireland's political figures, even down to the rank of gentlemen, and also with English personnel serving in Ireland and their campaigns. As a result of increased personal contacts with Irish lords and gentlemen, who either travelled to France or corresponded with French monarchs and courtiers, the first sustained direct (if unofficial) political links were established between Irish dissidents and the French court during this period.

French ambassadors and agents employed in England and Scotland constituted a second vital channel through which regular reports of Irish affairs reached the French court. Apart from Monluc and Fourquevaux, Antoine de Noailles and d'Oisel both exhibited a remarkably keen interest in promoting disturbances in Ireland and contributed enormously to expanding French knowledge of Irish affairs during the 1550s. They provided regular updates on engagements and reported the substance of rumours about a French or combined Franco-Scottish invasion of Ireland. A high degree of scepticism is, however, required in assessing the credibility of these reports as some, such as those circulating in 1540–50 and again in 1565–7, had a solid basis whereas others were little more than fabrications and boastful speculations. None the less, the de Noailles brothers and d'Oisel provided details of Irish dissidents' overtures to them along with descriptions of the country's principal patrimonies, and intelligence regarding the best routes by which invading forces should approach the island.[105] By the late 1560s the acquaintance of the French king and courtiers with Irish politics had advanced significantly beyond that of the 1520s and 1530s when contacts were confined to visits to court by emissaries of the most renowned Irish noble families, the Fitzgeralds and the O'Donnells, and ambassadors' reports at best provided mere vignettes of Irish affairs through oblique allusions to anonymous 'sauvages'.[106]

[105] The de Noailles occasionally devoted entire reports to coverage of developments in Ireland. See, for example, de Noailles to M. de Guise, 22 sept. 1559, 'Advis des choses qui se passent à p[rese]nt en Irlande', dépêches et mémoires de MM de Noailles, 13, 616–17.
[106] See, for example, pièces sur la guerre d'Irlande, 1568 [1569], BN, MS Fr. 20793.

6

French Reaction to Catholic Counter-Reformation Campaigns in Ireland, 1570–1584

The last phase of sixteenth-century French–Irish intrigue had its origins in two major insurrections headed by young Anglo-Irish lords, both of whom were militant supporters of the Catholic Counter-Reformation. The first of these, James Fitzmaurice Fitzgerald, first cousin of the fourteenth earl of Desmond, staged two rebellions in Munster, in 1569–72 and again in 1579–83, while the second insurgent, Sir James Eustace, third Viscount Baltinglass, led a rebellion in south Leinster in 1580–1 that spawned the so-called Nugent conspiracy of 1581–2. Of the two, the challenge posed by Fitzmaurice was of the greatest consequence in terms of Irish intrigue with the French crown and the Guise faction. Both Fitzmaurice and the ringleaders of the Nugent conspiracy sought the assistance of Catholic continental powers in shows of resistance not against the legitimate monarch of England but against Elizabeth whom they styled a tyrant.[1] In so doing, they gradually gravitated away from the French court towards the papacy and, in particular, towards Philip II who emerged from the mid-1580s onwards as the most promising source of military support for Irish campaigns of resistance to the Elizabethan *régime*.

Yet in the 1570s Fitzmaurice's targeting of the French monarchy and the Guise faction with requests for financial and military aid for his campaign was well conceived. He arrived in France in March 1575 at a time when French Catholic public opinion was highly sensitised to the need to preserve the Catholic religion in France and elsewhere in western Europe in the face of the threat posed by Protestantism. The Catholic League, established in 1576, tapped this desire for a pan-European alliance in opposition to Protestantism, and near contemporaries in France testified to the importance of Ireland in the rhetoric, if not in the real plans, of the Catholic League; Ireland was cited as one of several countries throughout Europe and Scandinavia in which Protestantism had already made advances at the expense of Catholicism.[2] Yet the disappointing outcome to the Irish dissidents' appeals at the French court

---

1 MacCraith, 'Gaelic reaction', 144–5.
2 *Histoire de la Ligue: oeuvre inédit d'un contemporain*, ed. Charles Valois, Paris 1814, 94; R. J. Knecht, *The French wars of religion, 1559–1598*, 2nd edn, Harlow 1999.

in the 1570s and early 1580s was not surprising. Their arrival in France came at a time when both Elizabeth I and Henri III were preoccupied with more serious domestic and foreign interests, and when a major realignment of continental alliances involving France, England and Spain was slowly taking more definitive shape, obliging Elizabeth's Irish opponents and their envoys to concentrate their efforts on the Spanish court from the mid-1580s onwards.

I

This reorientation in the Irish position reflected the fundamental shift in relations between the continental powers and the kingdoms of the British Isles which took place in the course of the 1560s, 1570s and early 1580s. In the early stages of Elizabeth's reign, the French had been England's greatest opponents, but from 1564 onwards a perceptible change in English policy *vis-à-vis* France occurred, stemming from two independent developments. The first was a deterioration in England's relations with Spain that necessitated the partial abandonment of traditional anti-French sentiments in the interests of winning over a continental ally in opposition to Philip II. The second was the threat posed by the powerful Guise faction in France, which had previously proved troublesome in its intervention in Scottish affairs and whose aggressive Catholicism, it was feared, might press them to form an alliance with the Spanish king against England.[3] During the early 1560s both Elizabeth and Philip were united in their suspicion of the Guises. It was largely for this reason that the Spanish king strove to dissuade the pope from excommunicating Elizabeth, being of the view that 'better a Protestant Tudor queen of England than a Catholic Stuart queen when the latter was a tool of the Guises'.[4]

While France was submerged in the second and third rounds of the wars of religion during the years 1567–70, Spain assumed the role of England's most formidable opponent and was widely believed to be the most likely to orchestrate a descent upon England or Ireland.[5] That is not to say that either Elizabeth or Philip was anxious to go to war at that time: the exact opposite was in fact the case. Rather, the period 1568 to 1573 has been regarded as a 'dress rehearsal' for the wholesale Anglo-Spanish conflict of the 1580s, the

---

[3] For surveys of Elizabethan foreign policy see R. B. Wernham, *Before the Armada: the growth of English foreign policy*, London 1966; Paul Crowson, *Tudor foreign policy*, London 1973; Wallace MacCaffrey, *Queen Elizabeth and the making of policy, 1572–88*, Princeton 1981; Smith, *Emergence of a nation state*, 155–61; Ramsay, 'Foreign policy of Elizabeth I', 147–68; John Warren, *Elizabeth I: religion and foreign affairs*, London 1993, ch. v; Palmer, *Problem of Ireland*, ch. vi; Nicholls, *Modern British Isles*, chs xiii–xv.

[4] Warren, *Elizabeth I*, 102.

[5] Janine Garrisson, *Guerre civile et compromis, 1559–98*, Paris 1991, 164, and *Sixteenth-century France*, 271; Palmer, *Problem of Ireland*, 91.

essential difference being that in 1568 Philip was still undecided as to the most appropriate manner in which to deal with Elizabeth, vacillating between feelings of hostility towards her and realisation of her value to him as a 'bulwark against Guise power in Europe'.[6] It was the diplomatic crisis precipitated by the duke of Alva's seizure of English ships and property in the Netherlands, and the suspension of trade between England and Spain in 1569, that spurred Elizabeth to court French support in anticipation of a possible Spanish offensive. She therefore authorised her officials to engage in deliberately protracted negotiations for a marriage alliance with the Protestant Henri, duc d'Anjou, in the period 1570–1.[7]

During this phase of 'low tension' between England and Spain (1568–73), Philip consistently refused to back conspiracies to undermine Elizabeth or to advance the cause of Mary Stuart. The immediate recovery of the Guises after the St Bartholomew's Day massacre in 1572 confirmed Philip in his belief that for the time being it was not opportune for him to have 'a flat falling out' with Elizabeth.[8] However, in 1569 Elizabeth and her councillors were anxious about the prospect of French or Spanish invasion as they struggled to contend with a serious British security problem arising from insurrections in Ireland and northern England.

In June of that year James Fitzmaurice staged a serious revolt in reaction to the threat posed to aristocratic lands and liberties by English colonisation in Munster. He led an attack on the Kerrycurrihy colony, Tracton and Carragaline castle in County Cork. Fitzmaurice's action provided a rallying-point for the nobility and gentry of the province who rejected Lord Deputy Sir Henry Sidney's reform programme, and he had the martial capabilities to compel reluctant collateral Geraldines and vassals to follow his lead. From the outset he adopted the rhetoric of the Catholic Counter-Reformation and actively supported Maurice Fitzgibbon, papal archbishop of Cashel, in his appeals for assistance from Philip II of Spain, the papacy and the French, though no aid was forthcoming at that time. The seriousness of the insurrection that engulfed the entire southern half of the country was manifest in the joint action of Fitzmaurice, MacCarthy, earl of Clancare, and the Butler brothers, who, with 4,500 men, laid siege to Kilkenny, the heart of the earl of Ormond's patrimony, in July 1569. Sidney appointed Humphrey Gilbert as colonel and governor of Munster in September 1569 and he fiercely suppressed the worst of the rebellion. By the end of the year, the earl of

---

6 Crowson, *Tudor foreign policy*, 190. See also Ramsay, 'Foreign policy of Elizabeth I', 159.
7 Ramsay, 'Foreign policy of Elizabeth', 156; Warren, *Elizabeth I*, 97. For discussion of the Anjou match negotiations see Wallace MacCaffrey, 'The Anjou match and the making of Elizabethan foreign policy', in Peter Clark, A. G. R. Smith and Nicholas Tyacke (eds), *The English Commonwealth, 1547–1640: essays in politics and society*, New York 1979, 59–75.
8 Crowson, *Tudor foreign policy*, 195.

Clancare and the majority of the Geraldines had submitted, though Fitzmaurice remained at large in the Glen of Aherlow in Tipperary.[9]

Meanwhile, in northern England, the earls of Northumberland and Westmorland sought military aid from Spain and from the pope when they rose in revolt in October 1569. By the end of December this disturbance too had been suppressed, though the English authorities were unnerved by news of the flight of two of the northern rebels to join forces with Fitzmaurice in Ireland.[10] The increasingly strong ties between the Gaels of Ulster and Scotland in the late 1560s also stirred concern in government circles. Turlough Luineach O'Neill's marriage to Lady Agnes Campbell, sister of the earl of Argyll, and a woman well renowned for her ability to muster Scottish troops and to dominate her husband, augured badly for English interests in Ireland. The marriage in 1569 of Lady Agnes's daughter, Finola, and Hugh Dubh O'Donnell, gave rise to further disquiet as she too provided her husband with a substantial private Scottish army.[11]

Soon after the disturbances in Ireland and northern England had been quelled, events in Scotland took a sinister turn, once again arousing English fears of a French conspiracy with the Scots (and possibly the Irish) designed to undermine the Elizabethan *régime*. In January 1570 the Scottish Protestant pro-English regent, the earl of Moray, was assassinated, plunging Scotland into a state of political disarray, while Mary Stuart's supporters increasingly looked set to achieve political ascendancy.[12] Fears of French collusion with the Scots in designs to launch an attack on Ireland early in 1570 were accentuated when news broke in April that O'Neill had sent his wife, Agnes, into Scotland to muster troops on his behalf.[13]

Back in Munster, where Gilbert continued to stamp out the embers of Geraldine insurgence in the early months of 1570, the earl of Ormond undertook to rescue Sir Edward Fitton, the hard-pressed president of Connaught, by opposing his own cousin, Conor O'Brien, earl of Thomond. He led a campaign into Thomond's patrimony and forced his kinsman to surrender all his prisoners and his 123 castles, on the understanding that Conor would be allowed sail for England where he might present his case in person to the queen and afterwards serve against Fitzmaurice. However, O'Brien reneged on his promise and in summer instead set sail for France to seek support for his rebellious stance against the queen. Following his arrival at the French court at Paris, he pursued a double-sided strategy whereby he spent a month interceding with Henri III for aid while assuring the then English ambassador

---

[9] Lennon, *Sixteenth-century Ireland*, 213–15.

[10] Warren, *Elizabeth I*, 68–70; Ellis, *Ireland in the age of the Tudors*, 296–7; Palmer, *Problem of Ireland*, 93.

[11] Ellis, *Ireland in the age of the Tudors*, 297; Lennon, *Sixteenth-century Ireland*, 275–6; Palmer, *Problem of Ireland*, 94.

[12] Nicholls, *Modern British Isles*, 291.

[13] Nicholas Malby to Cecil, 8 Apr. 1570, SP 63/30/72.

to France, Sir Henry Norris, of his loyalty to the queen. He presented himself to Norris as a victim of Fitton's harsh policies, and requested that the ambassador arrange an audience for him with Elizabeth I.

Norris, however, saw through O'Brien's false protestations and notified Elizabeth that the earl had pledged to deliver forts and castles in Ireland to the French, warning that if they refused to help, he would instead offer his property to Philip II.[14] Yet beyond Charles IX's initial show of enthusiasm for the Irishman's cause, and the queen regent, Catherine de Médicis's gift of 200 *pistols* (French gold coins), no substantial aid was forthcoming from the French. A disheartened O'Brien was left with no alternative but to travel to England to make his personal submission to Elizabeth who granted him a pardon and bound him to remain an obedient subject by a recognisance of £10,000.[15] Meanwhile, in Ireland, Fitzmaurice continued to evade capture in the Glen of Aherlow, and Archbishop Fitzgibbon of Cashel, who lobbied for aid in Spain, France and Rome in support of Fitzmaurice's resistance, repeatedly encouraged the Irish to persist in their rebellion.[16]

The reluctance of the Spanish king to offer any more than fair words in response to the pleas for aid made by his envoys caused Fitzmaurice to concentrate his personal efforts on the French. Significantly, it was a member of the Guise faction rather than the French crown who furnished him with a small fleet under the command of a Breton captain named de la Roche. As events of the following eight years were to show, de la Roche occasionally became the subject of intense English suspicion and was discovered to have conspired to help Fitzmaurice in 1570 and again in 1575 when the Irish rebel visited the French court. It was in June 1570 that this captain first came to Elizabeth's attention as a result of a report that he had set sail with 500 Breton arquebusers, destined for Scotland.[17] By October he and Fitzmaurice were co-ordinating plans for a fleet of ships to convey French troops to Ireland in support of the rebellion. In spite of the English ambassador's advice to Charles IX that the governors of Brittany should be instructed to prevent any such expedition from taking place, de la Roche set sail and arrived in Ireland in December.[18] He immediately seized the earl of Desmond's castle at Dingle in Kerry and held discussions with Fitzmaurice regarding the possibility of providing further French aid in return for recognition of French sovereignty over Ireland. Encouraged by this unprecedented show of practical French

---

14 Sir Henry Norris to Cecil, 22 July 1570, *CSP Foreign, 1569–71*, 296; Norris to the earl of Leicester, 9 Aug. 1570, ibid. 311; Lennon, *Sixteenth-century Ireland*, 242–3.
15 C. R. Sasso, 'The Desmond rebellions, 1569–73 and 1579–83', unpubl. PhD diss. Chicago Loyola 1980, 142–3.
16 Ibid. 146; Lennon, *Sixteenth-century Ireland*, 215.
17 Bertrand de Salignac de la Mothe Fénélon to Catherine de Médicis, 19 juin 1570, *Correspondance diplomatique de Bertrand de Salignac de La Mothe Fénélon, ambassadeur de France en Angleterre de 1568 à 1575*, ed. Auguste Teulet, 7 vols, Paris 1838–40, iii. 203.
18 La Mothe Fénélon to Charles IX, 15 oct. 1570, ibid. vii. 137–8; Charles IX to la Mothe Fénélon, 8 fév. 1571, ibid. vii. 181

support, albeit modest, Fitzmaurice's supporters made fantastic claims that the French had promised the Irish lord 10,000 men, in addition to royal artillery support, and that the French king had undertaken to reward Fitzmaurice for his loyalty by conferring upon him the earldom of Ormond and Ossory.[19] De la Roche took one of Fitzmaurice's sons back to Brittany as a guarantee of the Irish lord's pledge to serve Charles IX.[20]

Anxious not to antagonise the French king, Elizabeth applied gentle pressure upon him, indicating that she knew of de la Roche's 'seditious' activities and urging him to ensure that the Breton and his allies in Ireland be compelled to draw an immediate halt to their schemes.[21] Charles claimed to have been completely unaware of such an expedition, which is entirely possible, and the English secretary of state, Sir Francis Walsingham, testified to the king's ignorance of de la Roche's practices in Ireland. The French king was affronted that Elizabeth suspected him of allowing his subjects to undertake any designs to undermine her authority in Ireland. He categorically disowned de la Roche and undertook to inflict exemplary punishment upon him if he were to be captured. Yet the fact that this threat was never carried out may be construed as indicative of the insincerity of the king's protestations. It also intimates Charles's appreciation that, although de la Roche's movements may have been harmless and irrelevant to English interests, he could make political capital from his handling of the Guisard's perceived threatening actions to warn Elizabeth against taking French amity for granted.[22]

In the broader scheme of international political relations at this time, Fitzmaurice and his involvement with de la Roche, and even the king's suspected support for their collaboration, did not place more than a slight strain on Anglo-French relations. This is a measure of the perceived gravity of the threat posed by Fitzmaurice's intrigue with the French. Even though de la Roche's expedition to Ireland in December 1570 was the first and only French fleet to materialise as a result of successive attempts to secure French aid since the 1520s, it stirred but a short-lived reaction from Elizabeth. By March of the following year the hollowness of the propaganda generated by Fitzmaurice supporters at the time of de la Roche's arrival in December 1570 was all too apparent, with no signs of the promised men and munitions. Elizabeth therefore overcame her preoccupation with de la Roche and Fitzmaurice and concentrated upon affirming her amicable relations with France.[23]

Yet Sir Francis Walsingham, a former special ambassador to France and

---

[19] Testimony of the dean of Cashel's son, Redmond Stacbolde, 16 Oct. 1571, CSP Ireland, 1509–73, 461.
[20] Sasso, 'Desmond rebellions', 147.
[21] La Mothe Fénélon to Charles IX, 23 jan. 1571, Correspondance diplomatique de La Mothe Fénélon, iii. 444–5; Charles IX to la Mothe Fénélon, 8 fév. 1571, ibid. vii. 181.
[22] Ibid. vii. 182.
[23] La Mothe Fénélon to Charles IX, 23 mars 1571, ibid. iv. 30.

one of Elizabeth's most influential privy councillors, was acutely sensitised to the threats posed to England and Ireland by French and Spanish intervention. He set about taking practical pre-emptive steps to negate the threat of foreign invasion of Ireland by neutralising some of the key parties to Irish intrigue with France and Spain. He sought a pardon for Archbishop Fitzgibbon of Cashel, Fitzmaurice's leading envoy on the continent. He also held an audience with the cardinal of Lorraine who was known to have been directly targeted by Fitzmaurice's associates with requests for military aid, and advised Elizabeth to dispatch an ambassador to Spain in order to monitor the seditious practices of the many Irish rebels who had sought refuge and assistance there.[24] But the English privy council was especially anxious about the possibility of the Guise faction orchestrating an invasion of Ireland. This was particularly true following the Ridolfi conspiracy in England in 1571 when it was feared that if the English did not show due encouragement in their dealings with the French, 'the house of Guise are likely to bear sway, [and] . . . will be . . . forward in preferring the conquest of Ireland'.[25]

II

Eighteen months after he staged his rebellion, Fitzmaurice resolved to intensify his lobby for support in France. Whereas in 1570 he had relied upon the representations of Archbishop Fitzgibbon in France and had concentrated his own energies on securing military assistance from the Guise faction through his negotiations with de la Roche, towards the end of 1571 he boosted his drive to win further French support by directly targeting the French monarchy, the Guises, other influential courtiers and their followers. He dispatched his emissary, Dennis O'Dussane, to Paris with letters addressed to the cardinal of Lorraine and the comte de Candale, a descendant of the nobleman with whom Fitzmaurice's kinsman, the tenth earl of Desmond, had conducted negotiations in 1522–3. He also maintained close contact with de la Roche who, on several occasions, conducted talks with a French-speaking Irish gentleman in Fitzmaurice's service who was dispatched on embassies to the cardinal of Lorraine and to Rome.[26]

With Fitzmaurice still at large in Munster in the early 1570s, English privy councillors and ambassadorial officials were concerned at the prospect of a French descent on Ireland.[27] In 1571 Walsingham admitted his fear of the determination of the Guises, the papacy, Philip II of Spain, the majority of the Irish nobility and several Englishmen 'of good quality' to challenge

24 Palmer, *Problem of Ireland*, 96–7.
25 Sir Francis Walsingham to Lord Burghley, 26 Sept. 1571, CSP *Foreign, 1569–71*, 539. See Crowson, *Tudor foreign policy*, 194–5.
26 Sasso, 'Desmond rebellions', 163.
27 Ramsay, 'Foreign policy of Elizabeth I', 155; Palmer, *Problem of Ireland*, 94–5.

English authority in Ireland and advised Elizabeth that England's need for an alliance with France was particularly pressing.[28] The queen's anxiety to win over the French was briefly allayed when France and England signed the Treaty of Blois in April 1572 which neutralised French designs on Scotland and provided her with the continental defensive counterweight against Philip II that she needed.[29]

However, public outrage in England at the massacre of St Bartholomew's Day in 1572 jeopardised this union and had important negative reverberations in Ireland as it illustrated what militant continental Catholic powers were capable of, and inspired numerous Irish friars to emerge from hiding, mainly in Ulster. Throughout 1572 they travelled about the country, openly preaching a Catholic crusade and making impassioned pledges 'to subvert the English government and set up their own wickedness'.[30] While the French were immersed in the disturbances that followed the massacre, Elizabeth adopted a neutral stance. That way she hoped to avoid any provocation of Philip.[31] The accession of the aggressively militant Gregory XIII to the papacy in 1572 brought about increased papal engagement in talks with champions of the Counter-Reformation struggle against Protestant rulers. James Fitzmaurice was quick to capitalise on Ireland's potential as an important instrument in the Catholic crusade against England in order to win the practical support of Gregory XIII for his campaign.[32] At that time more than thirty English and Irish Catholics, including Archbishop Fitzgibbon, were actively soliciting military and financial support for Fitzmaurice's campaign in Brittany.[33] Their efforts, along with Fitzmaurice's persistent defiance, and the plotting of the English adventurer, Sir Thomas Stukeley, with the papacy to launch an attack on England, pointed to the link between what William Palmer has termed 'international Catholic recovery' and developments in Ireland.[34]

Meanwhile, Philip still refused to provoke Elizabeth: in April 1573 he entered into a two-year commercial treaty with England which he confirmed in the Treaty of Bristol in August 1574, and all the while Irish and English rebels and their representatives persisted in unsuccessful attempts to secure

---

[28] Walsingham to Cecil, 8 Feb. 1571, PRO, SP 70/116/78–9. Walsingham was special ambassador from 11 Aug. 1570 to 29 Aug. 1570. See also Elizabeth I to Walsingham, 11 Feb. 1571, SP 70/116/80.

[29] J. H. Elliott, Europe divided, 1559–98, London 1968, 206; Warren, Elizabeth I, 97; Palmer, Problem of Ireland, 97.

[30] Fitzwilliam to Elizabeth I, 7 Dec. 1572, CSP Ireland, 1509–73, 490.

[31] Warren, Elizabeth I, 104.

[32] Palmer, Problem of Ireland, 101, 103. Many of Gregory XIII's cardinals and bishops corresponded regarding Ireland's potential in undermining the Elizabethan regime.

[33] Sasso, 'Desmond rebellions', 152, 198.

[34] Palmer, Problem of Ireland, 101. For further discussion of this theory of international Catholic conspiracy see Thorp, 'Catholic conspiracy', 431–8.

Spanish aid.[35] Elizabeth steered a middle course in her relations with France and Spain. She initiated negotiations with both the French monarch and the French Huguenots. After Charles IX's death in 1574, she renewed the Treaty of Blois but to the chagrin of the new king, Henri III, she continued to send aid to the Huguenots. Between 1573 and 1578, when events in the Netherlands seemed to be advancing towards the compromise solution she had sought, Elizabeth maintained amicable relations with Philip II whilst cultivating revived interest in a match with Anjou.[36] In 1574 the English privy council received reports of rumours of an imminent Spanish invasion of Ireland, led by Sir Thomas Stukeley, and Desmond was alleged to have sought munitions and powder in France.[37] Concern for Ireland's security on the part of the Whitehall and the Dublin administrations was further heightened in July by reports of a Catholic fleet in the Bay of Biscay which, they erroneously believed, was destined for Ireland.[38] In France, the massacre of 1572 had deepened the existing divisions within the kingdom and severely reduced the crown's moral and political credibility.[39] At the time of James Fitzmaurice's arrival there in March 1575 a weak French monarchy was struggling to contend with the country's fifth war of religion (1574–6) in which Henri III was opposed by both Catholic malcontents and Huguenots, the latter supported by Elizabeth.[40] With France in such a disturbed state, the Valois régime could cope with little more than the most pressing problems either at home or abroad.[41]

III

James Fitzmaurice's departure did not come as a shock to the English administration in Dublin. He had previously intimated to Ormond that he feared for his safety in Ireland and that he was seeking a royal pardon. This was evidently a clever ploy conceived to lead the Dublin administration to believe that his intentions were honourable and that he had no option but to leave the country. His choice of France as his destination was perhaps to be expected. After six years of sustained canvassing by Fitzmaurice's envoys,

---

35 Sasso, 'Desmond rebellions', 199; Warren, *Elizabeth I*, 98.
36 Crowson, *Tudor foreign policy*, 199; Warren, *Elizabeth I*, 98; Palmer, *Problem of Ireland*, 104. See MacCaffrey, 'The Anjou match'.
37 Fitzwilliam to the privy council, 25 Apr. 1574, SP 63/45/221.
38 Dr Valentine Dale to Thomas Smith and Walsingham, 7 July 1574, *CSP Foreign, 1569–71*, 527. The fleet in question was dispatched to Flanders. See Sasso, 'Desmond rebellions', 300.
39 Robin Briggs, *Early modern France, 1560–1715*, Oxford 1977, 24.
40 Knecht, *French wars of religion*, 62–4.
41 Elliott, *Europe divided*, 252; Briggs, *Early modern France*, 24–5; H. G. Koenigsberger, G. L. Mosse and G. Q. Bowler, *Europe in the sixteenth century*, 2nd edn, London 1989, 308–9; Garrisson, *Guerre civile et compromis*, 184–5, and *Sixteenth-century France*, 365–7.

Philip II had failed to provide him with any support whereas the French had at least dispatched the small fleet under de la Roche in December 1570. Accompanied by his wife, Catherine Burke, their children, and three of the principal lords of Desmond (the son of the White knight, the son of the knight of the Valley and, lastly, the seneschal of Imokilly), Fitzmaurice sailed for France on board the *L'Arganys* in March 1575.[42] Following their arrival in Saint-Malo, the party was met by de la Roche and received an hospitable reception from the town's captain, the governor of Brittany and the bishop of Nantes. By late April Fitzmaurice had arrived at the court in Paris while Catherine, his wife, remained in Saint-Malo where presumably she was united with her son who had been in de la Roche's custody since 1570.[43] Not surprisingly, when Elizabeth I learned that both de la Roche and Fitzmaurice were at the French court, she doubted the honesty of Henri III's and Catherine de Médicis's protestations of their unwavering indifference to the requests of these two conspirators with whose cause they were well acquainted.

Throughout the early 1570s Bertrand de la Mothe Fénélon, the French ambassador to England, had kept Charles IX and Catherine de Médicis briefed regarding Fitzmaurice's campaign, as well as the progress of Thomas Stukeley's adventures and Spanish designs on Ireland. Significantly, on occasion his reports were in response to the queen regent's specific queries.[44] Especially in the months immediately prior to Fitzmaurice's arrival in Paris in 1575, the ambassador provided Catherine, Charles IX and his brother, Henri III, with regular reports on the state of affairs in Ireland, commenting specifically on the earl of Desmond's campaign in Munster, Turlough Luineach's collusion with the Scots, the reduction of Desmond, as well as on the earl of Essex's need for more provisions and his altercation with Lord Deputy Sir William Fitzwilliam.[45] Henri III was therefore reasonably well informed of the immediate circumstances that precipitated the rebel's flight to seek refuge and military aid in his realm.

Responding to Fitzmaurice's overtures, Henri III interceded with Elizabeth in June 1575 in order to secure a pardon on the Irish lord's behalf. From that point onwards, his direct contact with Fitzmaurice made it increasingly difficult for Henri and his mother to maintain an appearance of complete co-operation with Elizabeth. Throughout the following three years Henri

---

[42] Both sons had been deprived of their inheritance through forfeiture to English hands. The seneschal was a close ally of Sir John of Desmond: *Annála ríoghachta Éireann*, iv. 1683; Don Philip O'Sullivan Beare, *Ireland under Elizabeth*, trans. Matthew J. Byrne, Dublin 1903, 19.

[43] Catherine Burke to John O'Duyn, 28 Apr. 1575, SP 63/51/81–2; Catherine to her mother, Margaret Power, 28 Apr. 1575, SP 63/51/83.

[44] See *Correspondance de la Mothe Fénélon*, iii. 65–6, 95, 258–9, 479; iv. 1–2, 239, 268, 281, 290, 339–41, 359, 384–5, 388, 397, 470–1; *Papiers d'état*, ii. 322.

[45] See *Correspondance de la Mothe Fénélon*, vi. 36–7, 43, 48, 75, 96, 146, 253–4, 353, 377–8, 401–2, 412, 414, 429, 441, 443.

adopted a strategy of lending tacit, and at times passive, support to Fitzmaurice, his envoys and French supporters. He used the Irishman as a lever to apply pressure on Elizabeth to honour the terms of the Treaty of Blois by ending her military and financial support for his Huguenot opponents. All the while Henri projected an appearance of full co-operation with England, deliberately manipulating the true facts of his dealings with Fitzmaurice in order to prevent England becoming complacent regarding French amity. His correspondence and that of his mother was fraught with ambiguity, leaving Elizabeth's councillors incapable of ascertaining the extent of French contact with Fitzmaurice while affording the latter ample scope to circulate highly exaggerated propaganda regarding the French crown's commitment to supporting his rebellion.

Henri claimed to believe that the rebel and his followers were genuinely contrite and at pains to be readmitted to royal favour, and he was confident of a positive response to his representations to Elizabeth on Fitzmaurice's behalf.[46] He requested that the pardon be delivered in triplicate, with one copy being dispatched to Sir William Fitzwilliam, lord deputy of Ireland, another to the earl of Desmond and the third to Fitzmaurice. In a further effort to secure favourable terms on the rebel's behalf, the king also charged his ambassador to persuade Elizabeth to command the earl of Desmond to return those lands rightfully belonging to Fitzmaurice and his supporters that he had confiscated.[47]

La Mothe Fénélon subsequently went to great lengths to convince Elizabeth of the inaccuracy of a report then in circulation to the effect that de la Roche had introduced Fitzmaurice to Henri III before travelling to Brittany to muster forces on the rebel's behalf for an expedition to Ireland. Henri was insistent that the Breton captain had remained in Paris all the while, 'dragging' behind him, that he never incited Fitzmaurice to continue with his rebellion, and that he never offered him ships, men, munitions or money.[48] This sparked suspicion that de la Roche deliberately remained in Paris in an effort to interest the queen regent and the king in an Irish expedition.[49] Elizabeth greeted the French king's assurances of his indifference to the rebel lord's cause with surprise and relief. His testimony was, she said, a welcome contradiction to the propaganda which the rebel had conveyed to his allies in Ireland in late May, wherein he provided assurances that Henri III had

---

[46] Henri III to Elizabeth I, juin 1575, *Nouvelles Additions aux mémoires de Michel de Castelnau, seigneur de Mauvissiere*, ed. Jean Le Laboureur, 3 vols, Brussels 1731–2, iii. 455; Henri III to la Mothe Fénélon, juin 1575, ibid. iii. 454–5; *Lettres de Henri III, roi de France*, ed. Pierre Champion, Bernard Barbiche and Henri Zuber, 4 vols, Paris 1959–84, i. 186.
[47] Ibid.
[48] Henri III to la Mothe Fénélon, 7 juill. 1575, *Nouvelles Additions*, iii. 458–9; la Mothe Fénélon to Henri III, 13 juill. 1575, *Correspondance de La Mothe Fénélon*, vi. 466.
[49] Sasso, 'Desmond rebellions', 218–19.

supplied him with eight men-of-war, 2,000 arquebusers and a sum of 3,000 *écus*.[50]

Despite Henri's protestations of loyalty and his ambassador's sustained efforts to dispel her doubts regarding his master's collusion with Fitzmaurice and de la Roche, Elizabeth remained suspicious of the king. She was particularly resentful of his association with de la Roche whom she knew had conspired with the Geraldine lord in 1570–1 and whom Charles IX had four years previously denounced and promised in vain to punish. Elizabeth, her ministers and her ambassador in Paris would not have their fears allayed by the protestations of Henri and la Mothe Fénélon alone. Meanwhile, in Ireland, officials anxiously ferreted out reports on the fugitive lord's movements. Late in July 1575 two of Fitzmaurice's close associates, the seneschal of Imokilly, who had accompanied him to France in March, and John McUlick were intercepted and questioned by English officials upon their return to Ireland. They were found to have in their possession several copies of Henri III's letters to his ambassador in England and to Elizabeth wherein he interceded on Fitzmaurice's behalf.[51] It is, however, highly probable that the capture of the two Geraldine supporters was anticipated by Fitzmaurice and that the content of the planted letters was deliberately aimed to deflect English suspicions away from the true nature and intent of his continental activities.[52]

The French regent and Henri III persisted in their endeavours to distance themselves from any allegations of conspiracy with Fitzmaurice or other Irish dissidents. Towards the end of July Catherine de Médicis availed herself of an opportunity to demonstrate clearly her indifference to the Irish lord by the manner in which she responded to the overtures of an Irish captain, Thomas Bathe, who claimed to have conferred with de la Roche in Brittany prior to his arrival at the French court in Paris.[53] Catherine brusquely rejected Bathe's pleas to assist him in stirring up trouble in Ireland, informing him that she did not wish to see him again: her son took a similar stand in a contrived demonstration of his exemplary adherence to the terms of the Treaty of Blois. After subsequently discovering that Bathe had stayed on in Paris, the queen regent ordered his arrest and condemned him to death by hanging. Yet the leniency displayed by Charles IX in dealing with de la Roche was also evident in Henri III's commuting Bathe's sentence to exile from France, thereby fuelling English suspicions of the king's integrity in this matter.

[50] La Mothe Fénélon to Henri III, 13 juill. 1575, *Correspondance de La Mothe Fénélon*, vi. 467.
[51] Dowdall, Nicholas Walshe and James Meagh to the lord deputy, 20 July 1575, SP 63/52/83–4.
[52] Sasso, 'Desmond rebellions', 219.
[53] Catherine de Médicis to Henri III, 29 juill. 1575, *Nouvelles Additions*, iii. 460; *Lettres de Catherine de Médicis*, ed. Hector de la Ferrière and Gustave Baguenault de Puchesse, 10 vols, Paris 1880–1943, v. 127–9.

In spite of their ostensibly decisive stance in dismissing this Irish conspir-ator, the role of Catherine and Henri in Fitzmaurice's plans was continually probed by the English ambassador to France, Dr Valentine Dale. He confronted the queen regent with reports that Fitzmaurice, with the backing of de la Roche, was plotting to land another expedition off the coast of Ireland. Again Catherine protested her honourable conduct and stressed that her son's letters to Elizabeth requesting that the rebel be pardoned were the sum of his involvement with Fitzmaurice. The regent also displayed her manipulative capabilities by planting doubt in the suspicious ambassador's mind as she tendentiously alluded to the possibility that, unknown to her, Henri may well have lent a willing ear to de la Roche's overtures.[54]

Meanwhile, Fitzmaurice followed up Henri's representation to Elizabeth on his behalf by addressing two letters to a member of the English privy council, thought to have been Walsingham. In the first he requested a royal pardon and restoration of his lands, and in the second, a guaranteed protec-tion for himself for the duration of twenty-one years. The council's response was swift: on 8 August his suit for a pardon was granted 'at the French king's request and on your own submission'. However, the councillors were by no means duped by Fitzmaurice's pretence that he remained in France for fear of recrimination if he returned to Ireland. They therefore declined to afford him the protection that he sought on the grounds that it was 'unwanted', unheard of, and could not be conferred with honour.[55] In compliance with Henri's stipulations, Elizabeth dispatched a copy of Fitzmaurice's pardon to Sir John Perrot, president of Munster, the province in which he had committed treason against her. However, since Fitzmaurice refused to return to Ireland to receive his pardon in person, she refused to concede him another and there-fore submitted the matter to the French king's judgement.[56]

Again, Henri's response was evasive: he declared that he was helpless in this regard, having heard no report of Fitzmaurice since he had written letters to her recommending that the rebel be pardoned. Neither was he aware of the fugitive's whereabouts since they last met when the king presented him with a passport and chartered a ship in Brittany to transport him back to Ireland. Henri would have Elizabeth believe that as far as he was concerned, Fitzmaurice had given an undertaking to return to Ireland once he learned the queen had granted him a pardon and he presumed that this was what the rebel had done.[57] Yet in December the king was forced to admit to Elizabeth

---

54 Henri III to la Mothe Fénélon, 29 juill. 1575, *Nouvelles Additions*, iii. 461; *Lettres de Henri III*, ii. 203–4. See la Mothe Fénélon to Henri III, 20 août 1575, *Correspondance de La Mothe Fénélon*, vi. 492–4; Catherine de Médicis to Henri III, 29 juill. 1575, *Nouvelles Addi-tions*, iii. 460; *Lettres de Catherine de Médicis*, v. 128–9.

55 Sasso, 'Desmond rebellions', 220–1.

56 La Mothe Fénélon to Henri III, 1 août 1575, *Correspondance de La Mothe Fénélon*, vi. 482.

57 Henri III to la Mothe Fénélon, 7 août 1575, *Nouvelles Additions*, iii. 464; *Lettres de Henri III*, ii. 207–8.

that he knew the fugitive was still in France when he had occasion to write to her requesting a passport for one of Fitzmaurice's men who was to be dispatched to Ireland to ascertain whether the measures stipulated in his royal pardon had been implemented.[58]

In fact Fitzmaurice had no intention of submitting to Elizabeth or of immediately returning to Ireland. Instead, he pressed ahead with his solicitations to the French court and the Guise faction.[59] Meanwhile, English officials in Ireland and in France continued to monitor closely Fitzmaurice's movements. In February Sir Henry Sidney, who had recently been reappointed lord deputy of Ireland, observed that though 'he hath not much relief from the French king', Fitzmaurice was none the less 'subtle, malicious, and hardy, a papist in extremity and well esteemed, and of good credit among the people'. Owing to his reputation, Sidney feared that

> if he come [to Ireland], and be not wholly dealt withal at first . . . all the loose people of this province [Munster] will flock unto him [and] . . . the lords, though they would do their best, shall not be able to keep them from him.[60]

While Fitzmaurice persistently lobbied the French regent and Henri at court in the early summer of 1575, it was in Rome that the most promising developments were unfolding. The cardinal of Como, papal secretary, concluded confidential discussions with Philip II and Gregory XIII, and drafted preliminary proposals for an expedition destined for either England or Ireland, the precise details of which were to be decided at a very important conference convened that summer in Rome by the pope. In attendance were several influential English Catholic exiles, including Dr Nicholas Sanders, a priest and leader of the English Catholic refugee community in Spain. The Jesuit, Fr David Wolfe, along with a Franciscan, Patrick O'Hely, who was later appointed bishop of Mayo, represented Irish interests in the assembly. Though invited, crucially Fitzmaurice did not attend that meeting, much to the vexation of the cardinal of Como, and as a result the Irish cause suffered. Instead, he remained in France upon the advice of Fr Wolfe, though this arrangement undoubtedly suited the Irish lord whose expectations of a favourable outcome to the negotiations were low from the outset. Wolfe is believed to have prevailed upon Fitzmaurice to stay in France in the hope that, in his absence, Wolfe himself could more effectively persuade Philip II of the necessity for both Fitzmaurice and Stukeley to lead the proposed expedition to Ireland.[61]

---

58 Henri III to Michel de Castelnau, seigneur de Mauvissiere, 27 déc. 1575, *Nouvelles Additions*, iii. 475–6; *Lettres de Henri III*, ii. 331–2.
59 *Ibernia Ignatiana; seu Ibernorum Societatis Jesu patrum monumenta collecta*, ed. Edmund Hogan, Dublin 1880, 21–2.
60 Sidney to the privy council, [27] Feb. 1576, *Carew MSS, 1575–88*, 42.
61 Sasso, 'Desmond rebellions', 224–30.

Following the conference, the momentum for an invasion passed to the English conspirators and Irish schemes were temporarily relegated to secondary importance. The English project remained dominant throughout 1576, while Irish exiles in Rome, Spain and France, backed by the papacy, continued to make overtures for a Catholic army to be dispatched to Ireland. Although Philip exhibited enthusiasm for mounting an attack on England, he was also acutely aware of his need to pacify Flanders as a prerequisite to any offensive action against England with whom he remained on superficially amicable terms: hence, nothing came of these plans.

However, towards the end of 1576, the prospects for Fitzmaurice again seemed bright as the papacy's interest increasingly gravitated towards an invasion of Ireland.[62] Although operating beyond the more critical and promising arena of papal and Spanish negotiations, James Fitzmaurice remained a source of constant annoyance to the English administrations in Ireland and England. In September he returned to the French court where he was welcomed by Henri III and Catherine de Médicis. Significantly, this time, on his departure from the court for Saint-Malo, he was presented with a gift of 5,000 crowns to fund his activities on the continent, leaving little ambiguity as to the French crown's stance *vis-à-vis* his cause.[63]

While the queen regent and Henri had consistently protested their innocence of allegations of complicity with Fitzmaurice since his arrival in France the previous year, the mounting evidence of their partiality in their dealings with him served to deepen English suspicions of French duplicity. Admittedly they failed to provide Fitzmaurice with the military and financial backing that he sought. Yet they had granted several audiences to him and had never moved to secure his arrest. They interceded with Elizabeth on his behalf. They misleadingly denied any knowledge of his whereabouts. They failed to punish or imprison de la Roche, whom they knew to have been involved in transporting French troops to Ireland in support of the rebel's insurrection. They permitted Fitzmaurice to return to Saint-Malo and afforded him a substantial financial support in order that he might continue his campaign to undermine Elizabeth's authority in Ireland. Not surprisingly, therefore, Elizabeth and her ministers were convinced that Henri and his mother covertly supported this fugitive rebel in his treasonous opposition to her.

IV

Having spent almost two years at a remove from the cut and thrust of his envoys' more lively engagements in Rome and Madrid, Fitzmaurice had little to show for all his endeavours to solicit significant military aid from the French king. Disappointed, he departed France for Rome early in 1577, trav-

---

[62] Ibid 233–4.
[63] Dale to Burghley, 10 Sept. 1576, *CSP Foreign, 1575–7*, 371.

elling via Spain in order to confer with his emissaries there and to brief himself on the Spanish king's response to his envoy's representations. Before leaving Brittany, he secured a pledge of future support from de la Roche. Between the months of February and July English agents and merchants closely observed the preparation of French ships and men whom they suspected of being destined for Ireland as it was widely believed that 'the French king meant shortly to have some service on the coast of Ireland and wanted pilots'.[64]

In April Sir Nicholas Malby, the president of Connacht, received intelligence from France that the rebel leader had been promised six tall ships and 1,200 French soldiers under the joint command of de la Roche, a Monsieur Daukin, and his brother. It was alleged that Fitzmaurice intended to employ the French fleet in an attack on Munster. The Spanish and Portuguese were also said to have been prepared to assist him with men and money. The following month there were several reports that Fitzmaurice had been appointed commander of an army comprising 4,000 Frenchmen and several of the principal gentlemen of France for a descent on Ireland.[65]

The Irish council took a very serious view of this intelligence; the English privy council was more reserved and predictably parsimonious in its response. Lord Deputy Sir Henry Sidney requested that the earl of Leicester expedite the ammunition, money and men needed to withstand such an attack. Thus equipped, Sidney was confident that the French force could be easily dealt with.[66] Sidney urged Elizabeth to respond immediately to his request, reminding her how 'Calais, the jewel and honour of England, was lost for lack of forces in readiness' during her sister's reign.[67] In June the prospects seemed very encouraging: the English privy council informed Sidney that the troops that he had requested would be placed in readiness in south-west England. Several ships had been commissioned, 500 additional calivers were to be dispatched and an extra £5,000 was earmarked for Irish defences. However, these supplies were put on reserve, only to be released in the event of an invasion. Thus, while the prospect of a French invasion engendered near panic in Lord Deputy Sidney in the summer of 1577, the English councillors' preoccupation with cost caused them to adopt a 'wait and see' strategy.

During the early summer months, Catherine de Médici's and Henri III's manipulation of their association with Fitzmaurice was exposed. In June the

---

[64] Intelligence, 19 Feb. 1577, *CSP Ireland, 1574–85*, 112–13 (enclosure); James Fitzmaurice, 9 June 1577, *Carew MSS, 1575–88*, 83–5; Sir Amyas Paulet to Walsingham, 9 June 1577, *CSP Foreign, 1575–7*, 594; John Calis to Walsingham, July 1577, HMC, *De L'Isle and Dudley MSS*, ii. 59.

[65] Sir William Drury to Walsingham, 14 Apr. 1577, SP 63/58/24–6; intelligence from France, 16 Apr. 1577, SP 63/58/28–31v (enclosure); Examinations . . . relative to the proceedings of James Fitzmaurice and his wife, 10 May 1577, SP 63/58/51–2v); Sidney to Elizabeth I, 20 May 1577, SP 63/58/93.

[66] Sidney to Elizabeth I, 20 May 1577, SP 63/58/93.

[67] Sidney to Leicester, 20 May 1577, SP 63/58/86–9; *Carew MSS, 1575–88*, 480.

English ambassador to France, Sir Amyas Paulet, believed that Fitzmaurice had 20,000 horsemen at his disposal and that he hoped to receive eight galleys from Gregory XIII along with aid from the French king.[68] Paulet confronted Henri with a report that Fitzmaurice intended orchestrating another series of disturbances in Ireland, that he had received a promise of support from Henri and the pope and that de la Roche had already equipped ships in Brittany for an expedition to Ireland. The ambassador sought the French king's assurance that he would no longer tolerate the rebel's remaining in France and reminded Henri of Elizabeth's expectation that he would forbid de la Roche to undertake any enterprise that was in contravention of the terms of the Treaty of Blois.

Henri claimed that, prior to their conversation, he had known nothing of Fitzmaurice's deliberations and just as little about de la Roche's activities. He also emphatically reaffirmed his resolve to remain on favourable terms with the English queen. In yet another of his pointed references to his displeasure at Elizabeth's support of French Huguenots, Henri stressed his expectation that his compliance with her wishes in this matter would be reciprocated by her refusal to favour or receive subjects who disturbed the peace in France.[69]

In mid-July the queen responded by pressing for a final, definitive statement from Henri on his real position with respect to the rebel's approaches for assistance. She directly challenged the king to dispense with his former pretence and oblique self-defence and to state categorically that he was 'not acquainted with any such matter' and to 'give such order that we might be clearly out of doubt'.[70] She confronted him with 'proof' of his involvement with Fitzmaurice in confiscated letters that the Irish lord had written to his wife. These, she claimed, set down 'in plain terms what promise of aid he had conceived of ...[Henri III] for his intended invasion of Ireland'. The letters, combined with Henri's permitting Fitzmaurice to reside in his realm, convinced Elizabeth that the French king had persistently defied her by supporting the rebel. In her strongest terms to date Elizabeth threatened Henri that if de la Roche were not prevented from proceeding with his preparations of his fleet, and if English sailors whose ships had been damaged or confiscated by French vessels did not have justice done to them in France, then she would be 'forced to resort to such remedies as we would be loath to put in execution'.[71] Henri appeased Elizabeth, emphasising that, like her, he wished to observe the terms of the Treaty of Blois but his own resentment at the queen's contravention of its terms is manifest in his jibe that 'il fallait aussi que de sa part elle en fait de même'.[72] He reiterated that he had no

68 Paulet to Walsingham, 9, 25 June 1577, CSP Foreign, 1575–7, 594, 604.
69 Henri III to de Castelnau, 20 juin 1577, ibid. 295–6; Nouvelles Additions, iii. 516–17.
70 Elizabeth I to Paulet, 13 July 1577, CSP Foreign, 1577–8, 16.
71 Ibid.
72 Henri III to de Castelnau, 1 août 1577, Nouvelles Additions, iii. 524; Lettres de Henri III, iii. 337).

knowledge of Fitzmaurice's whereabouts and gave an assurance that neither the rebel nor any other insurgent need expect any help from him which might be prejudicial to the friendship between France and England. In response to Elizabeth's allegations regarding de la Roche, Henri explained that he had made inquiries of the Breton captain as to his purpose in arming and equipping his ships, and had been assured that de la Roche was not engaged in any enterprise that conflicted with the queen's interests. Consequently, Henri refused to comply with Elizabeth's insistence that he ban de la Roche from embarking on his voyage.[73] Catherine de Médicis, however, provided a somewhat contradictory and more accurate account of Fitzmaurice's manoeuvres: she informed Paulet that 'Fitzmaurice . . . était mal-content de nous', as a result of which he had departed France for Rome in the hope of receiving a more favourable response at the papal court. The queen regent claimed to have extracted a promise from de la Roche that he would not undertake any expedition that was contrary to Elizabeth's interests.[74]

This intense exchange of allegations and rejoinders during the early summer months exposed recurring inconsistencies in the replies of Henri and Catherine de Médicis to the English ambassador's queries. This served to undermine the effectiveness of the smoke screen that both endeavoured to maintain in order to manipulate Elizabeth into withdrawing her assistance to the Huguenots. Elizabeth availed herself of every opportunity to remind the French king of her suspicions concerning his involvement with Fitzmaurice, but by mid-August tensions between the monarchs had eased when any surviving Irish hopes of French military support were dealt a decisive blow.[75] The French king gave repeated assurances that he would not assist Fitzmaurice and that he would not allow de la Roche to return to his realm should the captain lend his support to Fitzmaurice's cause against his royal will. In return, he sought a promise from Elizabeth that she would not furnish aid to the Huguenot leaders in France or to John Casimir, the son of the elector palatine and commander of the German forces, who had been allied with the Huguenots.[76] The queen initially gave her consent to the agreement, but subsequently contravened its terms by supporting Casimir.[77]

Throughout the second half of 1577 Elizabeth remained suspicious of Henri's involvement with de la Roche as the uncertainty surrounding the captain's manoeuvres and intentions continued to give rise to a significant

---

[73] Ibid.
[74] Catherine de Médicis to de Castelnau, 1 août 1577, *Nouvelles Additions*, iii. 526; *Lettres de Catherine de Médicis* v. 268.
[75] Paulet to Leicester, 7 Aug.[?] 1577, *CSP Foreign, 1577–8*, 58–9; Leicester to Walsingham, 16 Aug. 1577, ibid. 81.
[76] Henri III to de Castelnau, 1 août 1577, *Nouvelles Additions*, iii. 523–4; *Lettres de Henri III*, iii. 337. See also Sasso, 'Desmond rebellions', 242.
[77] Sasso, 'Desmond rebellions', 242.

level of unease in English circles.[78] A report sent by Sir Francis Walsingham to Sir William Drury, president of Munster, in August 1577 claimed that de la Roche was at Vannes in Brittany with 1,000 men, four galleons and other vessels. As a precautionary measure in the event of a sudden attack, the royal navy were ordered to continue patrolling the Irish coast, at least until mid-September.[79]

Members of the Irish council, too, were mindful of their need to initiate extraordinary measures in anticipation of an invasion. Early in September the lord deputy, Sir Henry Sidney, requested that the sheriff and other officials of Devon assemble 400 soldiers 'required by the intended French invasion' who were to sail for Waterford.[80] Sidney asked that a further 2,000 soldiers be sent to defend Ireland for fear of designs by de la Roche and Fitzmaurice.[81] Yet he was not overly anxious about an invasion as is evident in his advice that the English privy councillors should halt their dispatch in the event of the alarm subsiding. The councillors' eventual decision to do so testified to the waning threat posed by the French. Nevertheless, the sheer scale of the preparations bore witness to the perceived seriousness of the French invasion scare during the summer of 1577.[82]

Fitzmaurice meanwhile grew increasingly restless and anxious to lead an expedition back to Ireland. Having failed to secure aid from Henri III or even from de la Roche, he left France for Rome with the intention of joining forces with the team of envoys soliciting support at the Spanish, papal and Portuguese courts. En route to and from Rome, he visited Spain where he held talks with Bishop O'Hely and Dr Nicholas Sanders, both of whom were to the fore in the Irish party's negotiations with Philip II. Fitzmaurice pinned all his hopes on the papacy and the Spanish king at this stage, having secured a pledge from Pope Gregory XIII to send a force of 6,000 Spanish troops to Ireland by 1578 with Philip's support. Upon his return from Rome to Madrid, much to his disappointment and in contrast with his treatment at the French court, Fitzmaurice was refused an audience with the Spanish king. In addition, he received only token support in the form of a letter from the king to his ambassador in Portugal asking him to assist the Irish lord in arranging his passage back to Ireland. He travelled to Lisbon where he arrived on 5 July 1577. There he sought the assistance of the Spanish ambassador but was refused an audience with Sebastian, king of Portugal.

Frustrated by these rebuffs and the loss of time, Fitzmaurice resolved to muster what few resources and troops he could and return to Ireland. With the help of Robert Fontana, the apostolic collector in Lisbon, he acquired

---

[78] Paulet to Walsingham, 24 Sept. 1577, *CSP Foreign, 1577–8*, 189; Walsingham to Sidney, 18 Jan. 1578 (enclosure, 10 Dec. 1577), HMC, *De L'Isle and Dudley MSS*, ii. 75.
[79] Walsingham to the lord president of Munster, HMC, *De L'Isle and Dudley MSS*, ii. 60.
[80] Sidney to the sheriff &c. of Devon, 5 Sept. 157, ibid. ii. 63.
[81] Sidney and council to the privy council, 6 Sept. 1577, *CSP Ireland, 1574–85*, 120.
[82] Walsingham to Sidney, 15 Sept. 1577, HMC, *De L'Isle and Dudley MSS*, ii. 69.

munitions and powder and approximately 100 soldiers. In late October, following further delays, he decided that he could wait no longer.[83] In a letter to the papal secretary, Ptolemy Galli, the cardinal of Como, he resigned himself to the pathetic outcome to all his continental solicitations and negotiations and declared that he was determined to set sail from Lisbon to Ireland in spite of his being 'sine armis, sine classe, et sine hominibus' ('unarmed, without a fleet, and without men').[84] Fitzmaurice was acutely aware of the negative impact of his prolonged absence on his supporters in Munster. His disillusionment was palpable in his admission to the cardinal that 'I have looked for aid and having failed to find it, my friends, who have been eagerly expecting me, will be lukewarm and dispirited, while my foes will be all the more ready to face me, when they see me coming back unarmed and unaided'.[85]

Towards the end of summer 1577 it became clear to the papacy that in spite of endeavours to persuade Philip II to provide practical assistance for Fitzmaurice's campaign, neither the Spanish king nor King Sebastian of Portugal was prepared to do so on an immediate basis. Feeling compelled to honour their promise to Fitzmaurice, Gregory XIII and the cardinal gave an undertaking to shoulder the burden of funding the entire enterprise. In October the cardinal of Como informed the Spanish nuncio that the pope had decided to send Sir Thomas Stukeley on an expedition to Ireland. While Philip continued to display interest in plans to launch an attack on England, he still refused to respond to Irish pleas with any aid whatsoever.[86]

V

Fitzmaurice's last interlude in France before returning to Ireland was determined by chance rather than design, and provides further evidence of Henri III's modest and passive but ultimately worthless support. Having departed Lisbon on 19 November 1577, Fitzmaurice and Bishop O'Hely set sail in a small convoy under the command of the Breton captain, Thomas Lestrubec. Within days of embarking violent sea storms forced them to take shelter in the harbours of Bayona, in Galicia, and Monuiero, near Corunna. Their departure from this last port was delayed owing to inclement weather, desertions and Lestrubec's refusal to proceed with the journey. Fitzmaurice was forced to take legal action against his captain and as a result Lesturbec and the crew were imprisoned. However, while Fitzmaurice was at mass on 5 January 1578, Lestrubec and his men managed to escape and make their way

---

[83] Sasso, 'Desmond rebellions', 237–40.
[84] James Fitzmaurice to Ptolmy Galli, cardinal of Como, 5 Nov. 1577, CSP Rome, 1572–8, ii. 347.
[85] Ibid.
[86] Sasso, 'Desmond rebellions', 243–4.

to their ship where they found all the provisions, arms and money belonging to the Irish lord and bishop still on board. They stole the ship and sailed for France. Fitzmaurice and O'Hely followed them overland. Fitzmaurice made his way to Saint-Malo where he was reunited with his family and O'Hely headed for Paris, where he sought a royal warrant for the restitution of their stolen property.[87]

The coincidence of the Irish rebel's reappearance in Brittany in early 1578 and de la Roche's preparation of a large expedition in Brittany once again gave rise to English suspicion of French backing for the rebel in another round of ultimately futile speculation centred on the Guisard's movements. De la Roche insisted that there was nothing irregular in his preparation for this expedition. However, when it was discovered that his story that he intended travelling to India was in fact a fabrication, his activities fuelled intense English anxiety.[88] At the same time, in Ireland, Sidney had also been alerted to the revival of the 'traitorous' devices of Fitzmaurice and to reports that de la Roche and others were in the throes of preparing another expedition to Ireland.[89] Paulet was convinced that rumours that de la Roche's fleet was destined for Ireland where he had contact with several rebels were little more than diversions designed to frighten Elizabeth into withdrawing aid to the French Huguenots. Meanwhile, de la Roche's use of three or four of his ships as pirate vessels gave rise to further speculation as to the true intentions behind his manifestly grander plans for the fleet. The ambassador viewed de la Roche as an opportunist, primarily set upon inflicting injury on La Rochelle, Ireland, Scotland, Zealand, England, Guernsey or Jersey.[90]

In February Henri III endeavoured to allay English suspicions by summoning de la Roche to court to meet Paulet. The Guisard captain described how he had recently been engaged in the preparation of an expedition with 2,500 arquebusers and admitted that he was aware of Elizabeth's suspicion regarding the purpose of his voyage, 'as if he intended to make some attempt to her prejudice'.[91] However, he took great pains to stress Henri's honourable conduct, explaining that the king had ordered him to 'enterprise nothing that might tend to disquiet in any part of her dominions', and went to considerable lengths to assure Paulet of the propriety of his intentions. In an oblique reference to his previous known involvement with Fitzmaurice in 1570–1, the Breton captain admitted that in the past he had 'some familiarity with some that were not the best affected to the State of England', having 'spent much time fondly and foolishly'. Yet he insisted that during the past five or six years, 'he had done nothing that would offend her majesty or the least of her subjects' and would 'never conceive to practice anything that

---

87 Henri III to the seneschal of Nantes, 7 Apr. 1578, CSP Foreign, 1577–8, 602–3.
88 Paulet to the English secretaries, 10, 12 Jan. 1578, ibid. 452, 455.
89 Walsingham to Sidney, 18 Jan. 1578, HMC, De L'Isle and Dudley MSS, ii. 75.
90 Paulet to the English secretaries, 24 Jan. 1578, CSP Foreign, 1577–8, 469.
91 Paulet to the English secretaries, 19 Feb. 1578, ibid. 508–9.

might disturb' the amicable relations between England and France. Paulet, however, was not convinced. He cautioned de la Roche against conspiring with fugitives or traitors as this would constitute an offence against Henri III and 'the sequel might be dangerous to both realms', and was highly sceptical of the captain's claim that he had neither seen nor heard of Fitzmaurice who was staying in Saint-Malo at that time.[92]

Still unconvinced by these protestations, throughout the spring of 1578 Elizabeth remained wary of de la Roche who continued to enjoy Henri's support until English interest in him eventually subsided.[93] In early April the French king demonstrated further tacit support for Fitzmaurice when he granted 400 francs to his consort, Bishop O'Hely, and instructed the sene-schal of Nantes to attend personally to the case for restitution of the Irish party's goods stolen by Lestrubec.[94] However, even in this routine case, Henri's intervention yielded little by way of immediate results. While Fitzmaurice and O'Hely impatiently sought restitution of their stolen ship and supplies in order to resume their long-deferred expedition as quickly as possible, the international situation, and specifically Anglo-Spanish re-lations, were entering a decisive phase owing to developments in the Nether-lands. The duke of Parma's arrival there in January 1578 effectively heralded the end of the five-year period of superficially amicable relations between Elizabeth I, Philip II and the duke of Alva. An outburst of overt Spanish hostility towards Elizabeth seemed imminent; yet once again, Philip avoided any outright provocation of the queen.

Meanwhile, Sir Thomas Stukeley set sail from Città Vecchia, north of Rome, for Cadiz with a troop of 600 papal soldiers and arms for 3,000 men, at a cost of 40,000 crowns to the pope who lobbied Philip II to match the papal force.[95] From the beginning of 1578 Paulet grew increasingly alarmed at these developments, believing that a holy league consisting of Philip II, Henri III, Gregory XIII and several other powerful Italian figures had been revived in Rome, and speculating that Stukeley's galley and troops might soon be augmented by either the Spanish or the French king.[96] He was convinced that the French intended to embark upon an expedition in support of Mary Stuart, and feared that in doing so they might also gain the support of the Spanish.[97] But while Paulet and Walsingham worried about the possibility of a French attack on Ireland, by the end of March Bishop O'Hely despaired of ever receiving aid from the French king, despondently admitting to the

---

[92] Ibid.
[93] Paulet to the English secretaries, 1, 16 Mar. 1578, ibid. 520, 544. See also Henri III to de Castelnau, 15 fév. 1578, *Nouvelles Additions*, iii. 542; *Lettres de Henri III*, iii. 471; Henri III to de Castelnau, 19 fév. 1578, *Nouvelles Additions*, iii. 543; *Lettres de Henri III*, iii. 477.
[94] Henri III to the seneschal of Nantes, 7 av. 1578, *CSP Foreign, 1577–8*, 602–3.
[95] Sasso, 'Desmond rebellions', 248–9.
[96] Paulet to the English secretaries, 24 Jan. 1578, *CSP Foreign, 1577–8*, 470.
[97] Palmer, *Problem of Ireland*, 106.

cardinal of Como that France was refusing to help them.[98] Sebastian of Portugal and Philip II continued to exhibit little more than indifference to Fitzmaurice's cause, leaving the papacy the only likely source of aid for the Irish in the immediate term. O'Hely believed that Fitzmaurice would soon travel to Rome again and that conditions in Ireland were particularly ripe for rebellion, with three influential noblemen, namely O'Neill, O'Donnell and O'Rourke, ready to revolt. The bishop therefore set about cultivating the support of the papal nuncio in Paris with the object of advancing Fitzmaurice's campaign with the cardinal of Como and Gregory XIII.[99]

However, both O'Hely and Fitzmaurice's more immediate challenge remained that of securing restitution of their stolen property. O'Hely sought the cardinal of Como's intervention on their behalf. Initially the papacy was reluctant to help. Gregory XIII was disgusted at having wasted money on failed campaigns such as Fitzmaurice's, and frustrated at Philip II's persistent apathy and inertia. Suspicious of the ubiquitous Stukeley's proposal that his expedition be allowed to join forces with King Sebastian of Portugal's fleet, destined for Africa, the pope grew wary of Fitzmaurice too. He thought that the story of the capture of this ship by Lestrubec might have been invented so that Fitzmaurice could avoid returning to Ireland and instead settle into a comfortable lifestyle in Saint-Malo.[100] By May 1578, however, the papacy evidently regained cautious confidence in Fitzmaurice, though O'Hely was warned that the pope would make no decision in response to his appeal for restitution of his stolen property until he received a letter from Fitzmaurice contradicting a report that he had in fact already had his goods restored and was therefore able to resume his expedition.[101]

Throughout June and July Fitzmaurice and O'Hely both received practical assistance from Fabio Mirto Frangipani, extraordinary papal ambassador to France in 1578, as well as from the papal nuncio, Anselmo Dandino. The latter was instructed by the cardinal of Como to intercede with Henri III in favour of the Geraldine rebel. By early June Fitzmaurice had visited the nuncio to inform him that he had reclaimed a portion of his goods and that he was ready to proceed with his expedition to Ireland.[102] No doubt he also drew the nuncio's attention to the inaccuracy of a report that alleged that he had departed for Ireland from Brittany with six ships and 2,000 soldiers supplied by a Breton lord.[103] He presented Dandino with a letter addressed to the cardinal of Como in which he advised that two or three Jesuits be

98 *Correspondance du nonce en France: Anselmo Dandino, 1578–81*, ed. Juan Cloulas, Rome 1970, 85, 780.
99 Ibid. 780–1.
100 Sasso, 'Desmond rebellions', 255.
101 Dandino to the cardinal of Como, 26 mai 1578, *Correspondance du nonce: Dandino*, 159 and n.
102 Dandino to the cardinal of Como, 8 juin 1578, ibid. 166.
103 Cardinal of Como to Dandino, 2 juin 1578, ibid. 162.

dispatched to Ireland and to Scotland with instructions to stir up support prior to his return home.[104] Fitzmaurice presented a similar proposal to Mercurian, general of the Jesuits. However, he received a negative response in June 1578 on the grounds that it was not, in the general's view, a fitting time to send his men to either country, though he did give an undertaking to do so in the event of a favourable opportunity presenting itself in the future.[105] Thanks to the representations of the nuncio, Fitzmaurice and O'Hely received a donation of 1,000 crowns from the papacy, and Frangipani continued to lobby for restitution of the remainder of James's goods, for which he secured a bill of exchange.[106] Having recouped his losses, Fitzmaurice departed France and sailed for Madrid where he arrived on 26 August 1578.[107] This effectively marked the end of his dealings with France.

<h2 style="text-align:center">VI</h2>

The similarities between Fitzmaurice's experience in France and that of his kinsman, Gerald Fitzgerald, eleventh earl of Kildare, are striking. In both cases Saint-Malo was regarded as a safe haven, and on both occasions the Irish lords were received in accordance with their aristocratic station. The two used their Catholicism to forge links with Rome in an effort to secure assistance for their political ends, though Fitzmaurice did so much more aggressively and to greater effect at a time when the Catholic Counter-Reformation was at its most militant. Within the broader schema of international diplomacy, Anglo-French relations in the mid-1570s resembled those of the early 1540s in that both countries were struggling, in the main succesfully, to adhere to the terms of truces and treaties, namely those signed at Nice (June 1538) and at Blois (April 1572). In the mid-1570s the revival of negotiations for a match between Elizabeth and Anjou denoted English interest in the pursuit of a pro-French line in foreign policy and it was hoped that one of the lateral effects of such a policy would be the negation of French designs on Ireland.[108] With France wracked by civil war and faced with mounting Huguenot resistance, Henri III had a vested interest in maintaining peace with England.

Thus, in both instances, the French kings were loath to provoke their English counterparts and *vice versa*, though François I and Henri III realised the diplomatic possibilities presented by Irish overtures in their manipulation

---

[104] Sasso, 'Desmond rebellions', 255–6.

[105] Everard Mercurian to James Fitzmaurice, 28 June 1578, SP 63/61/23–4.

[106] Fabio Frangipani to cardinal of Como, 14 juill. 1578, *Correspondance du nonce en France: Fabio Mirto Frangipani, 1568–72, 1586–7: nonce extraordinaire en 1574, 1575–6 et 1578*, ed. A. Lynn Martin and Robert Toupin, Rome 1984, 299; Sasso, 'Desmond rebellions', 256.

[107] Sasso, 'Desmond rebellions', 256.

[108] See Palmer, *Problem of Ireland*, 107.

of England's vulnerability. Both French rulers consciously exploited their dalliance with these Geraldine lords, not so much to antagonise, as to manipulate cleverly Henry VIII and Elizabeth I in their pursuit of England's continental interests and in their conduct of monarchical relations in accordance with a code of honour. Both François I and Henri III were masters of disguise. Their shows of favour to the Irish lords were viewed by English officials and the Tudors as sufficient evidence to substantiate rumours of French royal assistance to Geraldine causes. Yet neither Sir John Wallop nor the astute Sir Amyas Paulet could present a shred of concrete evidence to incriminate definitively either king of France. What is evident is the recurring readiness of the French kings to use Irish lords as bargaining instruments in balancing their relations with England.

Fitzmaurice's campaign for French aid for his campaign also resembled that of his ancestor, the tenth earl of Desmond, but was in contrast with the conspiracies of the 1550s and 1560s as it involved direct contact between the French court and a leading Munster lord without any dependence on Scottish support for undertaking an enterprise against Elizabeth. It also brought about renewed contacts between the Geraldines and the comtes de Candale. The fact that Fitzmaurice managed to elicit some response from both the French monarchy and Guise supporters testified to the strength of the Geraldine cause in mustering continental aid for Irish resistance to the Tudor *régime*. Fitzmaurice and his envoys also drew on the experience of Irish dealings with the French in the previous two decades by specifically targeting the Catholic Guise faction at the French court for assistance.

In spite of his failure to gain significant military or financial aid from Charles IX or Henri III for his expedition to Ireland, James Fitzmaurice's sojourn in France during the years 1575–8 was more than a mere re-enactment of his kinsman's exile thirty-five years before. Fitzmaurice's success in harnessing the Catholic Counter-Reformation to whip up continental support for his cause resulted in his representations generating significantly greater interest in French intervention in Ireland and in the arrival of a small fleet in December 1570. Unlike Gerald Fitzgerald, Fitzmaurice received more than a welcoming reception in Saint-Malo and hospitality from the governor of Brittany. Rather, he received an assurance (albeit empty) of a dozen French ships and 12,000 men. He gained personal access to the French queen regent and to her two sons, Charles IX and Henri III, and received a substantial financial contribution to sustain him in his continental solicitations and negotiations. He also enjoyed the support of provincial authorities and the papal nuncios in France in securing restitution of his stolen property. In addition, his intrigue on the continent encouraged diplomatic and ecclesiastical personnel to focus on Irish political events on a regular and unprecedented basis.[109] One of the most significant legacies of Fitzmaurice's concerted

---

[109] See *Correspondance du nonce: Anselmo Dandino*; *Correspondance du nonce en France:*

campaign to win support at the French, Spanish and papal courts was the invaluable practice and training that it afforded negotiators such as Fitz-gibbon, O'Hely, Wolfe and countless others in the skills of formulating and presenting proposals at these courts, in complying with courtly protocol and in mastering the intricacies of court factionalism, all of which the Irish were to use to good effect in soliciting Spanish aid throughout the 1580s and 1590s.

While the French court was being steadily overshadowed by the papacy and Spain as the most promising source of military aid for Irish insurgents in the late 1570s and early 1580s, Philip II remained reluctant to respond to Irish pleas for assistance. Consequently, those involved in the Baltinglass rebellion and the Nugent conspiracy in Leinster in the early 1580s still held out some slim hope of securing aid from the French crown. However, in 1579 Fitzmaurice was left with no option but to proceed with what forces he had along with the remains of Stukeley's papal force. While Philip still refused overt support for the expedition, he granted the Irish lord permission to embark on his expedition to Ireland. On 17 June Fitzmaurice, accompanied by his wife, his chaplain, Dr Nicholas Sanders, and several Irish clerics, set sail for Ireland with four vessels and an army of Spaniards and Italians in the pay of Pope Gregory XIII and arrived in Smerwick on 17 July 1579.[110] Relying on promises of strong reinforcements to follow, Fitzmaurice had departed with a landing force of no more that 100 soldiers and possibly even as few as fifty men.

William Palmer regards the expedition of July 1579 as a landmark in Irish history, 'the most visible manifestation of the power politics of the Catholic Counter-Reformation coming to bear on Tudor policy in Ireland', and proof that during the 1570s considerations regarding Ireland affected vital elements of English foreign policy.[111] Fitzmaurice's canvass for continental support taught him and his associates that their adept harnessing of the crusading cause had won them the support of the papacy and earned them a hearing at the Escorial. Notwithstanding the failed outcome to his solicitations in France, Fitzmaurice's use of the Catholic Counter-Reformation cause in order

Giovanni Battista Castelli, 1581–3, ed. Robert Toupin, Rome 1967; *Girolamo Ragazzoni évêque de Bergame, nonce de France, correspondance de sa nonciature 1583–6*, ed. Pierre Blet, Rome 1962.

[110] J. H. Pollen, 'The Irish expedition of 1579', *The Month* ci (1903), 80–1; David Mathew, *The Celtic peoples and Renaissance Europe*, London 1933, 167; Silke, *Ireland and Europe*, 13; G. A. Hayes McCoy, 'The completion of the Tudor conquest, and the advance of the Counter-Reformation, 1571–1603', in Moody, Martin and Byrne, *New history of Ireland*, iii. 105; J. J. N. McGurk, 'The fall of the noble house of Desmond, 1579–83', *History Today* xxix (1979), 671; Ellis, *Ireland in the age of the Tudors*, 309–10; Brady, *Chief governors*, 200; Lennon, *Sixteenth-century Ireland*, 223; Palmer, *Poblem of Ireland*, 108, 110.

[111] Palmer, *Problem of Ireland*, 108. A similar view is expressed by Margaret MacCurtain in 'The fall of the house of Desmond', *Journal of the Kerry Archaeological and Historical Society* viii (1975), 36.

to muster support for his campaign was cleverly conceived. The fact that Philip tacitly supported the involvement of Spanish soldiers in his campaign, and granted him permission to undertake his expedition, was undoubtedly interpreted as a promising sign for future Spanish assistance. Following the arrival of the fleet in Kerry in July, Sir Humphrey Gilbert, president of Munster, was convinced that 'this spark of rebellion is attended with bellows, both French, Spanish, Portingals [sic], Italians, and all sorts of papists throughout Christendom'.[112]

Although French involvement in the Desmond rebellion was minimal compared with that of the Italians and the Spanish, a number of French soldiers fought on the side of James Fitzmaurice and held his castle at Castlemaine on the rebel's behalf.[113] In August the common report in Paris was that the rebellion was proceeding with great success even though Fitzmaurice died in a skirmish with the Burkes of Castleconnell on the 18th of that month.[114] Lord Justice Drury struggled with what resources he had to suppress the rebellion and was forced to resort to expediency. In late September he was encouraging the earl of Desmond to crush the revolt in his own way while the lord justice awaited reinforcements from England, namely 2,500 men and five frigates, to patrol the coast of Munster which were ordered, countermanded and reordered as reports arrived of the progress of Fitzmaurice's insurrection. As the reinforcements dribbled into Ireland, Drury's health was fading and he was carried away to Waterford where he died soon after. When Ormond took the field against the rebel forces in December, his army was hopelessly inadequate. Consisting of 950 men who were 'sickly, unapparelled, . . . almost utterly unvictualled', and lacking sufficient ordnance and supplies, the earl's men could achieve little.[115]

In February of the following year the floundering earl of Desmond, who had been declared a rebel in October 1579, was discovered to have held a conference with French and Spanish messengers who visited him in his house at the Island in Kerry. These men reported that Philip and Henri III had been informed that none of the Geraldines were alive. The earl was also notified that Philip had appointed 30,000 men, along with governors and two of Fitzmaurice's sons, to be dispatched to Ireland. Desmond was allegedly told that Henri would supply him with a number of soldiers after some time had

---

112 Sir Humphrey Gilbert to Lord Justice Drury, Aug. 1579, *The Walsingham letter-book or register of Ireland, May 1578 to December 1579*, ed. James Hogan and M. McNeill O'Farrell, Dublin 1959, 121.
113 The privy council to the earl of Desmond, [9] Jan. 1579, ibid. 32. For accounts of other French soldiers in Ireland at this time see Lord Justice Drury and the council in Ireland to the privy council, 12 Sept. 1579, ibid. 173; examinations taken before Sir Nicholas Malby, 10 Sept. 1579, ibid. 180–1.
114 Burghley to the earl of Ormond, 26 Jan. 1580, SP 63/71/59–60v; Ellis, *Ireland in the age of the Tudors*, 311–12.
115 Ellis, *Ireland in the age of the Tudors*, 312–13.

elapsed.[116] The Spanish messenger promised that a force would arrive within a month of their departure but this failed to materialise.

Fear of another foreign invasion exerted a pronounced catalytic effect on English defence policy as was evident in increased English vigilance and expenditure on troops and supplies for Ireland. Dr Nicholas Sanders's preaching a crusade and extolling rebel successes in letters addressed to correspondents in France and Spain convinced Elizabeth of the necessity for reinforcements and by February the English garrison had been increased to 2,800 men.[117] While English officials remained alert throughout the summer months to reports of ships in Spanish ports preparing to depart for Ireland in support of the Geraldine cause, the second Desmond rebellion was slowly nearing an end. The earl's appeal for peace, combined with widespread starvation and deprivation in Munster, and evaporating support for the rebels, all pointed to an imminent end to the protracted hostilities.

During the course of the two Desmond rebellions (1569–72 and 1579–83), the rounds of concerted negotiations conducted by James Fitzmaurice and his team of envoys employed in Paris, Madrid, Rome and Lisbon yielded paltry results. In spite of all the promises, the French and the papacy only dispatched small fleets in 1570 and 1579 respectively. Yet their protracted engagement with Europe's Catholic leaders exerted an important catalytic impact on the course of the rebellions and the manner in which the English authorities in Whitehall and in Ireland dealt with the insurgents. It caused Fitzmaurice's hopeful followers to drag out a campaign that, by his own admission, steadily lost its momentum and direction in his absence and therefore contributed to the wholesale destruction of Munster and accentuated the hardship inflicted on both English and Irish inhabitants in the province. It demonstrated to Elizabeth and her ministers that the Irish were deliberately and very effectively using their Catholicism to annex their cause to that of the continental Catholic powers in an effort to undermine her position.

Moreover, Fitzmaurice's success in securing continental backing in two expeditions within the space of nine years forced the English administration in Whitehall begrudgingly to spend comparatively extraordinary amounts to secure Ireland's defence. Throughout the 1570s and 1580s the 'policies' of the English administrations in Whitehall and Dublin in respect of Ireland's defence remained the product of expediency. For Whitehall officials, the maintenance of the island kingdom was secondary to England's more vital struggles with the French and the Spaniards, particularly in relation to the Netherlands and to religious confrontation with the papacy. For their counterparts in the Dublin administration, the refusal of the queen and the English privy council to dispatch the requisite men, munitions and supplies resulted in their being forced to make the best of the inadequate resources

---

[116] Sir William Pelham to the privy council, 11 Feb. 1580, *Carew MSS, 1575–88*, 216; Lord Roche to Ormond, 11 Feb. 1580, ibid. 217.
[117] Ellis, *Ireland in the age of the Tudors*, 313.

they had to suppress all disturbances. However, the appearance of a real threat of foreign invasion did impact on English reactions, goading the privy council into authorising the muster of a substantial standby force in September 1577 and forcing Elizabeth to augment the English garrison in February 1580.[118]

The shift in Irish solicitations from France to Rome and Madrid was evident between the first and second Desmond rebellions. In 1569–72 Fitzmaurice concentrated much of his effort on securing French assistance, and his modest success in doing so undoubtedly caused him to target the French court when he prepared to mount a second rebellion in the late 1570s. However, by 1577 he realised that his efforts in France were in vain and therefore transferred his energies to targeting the papacy and Philip II, though developments in domestic politics in Scotland meant that he never entirely abandoned hope of French and specifically Guise assistance.

VII

The unexpected outbreak in Leinster of another rebellion, led by a young Catholic gentleman of the Pale, James Eustace, third Viscount Baltinglass, in 1580 opened a last brief and ill-fated round of Franco-Irish intrigue that ended in 1584 and that was far less consequential than Fitzmaurice's designs. Thereafter, all Irish appeals were definitively deflected away from the French court towards the increasingly well-disposed Escorial. Eustace, who had recently returned from Rome, fired with enthusiasm for the Catholic Counter- Reformation, had been in contact with the rebels in Munster prior to joining the disaffected chief of the O'Byrne clan, Feagh MacHugh, in attacking the New English seneschal of Wicklow. He displayed the papal banner in mounting his attack and invited the support of Gerald, eleventh earl of Kildare. He provocatively declared that 'a woman uncapax of all holy orders' had no right to be supreme governor of the Church, and that Ireland had witnessed 'more oppressing of poor subjects under pretence of justice' during Elizabeth's reign than ever before.[119]

The Dublin administration took an especially serious view of Eustace's revolt since he was an important Tudor noble whose family had been traditional enemies of the O'Byrnes and who had heretofore, in the main, been loyal servants of the crown. He was soon joined by Fitzmaurice's close ally, Dr Nicholas Sanders. In reality the revolt was a fiasco, being almost exclusively confined to Gaelic clansmen while the Pale community, excepting a handful of fervently Catholic lawyers and leading Dublin merchants, remained unsympathetic. As a result it quickly collapsed. The newly-

[118] Sasso, 'Desmond rebellions', 162.
[119] Ellis, *Ireland in the age of the Tudors*, 314–15.

appointed lord deputy, Arthur, Baron Grey de Wilton, launched a savagely repressive campaign against the insurgents, deploying his 6,500-strong army about the southern Pale and its marches throughout the autumn and winter of 1580. This, combined with his pursuit of a scorched earth policy in Munster, and the massacre of the Italian and Spanish troops by English forces at Smerwick in November 1580, ensured the effective and immediate suppression of disturbances in the Pale and the confinement of unrest to Munster. By Christmas the threat of the insurrection had receded and Grey had imprisoned the earl of Kildare and the baron of Delvin in Dublin castle on suspicion of having abetted Baltinglass.[120]

Devlin's imprisonment precipitated another conspiracy in Leinster. His brother, William Nugent, conspired to release him and gained the support of several gentlemen, most of them from Meath and Westmeath. Nugent also secured the assistance of Brian Macgeoghegan and Brian O'Rourke, two Gaelic lords from the northern midlands. However, by late 1581 the conspiracy had disintegrated and a number of its leaders were under arrest. In 1581 and 1582 the rebels' flagging struggle suffered a succession of further fatal blows. Nicholas Sanders died. James, Viscount Baltinglass, fled to Spain. William Nugent and Brian Macgeoghegan escaped via Ulster and Scotland into France where Macgeoghegan stayed while Nugent, accompanied by Fr Leonard Fitzsimons and one servant, travelled to Rome.[121] Like O'Brien of Thomond in 1570 and Fitzmaurice in the 1570s, Macgeoghegan adopted a two-fronted strategy, allowing the English ambassador, Sir Henry Cobham, to believe that he was a contrite subject seeking a royal pardon while actively seeking French support for his resistance to the queen. Unlike Fitzmaurice, however, he does not appear to have been granted an audience with Henri III.[122] His concerted targeting of the Guise faction in France in preference to the French king was undoubtedly determined by the fact that the Guises alone had furnished Fitzmaurice with a fleet. It may also be seen as symptomatic of the Irish dissidents' sensitivity to the changes in French domestic politics and in international political alignments that had been crystallising since the late 1570s as the Guises grew steadily closer to forging an alliance with the Spanish crown.

Like Gerald Fitzgerald and James Fitzmaurice, Macgeoghegan and Nugent sought to incorporate Ireland within a pan-European Catholic alliance against the Protestant queen of England. While Irish hopes hinged primarily

120 Ibid. 314; Lennon, *Sixteenth-century Ireland*, 202–3; Brady, *Chief governors*, 204–6, 209–12; Palmer, *Problem of Ireland*, 113.
121 Examination of Nowland Tadee relative to the journey of William Nugent . . ., 23 Jan. 1584, SP 63/107/ 8–9. See also Ellis, *Ireland in the age of the Tudors*, 316–18; Palmer, *Problem of Ireland*, 114. For a detailed discussion of Nugent's rebellion see Helen Coburn Walsh, 'The rebellion of William Nugent, 1581', in R. V. Comerford, Mary Cullen, J. R. Hill and Colm Lennon (eds), *Religion, conflict and coexistence in Ireland: essays presented to Monsignor Patrick J. Corish*, Dublin 1990, 26–52.
122 Brian Macgeoghegan to Walsingham, 28 Oct. 1582, SP 63/96/111–v.

on a positive response from the Spanish and papal courts, Macgeoghegan's independent overtures to the papal nuncio in France and to the Guises were well conceived. Henri III was acutely conscious of the duc de Guise's increasingly close ties with Philip II in the 1570s: it was fear of them that spurred the French king to assume leadership of the Catholic League in France in 1576.[123] Early in 1578, following several years of tension with Henri, the Guises temporarily withdrew from the French court following a duel staged between the king's *mignons* and a number of Guise allies.[124] Brian Macgeoghegan's targeting of the Guise faction at this juncture is therefore unlikely to have been motivated by a hope that the French *grandees* would lobby Henri III to provide him with military aid. Rather, it is more probable that they were targeted in their own right as France's powerful militantly Catholic dynasty with very substantial military resources at their disposal who had an active interest in Scottish affairs, who were growing ever closer to the Spanish monarch and whose supporter, de la Roche, had previously honoured a promise of aid to Fitzmaurice. All of these factors boded well for the prospect of a foreign invasion of Ireland.[125]

In contrast with Fitzmaurice's campaign for direct continental aid for his rebellion, and in a manner reminiscent of the 1550s and 1560s, Irish lords and their envoys seeking continental backing for their resistance to the Elizabethan *régime* in the early 1580s investigated the possibility of annexing their campaign to plans for mounting a French attack on Elizabethan England *via* Scotland. Throughout much of the 1570s, while Mary Stuart was detained in England, Scotland was left to resolve its own problems as France, and specifically the Guises, were immersed in domestic wars and displayed little interest in involvement in Scottish affairs. As a consequence, England was temporarily relieved of France's episodic pursuit of ambitions in the north and was content to see Scotland neutralised as an international player.[126]

However, in the late 1570s the Guises attempted to revive their strong dynastic ties with Scotland as they resolved to restore their niece, Mary Stuart, to the Scottish throne and to re-establish Catholicism in her realm. To that end, in September 1579, the French *grandees* dispatched an emissary, Esmé Stuart, seigneur d'Aubigny and later duke of Lennox, to Scotland where he immediately became a favourite of the young King James VI.[127] By June 1581 Elizabeth again faced the threat of French intervention in

123 Garrisson, *Sixteenth-century France*, 276.

124 Knecht, *French wars of religion, 1559–1598*, 63–4.

125 Crowson, *Tudor foreign policy*, 202.

126 See Gordon Donaldson, *All the queen's men: power and politics in Mary Stuart's Scotland*, London 1983; George Hewitt, *Scotland under Morton, 1572–80*, Edinburgh 1982; Nicholls, *Modern British Isles*, 289.

127 Crowson, *Tudor foreign policy*, 208; Wernham, *Before the Armada*, 363–4; Nicholls, *Modern British Isles*, 294.

Scotland. Agents representing Philip and the Guises were stationed in Edinburgh, plotting the 'enterprise' whereby England would be overrun by simultaneous attacks from north and south.

Esmé Stuart's design to win Scotland over to Catholicism in autumn 1582
collapsed in August with the Ruthven raid in which James VI was kidnapped
by Stuart's Scottish opponents. As a result of the raid, and forsaken even by
his closest friends, Stuart returned to France in December.[128] Thereafter
James's increasingly close contacts with the Guises and the pope led Elizabeth
to suspect that he intended to convert to Catholicism and lent further weight
to her suspicions of a Catholic conspiracy against her.[129] In the highly
charged climate of international politics, Macgeoghegan and Nugent's solicitations in Paris and Rome during the period 1582 to 1584 served to heighten
Elizabeth's anxiety at threats to British security.[130] Throughout 1583 officials
in Whitehall and Dublin were repeatedly briefed on reports of imminent
French, Spanish and papal-backed attacks on Ireland, England and Scotland.[131] By early December Macgeoghegan was in Rome, having refused to
accept the conditions for a royal pardon offered to him by the English ambassador to France, Sir Henry Cobham.[132]

Late in January the following year the prospects of the Irishmen securing
continental aid in the immediate future seemed particularly promising. The
cardinal of Como held regular meetings with Nugent and Macgeoghegan to
apprise them of the most recent reports from the Escorial and 'put them in
comfort that they shall have succour shortly'. If plans proceeded as scheduled,
the pope would dispatch Macgeoghegan to Paris, and then into Scotland and
Ireland, to alert Gaelic allies to be 'in readiness'.[133]

At Easter 1584 the papacy was optimistic regarding the possibility of
merging Scottish interests with those of the Irish fugitives. The cardinal of
Como sent Macgeoghegan and his son to Paris where the nuncio and James
Beaton, bishop of Glasgow, referred them to the duc de Guise. He in turn
arranged for them to meet with certain Scottish lords and entrusted them
with letters addressed to King James VI.[134] The fears of councillors in both
Whitehall and Dublin at the Scottish king's collusion with the Guises and

---

[128] Wernham, *Before the Armada*, 364; Crowson, *Tudor foreign policy*, 209; Nicholls,
Modern British Isles, 296.
[129] Quoted in Crowson, *Tudor foreign policy*, 209.
[130] Sasso, 'Desmond rebellions', 344.
[131] Sir Patrick Walshe to Walsingham, 5 Mar. 1583, *CSP Ireland, 1574–85*, 432; Wallop to
Walsingham, 17 Mar. 1583, ibid. 434; lords justices and council to the privy council, 17
Apr. 1583, ibid. 442; Richard Whyte to the lords justices, 27 June 1583, SP 63/103/24–5v
(enclosure); mayor and recorder of Limerick to Ormond, 1 Sept. 1583, SP 63/104/164;
lords justices to Walsingham, 20 Oct. 1583, *CSP Ireland 1574–85*, 475; Macgeoghegan to
Walter Hope, 2 Dec. 1583, SP 63/106/2.
[132] Macgeoghegan to Hope, 2 Dec. 1583, SP 63/106/2.
[133] Examination of Nowland Tadee, 23 Jan. 1584, SP 63/107/28–9.
[134] True and simple declaration delivered by William Nugent to Lord Deputy Sir John
Perrot, 4 Dec. 1584, SP 63/113/24.

the papacy reached new heights in April owing to a report that 1,000 French troops had arrived in remote areas of Scotland.[135] It was in Ireland that evidence of a Hiberno-Scottish conspiracy was uncovered. In August Lord Deputy Sir John Perrot foiled a seditious plot in which Turlough Luineach, assisted by the Scottish king's forces, the rebels of Munster and Connaught and Spaniards due to land at Sligo, intended to stage an insurrection. William Nugent was identified as a party to that plot on the grounds that he had lately travelled from France to Scotland, whence he had recently departed.[136]

By August 1584, however, English fear of French or Spanish designs on Scotland was diminished though not eliminated when James accepted a gift of £5,000 from the English ambassador and assented to a possible military alliance with England.[137] Upon his return to Ireland from Scotland, William Nugent was captured by Sir John Perrot. Under interrogation, he declared that the duc de Guise had been in regular correspondence with the pope, Spain and Scotland and claimed that a Spanish expedition, funded largely by the papacy, would be dispatched to Ireland by the end September at the very latest, though this fleet failed to materialise.[138]

On the 31 August Philip II and the duc de Guise signed the Treaty of Joinville and formed an alliance whereby Philip undertook to subsidise the Catholic League.[139] According to Paul Crowson, the treaty resulted in the relegation of the Guises to the status of 'subsidized dependants of Spain'.[140] From that point onwards, both parties' interests were pursued in tandem and independent French designs on Ireland were effectively abandoned, demonstrating the crucial importance of the Guises as the primary agents in Franco-Irish intrigue. In 1585 Walsingham was warned that 'the duke of Guise himself will invade England by way of Scotland, and other Spanish forces are to enter Ireland'.[141] By that stage, however, Scotland was no longer a priority for Elizabeth and her councillors. The death of the fifth earl of Argyll, a former ally of the Ulster lords, in 1573, the conclusion of the Treaty of Berwick with the Scots in July 1586 and, in particular, Mary Stuart's execution in February of the following year, terminated the Guise faction's interest in Scottish affairs, effectively relegating Scotland to a very low position on the English agenda and diminishing the likelihood of a Franco-Scottish invasion of Ireland.[142]

---

135 Lords justices to Walsingham, 14 Apr. 1584, SP 63/109/69–v; Captain Dawtrey to the Lord Justice Wallop, 16 Apr. 1584, SP 63/109/94–5.
136 Lord deputy and council to the privy council, 6 Aug. 1584, SP 63/111/44r–v.
137 Crowson, *Tudor foreign policy*, 210.
138 True and simple declaration delivered by Nugent to Perrot, 4 Dec. 1584, SP 63/113/24.
139 Knecht, *The French wars of religion*, 66.
140 Crowson, *Tudor foreign policy*, 202.
141 Thomas Rogers's report to Walsingham, 11 Aug. 1585, *CSP Foreign, 1584–5*, 716.
142 See *DNB* viii (1886), 318; Mason, *Scotland and England*; Michael Lynch (ed.), *Mary Stewart, queen in three kingdoms*, Oxford 1988; Jenny Wormald, *Mary Queen of Scots: a study in failure*, London 1988; Nicholls, *Modern British Isles*, 298.

VIII

Throughout the 1570s the monarchs of England, France and Spain respectively had shown themselves loath to become involved in the domestic affairs of each other's realms. Elizabeth was cautious in her dealings with the Dutch rebels, fearing reprisals at the hands of Philip and she was careful to lend support to the French Huguenots on a clandestine basis. Henri III resisted the temptation to become overtly involved with Fitzmaurice, and Philip II concealed his role in plots to undermine the Elizabethan *régime* in England and in Ireland. Their reluctance to back Fitzmaurice in the 1570s must be assessed in the light of its implications for both monarchs' relations with Elizabeth, with each other, with the Netherlands and with powerful court factions within each country. However, Philip's gravitation towards overt hostility to Elizabeth became evident in his resort to increasingly provocative measures in dealing with the English queen during the early 1580s and culminated in the Armada in 1588.[143] This served to strengthen the appeal of Spain as the most likely source of assistance to Irish dissidents and any fears of French intrigue with Irish rebels faded into insignificance during the remaining years of the sixteenth century, ending this unprecedented phase of tentative political relations between Ireland and France. The explanation for this is largely to be found in developments in French domestic politics that exerted a direct effect on Anglo-French relations, rendering them forcibly amicable.

During the Spanish Armada crisis, Elizabeth was fortunate to have benefited from the refusal of French royalist governors at Brest, Saint-Malo, Le Havre, Dieppe, Boulogne and Calais, to allow Spaniards access to their deep-water harbours, thereby undermining her enemy's chances of success. The accession of the Huguenot Henri of Bourbon to the throne as Henri IV, following the assassination of Henri III in 1589, also augured well for Anglo-French relations. At that stage Henri's priority was the very real Spanish threat to France. Philip II had supported the Catholic League through subsidies to the duc de Guise from 1585. He had sent a Spanish army under the duke of Parma to take Paris and Rouen in 1590 and 1592. In 1594, when the Nine Years' War proper commenced in Ireland, the French king had far greater issues to occupy his attention as his realm was in the throes of the last of the century's wars of religion. Henri IV's conversion to Catholicism a year earlier had paved the way for his reconciliation with the majority of the leadership of the Catholic League and the concomitant submission of league cities including Rouen, Saint-Malo, Rheims, Amiens, Lyons and, most importantly, Paris by 1594. None the less, Spain supported Marseilles's opposition to Henri until 1596 and supplied subsidies and troops to hard-line elements of the League, notably the duc de Mercoeur in Brittany, the duc de

---

[143] See Wernham, *Before the Armada*, ch. xxvii.

Joyeuse in Languedoc, Charles Emmanuel in Lyons and the duc de Lorraine in north-eastern France, who held out against Henri IV until 1598. Fearful of League opponents within France and of their Spanish allies, Henri appealed to Elizabeth I for support on successive occasions during the 1580s and 1590s. The queen responded generously with over 11,000 English troops to serve in Henri's campaigns in Normandy, Picardy and Brittany, leaving the king acutely conscious of his enforced position of dependence upon Elizabeth's continued goodwill towards him.[144] When in 1596, just a year after he had declared war on Spain, Henri's campaign against the Spanish was floundering, Elizabeth once again supplied her ally with troops. Two years later (in 1598), Henri reached a peace agreement with Spain and became reconciled with the last of the hard-line Catholic League leaders.

Throughout the greater part of the Nine Year's War in Ireland, therefore, Henri's complete reliance on Elizabeth's support for his campaigns against the League and the Spanish precluded even the possibility of any collaboration between the French crown and the Ulster lords who were allies of his Spanish enemies. Prior to the cessation of hostilities in France and the signing of the peace treaty with Spain in 1598, Henri constantly strove to ensure that Elizabeth had no grounds for suspecting him of offering any form of support or assistance to her Irish rebels. At no point, then, in the course of the Nine Years' War did Henri lend encouragement to the rebel forces in Ireland: nor, it appears, did any Irish lord approach the French king for military or financial support after James Fitzmaurice's appeal to Henri III in the mid- to late 1570s. In spite of Henri IV's conversion to Catholicism in 1593, he made no attempt to embark upon a defence of Catholicism in Ireland. Indeed, one cannot but be struck by his indifference to the war in Ireland, and by the extremely limited interest that Ireland evidently held for him, when reading a letter that he wrote to the earl of Essex, in late 1595 or early 1596. Henri asked the earl to send him a pair of Irish hares, one male and one female, so that he could breed them for hunting, his favourite pursuit.[145] However, in his defence, Henri could hardly be expected to involve himself in a foreign campaign given that he was struggling to assert his right to the French crown and was hard pressed in terms of men and money to continue with his protracted campaigns against the Catholic League and the Spanish within France.[146]

Like Henri IV, the Catholic League's forces were too deeply immersed in waging their domestic campaign against the king to be in a position to contemplate serious involvement in Irish affairs. Consequently there is only anecdotal evidence of the most modest planned collaboration on the part of individuals resident in pro-Catholic League cities and towns in France with rebel forces in Ireland both immediately prior to and during the Nine Year's

144 Crowson, *Tudor foreign policy*, 185–6.
145 Henri IV to Essex, 29 Dec.–8 Jan. 1595–6, HMC, *Salisbury MSS*, v. 511.
146 Warren, *Elizabeth I*, 100–1.

War. Certain influential French ecclesiastics and ardent supporters of the Catholic League did lend their support to the Irish in the war. These included the cardinal of Joyeuse, one of France's most high-profile clerics and member of a hard-line Catholic League dynasty, who had Bernard O'Donnell, a leading clerical envoy of the Irish lords, reside in his palace at Toulouse for a period of ten months in 1592 while he was engaged in a round of negotiations on the continent in the early 1590s. Three years later the cardinal was in Brussels when news of the success of the Irish side in the Battle of the Yellow Ford came through, and he and those Irish there were reported to have rejoiced at the good news. The seminary at Rheims, the symbol of Catholic France and a bastion of the Catholic League, was singled out in early 1596 by Sir John Dowdall, an English captain in charge of Dungannon fort, for being especially instrumental in inciting sedition in Ireland through its practice of issuing young Irish and Englishmen with instructions to 'seduce the people to disobedience and rebellion'.[147] These were exception, however. Overall, Henri IV's rigid adherence to a neutral stance during the Nine Years' War eliminated the possibility of Franco-Irish intrigue, and as a consequence Anglo-French relations remained on an even footing throughout the 1590s and into the first decade of the seventeenth century.

[147] Dowdall to Lord Burghley, 9 Mar. 1596, CSP Ireland, 1592–96, 484–8. See also Mary Ann Lyons, 'Reluctant Collaborators'.

7

France and the Fall-Out from the Nine Years' War in Ireland, 1603–1610

The opening years of the seventeenth century heralded a series of changes in politics in Ireland, France and on the international stage that brought to an end the episodic political engagement of the sixteenth century between Irish dissidents and the French for several decades to come. After the Spanish Armada, and throughout the 1590s, disaffected Irish lords consistently directed all their pleas for military aid at the Spanish and papal courts. However, a slight glimmer of hope for a possible French invasion of Ireland still survived so long as Hugh O'Neill, earl of Tyrone, and Hugh Roe O'Donnell of Tyrconnell led their campaign to forestall the Anglicisation of Ulster. Elizabeth I's decisive defeat of the joint Gaelic and Spanish forces led by O'Neill, O'Donnell and Don Juan del Águila at the battle of Kinsale in 1601, in the final challenge to the Tudor regime, and the departure from Ireland in 1607 of O'Neill and Rory O'Donnell (Hugh Roe's brother), the last of the greatest potentates of the Gaelic polity, effectively quashed the possibility of any further collusion between Irish rebels and the French. Henri IV's unwillingness to annoy James I, who concluded the Treaty of London with Spain in 1604, James's search for a Spanish or French bride and his resolution to concentrate on securing his position in England meanwhile proved decisive in ensuring the maintenance of stable amicable relations between the three monarchs in the first decade of the seventeenth century.[1] Consequently, in the early years of the century Franco-Irish relations reverted to those traditional contacts based on commerce, military service and migration which had been maintained throughout the sixteenth century notwithstanding sporadic and ill-fated attempts to establish tentative political relations between the two countries.

In the late sixteenth and early seventeenth centuries new trends were manifest in the patterns of Irish migration to France. While the perennial migration of Irish soldiers, clerics and clerical students that dated from the late medieval era continued,[2] from the early years of the reign of Elizabeth I the number of clerics, both secular and regular, who resorted to French

---

[1]   Philip II died in September 1598 and was succeeded by his son, Philip III. See Godfrey Davies, *The early Stuarts 1603–1660*, repr. Oxford 1976, 47–67.
[2]   Astrik Gabriel, 'Les Étudiants étrangers à l'Université de Paris au XVe siècle', *Annales de l'Université de Paris* xxix (juill.–déc. 1959), 377.

universities and colleges to pursue their studies swelled to an unprecedented degree as a result of increasingly strident moves to enforce conformity to the Protestant faith.[3] The establishment of the Irish college in Paris in 1578 by Fr John Lee and six other Irish clerics is testimony to the real need that existed for permanent accommodation for the many Irish students who studied for degrees in the theology faculty of the University of Paris in the late sixteenth century.[4] In the 1580s there were sufficient Irish clerics in Rouen to cause the French papal nuncio to recommend that a college be founded in that city too.[5] In the early years of the seventeenth century this community, under the supervision of Stephen Duffy, was dependent upon the city's ecclesiastical establishment for alms.[6] A County Cork cleric named Dermot MacCarthy founded an Irish college in Bordeaux in 1603.[7] In each of their host cities or towns these Irish clerics enjoyed the patronage and protection of either key public or ecclesiastical figures or of the local ecclesiastical establishment. In the case of the Irish college in Paris, it was the baron de l'Escalopier, one-time president of the *parlement* of Paris, who assumed the role of benefactor to the community of priests. The Irish college in Bordeaux had perhaps one of France's strongest supporters of Counter-Reformation Catholicism, Cardinal de Sourdis, as its patron. The small community of Irish clerics in Rouen had, as noted, the financial support of the ecclesiastical establishment in that city, though the lack of any single sponsor explains its precarious history.

However, the benevolent patronage afforded Irish Catholic clerics was reserved for them alone amongst Irish immigrants who fled to France in the sixteenth and early seventeenth centuries. The reasons for this are clear. Their numbers were small. They were clearly identifiable as genuine religious

[3] See Boyle, *The Irish college in Paris*; 'The Irish college at Paris, 1578–1901'; and 'The Irish college at Bordeaux'; Daumet, 'Les Établissements religieux: fin'; O'Boyle, *The Irish colleges on the continent*; Walsh, *The Irish continental college movement*; Ó Fiach, *The Irish colleges in France*; Swords, *Soldiers, scholars, priests*; Flynn, *The Irish Dominicans*, 210–12; Brockliss and Ferté, 'A prosopography of Irish clerics', and 'Irish clerics in France: a statistical survey'.

[4] Collège des Irlandais, Paris, file 3 B2, A no. 1 (3); L'Abbé Lebeuf, *Histoire de la ville et de tout le diocèse de Paris*, new edn, 5 vols, Paris 1864, ii. 733; Boyle, *The Irish college in Paris*, and 'The Irish college at Paris'; Daumet, 'Les Établissements religieux', 89–91; Hayes, *Biographical dictionary*, 155; Ó Fíaich, *The Irish colleges in France*, 8; Swords, *Soldiers, scholars, priests*; Brockliss and Ferté, 'A prosopography of Irish clerics'.

[5] *Girolamo Ragazzoni*, 332–3.

[6] Tomás Ó Fíaich (*The Irish colleges in France*, 9) claims that a college was established in Rouen in 1612. However, such a college was not comparable to those in Paris or Bordeaux since there is little evidence to suggest that it had any permanent premises and its existence appears to have been very short-term. For details of grants of alms to the Irish clerics see AD, Seine-Maritime, Rouen, G.2187, G.2315, G.2319, G.2320.

[7] Antoine-Louis Bertrand, *Histoire des séminaires de Bordeaux et de Bazas*, 3 vols, Bordeaux 1894, i. 322ff.; Boyle, 'The Irish college at Bordeaux'; Walsh, *The Irish continental college movement*, ch. ii.

refugees. They fulfilled religious duties in their parish communities. They begged for alms under licence from the municipal authorities. As such, they were identified as legitimate beneficiaries of sponsorship.[8] However, in the wake of the Nine Years' War in particular, there occurred an unprecedented though short-lived surge of outward migration from Ireland to England, Wales, Spain and France of several thousand Irish servicemen and peasants down to *c.* 1610. The sheer number of these impoverished immigrants with whom the French authorities were suddenly burdened provoked a unilaterally inhospitable reception, which contrasts sharply with that afforded their clerical compatriots and the earls from Ulster who passed through France in 1607.

I

The most profound and immediate impact of the Nine Years' War on France was the arrival of Irish migrants in its ports, cities and towns from the 1590s onwards. Arising from the protracted war and a scorched earth policy on both sides, large sections of Ireland lay devastated, crops were burned, herds of cattle were slaughtered and buildings completely razed. Ulster was a virtual wilderness. In Munster, the area to the west of Cork was left almost uninhabited. The country's trade was seriously disrupted, its coinage debased, towns ruined or languishing in decline, and the population decimated by famine.[9] Fynes Moryson, secretary to Lord Deputy Sir Charles Blount, Lord Mountjoy (1600–3), provided graphic accounts of the dire circumstances to which the inhabitants of Ulster had been reduced by 1603:

> No spectacle was more frequent in the ditches of towns, and especially in wasted countries, than to see multitudes of these poor people dead, with their mouths all coloured green by eating nettles, docks, and all things they could rend up above the ground.[10]

Such extreme hardship experienced by the population as a whole rendered a substantial proportion of Gaelic peasants and their families destitute, notably in the province of Munster in the south, and to a lesser extent in the western and northern provinces of Connaught and Ulster, leaving them with little choice but to emigrate. Moreover, immediately the war ended, several thousand galloglas and kerne suddenly found themselves unemployed. Those who left Ireland following the cessation of the Nine Years' War did so because peace-time opportunities for employment were overwhelmed by their rapid

---

8   See n. 3 above.
9   Ellis, *Ireland in the age of the Tudors*, 353. See O'Sullivan Beare, *Ireland under Elizabeth*, 181, for a Gaelic perspective. See also Clarke, 'The Irish economy', and Gillespie, *Transformation*; Lyons, ' "Vagabonds, "mendiants", "gueux" '.
10 Quoted in D. B. Quinn, *The Elizabethans and the Irish*, New York 1965, 140.

demobilisation. It is estimated that from the early 1600s onwards, an average of 1,000 Irish soldiers and their dependants migrated annually to continental Europe and England in search of employment.[11]

The Nine Years' War accelerated the ongoing trickle of emigration that had followed the devastation of Munster in the 1580s. As Patrick Fitzgerald's work has illustrated, England and Wales were the principal destinations for Irish migrants in the 1580s following the second Desmond rebellion in Munster (1579–83). As early as December 1583 the English privy council referred to the 'great number of poor Irish people . . . begging in and about this city [London]'. By the mid-1590s they were arriving 'bag and baggage' in Bristol. Such was the scale of the problem that in 1601 the city council was obliged to appoint a special official to oversee their repatriation. Two years later Pembrokeshire in south-west Wales was said to have been inundated with Irish migrants who had fled the 'late wars in Ireland'.[12] In addition, the war and its aftermath precipitated a sharp acceleration in the rate of Irish migration to Flanders, Spain and France where redundant Gaelic galloglas and kerne had enlisted in continental regiments from the 1580s onwards.[13]

From the late 1590s the Dublin administration had been mindful of the magnitude of the problem of troublesome redundant Gaelic servicemen remaining in Ireland and presented the English privy council with a formal request to have Gaelic troops deployed in the queen's service in the Low Countries or France. However, Whitehall dismissed this suggestion as impractical. On several occasions during the early 1600s the proposal to deport Gaelic soldiers was revived: in 1601 Charles Blount, Lord Mountjoy, had hoped that Irish soldiers might migrate to the Low Countries or to the Indies. There was a suggestion that Irish soldiers be sent to colonise Virginia in 1607, and in 1609 approximately 1,000 soldiers were shipped from Ulster to Sweden under the command of Colonel Stewart.[14] In the event, the failure to implement the majority of these proposals was compensated for by the 'spontaneous' emigration of several thousand Irish soldiers and peasants, along with their families, to Wales, England and continental Europe in the wake of the battle of Kinsale. But if the Dublin and Whitehall administrations had anticipated the problem of redundant Gaelic servicemen, they

---

[11] Cullen, 'The Irish diaspora', 121–2, 138–9.

[12] Fitzgerald, 'Poor Irish migrants in England', 13–35.

[13] See Henry, *The Irish military community*.

[14] Lords Justices Archbishop Adam Loftus and Robert Gardiner, Ormond and the council to the privy council, 4 May 1598, *CSP Ireland, 1598–9*, 138–9. See also privy council to Loftus and Gardiner, Ormond and the rest of the council, 28 May 1598, ibid. 156; [Hugh Cuff] to [Sir George Carew], Aug. 1600, *CSP Ireland, 1600*, 401; Lord Deputy Sir Charles Blount, Lord Mountjoy, to the privy council, 1 May 1601, *CSP Ireland, 1600–1*, 305. See also Fynes Moryson, *An itinerary . . .*, 3 pts, London 1617; new edn in 4 vols, Glasgow 1907–8, ii. 379; Quinn, *Elizabethans and the Irish*, 119–20; 'Documents relating to the Irish in the West Indies', ed. Aubrey Gwynn, *Analecta Hibernica* iv (1932), 157–8; Henry, *The Irish military community*, 23, 28–9, 32, 41, 71, 107, 112.

failed to foresee or, more important, to make provision for forestalling the exodus of Gaelic Irish which began during the later stages of the Nine Years' War.

The first significant wave of large-scale Irish migration to France reached a climax in the years 1605–7 and stirred the French authorities to adopt immediate legislative measures to stem the influx and to expel the Irish from their jurisdiction. The migrants congregated in Paris, Nantes, Angers, Morlaix, Saint-Malo and Rouen as well as elsewhere in Normandy and Anjou in particular. Like their counterparts who sought relief and employment in Flanders and Spain, those who fled to France were in a particularly disadvantaged state upon their arrival. They had no knowledge of the French language and the majority did not appear to have had a vocational profession by which to earn a living. They were therefore completely dependent upon the charity of the authorities and of the residents of their host cities and towns. Their presence exerted extraordinary pressure on the limited resources of even the most affluent of these urban centres. From the outset they were seen and treated primarily as a threat to public health and order. On those grounds the French crown, provincial government agencies and municipal authorities unilaterally felt compelled to sanction rigorous measures to deal systematically with the problems posed by Irish immigrants, though they appear to have been largely ineffective in ensuring their implementation.

II

From the outset, the Irish were viewed by the French government and municipal bodies as distinct from the Italian, Spanish, Portuguese and German immigrants who had settled in France in the sixteenth century and who had become integrated into the social and economic life of their adopted country.[15] Both French and the English authorities alluded to the Irish migrants collectively, using a stock of indiscriminate, pejorative terms including 'gueux', 'vagabonds', 'mendiants', 'beggars', 'base people', 'wandering Irish', each of which reflected their predominant perception of the Irish as liabilities who eked out an existence by begging, regardless of their profession. More discerning English government officials, and the Gaelic annalists, distinguished between two types of migrants who fled Ireland in the 1590s and early 1600s, 'the wandering Irish' who subsisted as 'poor, indigent, helpless paupers', and those who 'offered themselves as soldiers to foreigners'. However, in reality the division between military service and mendicancy proved extremely tenuous and fluid.[16] This was evident when in 1608 the 'Irish beggars' in France were considered fit subjects to be pressed into English

15 See Lequin, *La Mosaïque France*; Dubost, *Les Étrangers en France*, 86–8.
16 Henry, *The Irish military community*, 48; Ó Cosáin, 'Les Irlandais en Bretagne', 155.

companies. The fact that migrants in France were said to have travelled in 'great companies', combined with the predominantly male composition of the group based in Paris in 1605–6, strongly suggests that a substantial proportion of those who emigrated to France at this time were 'idle swordsmen' by profession.[17]

As in the case of those who resorted to Spanish Flanders, the majority of Irish migrants in France were natives of Munster, with a smaller proportion originating from Connaught and Ulster.[18] The scale of migration from Munster is referred to in a statement by William Lyons, bishop of Cork, Cloyne and Ross, in 1607. He alleged that, 'by credible report, 4,000 or 5,000 are departed [from his dioceses since 1601], some for France, some for Spain'.[19] Most apparently travelled directly from Ireland though there were a number of isolated cases of individuals crossing from England to Breton ports such as Saint-Malo. They paid for their passages, which took at least two days if they sailed from Munster to western Brittany. In general they made the crossing in ships used by merchants to transport cargoes of hides from Ireland.[20]

Apart from the related reasons of unemployment and extreme penury, their motives for migrating to France were varied. Both Lord deputy Sir Arthur Chichester (1604–15), and Fynes Moryson believed that many emigrated to the continent to seek short-term relief and that they intended to return to Ireland *via* England when conditions back home had improved. Chichester also suspected that a large proportion of those who crossed to France and Spain did so with the calculated intention of returning soon after to their true intended destination, England, as they were prohibited from travelling directly from Ireland to England. Again, he identified their primary motive as seeking relief.[21] Others such as Charles Cornwallis, English ambassador to Madrid, held the view that the 'wandering Irish in France and Spain' were biding their time before responding to an anticipated summons to participate in an invasion of Ireland which was to be orchestrated by the

---

[17] Sir Charles Cornwallis to the earl of Salisbury, June 1608, CSP Ireland, 1607–8, 584; advertisement from Brussels, Apr. 1608, ibid. 653.

[18] Sir Arthur Chichester to Salisbury, 2 Nov. 1605, CSP Ireland, 1603–6, 345; instructions for Ireland, 7 June 1606, ibid. 499; the king's instructions to Chichester, 28 Jan. 1607, CSP, Ireland, 1606–8, 98; Henry, The Irish military community, 44–5.

[19] Bishop William Lyons to Chichester, Mar. 1607, CSP Ireland, 1606–8, 132.

[20] Pomponne de Bellièvre to Nicolas de Neufville, sieur de Villeroy, 2 nov. 1605, BN, MS Fr. 15578, fo. 246; Buisseret, 'The Irish at Paris', 60; Département d'Ille-et-Vilaine, ville de Saint-Malo: inventaire sommaire des archives communales, 1393–1800 (n.p. 1991), GG14, registre.

[21] Chichester to the privy council, 29 May 1606, CSP Ireland, 1603–6, 486–7; Chichester to the earl of Salisbury, 4 July 1606, ibid. 512. See also the lords of the council to the lord warden, 7 June 1605, HMC, Thirteenth report, app., pt iv, 132; Quinn, Elizabethans and the Irish, 140.

exiled lords of Ulster around the year 1609.[22] A handful of these migrants cited religious persecution in Ireland as the motive for their flight to France.

It is very likely that a substantial proportion of the Gaelic soldiers and their retinues who were in France in the early 1600s were in fact passing through *en route* from either Ireland or Spain to their ultimate destination, Spanish Flanders, where they enlisted in the army of Albert, archduke of Austria. There is certainly ample evidence of soldiers from Ireland having received licences to pass through France at this time. In June 1606, for example, the Flanders army records the recent arrival of forty-three Irishmen who had journeyed 'from Spain by way of France'. In addition, many Irish immigrants used France as their temporary base when they first arrived on the continent. In the early 1600s Charles O'Daly, for example, left Ireland along with 200 of his relations, kinsmen and friends, most of whom stayed in France while he proceeded to Flanders with the purpose of enlisting them in the service of the Spanish king and obtaining for himself a commission as their captain.[23]

III

Sir Arthur Chichester's assertion in 1603 that a great many fugitive beggars had fled Ireland during the Nine Years' War is corroborated by the response of the provincial *parlement* of Brittany to their arrival in the early 1600s. By 1603 the problem of Irish vagrants roaming the province had grown so serious as to cause the *parlement* at Rennes to order its *substituts généraux* to compile a report recording the number and names of Irish migrants who had arrived as well as the names of those mariners who had transported them in their ships to Brittany.[24] The Irish were not the only immigrant group to be targeted by the Breton *parlement* at this time: in 1598, an order was issued to effect the immediate expulsion of all gypsies ('*Egyptians*' or '*bohemiens*' in contemporary nomenclature) who had settled in the suburbs of Rennes.[25] The *états* of Brittany invoked the *parlement* to prohibit all mariners from facilitating the passage of any further Irish migrants into the ports of the province. Henri IV lent his support to the legislative measures adopted by the provincial authorities by issuing letters in 1606 in which he commanded all Irish '*mendiants*' and '*gueux*' who had sought refuge in his realm to return to their own country immediately. These letters were to be posted or read in the ports of France and,

---

22 Advertisement from Brussels, Apr. 1608, *CSP Ireland, 1606–8*, 652–3; Henry, *The Irish military community*, 47–8. For a study of the earls' intrigues on the continent see Kerney Walsh, *An exile of Ireland.*
23 Henry, *The Irish military community*, 45, 71.
24 Lyons, ' "Vagabonds", "mendiants", "gueux" ', 366. Regrettably this report has not survived.
25 Carré, *Essai*, 490.

in the cases of Rouen and Saint-Malo, publicised to the sound of trumpets and drums.[26]

The municipal authorities in Morlaix were among the first to adopt stiff measures to eradicate the problem of the growing number of Irish who arrived in the port in the early 1600s. Morlaix was a small town and had few resources to meet the demands made by the unwelcome Irish. More particularly, in the aftermath of the wars of the Catholic League, the town's hinterland was devastated and its population, having withstood an outbreak of plague and reduced to famine, gravitated towards local towns and villages in search of alms.[27] Morlaix's ramparts lay in ruins and the municipal authority was in debt to the tune of 42,000 *livres*. At the time of the arrival of the Irish, there is evidence of their being a *hôtel-dieu* in the town with the poor being accommodated in a *hôpital*.[28] In the early 1600s Morlaix was therefore undergoing a phase of major structural repair and its municipal authority, the *communauté*, needed all available resources to fund it.[29]

In April 1605 the police were ordered to command all Irish migrants in the town and its suburbs to return to their country. By order of the *ministère de l'exécuteur de la haute justice*, they were to return to Roscoff whence they were to depart for Ireland.[30] The town's sergeant, Nicolas Cubert, and a clerk were hired to oversee the expulsion of the Irish and several payments were made to the officials involved in expediting it the following year. Clearly, by virtue of their number, the Irish were regarded as posing a particularly pressing problem for the Morlaix authorities at a difficult time. However, the simultaneous expulsion of other mendicants suggests that the presence of the Irish merely served to accentuate existing problems of vagrancy and deprivation in the aftermath of the League wars which the *communauté*, the police and the *hôpital* struggled to contend with in the early years of the seventeenth century. Moreover the drive to expel them in 1606 evidently failed to rid the town of Irish migrants as in 1609, new orders had to be issued for their deportation.[31]

Nantes was the destination of a substantial number of Irish migrants since Irish mariners were familiar with this port town and it enjoyed a reputation as a safe haven for Catholic asylum-seekers during the Elizabethan period. However, the migrants who arrived there in the early 1600s were afforded a

---

[26] Ó Ciosáin, 'Les Irlandais en Bretagne', 154; Lyons, ' "Vagabonds", "mendiants", "gueux" ', 367.

[27] Concern at the possibility of another outbreak of plague in the town predated the arrival of the Irish: Joseph Daumesnil, *Histoire de Morlaix*, Morlaix 1976, 100.

[28] Joachim Darsel, *Histoire de Morlaix des origines à la révolution*, Rennes 1942, 67, 68, 70, 73.

[29] Bernadette Lécureux, *Histoire de Morlaix des origines à la révolution*, Morlaix 1983, 65.

[30] Daumesnil, *Histoire de Morlaix*, 100; Ó Ciosáin, 'Les Irlandais en Bretagne', 154; Lyons, ' "Vagabonds", "mendiants", "gueux" ', 367.

[31] AD, Ile-et-Vilaine, Rennes (hereinafter cited as AD, I-et-V), sous-série, fonds Henri Bourde de La Rogerie, 5J 71; Daumesnil, *Histoire de Morlaix*, 100.

decidedly inhospitable reception. Like all urban centres at this time, Nantes was subject to intermittent outbreaks of plague and contagious diseases, the most recent having occurred in the summer of 1602 and in May 1605.[32] An expulsion edict against the Irish migrants, passed on 15 May 1605, was, therefore, an emergency measure sanctioned by the corporation in its drive to check the spread of disease. The edict stipulated that the large number of Irish vagabonds in the town and its suburbs, who were viewed by members of the corporation as potentially a serious threat to public health and public order, were to be deported in ships provided at the expense of the townspeople. A sum of between 800 and 900 *livres* was allocated to cover the anticipated cost. The objections to the Irish advanced by the corporation of Nantes were precisely those reiterated by several of the other French municipal authorities that were similarly forced to contend with the impositions which these immigrants placed upon them. They also echoed the reasons advanced by municipal authorities in Dublin and in England in their efforts to address the problem of vagrancy in their jurisdictions.[33]

A broader view of the context within which the expulsion order was delivered suggests that a more widespread culture of opposition to immigration was prevalent in the town at this time. Immediately before the arrival of the Irish, Nantes had played host to another group of unwelcome migrants. By December 1603 in excess of 500 Portuguese *marranes*, including women and children, had taken up residence in the town following a renewed wave of persecution in Portugal by the Spanish crown.[34] Their reception provides a valuable point of comparison when examining the authorities' handling of the Irish migrants eighteen months later. The townspeople's resentment at the Portuguese influx caused Hercule de Rohan, duc de Montbazon, governor of Nantes, to convene an assembly on 7 December 1603 in order to consider strategies to tackle the problem. The assembly delivered a decision to expel the Portuguese. Their decision was based on two grounds. First, the migrants were suspected of having offended the Catholic Church authorities who alleged that they practised Judaism in the town. Second, members of the assembly claimed that King Henri IV thought that the Portuguese were seeking to monopolise Nantes's trade with Iberia. However, having assured all Portuguese *marranes* who had fled to Languedoc, Gascony and Guyenne of his protection, the king allowed their compatriots in Nantes to remain in the town and guaranteed them the same rights as those enjoyed by French

---

[32] Nicolas Travers, *Histoire civile, politique et religieuse de la ville et du comté de Nantes*, 3 vols, Nantes 1836–41, iii. 140, 141, 150.

[33] See Walsh, 'The Irish in Brittany', 317; 'Annales de Nantes', comp. F. C. Meuret, 2 vols, Paris 1830–1, ii. 151; Travers, *Histoire civile*, iii. 150; Mathorez, *Notes sur la colonie irlandaise*, 172; Fitzgerald, 'Poor Irish migrants in England', 25.

[34] *Marranes* or *marranos* were Jewish converts to Christianity. See Ivan Cloulas, 'Les Ibériques dans la société rouennaise des XVIe et XVIIe siècles', *Revue des sociétés savants de Haute Normandie* lx (1970), 20–21; Dubost, *Les Étrangers en France*, 90–1.

Catholics.[35] The townspeople's concern at the threat posed to their commercial interests suggests that, in the main, the Portuguese were traders or mariners by profession. They were, therefore, unlikely to draw on the corporation's poor relief funds, and consequently were reluctantly tolerated.

By contrast, the Irish migrants were consistently perceived as vagrants. An interesting aspect of the difference between the experience of the Irish and of the Portuguese centres on the failure of the French authorities to be influenced by religion in their strategies for dealing with the two groups. In 1603 Nantes's corporation favoured the extreme measure of expulsion of the Portuguese partly on the grounds of suspected Judaism. Yet in 1605 its members sanctioned the same measure against Catholic migrants from Ireland, indicating that the authorities were motivated less by sentiments of religious solidarity and more by practical concerns, namely fear of economic monopolisation in the case of the Portuguese and concern for public health and order in that of the Irish.

The subsequent history of Irish migrants in Nantes proves that this was the case. They remained in the town following the publication of the expulsion order directed against them in mid-May, and they do not appear to have contributed to the spread of disease. Once the initial crisis of the plague that was foremost in the minds of the corporation members had subsided, they resigned themselves to tolerating the continued presence of the Irish, in spite of their poverty, just as they had done in the case of the Portuguese. A handful of Irish migrants applied to be naturalised as French subjects and became quickly integrated into Nantes society. When Irish and Portuguese immigrants applied for naturalisation, both were examined on their behaviour and Catholicism. Those Irish who resorted to neighbouring towns received a similar reception: in Angers four officials termed 'chasse gueux' were charged with rounding up Irish mendicants and other vagabonds in the town and its surrounds, though no evidence exists to suggest that the Irish were in fact deported.[36]

Saint-Malo had a long-standing tradition of commercial relations with Ireland which, as shown above, facilitated the harbouring of Irish political dissidents and religious refugees in that town during the sixteenth century. It was, therefore, to be expected that the port would be sought out by some of the Irish migrants in the early seventeenth century. Upon their arrival, the

---

[35] Meuret, *Annales de Nantes*, ii. 150; Travers, *Histoire civile*, 146–7; Roland Francisque Michel, *Les Portugais en France: les français en Portugal*, Paris 1882, 187–8; Carré, *Essai*, 490; Gérard Nahon, 'La Nation juive portugaise en France XVIème–XVIIIème siècle: espaces et pouvoirs', *Revue des études juives* cliii (juill.–déc. 1944), 356; Cloulas, 'Les Ibériques', 29; J. H. Elliott, 'The Spanish monarchy and the kingdom of Portugal, 1580–1640', in Mark Greengrass (ed.), *Conquest and coalescence: the shaping of the state in early modern Europe*, New York 1991, 56.
[36] Travers, *Histoire civile*, 146–7; Gueriff, 'Recherches sur les "étrangers" ', 19; Léon Maitre, *Inventaire sommaire des archives départementales antérieurs à 1790*, Nantes 1902, 74, 75.

Irish had to evade prowling guard dogs who were unleashed each evening by the municipal authorities to roam the outer precincts of the town during the night and who were recalled in the morning to the sound of a trumpet. The reception accorded the Irish in Saint-Malo resembled that which their counterparts received in each of the French cities and towns to which they went. In June 1606 the town's seneschal, the sieur de Pré, published Henri IV's letter ordering all Irish mendicants to return immediately to their own country. He had been charged to advertise the king's proclamation to the sound of a trumpet at the town's crossroads and in the district generally in order that nobody could claim to have been unaware of the expulsion order.[37]

As at Morlaix and Nantes, fear of plague determined the *malouin* authorities' response to the influx of Irish. In March 1606 the *malouin* population had been subjected to an outbreak of plague and the municipal authorities had reacted by issuing an expulsion order against all able-bodied beggars, instructing them to flee the town within twenty-four hours on pain of flogging. Yet their treatment of the Irish was more benevolent in practice than the legislation suggests. This is exemplified by isolated cases in which small groups of Irish migrants or individuals received donations from the authorities of the *hôtel-dieu*.[38]

The city of Rouen was larger and wealthier than Morlaix, Nantes, Angers or Saint-Malo and was the most accommodating in terms of the provisions it made for Irish immigrants. Irish mariners were familiar with the port and, like Nantes, it had served as a refuge for Irish Catholics from the Elizabethan era onwards. Not surprisingly, therefore, Rouen was the destination of a large number of Irish immigrants in the early 1600s. Rouen's indigenous poor dependants constituted approximately 5 per cent of its population in ordinary times in the late sixteenth century: in crisis years their numbers swelled to in excess of 20 per cent. The city's vagrancy problem persisted in times of prosperity and predated the influx of Irish migrants. In 1598, for example, a year of prosperity in Rouen, a total of 800 beggars, vagabonds and able-bodied poor, not including the elderly, the infirm or children, was recorded in the city.[39]

Rouen was unique by contemporary standards in having an advanced financial and organisational capacity and framework to ensure adequate provision for its poor in times of crisis. This was exemplified in 1586 when in response to a serious harvest failure, a combined programme of public works and bread distribution that catered for 14,260 persons at the height of the crisis was instituted by the authorities.[40] Yet in spite of its wealth and the

---

[37] AD, I-et-V, sous-série 5J, fonds Henri Bourde de La Rogerie, 5J 71; Paul Banéat, *Le Département d'Ille-et-Vilaine: histoire, archaéologie, monuments*, 4 vols, Mayenne 1994, iii. 513, 552.

[38] Lyons, ' "Vagabonds", "mendiants", "gueux" ', 370.

[39] Philip Benedict, *Rouen during the wars of religion*, Cambridge 1981, 10–11.

[40] Ibid.

sophistication of its poor relief system, the city remained vulnerable to plague and to public disorder, and this determined the authorities' treatment of the Irish in 1606 and 1607. There had been outbreaks of plague in the town in 1589, 1592 and 1593, and the mid- to late 1590s was a period of particularly acute disturbance that was characterised by repeated unsuccessful attempts by the *parlement* to curtail an alarming degree of banditry in the city and suburbs, to expel the poor and to prevent the introduction of plague.[41] In 1597 criminals and prowlers who had decimated the surrounding countryside managed to penetrate the precincts of the city as far as the suburbs of Saint-Sever where they threatened to rob and hang the inhabitants. At that time there were in excess of 6,000 poor persons in Rouen and on 27 July they were issued with an ultimatum to leave within twenty-four hours, while those labourers amongst them were to be set to work on the city's fortifications. Not all of these were indigenous poor. In 1599 the problem of foreign mendicants in the city was such that the *parlement* was obliged to legislate for the construction of a tower in the city in which they were to be imprisoned. In spite of the authorities' efforts to 'quarantine' the city's population through the enforcement of a series of preventative measures, in 1602 and 1603 outbreaks of plague did occur.[42]

The impositions that the Irish migrants placed upon the municipal authorities in terms of demands for relief, and the threat that they posed as potential carriers of plague and sources of public disorder were not therefore unfamiliar, but they accentuated existing pressures on the city's poor relief system. Initially, Rouen's *parlementaires* adopted a hard-line approach in tackling the problem of the Irish. At two assembly meetings convened on 30 May 1606, they initiated proceedings to effect the immediate expulsion of the immigrants. At the first session, Pierre Pymont, a resident of Havre de Grâce, testified before the assembly to having received the sum of 10,000 *livres tournois* in cash from a nobleman named David Danviray, a royal councillor and *receveur général des finances* in the *generalité* of Rouen. Pymont claimed that he had been given this money to cover the cost of repatriating the Irish. The payment was authorised by the *trésoriers généraux* of France at Rouen in compliance with a royal edict and Pymont was ordered to furnish the ships. The second meeting, held at the residence of the president of Rouen's *parlement* on that same afternoon, was attended by the most senior

41 Nicétas Periaux, *Histoire sommaire et chronologique de la ville de Rouen*, Rouen 1874, 344, 354, 356, 366, 371, 372, 375; René Herval, *Histoire de Rouen*, 3 vols, Rouen 1949, ii. 111; Jean-Noel Biraben, *Les Hommes et la peste en France, dans les pays européens et méditeranéens*, Paris 1975, 385. For a detailed discussion of municipal administration in sixteenth-century Rouen see E. Le Parquier, *Contribution à l'histoire de Rouen: une année de l'administration municipale au XVIe siècle (année 1515)*, Rouen 1895. See also Benedict, *Rouen during the wars of religion*, 41–4.
42 Periaux, *Histoire sommaire*, 366, 371, 372, 375, 379.

parlementaires, a number of whom were also members of the *conseil privé* and the *conseil d'état*.

At both sessions the enactment of letters patent issued by Henri IV at Fontainebleau on 27 May concerning the repatriation of the Irish were discussed. The assembly was informed that Pymont had undertaken to provide two or three ships within twelve days. These were to have the capacity to carry between 600 and 700 Irish persons who were to be rounded up in the kingdom of France and conveyed from the Breton port of Caudebec to the first port or harbour in Ireland which Pymont might reach. Pymont was required to ensure that on their return from Ireland, the ships' masters and mariners would present certificates testifying to their having delivered the migrants to Irish ports.[43] The following month, Mathurin Cusson, a notary and clerk at Rouen, received a payment of 500 *livres*, which was to be spent on provisions and other necessities for the Irish and to defray other costs incurred in expediting their repatriation.

While there is no explicit evidence to suggest that Pymont in fact fulfilled his undertaking, a writ issued by the *parlement* in March 1607 overtly testified to the failure of the measures approved the previous year for the expulsion of the Irish. The writ arose out of the *parlementaires'* having been informed that a large number of Irish migrants continued to reside at Rouen and several who appeared to have complied with the 1606 expulsion order had soon after returned. They assembled in the city and in its suburbs, or in the woods in the district, the habitual shelter of the indigenous poor. In the writ, which was read and publicised on 16 March at the city's bailiwick and announced to the sound of a trumpet at its crossroads, the *parlement* addressed a routine order to all Irish vagabonds specifically, charging them to leave the city within twenty-four hours and to return to Ireland. Any Irishman who failed to comply with this edict was to be sent to the galleys and any female offender was to be flogged without trial.[44]

In contrast with the severity of the edict's stipulations, the accommodating nature of the city's *parlement* is evident in its practical provisions for the Irish. The *receveur du bureau des pauvres valides* was instructed to compile a list of all those Irish resident in Rouen. He was also charged to provide each Irish person with 5s. and a loaf of bread worth 20d. The authorities' concomitant readiness to grant the Irish conditional permission to stay demonstrates that their objections to the immigrants stemmed from their being vagabonds and the '*inconvénients qu'ils pourraient apporter en cedit royaume*'. Those with a skill or craft, who could find a master to employ them in Rouen, in its suburbs or elsewhere in Normandy, were permitted to stay, provided they presented themselves to the local officials, bearing letters of credence written by their

---

[43] Beaurepaire, 'Expulsion des irlandais, 1606', 42–4.
[44] Ibid. This writ typified the approach of the *rouennais* authorities to the general problem of vagabondage in the city and its environs.

masters, within twenty-four hours of the announcement of this amnesty.[45] Yet this writ too was only partly successful in redressing the problem of Irish vagrancy as it did not set all the immigrants to work nor did it achieve a complete expulsion of the remaining Irish mendicants.

In 1609, in a drive to adopt sterner measures to corral recalcitrant mendicants, Alexandre Faucon de Ris, the newly-appointed first president of Rouen's *parlement*, proposed that Irish vagabonds be put in chains and compelled to work on the land. This suggestion was by no means exceptionally punitive: labouring was a common occupation for both indigenous and foreign vagrants in Rouen and indeed in France during the 1600s.[46] However, his proposition was categorically rejected by the city's inhabitants whose opposition to their being enchained was symptomatic of a move towards a more lenient attitude to the city's vagrancy problem in the early decades of the seventeenth century. In the final analysis, the disparity between the draconian legislative measures passed and the actual treatment of the Irish who resorted to Rouen is attributable to the city's wealth, its sophisticated poor relief system and the resultant accommodating outlook of its *parlementaires*. It was these factors which set Rouen's treatment of the Irish apart from that of less well-endowed provincial towns such as Morlaix, Angers or Saint-Malo.

IV

By contrast, the response of the municipal authorities and of the government in Paris to the influx of Irish immigrants was unrelenting. On 2 November 1605 officials at senior government levels in both France and England simultaneously though independently expressed concern at the escalating problem of Irish migrants who arrived in the ports of both countries on a daily basis. In an alarmist address to Henri IV on the issue, the chancellor of France and chief of the council, Pomponne de Bellièvre, strongly urged Henri IV to expedite the immediate expulsion of the Irish. They were, he said, to be found in such large numbers in the capital that Parisians were seriously inconvenienced and apprehensive concerning the damage which the Irish inflicted on their persons and on their property by night. The Irish congregated at the site of the modern Place du Pont-Neuf, which was still under construction in 1605, and their behaviour contributed to the district's notoriety. In the evening, and during the night, the Irish were said to have been in the habit of grabbing pedestrians by the foot as they crossed the Pont-Neuf

---

[45] Lyons, ' "Vagabonds", "mendiants", "gueux" ', 372–3. There is insufficient surviving evidence on which to draw definitive conclusions regarding the types of employment secured by the Irish or the numbers involved.

[46] Ibid. 373. See Pierre Goubert, *The ancien régime: French society, 1600–1750*, repr. Paris 1976, 103.

and having robbed them hurled them into the Seine.[47] Apart from the threat which they posed to public safety and order, Bellièvre feared that the Irish would inevitably introduce the plague into the city if they were permitted to remain there for much longer as they were dying of hunger in the streets of several French cities and towns. At the same time, the chancellor sought the support of Nicolas de Neufville, sieur de Villeroy, secretary of state, for his efforts to have the Irish expelled from France. He drew Villeroy's attention to the manner in which the streets of Paris were teeming with Irish and warned him against expedient measures to redress the problem, arguing that their banishment from the city would only result in their inflicting harm to the indigenous *gens de champs* who were already very numerous.[48]

In endeavouring to persuade the king to take immediate action, Bellièvre described the pathos of the Irish ghetto settlement at Pont-Neuf in terms which bear comparison with William Waad's account of the tenements in London in 1605 and Parets's account of the Irish soldiers' ghetto in Barcelona in 1653–4.[49] He cited estimates that as many as 1,200–2,000 Irish men were in the group along with several women and children who were malnourished and who lived in filthy conditions.[50] The Parisian memorialist, Pierre de l'Estoile, did little to conceal his contempt for the Irish whom he described as

> en grand nombre, gens experts en fait de gueuserie et excellants en cette science par dessus tous ceux de cette profession, qui est de ne rien faire et de vivre aux dépens du peuple et aux enseignes du bon homme Péto d'Orléans: au rest, habiles de la main et à faire des enfants, de la manière de quelle Paris est tout peuplée.[51]

47 Pomponne de Bellièvre to Henri IV, 2 nov. 1605, BN, MS Fr. 15894, fo. 609; de Bellièvre to de Villeroy, 2 nov. 1605, MS Fr. 15578, fo. 246; 'Confession Catholique du sieur de Sancy', in *Oeuvres complètes de Théodore Agrippa d'Aubigné*, ed. Eugène Réaume and François Caussade, 6 vols, Paris 1873–92, ii. 360. See also *Histoire universelle par Agrippa d'Aubigné*, ed. le Baron Alphonse de Ruble, 9 vols, Paris 1886–97, ix. 384, 422. Similarly, in the contexts of England and Spanish Flanders, A. L. Beier and Gráinne Henry respectively have remarked that the Irish generally travelled in large companies which can be explained in part by their extended family structures: A. L. Beier, *Masterless men: the vagrancy problem in England, 1560–1640*, London 1985, 62–3; Henry, *The Irish military community*, chs iv, v.

48 De Bellièvre to Henri IV, 2 nov. 1605, BN, MS Fr. 15894, fo. 609; de Bellièvre to de Villeroy, 2 nov. 1605, MS Fr. 15578, fo. 246; 'Confession Catholique du sieur de Sancy', 359; Biraben, *Les Hommes et la peste en France*, 385–6.

49 Fitzgerald, 'Poor Irish migrants in England', 25; Peter Pyne, 'Irish soldiers in Barcelona, 1653–4', *Irish Sword* xix (winter 1995), 277.

50 De Bellièvre to Henri IV, 2 nov. 1605, BN, MS Fr. 15894, fo. 609. Fitzgerald highlights the fact that almost all the complaints made to the English privy council relating to the Irish migrants refer to their number including women and children: 'Poor Irish migrants in England', 23.

51 'Registre journal de Henri IV et de Louis XIII', in Jean-Jacques Champollion-Figeac and Aimé Champollion (eds), *Nouvelle Collection des mémoires pour servir à 'histoire de France depuis le XIIIe siècle jusqu'à la fin du XVIIIe*, i, 2nd ser., Paris 1837, 398. See also *Mémoires de*

Such was the scale of the general problem of mendicancy in Paris at the time that in 1595 Henri IV ordered the head of the municipal government to provide food for the deserving poor and arrange for the able-bodied poor to be set to work.[52] Extraordinary measures were also introduced to address the problem of public disorder and crime.[53] The reasons why the Irish congregated in Paris at this time and details of their provenance are not known with any certainty. However, substantial numbers of Irish soldiers were passing from Spain through France to join regiments in Spanish Flanders in the early 1600s, and Paris was the usual stopping-off point for soldiers travelling in either direction.[54] Given that this large number of mainly Irish men was congregated in Paris at precisely the time when Henry O'Neill, Hugh O'Neill's son, was recruiting soldiers and commissioning captains for the first Irish regiment in Spanish Flanders (September 1605–June 1606), it appears highly probable that this was the ultimate destination of the migrants with whom Bellièvre and L'Estoile were concerned.[55]

By late 1605 the Irish were compounding the French capital's existing problems of plague, poverty and associated crime as they did in London and Madrid. Moreover, to the great annoyance of the municipal authorities, they continued to arrive in Paris, causing Bellièvre to consider urgent, extreme measures to stem the influx into France and to explore all possible avenues for their removal. First he advocated their expulsion *via* the port of Conquet, a few miles west of Brest. Second, he stressed that ships travelling to Ireland in order to purchase Irish hides were to be prohibited from conveying any more Irish migrants to Brittany. Another suggestion was that the Irish be transported to the French colonies in Canada.[56] That proposal was not novel. Richard Beacon, writing in 1594, had suggested that masterless men from England be transported to colonise Ireland.[57] Several other proposals to transport the English poor to Ireland, the American colonies and elsewhere

l'Estoile, d'après les manuscrits originaux, ed. G. Brunet and others, 12 vols, Paris 1875–96, viii. 211.

[52] *Recueil des lettres missives de Henri IV*, ed. Jules Berger de Xivrey, 11 vols, Paris 1843–76, iv. 355; 'Registre journal de Henri IV et de Louis XIII', 262, 263, 361, 364, 368, 376, 407, 420; *Histoire générale de Paris: registres des délibérations du Bureau de la ville de Paris*, ed. Paul Le Guérin, François Bonnardot, Alexandre Tuetey, Léon Le Grand, Suzanne Clémencet and others, 20 vols, Paris 1883–1984, xiv. 40–1, ordonnance du parlement sur les pauvres, 18 jan. 1606.

[53] *Registres des délibérations*, xiv, 40–1 n. 2; Michel Félibien, *Histoire de la ville de Paris*, reviewed, augmented and updated by D. G. A. Lobineau, 5 vols, Paris 1725, iv. 14.

[54] Jennings, 'Irish swordsmen', 193, 200. In July 1602 more than thirty-eight Irish soldiers and their captains briefly stopped off in Paris while passing through from the Low Countries to Spain on their way to Ireland.

[55] Casway, 'Henry O'Neill and the Irish regiment', 481–8; Henry, *The Irish military community*, ch. iii.

[56] De Bellièvre to Henri IV, 2 nov. 1605, BN, MS Fr. 15894, fo. 609; de Bellièvre to de Villeroy, 2 nov. 1605, MS Fr. 15578, fo. 249.

[57] Richard Beacon, *Solon his follie, or A politique discourse, touching the reformation of*

were also made, and in 1598 English officials were empowered by statute to do so forcibly.[58]

However, Bellièvre was resigned to the fact that this was not a viable option for the French government in tackling the problem of Irish immigration. A gentleman named du Mont, who had returned from Canada in late 1605 and with whom Bellièvre discussed the proposal, rejected the idea on the grounds that the Irish would be of no use to the colonists. Du Mont claimed that 'pour rien il ne recevrait gens si inutiles et qui ne savent et ne veullent travailler'.[59] The chancellor had no choice but to deport the Irish migrants to England or Ireland. However, he was fully aware that given James I's prohibition on the admission to his realm of any 'estranger' who had no means of supporting him or herself, the Irish were not likely to be permitted to disembark in England. Bellièvre therefore advised that Henri IV's ministers elicit a guarantee from James I that the migrants would be admitted to one or other country.[60]

In order to justify his government's resort to this strategy, Bellièvre cleverly seized on an anomaly in James I's view of his relationship with the Irish migrants. The chancellor was aware that James categorised the Irish amongst those 'foreigners' denied entry into England owing to their lack of means by which to support themselves. Indeed, this perception of the Irish as foreigners in England was in common currency in the late sixteenth century.[61] Bellièvre then highlighted the constitutional status of the Irish migrants as 'subjects' of the king of England, irrefutably arguing that 'le roy d'Angleterre ne peut avec justice refuser de y recevoir ceux qui sont ses sujets'.[62]

Nevertheless, since June 1605 the English privy council had sought to do just that, attempting to stem the influx of Irish 'base people' who had been begging in France and who were deported to England where they congregated in London in particular.[63] Throughout the later months of 1605, and in early 1606, Sir Arthur Chichester, the Irish council and the English privy council were insistent that those migrants leaving Ireland, along with those expelled from either France or Spain, should not be allowed to disembark in English ports.[64] In October 1605, even before the French chancellor first voiced alarm at the problem of Irish immigration into France, English privy councillors had complained to Chichester and the Irish council about the presence

---

common-weales conquered, declined or corrupted, Oxford 1594, sig. 03r–v, quoted in Quinn, *The Elizabethans and the Irish*, 157.

58 Quinn, *The Elizabethans and the Irish*, 157.
59 De Bellièvre to de Villeroy, 2 nov. 1605, BN, MS Fr. 15578, fo. 246.
60 De Bellièvre to Henri IV, 2 nov. 1605, BN, MS Fr. 15894, fo. 609.
61 Quinn, *The Elizabethans and the Irish*, ch. xi.
62 De Bellièvre to de Villeroy, 2 nov. 1605, BN, MS Fr. 15578, fo. 246.
63 Fitzgerald, 'Poor Irish migrants', 24.
64 Lords of the council to Chichester and the Irish council, 12 Oct. 1605, *CSP Ireland, 1603–6*, 336–7; Chichester to Salisbury, 2 Nov. 1605, ibid. 345; 'Instructions for Ireland', 7 June 1606, ibid. 498–9.

of a group of more than 100 Irish soldiers in London.[65] The councillors bemoaned the fact that 'so many of the poor and miserable inhabitants of . . . [Ireland] are suffered to come thither with their wives and children . . . [that] the towns and villages of this country are put to continual charges, and the infection greatly augmented in England'. In their view, such migration occurred as a result of the abuse of a liberty granted by King James 'to all such of his subjects as would . . . seek employment under foreign princes in amity with his majesty'.[66] The following month Chichester claimed that only a few had left Ireland for overseas since he issued an order prohibiting their transportation abroad. In an effort to extricate himself from blame for permitting the Irish to continue to emigrate, he argued that the 'multitude' of Irish migrants in England were in fact the 'remnant' of those who had originally sought refuge there during the Nine Years' War. He believed that their increased numbers could be explained by the recent return of others from France and Spain where they had sought temporary refuge. Chichester also worked to regularise the transportation of Irish troops abroad by eliciting pledges from captains that they would 'land their men, rather in France, if need were, than in England'.[67]

During the months of April and May 1606, when the Parisian authorities were taking remedial steps to deal with the Irish immigrants, concern was expressed both in England and in Ireland at the problem posed by the Irish in English cities and towns. English privy councillors complained that parts of London and elsewhere were 'exceedingly pestered with a multitude of beggars of that country [Ireland], . . . most of them peasants with wives and children'. They blamed port officers and ship-owners for allowing the Irish entry into the country and were outraged at 'how great a dishonour it is, that strangers should behold them in the highways and streets', disparagingly referring to them as 'a great eyesore and burden . . . to His Majesty's subjects' in England.[68] In response to their complaints, Chichester and the Irish councillors undertook to implement more rigorous measures in policing the ports but warned that there was little chance of effecting a complete cessation of migration from Ireland because of the 'extreme misery' prevailing in the country. They favoured the expulsion of the Irish from England, believing that the English people 'should be eased of their burden, and in Ireland they might live if they would give themselves to labour'.[69]

Sir George Carew, the English ambassador to the French court, exerted his influence to encourage Henri IV to comply with James I's expressed request

---

[65] See Fitzgerald, 'Poor Irish migrants', 19.

[66] Privy council to Chichester and the Irish council, 12 Oct. 1605, *CSP Ireland, 1603–6*, 336–7.

[67] Chichester to Salisbury, 2 Nov. 1605, ibid. 345. Chichester did not specify the date of issue of this prohibition order.

[68] Privy council to Chichester and the Irish council, 30 Apr. 1606, ibid. 462.

[69] Lord deputy and council of Ireland to the privy council, 29 May 1606, ibid. 486–7.

not to have any more Irish migrants foisted upon his subjects in England. Prior to Bellièvre's communication with Henri IV on the matter in November 1605, Carew had his secretary advise the French chancellor on what he considered to be the most suitable strategy to address the problem. He recommended that the Irish be conveyed from Paris to Conquet, where the governor of Brest, René de Rieux, sieur de Sourdéac, would supervise their transportation directly to Ireland. Soon after, in November, the council of the *hôtel de ville* in Paris was instructed to redirect one or two thousand *écus* in order to cover the costs of repatriating the Irish migrants to the first port that the ships reached in Ireland.[70] However, at that time Henri IV was prepared to go to considerable lengths to avoid destabilising relations with James I (with whom his ministers were conducting negotiations towards signing a commercial treaty) by the wholesale repatriation of the Irish either to England or Ireland. Moreover, he could not afford to annoy the English monarch who had recently concluded a treaty with Spain (1604) and who had served as mediator in the negotiation of a treaty between France and Spain that same year.[71] Bellièvre's recommendations on the repatriation of the Irish would therefore have been perceived by other members of the *conseil d'état* as too strident and potentially diplomatically harmful to French relations with England.

Early in 1606 the *parlement* of Paris instigated a rigorous policy to tackle the escalating problem of vagrancy in the city and it was as part of this drive that extraordinary measures were taken to rid the capital of the Irish. One of the steps taken was an order to all mendicants to return to their place of birth or residence within twenty-four hours on pain of flogging for a first offence and the galleys for a second. This was the standard response, similar to that sanctioned in Rouen, in dealing with the Irish migrants and with the indigenous poor at the time.[72]

In May 1606 the first steps in a concerted effort to expel the Irish were taken by the municipal authorities in Paris. On 18 May the *bureau de la ville* issued a directive that an extraordinary levy to provide assistance to the city's poor and to fund the expulsion of the Irish was to be imposed with immediate effect. The following day the municipal guards were instructed to station themselves at the city gates and at other strategic points throughout the city's precincts to ensure that the Irish were rounded up and captured. Charles Marchant, captain of the city's archers and arquebusers, was ordered to station his archers at the entrance to the market of Saint-Germain, at the Cimitière des Innocents, and at the city gates at Neuve, Saint-Honoré, Montmartre, Saint-Denis, Saint-Martin, the Temple and Saint-Antoine,

70 De Bellièvre to Henri IV, 2 nov. 1605, BN, MS Fr. fo. 609.
71 See David Buisseret, *Sully and the growth of centralised government in France, 1598–1610*, Paris 1968, 35; Jean-Pierre Babelon, *Henri IV*, Paris 1982, 928–32; Mark Greengrass, *France in the age of Henri IV: the struggle for stability*, 2nd edn, Paris 1995, 175.
72 *Registres des délibérations*, xiv. 40–1, 82–3.

Saint-Bernard, Saint-Victor, Saint-Marcel, Saint-Jacques, Saint-Michel, Bussy and Nesle. They were to take up positions at daybreak and all Irish people were to be allowed into the city but none were to be permitted to leave. Those detained were to be rounded up at the Place de la Halle Saint-Germain et Saint-Innocent where they were to be handed over to the police who were responsible for supervising their deportation.

On 20 May the principal sergeant of Paris received orders to provide the *bureau de la ville* with a fully equipped boat capable of carrying 500 men. A widower named Thoré, a baker in the city, was employed to bake 1,500 twelve-ounce loaves and 1,000 six-ounce loaves of white bread, and to deliver them to the *hôtel de ville* by eight o' clock on the following morning, at which stage he would receive payment. François Miron, civil lieutenant of the municipal government in Paris, oversaw the expulsion of the Irish migrants in May 1606, and received the full backing of the members of the *bureau de la ville* in expediting their repatriation.[73]

Pierre de l'Estoile was another Parisian who was relieved by the departure of the Irish. Writing on Saturday 20 May, he remarked how they were boarded on ships manned by archers and sent back to their own country, and described their expulsion as a 'belle décharge pour la ville de Paris, dès longtemps attendue, mais différée à l'extrémité'.[74] Two boats, with a combined capacity of approximately 1,000 passengers, are said to have set sail from Paris for Ireland.[75] However, there is only one explicit record of a small number of Irish migrants returning from France to Ireland in the immediate aftermath of the expulsions from Paris and Rouen. On 4 July 1606 Arthur Chichester reported that some eighty men, women and children, 'people in the habit of beggars' who, 'being searched were so conceived', had recently arrived in Waterford. They claimed that many more were to follow from France and Spain. In anticipation of this, Chichester instructed the officers of the Irish ports to examine recently returned migrants. Having done so, the officials were charged to ensure that the migrants were conveyed to their birthplaces where the lord of the patrimony was obliged to vouch for them, to employ them or otherwise to occupy them in order to prevent their 'wandering abroad' again.[76]

---

73 Félibien, *Histoire de Paris*, iv. 35.
74 'Registre journal de Henri IV et de Louis XIII', 398, quoted in *Registres des délibérations*, xiv. 82 n. 1.
75 See *Letters of John Chamberlain*, ed. N. E. McClure, 2 vols, Philadelphia 1939, i. 231.
76 Chichester to Salisbury, 4 July 1606, *CSP Ireland, 1603–6*, 512. This strategy resembled that adopted by the London administration in 1587: Fitzgerald, 'Poor Irish migrants', 24.

V

The dearth of other records of Irish migrants disembarking in Irish or English ports, the naturalisation of Irish migrants as French subjects in the 1600s and 1610s, the repeated attempts by the authorities in French cities and towns to expel the migrants, and one Captain Simonds's efforts to press the Irish in France into companies in 1608 all suggest that the French expulsion orders (excepting those of the Parisian authorities), were not strictly enforced, for both diplomatic and practical reasons.[77] The ineffectiveness of the Dublin government's efforts and the failure of port officials to stay the exodus of migrants travelling to France is corroborated in the records of the *états* of Brittany in November 1607. The *états* declared that France 'se remplit journellement d'étrangers irlandois tous mendiants', transported in ships mooring in Breton ports and harbours, and denounced the ship's masters and others for making a profit on their illegal traffic by charging these migrants whom they carried aboard their vessels. In their attempt to address the same problem, the members of the *états*, like the English privy councillors, complained that the province's towns and villages teemed with Irish who forced local residents to provide them with lodgings, frequently by resorting to violence.[78] King James I and the governments in Whitehall and Dublin were infuriated and embarrassed by the flight of 'many poor, idle and vagrant [Irish] persons' to France and were particularly incensed at their pretence at having been 'banished for cause of religion', a claim which the English privy councillors dismissed as the abuse of religion 'for colour to move commisera-tion'. The Irish were rebuked for having 'raised a scandal to the governors there without cause' and Bellièvre's view that James ought to honour his responsibilities to his Irish 'subjects' only aggravated the king's sensitivity to the problem all the more.[79]

In reality, however, concern that the Irish migrants in France as a whole were appealing for or being granted asylum on the grounds of religious perse-cution was largely unfounded. In the case of Nantes, Angers, Morlaix, Saint-Malo, Rouen and Paris, it is clear that pragmatic concerns, notably the preservation of public health and order, took precedence over any show of confessional solidarity or sympathy on the part of the king, the provincial *parlements* or municipal authorities. There is no evidence to indicate that the Irish were perceived collectively as a politically or religiously victimised group. Neither is there evidence of their basing appeals for assistance or permission to stay on a collective basis on the grounds of religious persecu-tion. There is no record of the immigrants having sought the assistance of Irish clerics based in Paris or Rouen. A handful of lay Irish migrants declared

---

[77] 'Advertisements from Brussels', Apr. 1608, *CSP Ireland, 1606–8*, 653.

[78] Lyons, ' "Vagabonds", "mendiants", "gueux" ', 366

[79] Lord deputy and council of Ireland to the privy council, 29 May 1606, *CSP Ireland, 1603–6*, 486; 'Instructions for Ireland', 7 June 166, ibid. 498.

that their flight to France was the result of religious persecution, describing themselves as 'Hyrois fugitifs de leur pays, . . . commes Catholiques'.[80] Yet in general the French elite does not appear to have regarded these Irish immigrants as genuine victims of a Protestant *régime* and those who did so were considered worthy targets of satire in the work of acclaimed French writers including Théodore Agrippa d'Aubigné.[81]

VI

In spite of the large number of Irish who fled to France before 1609, their presence there ultimately proved ephemeral. With the exception of a very small number of individuals who settled in Nantes, Saint-Malo and Quimper, and who became naturalised citizens in the period 1606–28, the majority were temporary migrants.[82] While it is impossible to draw definitive conclusions as to their eventual fate, what evidence there is strongly suggests that a significant proportion moved on to serve in the archduke's army in Spanish Flanders. It also appears that a large number returned to England either of their own volition through clandestine means or through expulsion, while others returned directly to Ireland under similarly varied circumstances.

Of the very small proportion of migrants who settled permanently in France, an even smaller number applied for naturalisation in the 1600s and 1610s. These were typically people who had acquired property, for this was liable for confiscation by the monarch if they died in France without having been naturalised. Like all immigrants resident in France the Irish followed the standard procedures of applying to the king for naturalisation which would entitle them to the same rights and privileges as French subjects. They were generally required to present details of their origins, their social status, their parents' names, their own marital status and whether they had children. They also presented information concerning the duration of their residence in France. In some cases they were obliged to undergo an examination of their characters and of their Catholicism before being issued with declarations of naturalisation. Once granted, the royal letters had to be verified by the *chambre des comptes* before being recorded in the treasury chamber or court. At that stage the letters conferred in full the privileges of French subjects on the applicants. However, it was not until the 1620s that a significant number of Irish immigrants began to apply for naturalisation.[83]

---

[80] See Ó Ciosáin, 'Les Irlandais en Bretagne', 166.
[81] 'Confession Catholique du sieur de Sancy', 359–60.
[82] Ó Ciosáin, 'Les Irlandais en Bretagne', 158.
[83] See Maitre, *Inventaire sommaire des archives départementales antérieurs à 1790: Loire-Inférieure . . .*, 34, 35, 74, 80; Dubost, *Les Étrangers en France*, 24–9, and *La France italienne*, 146–7; Dubost and Sahlins, *Et si on faisait payer les étrangers?*.

This first wave of Irish migration to France was distinctive in that the scale of the exodus from Ireland was unprecedented. Like the Gaelic Irish who departed Ireland in the wake of the second Desmond rebellion in the 1580s, those who migrated to France in the early 1600s did so in order to escape the political and economic turmoil which characterised the Nine Years' War and its immediate aftermath and to seek relief or employment abroad. An embarrassment for the English monarchy and government, they were perceived and treated by the French as unwelcome beggars who were categorised indiscriminately and exclusively on the basis of their mendicant lifestyle and their collective dependency upon the municipal authorities and charitable agencies. Unlike their counterparts in Spain, they were without a cohort of nobility to articulate their grievances in official circles. When the Ulster lords passed briefly through France into Flanders in October 1607, they did not associate in any way with the poor Irish migrants.[84] Hence the complex political, economic and religious circumstances which precipitated the migrants' crossing to France remained largely unknown and of little interest to the municipal authorities onto whom responsibility for dealing with them had been devolved. Bereft of any recognisable political or religious influence or ideology, they were accorded similar treatment to indigenous vagabonds and were viewed as particularly menacing nuisances, who were given to crime, and who were unskilled, uncouth and idle.[85]

By the early 1610s the number of complaints regarding the Irish had declined, indicating that this wave of immigration had been the direct result of the fall-out from the Nine Years' War. Nevertheless, the Parisian authorities continued to wrestle with the problem of Irish immigrants. In 1614 the authorities at the Hôpital Sainte-Anne were instructed by the *parlement* to have the hospital in a state of readiness to provide one month's lodgings for a group of Irish who had congregated in the city and who were awaiting repatriation.[86] It seems that a modest level of Irish immigration continued throughout the 1610s before accelerating once again in the 1620s. This second wave was primarily motivated by the unfavourable economic situation at home, the migrants having been forced to leave Ireland to escape the hardships resulting from a series of bad harvests. Again, the French treated them as mendicants and in the late 1620s and 1630s they were banned from the Breton towns of Landerneau and Quimperlé: in St Pol-de-Léon the authorities even listed the Irish after dogs and swine in their interdicts. Although they were still too few in number and too widely dispersed to

---

84 See Tadhg Ó Cianáin, *The flight of the earls*, ed. Paul Walsh, Dublin 1916.
85 See René Pillorget, 'Louis XIV and Ireland', in Bernadette Whelan (ed.), *The last of the great wars: essays on the war of the three kings in Ireland, 1688–91*, Limerick 1995, 1. For a study of vagrancy and the reaction of authorities throughout Europe to this problem see Robert Jütte, *Poverty and deviance in early modern Europe*, repr. Cambridge 1996.
86 See *Inventaire-sommaire des archives hospitalières antérieures à 1790: Hotel-Dieu*, ii, Paris 1884, 106. Details of their provenance were not specified.

form distinct Irish communities in their host cities and towns, this second wave of migrants established a more permanent presence in France than had their predecessors.[87]

VII

Notwithstanding the stable and amicable state of relations between France and England in the early 1600s, and in contrast with the reaction to the ongoing influx of Irish migrants into France, when Hugh O'Neill, earl of Tyrone, and Rory O'Donnell, earl of Tyrconnell, were forced to seek refuge briefly in France while *en route* to Spanish Flanders in early October 1607, their sojourn sparked diplomatic tensions between Whitehall and Paris as the fugitive party received at least the tacit support of the French king and of the duc de Lorraine. Henri IV's desperate dependence upon England for the provision of troops to serve in the Brittany and Picardy campaigns against the Catholic League in the 1590s has already been emphasised. However, by the middle of the following decade, he had done much to secure his position in France and was sufficiently self-reliant to handle the diplomatic wrangling surrounding the earls' arrival from Ulster in an independent manner, similar to François I's dealings with Gerald Fitzgerald in 1540. This episode cannot be regarded as a revival of the political intrigue of the previous century for a number of reasons. First, there was no attempt on the part either of the earls, the French king or the duc de Lorraine to orchestrate a French intervention in Ireland. The Irish sought and were granted only protection of their persons during their passage through France and specifically Lorraine. Second, unlike in the case of Gerald Fitzgerald's flight to France in 1540, there was no confederation in Ireland which awaited the earls' return with continental forces in order to launch a campaign against James I. Exiled from Ireland, the fugitives' sojourn in France was of no consequence for Irish politics; rather its importance stemmed from the strain it exerted on Henri IV's relations with the new king of England. Third, whereas Gerald Fitzgerald's guardians had sought to annex his cause to Cardinal Pole's designs for a pan-European Catholic alliance against Henry VIII, in the early 1600s there was no continental intrigue to undermine James I's position in which the Ulster lords might have participated. By the time the earls arrived in France, the last of the wars of religion had ended, France was undergoing major reconstruction and Henry could deal with the diplomatic issues arising from the arrival of the lords from Ulster in an assertive, independent-minded manner, something he could not have done a decade before because of his enforced dependence on Elizabeth I.

---

[87] Ó Ciosáin, 'Les Irlandais en Bretagne', 155.

Of course the earls had not even considered France as a possible refuge when they departed Lough Swilly in September 1607. Rather, Spain was their destination, but inclement weather conditions thwarted their plans and forced them to change course for Le Croisic in western Brittany. Once they arrived in France, however, they were treated with considerable deference by most of those with whom they came in contact during their brief stay. A French mariner on board the ship on which they had made the crossing from Ireland volunteered to take the party to Normandy. On their arrival, the Irish readily secured the services of *rouennais* crewmen who endeavoured to pilot their vessel into the harbour before discovering that they were unable to moor the ship. The crewmen therefore berthed the vessel at Quilleboeuf, a small town situated at the mouth of the Seine, south of Rouen, about noon on 4 October. There, the earls and their retinue were again greeted as esteemed guests and the governor of the town dined with Hugh O'Neill. While at Quilleboeuf, the Irish party was assisted by local mariners in hiring boats in which they dispatched the Countess Catríona O'Neill, Nuala, daughter of O'Donnell, and their children, along with some of the gentry and their servants, to the nearby city of Rouen where they arrived around midday on Sunday 7 October.

Meanwhile, O'Neill, O'Donnell and their attendant lords and gentlemen proceeded to La Bouille, a town east of Quilleboeuf and south-west of Rouen. It was here that they first encountered an obstacle to their progress. On the 5 October the governor of Quilleboeuf was obliged to place them under 'arrest', and ordered them to present themselves to the governor and the chief marshal of Normandy. The earls complied, hired more horses, and made their way to Lisieux, formerly a Catholic League stronghold, where they were once again afforded an hospitable reception. They were received 'with honour and kindness' by the provincial governor, Henri Bourbon, duc de Montpensier, and his chief marshal, Guillaume de Hautemer, comte de Mauny, seigneur de Fervaques and lieutenant general of Normandy.[88] In Montpensier the Gaelic lords found a highly influential supporter with close ties with Henri whom he had served throughout the campaign against the Catholic League in Normandy and Brittany.[89] Their meeting with him in his capacity as the king's chief representative in Normandy was critical in assuring their protec-

---

88 Ó Cianain, *Flight*, 11–21; Meehan, *Fate and fortunes*; Lyons, 'Reluctant collaborators'; A. D. Ansélme, *Histoire de la maison royale de France et des grands officiers de la couronne*, continued by Caille du Fourny, 9 vols, 3rd edn, Paris 1726–1879, vi. 852–5; vii. 393–4; *Comptes rendus des échevins de Rouen avec des documents relatifs à leur élection, 1409–1701*, ed. Julien Félix, Rouen 1890, 190.

89 Henri de Bourbon, duc de Montpensier (1573–1608), was known as prince de Dombes until 1592 when, upon the death of his father, he assumed the latter's titles thereby becoming duc de Montpensier, pair de France, duc de Montpensier de Châtellerault et de Saint-Fargue, souverain de Dombes, prince de la Roche-sur-Yon, 'dauphin d'Auvergne', baron de Beaujolais, marquis de Mézières, comte de Mortain, vicomte héréditaire d'Auge et de Brosses, seigneur de Champigny et d'Argentan. See Ansélme, *Histoire de la maison royale*,

tion and safe passage through France as Henri deferred to Montpensier's judgement in alleviating their predicament. The speed with which both Montpensier and Henri reacted to the earls' presence in France testifies to both men's sensitivity to the diplomatic ramifications of the fugitives' seeking safe passage through their respective jurisdictions. Within three days of the earls' arrival at Lisieux, Montpensier had notified the king of their arrival in Normandy and requested instructions as to how they ought to be dealt with. O'Neill and O'Donnell were meanwhile charged to tolerate their detention until the king issued directives concerning their fate.

Too impatient to await the return of Montpensier's messenger from the court, Matthew Tully, O'Donnell's secretary, set out for the French court in Paris where he was afforded the rather exceptional privilege of being granted an audience with Henri within just two to three days of his arrival.[90] Equally remarkable is the speed with which the king had already taken steps to address the issue of the earls' seeking refuge in Normandy, and also his readiness to receive their representative even after he had issued Montpensier's messenger with instructions as to how they were to be dealt with. Henri heard first-hand from Tully of the circumstances that precipitated the Irish party's flight to the continent and of their having been detained in Normandy. While the king did not meet either O'Neill or O'Donnell, as a result of his audience with Tully, he was fully apprised of the earls' motives for fleeing Ireland, of their status as rebels who were sought after by the English authorities and, lastly, of their future plans. One finds further evidence of the king's real concern with the predicament of the Ulster lords in Tully's also being granted a meeting with the king's secretary of state, Nicolas de Neufville, sieur de Villeroy, whom he likewise briefed on his masters' circumstances. Villeroy proved equally well disposed to the earls, and assured Tully that no harm would come to them as a result of their detention and that the king had made provisions for their safety.[91] It is reasonable to assume that Montpensier and his chief marshal in Normandy were equally well acquainted with the Irishmen's fugitive status and their plans. This all suggests that, although the French monarchy, the secretary of state, the governor and the chief marshal of Normandy had these fugitives thrust upon them by an accident of fate, they were fully aware of the implications of their helping them to escape from their respective jurisdictions into Flanders. James I and his ambassador at the French court, Sir George Carew, therefore had good grounds for being disgruntled at the conspiratorial and partisan manner in which the French

---

i. 357–8; Maurice Veyrat, 'Les Gouverneurs de Normandie du XVe siècle à la révolution', *Études normandes* (1953), 577–8; *Nouvelle Biographie générale*, xxxv–xxxvi (1968), 380.

[90] According to James Bathe, Tully 'was driven to run away out of England in great danger from the earl of Salisbury' and travelled to Spain about Christmas 1605. He served as secretary to Tyrconnell: information of James Bathe, 7 Oct. 1607, *CSP Ireland, 1606–8*, 301.

[91] Ó Cianain, *Flight*, 21–3.

king and leading provincial officials knowingly orchestrated and authorised the earls' escape from the reach of the English authorities.

Henri instructed Montpensier to order the Irish party to travel to Flanders rather than directly to Spain as they had intended. In Montpensier the king had the perfect scapegoat in explaining his handling of the Gaelic lords during their sojourn in Normandy when he was eventually found by James I to have blatantly compromised himself in his management of this sensitive situation. From the very outset Henri had deliberately set out to mislead Carew in the entire affair. He told him that he thought the earls had arrived in Spain and declared that the king of Spain had done wrong to James I in receiving them in his realm.[92] Initially, therefore, Carew was hopeful of the French king's co-operation. But when Carew learned of the lords' arrival in Normandy, and of their having been granted safe passage to Brussels by Montpensier, he immediately made representations to Henri, requesting that the king detain the fugitives until such time as he (Carew) would receive instructions from England on how they were to be treated.

It was not long before Henri's duplicity came to light and when it did, he proved elusive and ultimately obstinate in accounting for his handling of the entire affair. The contrast in his treatment of Carew and of Matthew Tully only serves to confirm the surreptitious nature of his handling of the affair. Whereas he refused even to grant Carew an audience for a period of three days while he went hunting every day, he had been prepared to meet Tully within two to three days of his arrival at court and after a day's hunting. Several contemporaries, such as the duc de la Force, remarked upon Henri's frequent insistence on affording hunting precedence over government matters at this time; this demonstrates the importance he gave to his handling of the earls' sojourn in Normandy. In spite of the fact that Carew 'was doing his full best to injure and harm the princes [the Ulster lords] if he could . . ., his efforts were idle and of no avail' as he failed to persuade Henri to honour his formal request as ambassador to detain the earls.[93]

According to Tadhg Keenan (Ó Cianáin), a chronicler who was a member of the Gaelic party, it was only after Henri had received assurances that the earls were in a secure place that he notified the English ambassador of their having passed out of his jurisdiction. Unlike François I, who pretended to try to have Gerald Fitzgerald, future eleventh earl of Kildare, arrested when he

---

92 Minute, [Salisbury] to Sir Thomas Edmonds, 14 Oct. 1607, *CSP Ireland, 1607–8*, 624; Ó Cianain, *Flight*, 23–4; Thomas Birch, *An historical view of the negotiations between the courts of England, France and Brussels from the year 1592 to 1617*, London 1749, 276.

93 *Mémoires authentiques de Jacques Nompar de Caumont, duc de la Force*, ed. le marquis de la Grange, Paris 1843, i. 25, 460–1; minute, [Salisbury] to Edmonds, 14 Oct. 1607, *CSP Ireland, 1607–8*, 624. Notice of their arrival in Quilleboeuf was also conveyed to Chichester by the privy councillors on 26 Oct. (ibid. 308). See also Levinus Muncke (under-secretary to Salisbury) to Sir Ralph Winwood, 17 Oct. 1607, *Memorials of affairs of state*, ed. Edmund Sawyer, 3 vols, London 1725, i. 350.

passed through France into Flanders in 1540, Henri displayed open if diplomatically couched defiance of James I in defending his support of the fugitives. He acknowledged that he had made provision for O'Neill, O'Donnell
and their attendants to leave France but justified his favourable treatment of
them on the grounds of his duty to afford them his royal protection owing to
their being Catholics. He made it clear to Carew, and by extension to James I,
that even if he were to discover that the earls had not left France, 'he would
not do any injury to noblemen who would be obliged to leave their parental
inheritance because of their faith and the injustice done to them'. So long as
he was king, he declared, 'all Catholics were free to go without any interfer-
ence through the kingdom of France'.[94] Henri also defended his stance on the
grounds that Montpensier had already assured the Irish party of their safety
and he could not revoke that decision, although of course he could well have
overturned the marshal's directive had he been so inclined.[95] Henri and
Montpensier also helped Matthew Tully to travel ahead of the rest of the
group into Flanders. They did so in order that Tully might meet Hugh
O'Neill's son, Colonel Henry O'Neill, to notify him that his father and
several other Ulster nobles had unintentionally landed in France and were
now set to pass into Flanders. Tully made arrangements for Henry O'Neill to
meet the earls and their retinues at the French border. In addition, he
requested in advance a passport and warrant from the archduke similar to
that granted them by Henri IV for the duration of their sojourn in his
jurisdiction.

While Henri, Villeroy, Montpensier and the chief marshal may have been
benevolently disposed towards the Irish party, the same cannot be said of the
governor of Rouen who had 'shown his unkindness and ill feeling . . . to them'
during their stay in his city. He personally applied pressure on the Irish to
hasten their departure. On Saturday 13 October he visited the hostel where
the female members of the party were resident and ordered them either to
leave immediately or to return to the ship which had brought them to Rouen.
In the event, the women's request for leniency persuaded him to allow them
to remain in the city until the following Monday. On the evening of Sunday
14 October the earls and their womenfolk were reunited and were in possession of the passport and warrant issued them by Henri, which authorised
their passage across the border into Flanders. They stayed in the city over-
night and on Monday 15 October, twelve days after they had disembarked at
Quilleboeuf, they set out to cross the French border into Flanders and arrived
at Douai three days later.[96] Despite the French king's assertion of his readiness
to afford the Ulster earls his protection indefinitely on the grounds that they

94 Ó Cianain, *Flight*, 25.
95 Salisbury to Sir Charles Cormwallis, 18 Nov. 1607, *CSP Ireland, 1607–8*, 331–2;
minute, [Salisbury] to Edmonds, 14 Oct. 1607, ibid. 624; Edmonds to Salisbury, 28 Oct.
1607, ibid. 628; Sawyer, *Memorials*. ii. 357–8.
96 Ó Cianain, *Flight*, 25–7, 37.

were 'out of their own country for matter of religion and private discontentment', it was clear that he both extended and boasted about, according them this privilege safe in the knowledge that they had neither the intention nor the desire to stay in France any longer than was necessary.[97]

Henri had terminated all dealings with the fugitives before James I issued a declaration on 15 December 1607, addressed to all continental rulers, advising them not to lend support or assistance to the earls whom he denounced as rebels, criminals and infidels unworthy of political asylum. The fact that this royal declaration seems not to have appeared in Paris until August 1608, ten months after Henri had allowed the lords to pass through France, might have provided him with a legal loophole to absolve himself from blame on the grounds of his ignorance of the lords' rebel status. In reality, however, that was not a viable option as both James and his ambassador were only too aware of how well apprised the king was of the circumstances of the flight of the earls from Ulster. A particularly revealing development at this juncture is Henri's response to the publication of the declaration. Rather than using this loophole to explain away his involvement with O'Neill and O'Donnell, Henri took umbrage at what he perceived as James's attempt to dictate to him regarding his treatment of the fugitives within his realm. In Henri's view, the issue of his royal prerogative was at stake. His response was to issue a stinging reminder to James that in the light of England's strained relations with Spain at the time, the English needed his friendship much more than he needed theirs. Consequently, he warned, James would be well advised in the future not to seek to influence his decisions in respect of matters relating to his exercise of power within his own jurisdiction.[98] Henri thus sought to make political capital out of his handling of the chance arrival of the Gaelic lords in France. He used his treatment of them as a pretext for reminding James of his determination to exercise completely and autonomously his royal prerogative within his realm.

The publication of James's declaration in both English and French in France did little to curtail any further shows of support for the earls in France. In January 1608, just a month after the denunciation of the Ulster earls was issued in England, the English ambassador at the imperial court at Brussels, Sir Thomas Edmonds, notified the earl of Salisbury that Hugh O'Neill had sought and obtained a permit of free passage through the duc de Lorraine's territory in north-eastern France. O'Neill and his party had resolved to travel to the Spanish territory of Milan, there to await King Philip III's reply to their

---

97 Salisbury to Cornwallis, 18 Nov. 1607, *CSP Ireland, 1607–8*, 332; Sawyer, *Memorials*, ii. 357–8. Henri IV bade Carew 'be content as they would be gone [from France] presently'. Philip Benedict highlights the fact that the governorship of Normandy tended to be honorific and that the actual decision-making involved in administering the province was devolved onto essentially autonomous royal officials: *Rouen during the wars of religion*, 33.
98 'Registre journal de Henri IV et de Louis XIII', 71–2; Birch, *Historical view*, 424.

correspondence.[99] Edmonds also reported that O'Neill claimed to have been promised favourable treatment at the hands of the duke when he arrived in his jurisdiction. He immediately endeavoured to dissuade the duke from according the fugitive earl any such welcome. He wrote to Lorraine in an effort 'to acquaint him how matters have passed concerning Tyrone, whereof he supposes the duke is not informed'. He emphasised that both James I and Philip III regarded the earls as 'fugitives and rebels', and that on those grounds the Spanish king had refused them entry to his country. Edmonds counselled Lorraine to follow their example in order that he would not unintentionally allow anything prejudicial to James's interests or favourable to the advancement of the rebels' malicious cause to take place.[100] Whereas Carew had been constrained by a lack of instruction from London in endeavouring to effect the earls' arrest when they first arrived in France, the publication and widespread circulation of the declaration against the fugitives was intended to remove all scope for their being afforded hospitality by hosts who claimed ignorance of their transgressions in Ireland. Lest there should be any uncertainty on Lorraine's part in respect of the earls' fugitive status, Edmonds supplied the duke with a French translation of James's declaration.

However, Edmonds's efforts had little effect. When the Gaelic lords arrived at Nancy, the capital of the duchy of Lorraine, on 8 March the duke and his family evidently ignored his advice and extended an hospitable welcome to their guests. Lorraine entertained them at his own table, while his sister, the duchess of Brunswick, did the countess of Tyrone the honour of paying her a visit at the inn where she was staying.[101] When the Irish had passed beyond his jurisdiction, the duke replied to Edmond's correspondence in terms which greatly displeased the ambassador who complained of how one could 'perceive how much Tyrone's insinuations have wrought upon him [Lorraine]'.[102] For his part James I was so incensed by Lorraine's disregard of his expressed instructions in respect of the rebels that when the duke died shortly afterwards, on 14 May 1608, he sent no representative to the funeral. James justified his stand on the grounds that 'he would have more regret for the loss of that old man and would send messages of condolence to his children, has he not, before dying, caused him such grave displeasure by receiving the earl and by the manner in which he did so'.[103]

---

99   Edmonds to Salisbury, 13 Jan. 1608, *CSP Ireland, 1607–8*, 644–5; Edmonds to the duc de Lorraine, 12 Jan. 1608, ibid. 644–5 (enclosure). Charles de Lorraine, fourth duc de Guise, prince de Joinville, duc de Joyeuse, comte d'Eu, pair et grand-maître de France, amiral des mers du Levant, gouverneur de Champagne et de Provence: *Nouvelle biographie générale*, xxi–xxii, Paris 1966, 788–90.
100 Edmonds to Salisbury, 13 Jan. 1608, *CSP Ireland, 1607–8*, 644–5; Edmonds to the duc de Lorraine, 12 jan. 1608, ibid. (enclosure).
101 Edmonds to Salisbury, 22 June 1608, ibid. 663. See also Kerney Walsh, *'Destruction by peace'*, and *An exile of Ireland*, 74–5.
102 Quoted in Kerney Walsh, *An exile of Ireland*, 75.
103 Ibid.

While Henri IV had been extremely reluctant to become involved in the Nine Years' War, when the Gaelic fugitives did seek his assistance in enabling them to reach their ultimate destination, he, along with the duc de Montpensier, the chief marshal of Normandy, the duc de Lorraine and countless other French mariners and inn-keepers treated them with the deference that befitted their noble station. They both welcomed and afforded them preferential treatment. They assisted them in eluding the English ambassador and a number of English spies and agents and in ensuring their passage to safety on two occasions. In short, although their involvement with the Ulster lords was brief, at a critical juncture the French played a significant role in enabling the the fugitive party to resume their ultimately unsuccessful attempts to revive papal and Spanish interest in undertaking an expedition to Ireland.

Conclusion

I

The flight of the Gaelic lords from Ulster, and the delicately balanced relationship between Henri IV, James I and Philip III in the early 1600s, effectively eliminated the remote prospect of a revival of Franco-Irish intrigue and closed a chapter on Ireland's short-lived political relations with France that was not re-opened until the 1640s. For almost sixty years, between the early 1520s and the early 1580s, the Irish had become embroiled in intrigue with the French for a variety of reasons. All the protagonists – the tenth earl of Desmond, Gerald Fitzgerald, Con O'Neill, Manus O'Donnell, O'Doherty, Cormac O'Connor, MacWilliam Burke, Shane O'Neill, Conor O'Brien, James Fitzmaurice, Brian MacGeoghegan and William Nugent – were driven by essentially personal, dynastic or seigneurial motives. They sought French assistance to bolster their campaigns against the crown at times when they were experiencing particular difficulties in their immediate locales, and their rhetoric alone elevated their intensely localised disputes to the status of a 'national' cause. Some, such as James Fitzmaurice, sought French assistance to back their efforts to defend Catholicism in Ireland as part of their agenda for protecting their position and privileges in opposition to the advance of Anglicisation and Protestantism. Typically, when Gaelic lords such as Shane O'Neill and Manus O'Donnell were seeking better treatment from the English crown and the lord deputy and Irish council, they made political capital out of rumours of their alleged or real associations with the French in order to apply pressure on the English. Of course, on a purely pragmatic level, the Irish sought French support as they needed foreign aid in order for their campaigns to have any chance of successfully withstanding English forces. Blatant opportunism therefore led the Irish to forge links with the French. With the notable exception of the early and mid-1540s, disaffected Irish lords were always ready to take advantage of England's isolation from her continental neighbours by offering their allegiance to her opponents.

The French were equally opportunistic in availing themselves of chances to cultivate associations with aggrieved Irish lords, particularly on occasions when Anglo-French political relations were strained. In times of declared war, as in the early 1520s, the mid-1540s and the late 1550s, the French crown deliberately engaged in intrigue with the Irish as part of its grand British strategy to undermine the Tudor *régime* by stirring unrest on the periphery of the realm. At other times, such as the mid-1570s when Henri III took umbrage at Elizabeth I's clandestine support of his Huguenot opponents in contravention of the terms of the Treaty of Blois, the French used Irish lords such as James Fitzmaurice as levers to pressurise the English crown to desist from supporting its opponents. Even when France and England were on amicable terms, as in the early 1540s, French monarchs occasionally used their contacts with Irish dissidents to present the Tudors with sharp reminders against taking French amity for granted. The French cultivated Irish and English conspirators as a means of articulating their opposition to both anticipated and actual developments in the English polity, a practice best illustrated by Antoine de Noailles's intrigue in 1553–4 which was motivated by resistance to Mary I's decision to marry Philip II of Spain.

As a Catholic nation, it was incumbent upon the French at least to appear sympathetic to the cause of Irish Catholic subjects of a Protestant monarchy. The French crown, particularly Henri II, and more especially the militant Guise faction, were at least partly motivated by genuine sympathy and confessional solidarity in engaging in intrigue with the Irish when they had little choice but to succumb to the intense moral pressure brought to bear upon them by Cardinal Reginald Pole and later by the papacy, to join pan-European Catholic alliances in opposition to the Protestant English *régime*.

Despite the prolonged and occasionally intense nature of their diplomatic exchanges, Irish engagements with the French produced little of any consequence in terms of military aid for Irish campaigns. Taken as a whole, this intrigue might legitimately be viewed as a wasted exercise. However, even though the Irish did not in the main succeed in achieving their ultimate objective, each of these episodes was very significant in forging a tenuous political relationship between Ireland and France in the early modern period. In the process a minority of both the Irish and the French political elites learned valuable lessons. They each experienced a heightened sense of awareness and acquired a deeper knowledge of politics in the other's country. Together they succeeded in improvising quasi-diplomatic relations in the absence of formal diplomatic structures and official ambassadorial personnel.

The Irish in particular learned to broaden their political arena beyond Ireland, indeed even beyond the British Isles, as they became increasingly visible within political and diplomatic circles in France, Spain and Rome as the sixteenth century progressed. Although on the whole the individuals involved in intrigue with the French court changed from one decade to the next, families such as the Fitzgeralds of Desmond, the O'Neills and the O'Donnells maintained contact with the French court and with specific families in France as illustrated in the association between the earls of Desmond and the comtes de Candale from the 1520s to the 1570s. The Irish learned valuable lessons from their predecessors' and their own experiences in dealing with the French. The treatment afforded Gerald Fitzgerald, Cormac O'Connor, James Fitzmaurice and the Ulster earls, earned France a reputation among the Irish as a safe haven for political and religious exiles. There they could expect to find the protection of sympathetic locals, a welcome in accordance with their social status, and at least the tacit support of provincial government officials and the French crown.

The Irish also gained first-hand experience of the practical difficulties involved in endeavouring to develop and maintain relationships at the French court by means of alternative, ex-official diplomatic channels. As protagonists such as Fitzmaurice grew more aware of their dependence on continental aid for a successful outcome to their campaigns, they gained an appreciation of their need to publicise their military successes in propaganda directed at a continental audiences and to keep potential continental supporters apprised of their achievements in order to entice them to provide men and money. They were also increasingly aware that if their negotiations were to have any prospect of success, they needed to employ full-time envoys to represent their causes at the French court. Hence, whereas in the 1520s and 1530s Desmond and O'Donnell sent emissaries to the French court on brief visits, from the late 1540s onwards Irish lords employed full-time envoys such as George Paris, and in the 1570s, Archbishop Fitzgibbon and Bishop O'Hely, to provide the necessary momentum in lobbying the French court.

It was through canvassing the French rather than the Spanish for military backing that the Irish lords and their envoys learned how to conduct clandestine negotiations with continental rulers. They acquired a mastery of the protocol that governed court life. They were obliged to become adept in gauging and taking advantage of the shifting dynamics of court factions and in identifying the most appropriate targets for solicitations. The presence of Irish lords and emissaries at the French court, particularly from the late 1540s onwards, alerted them to the influence exerted over the French monarchy by the Catholic Guise faction. They were also quick to capitalise on the Guises' favourable disposition towards the Irish owing to their vested interests in Scotland. Earmarked as the most likely source of French military aid, the Guises were constantly targeted with solicitations from a succession of Irish dissidents, notably Shane O'Neill, James Fitzmaurice and MacGeoghegan and Nugent down to the mid-1580s.

Irish emissaries such as George Paris and dissidents who themselves attended the French court acquired the skills of professional diplomats by means of trial and error. They learned how to compete with rival suitors and professional diplomats in presenting their cases before the French monarch. They mastered the arts of diplomatic dexterity and duplicity. They effected the safe and accurate conveyance of intelligence between France, Ireland and Scotland and proved adept in using standard ploys to deflect the attention of the English authorities from their true intentions.

Their involvement with the French also provided the Irish with valuable training in tracing signs of shifts in continental and British diplomacy and politics which was particularly evident in the 1570s and early 1580s. They benefited from their contacts with the French by becoming proficient in the manipulation of rumour and intrigue in the formal diplomatic sphere in order to enhance their designs. They learned the importance of adopting the Counter-Reformation cause as a propaganda tool in soliciting continental support for their causes. Shane O'Neill and James Fitzmaurice used their contacts with the French court to manipulate the English administrations in Whitehall and Dublin, knowing that the prospect of foreign support for their campaigns would stir the councils to take a more serious view of their resistance. The Irish learned important lessons following each episode of intrigue as they ultimately resigned themselves to the realisation that, while the French kings might be prepared to afford them temporary protection as a demonstration of their monarchical honour, none was prepared to allow his involvement with Irish rebels jeopardise French relations with England. Gerald Fitzgerald and James Fitzmaurice recognised that, while the French may have considered a campaign in Ireland as part of a pan-European Catholic alliance against England, they were not prepared to take the initiative alone. Both men, along with Conor O'Brien, found that French monarchs were more ready to make representations on their behalf to the English monarch for pardons than they were to grant them any form of practical assistance.

Each of the Irish lords and their envoys who made overtures or engaged in negotiations with the French between the 1520s and the 1580s learned one particularly salutary lesson: that the French (like the Spanish) were content to court, use and dispense with them according to the dictates of fickle international politics. Through their frequent interaction with French ambassadors and military personnel during their sojourn at the Scottish court, particularly in the era of Marie de Guise between the 1540s and 1560s, the Irish became acquainted with the extent of French military resources which in turn encouraged George Paris and Cormac O'Connor in their hope for a possible French invasion of Ireland. The failed outcome to successive efforts to extend French military involvement in Scotland into Ulster was also instructive in that it provided the Irish parties with first-hand experience of the frustrations arising from their dependence on both the French and the Scots. All these skills and lessons were of enduring value when the Irish redirected their campaigns for military aid away from the French to the Spanish and papal courts from the 1570s onwards.

France's political elite likewise drew valuable lessons from its unprecedented contacts with Irish lords who provided them with first-hand accounts and insider analysis of the political culture of a country with which they were relatively unfamiliar. From the early 1520s onwards, a tiny number of Gaelic emissaries and Irish lords attended the French court. Through direct personal encounters with these individuals, a small coterie of the French political elite gained insights into Gaelic perspectives on how the country was being ruled and heard them articulate for themselves their sense of grievance at the loss of their ancestral property and titles to the English. This served as an important counterbalance to the steady stream of ambassadorial correspondence which, from the late 1540s onwards, provided ongoing if fragmented commentary on Irish affairs from an English government perspective. Both the ambassadors' reports and their personal encounters with various Irish dissidents educated the French in respect of the political geography of Ireland

and the country's strategic harbours. Through both channels they learned that the O'Neills, the O'Donnells, the MacCarthys, the O'Connors, the Geraldines of Desmond and Kildare, the O'Briens of Thomond, the Burkes of Clanricard and the Ormonds were the most important and powerful lords in Ireland. As the century progressed their knowledge of the country's lesser lords and their grievances expanded to a limited extent. Similarly, the two French diplomats who visited Ireland in 1549–50 informed their colleagues of what they learned about Irish lifestyles, housing, the conduct of politics, religious practices and beliefs, food, the countryside, the Irish language, Irish ammunitions and the characteristics of the Irish people amongst other topics.

From the initial stages of establishing tentative political ties with Ireland in 1522–3, the French realised that almost invariably disaffected elements in Ireland were ready to negotiate with them regarding possible French intervention in Ireland, the one notable exception being the early to mid-1540s. However, their negotiations in 1549–50 also alerted the French to the fact that the Irish were not content to render their allegiance unconditionally. Rather they found the Irish determined to have their own agenda honoured in order to protect their own interests. On the basis of their experiences with Irish dissidents, the French were dissuaded from undertaking an invasion of Ireland, partly owing to their well-founded apprehension that the Irish were beset by internal dissension. In the 1549–50 negotiations, this problem was particularly evident in Manus O'Donnell's refusal to meet the two French envoys, self-preservation being his paramount concern. Their reconnaissance also apprised the French of the limited military capabilities of the Irish in spite of their renowned fighting ability, which led to their conclusion that the Irish would be unsuitable as allies in a French invasion, being poorly armed and inexperienced in the use of artillery.

At a very early stage the French also grasped the vital importance of the Geraldine dynasty to Irish politics and as potential allies in any envisaged intervention in Ireland. Particularly from the 1540s, they displayed an appreciation for the potency of the Geraldine cause and Catholicism as the two fundamental canons in Irish politics and society. The substance of Franco-Irish intrigue throughout the period from the early 1540s down to the 1580s testifies to their belief that the use of one or the other cause, or the two together, would serve as grounds for legitimate French intervention in Ireland. While the French political elite's knowledge of Gaelic politics was advancing slowly, their understanding of the dynamics underpinning those politics remained extremely limited. None the less, a handful exhibited an appreciation of the close ties that bound together Ulster's Gaelic lords and their Gaelic counterparts in Scotland and they were quick to identify those bonds as a useful medium by which a French campaign might be extended into Ireland. They were apprised regarding the progress of English policies in Ireland from the late 1530s onwards and were undoubtedly aware that English defence of Ireland was poor, expedient and wholly inadequate. Each of the French monarchs displayed keen sensitivity to both the positive and negative implications for their relations with England of their association with Irish fugitives. François I, Henri II and Henri III succeeded in using their contacts with Irish dissidents occasionally to accentuate English insecurity and vulnerability. However, François I and Henri II both discovered that their involvement with Irish rebels could equally be used as a stick with which their Habsburg opponents could beat them in efforts to upset otherwise amicable relations between France and England.

The reasons for the failure of each round of Franco-Irish intrigue in the sixteenth century are varied and complex. The most serious engagements occurred when the rapport between France and England was strained or overtly hostile. However, once relations improved and it was no longer politically advantageous to maintain links with the Irish, the French typically dispensed with the latter as compromising evidence of their underhand dealings with rebels against the English crown. In short, the potential costs in terms of jeopardising Anglo-French relations far outweighed the possible returns from any intervention in Ireland. Ireland had no intrinsic appeal for the French as it possessed no lucrative mineral resources. Consequently, the Irish were only of value to the French as levers that could be used to apply pressure on the English crown to conform with the interests of the French king. Moreover, throughout the sixteenth century, continental politics and French domestic politics dictated that France needed either England's support or at least her neutrality to protect and advance French interests, usually against the Habsburgs. The degree of interest exhibited by the French crown in Irish overtures was therefore determined by this preoccupation with their potential ramifications for French relations with England.

Intrigue also failed to bring about an invasion because, with the exception of 1522–3, the French were never prepared to commit themselves to anything more than vague statements of interest in launching a military expedition to Ireland. Apart from the 1523 treaty, no formal enrolled treaties or legally binding agreements were signed, proving that even in the case of the most promising round of formal negotiations with the Gaelic lords, in Ulster in 1549–50, both French and Irish commitment to the project in hand was limited, cautious and conditional, which augured badly for the prospect of any real outcome to their talks. The changing fortunes of the Guise faction were decisive in the failed outcome to several plans for a French descent on Ireland. While in the late 1540s the Guises demonstrated enthusiasm and commitment to supporting their sister's Catholic *régime* in Scotland, from an early stage in 1550 their interest began to fade. By March they had grown weary of a Scottish campaign that was showing little signs of real progress and were mindful of the resentment that the inordinate cost of prolonging the campaign had engendered in French taxpayers. In April of that year Claude, duc d'Aumale and first duc de Guise, who had advocated French intervention in Scotland in support of Marie's rule, died. The Guises made their reputation through military service and, from the 1540s onwards, they were heavily involved in French foreign and domestic campaigns that diverted their attention from Scotland and by extension, from Ireland. They were dealt a serious blow when in 1563 the duc de Guise was assassinated in the first of the wars of religion which left only his brother, the cardinal of Guise, to promote the faction's interests in France and abroad. Throughout the period from the early 1560s to the 1580s, the Guises were immersed in the French wars of religion. Once their kinswoman, Mary Queen of Scots, was executed in February 1587, their dynastic links with Scotland were effectively severed and thus any prospect of a Guise-led attack on Ireland evaporated. Finally, in the late 1570s and early 1580s, it became obvious to the Irish lords and envoys involved in lobbying for military support on the continent that the French were unable to compete with the increasingly menacing Spanish who looked like the most promising source of assistance. As the spectre of the Spanish threat to both England and France grew in the 1580s, Henri III and Henri IV were keenly aware it was in the best interests of the French monarchy to affirm French ties with non-Habsburg allies, most important of whom were the English. Consequently, the French kings made known their disapproval of all insurgence in Ireland and dissuaded dissidents from directing solicitations to their court after the early 1580s.

The failure to bring about a French invasion cannot be attributed solely to the cavalier treatment of the Irish by the French crown and the Guise faction. The Irish, too, were partially responsible. They failed to present a united 'national' league under strong leadership, backed by a united, well-armed, well-disciplined military force with whom the French could conduct serious negotiations and on whom they could rely as allies in the event of invasion. Manus O'Donnell's efforts to convince Henri II in February 1550 that they could, with difficulty, transcend these dissensions testified to French anxiety concerning the risks involved in collaborating with the Irish in a French invasion. In addition, once the identity of the protagonists involved in the more serious plots was discovered by the English authorities and all their incriminating correspondence confiscated, the likelihood of a French invasion of Ireland was significantly reduced in the short term. Equally the French, embarrassed at the English authorities' discovery of their involvement with Irish dissidents, were at least temporarily cowed and reticent in resuming contact with the Irish. The fact that this intrigue at best ended in their connivance eluding the lord deputy and council or at worst, discovery and subsequent monitoring and reproaches from the Dublin administration, served to discourage the Irish from persisting with their conspiracies. In particular, figures such as Manus O'Donnell and Con O'Neill, who were found by the Irish council to have been involved in intrigue, were very wary about becoming implicated in further conspiratorial schemes.

The restoration of Gerald Fitzgerald to his dynastic inheritance in 1554 also dealt a fatal blow to Franco-Irish intrigue as it deprived the French of one of their two trump propaganda cards (the Geraldine cause and Catholicism) in their relations with the Irish. Without recourse to Fitzgerald as a rallying figure to legitimate a French attack on Ireland, the French could now invoke only Catholicism as a justification for intervention. However, by the 1570s the Spanish and the papacy, champions of the Catholic Counter-Reformation, held much greater appeal as targets for Irish requests while in France the Guises were considered the most likely source of aid. The Scots also bore responsibility for the failed outcome to Franco-Irish designs. Neither Archibald Campbell, fifth earl of Argyll, nor the MacDonnells could be relied upon to put the interests of an alliance with the Gaelic lords of Ulster before their own and before their intention to use the intrigue to settle old scores against the Irish. These tendencies are best illustrated in the 1549–50 episode when James MacDonnell used his alleged support for French negotiations with the Ulster lords partly as a smokescreen to enable him to capitalise on Manus O'Donnell's feud with his own son, Calvagh, in order that he might establish a foothold for himself in Ulster. Argyll used his connections with the French and the Gaelic lords in Ulster in a deliberate ploy to demonstrate to Elizabeth I that his allegiance could not be taken for granted by the English. He also used those associations to register his annoyance at having been slighted by the English administration's failure to avail itself of his offer to furnish troops for service in Ulster and also at Elizabeth's refusal to reciprocate his show of spontaneous support by lending her backing to his close ally, the Protestant earl of Moray, in 1565. The vicissitudes of Anglo-Scottish political relations also had a direct bearing on Franco-Irish intrigue as improvements in the former invariably resulted in the Irish dissidents being afforded a cool reception at the Scottish court.

To a limited extent the failed outcome to Irish engagement with the French can be attributed to the actions and fates of the protagonists. Several of the Irish lords and some of the envoys involved prejudiced the outcome to negotiations by placing self-interest before the good of those whom they claimed to represent. The longest-serving Irish envoy employed in the most important round of talks, George Paris, was not trustworthy. Henri II voiced his suspicions of Paris's character in October 1549. These were confirmed in 1552 when it was revealed that he was prepared to put self-interest before the preservation of the confidentiality of the French king and the Gaelic lords incriminated in correspondence which he offered to surrender to the English crown in return for a pardon. The untimely death of Irish protagonists, notably Shane O'Neill and Bishop Robert Wauchop, at points when domestic and international political circumstances appeared to augur well for the prospect of French intervention in Ireland, dealt a severe blow to efforts to achieve that goal. In addition, the accidental death of Henri II, of all the French kings the one who demonstrated a consistent interest in Irish affairs, represented a serious setback to Irish efforts to forge an advantageous political relationship with the French crown.

This study has highlighted the reasons why successive episodes in Franco-Irish intrigue between 1522 and the early 1580s ultimately ended in failure. The earl of Desmond's negotiations with François I in 1522–3, the French diplomatic mission of the winter of 1549–50, Shane O'Neill's overture to Charles IX in 1566 and 1567, and James Fitzmaurices's campaign for assistance in Paris and Brittany in the early 1570s have been identified as rare occasions when a very short-lived coincidence of several of the prerequisites for a successful realisation of plans for a French invasion of Ireland occurred. Yet at no stage did all of the requisite factors simultaneously converge, hence the failed outcome of each of these engagements.

II

While the tenuous political ties built up between France and Ireland over the course of the sixteenth century lapsed for a period of sixty years from the 1580s until the 1640s, their long-standing commercial connections remained the most enduring of all contacts between the two countries and regained primacy in the early 1600s. The opening years of the seventeenth century saw both Ireland and France emerge from decades of intermittent warfare and associated economic dislocation and resulted in an intensification in commercial activity between the two countries. From the 1590s onwards the Irish economy showed signs of significant improvement. Ireland's low inflationary economy trading with the high inflationary economy of England combined with price stability to give Irish merchants a considerable competitive advantage over one of the country's main trading partners. The rapid recovery of the Irish population in the early seventeenth century, largely the result of the resettlement of Munster after the Nine Years' War and Scottish and English immigration through formal plantation schemes and more informal initiatives, also represented a significant development by contemporary European standards. The expansion of the settlers' market system into native Irish areas in the late sixteenth and early seventeenth centuries caused the economy to become increasingly commercialised.[1]

At the same time, the French economy experienced a remarkably swift recovery. Grain prices decreased, farmers enjoyed a succession of good harvests from 1604 to 1609, population densities were restored to 1580s levels, low grain prices encouraged diversification to new cash crops. French towns also experienced revival. On the Atlantic seaboard, Saint-Malo, Brest and La Rochelle emerged as centres of new prosperity. The problems of English and Dutch encroachments on the French domestic market were temporarily overshadowed by the growth of the domestic textile market in which all interests could in the short term share the profits. Some of France's currency problems were also addressed with the cessation of the wars when the circulation of defective silver and of debased copper coins was halted

---

[1] Clarke, 'The Irish economy'; Gillespie, *Transformation*.

through reform of the mints and the enforcement of an edict issued in 1596.[2] The coincidence of their respective economic recoveries proved beneficial to both Irish and French merchants who maximised lucrative and mutually complementary market opportunities in the early decades of the seventeenth century.

From the 1540s Breton mariners regularly sailed beyond the southern and eastern coasts of Ireland and moored in various havens between Limerick and Donegal, in search of salmon, herring, hake and ling that they sold in Ireland and England at great profit.[3] By the late 1590s Breton ships exchanged cargoes of wine, salt and other commodities for fish, tallow and hides at the ports of Killybegs, Donegal, Ballyshannon and Sligo and fished for cod, ling, hake and conger off the Aran Islands and for dogfish and ray at Portrush in the north of Ireland.[4] Although French involvement in fishing off the Irish coast apparently slackened when Ireland's fish exports declined in the early seventeenth century, the abundant supplies off the north-western coast still drew Breton and Normandy fishermen every year in considerable numbers as did the southern ports of Baltimore, Crookhaven, Bantry and Berehaven, which continued to thrive as fishing centres while the Breton market for Irish ray and conger remained buoyant and lucrative.[5] So strong were commercial links with Brittany in particular that in the 1590s the mayor of Galway, James Lynch, claimed that the town's economy was largely dependent upon commerce with the province, especially with Saint-Malo, which had became the main market for Irish hides in the early 1600s.[6] By that stage ships from the lesser Breton ports of Morbihan, Le Conquet, Lannion, Audierne, Crozon, Vannes, Morlaix and Le Croisic had also become involved in trade with Ireland, though on a more modest scale, and Rouen's outport, Le Havre,

---

[2]   Greengrass, *France in the age of Henri IV*, 172–81.
[3]   Warner to Wallop, 22 May 1540, *LP Henry VIII*, xv (1540), 704; *SP Henry VIII*, iii/3, 211–13; 'For the reformation of Ireland' (probably by Robert Cowley) [Aug.–Dec. 1541], *SP Henry VIII*, iii. 347.
[4]   Captain Charles Plessington to the earl of Nottingham, lord high admiral, and Cecil, 3 Sept. 1601, *CSP Ireland, 1601–3*, 54; 'A project of Sir Thomas Phillips for the landowners' plantation in the county of Colerane and the Derry sent to Robert earl of Salisbury, lord high treasurer of England' [1611], *Carew MSS, 1603–14*, 150; *CSP Ireland, 1611–14*, 225.
[5]   Gustave Fagniez, *Le Commerce extérieur de la France sous Henri IV, 1589–1610*, Paris 1881, 7. See also *Advertisements for Ireland*, ed. George O'Brien, Dublin 1923, for a comment regarding continental encroachment on Irish fisheries. For discussions of the decline of other southern fisheries see Clarke, 'The Irish economy', 181; Cullen, *Economic history of Ireland*, 8; John de Courcy Ireland, *Ireland and the Irish in maritime history*, Dublin 1986, 95, 126; Donald Woodward, 'Irish sea trades and shipping from the later Middle Ages to *c.* 1660', in Michael McCaughan and John Appleby (ed.), *The Irish sea: aspects of maritime history*, Belfast 1989, 37; *High Court of Admiralty examinations*, no. 728; Lyons, 'Franco-Irish relations', 27–9.
[6]   James Lynch to Sir Richard Bingham, 23 Aug. 1591, SP 63/160/7 (enclosure); 'Hides', 1611, *Carew MSS, 1603–24*, 207; 'Select documents, XVI: The Irish wine trade, 1614–15', ed. H. F. Kearney, *IHS* ix (1954–5), 405.

had also developed commercial links with Ireland.[7] By the 1610s Bordeaux was the largest single exporter of wine to Ireland, with Londonderry and Coleraine having been added to the list of ports importing wine from there. Calais also emerged as one of the main ports in the wine trade, re-exporting Spanish wine to Galway, Cork, Waterford, Wexford and Drogheda in particular.[8] In contrast with Nantes which only ever filled a small though significant niche in the Irish market, La Rochelle had assumed a prominent role in the importation of wine into Ireland by the early 1600s, at which time its vessels frequented the ports of Londonderry and Coleraine.[9] Ireland's commercial ties with Bayonne and Saint-Jean-de-Luz in the extreme south-west of Aquitaine were indirectly strengthened by legislative restrictions imposed on commerce with the Iberian peninsula by the English government in the 1560s and in the 1580s. Since then, Irish merchants frequented both ports to take on cargoes for conveyance to Spanish and Portuguese ports with which Irish and English merchants were forbidden to trade.[10]

During the 1590s and early 1600s these established commercial routes between Ireland and the ports of Saint-Malo, Rouen and Nantes were harnessed as migrant paths by several thousand Gaelic soldiers, peasants and their families who fled Ireland for France. This was to be the first of successive waves of large-scale migration of thousands of Irish to French cities and towns during the seventeenth century. As such, it marked the beginning of a new chapter in Franco-Irish relations in the early modern era for several reasons. At that time Irish emigration became part of the phenomenon of modern migration of the population of western Europe from periphery to core or central areas. The mass movement of members of the poorer strata of Irish society, mainly redundant soldiers and peasant farmers, marked a radical departure from the established pattern of perennial migration of clerics, clerical students and more modest numbers of soldiers seeking employment in continental armies. It thrust French society into unprecedented sudden, wholesale face-to-face exposure to thousands of Irish men, women and children drawn from the lower social order within Gaelic society. This encounter challenged French preconceptions of the Irish and significantly reaffirmed their generally negative views. Such was the scale of the influx of migrants that special legislative measures had to be devised to tackle the problems

---

[7] Lyons, 'Franco-Irish relations', ch. i; *High Court of Admiralty examinations*, nos 44, 45, 59, 173, 272, 322, 407, 470, 829; Wotton to de Montmorency, 23 fév. 1554, dépêches et mémoires de MM de Noailles, xii. 650bis–652.

[8] 'The Irish wine trade', 405; *High Court of Admiralty examinations*, nos 67, 675, 685, 691, 706, 1254, 1255, 1296.

[9] Trocmé and Delafosse, *Le Commerce rochelais*, 84 (see tables v and vi); 'The Irish wine trade'. The growth of Spanish trade in *rochelais* wine in Ireland in the post-1485 period resulted from the establishment of a Spanish colony in the town. See O'Brien, 'Commercial relations', 50–1.

[10] See 'The Irish wine trade'; Lyons, 'Franco-Irish relations', 59–65.

posed by their arrival and their dependence on municipal authorities for relief. Their flight to France caused political embarrassment and a significant strain on Anglo-French relations as the French wished to expel the migrants to England. Confessional concerns have been shown to have played little real part in determining the reception afforded the Irish in France. In the long term, however, this first wave of immigrants failed to establish a significant permanent Irish presence in France and it was not until the 1640s and 1650s that embryonic Irish communities could be identified in the cities and towns of Brittany in particular.

Intrigue, migration and trade were therefore vital dynamics that profoundly transformed the relationship between Ireland and France during the period 1500 to 1610, by the end of which time Franco-Irish relations had come full circle. Following a sixty-year interval, from the early 1520s to the early 1580s, during which the dynamic of 'normal' relations was significantly altered as unprecedented political contacts were cultivated and ultimately floundered, trade and migration, traditionally the main lines of contacts in the early sixteenth century, once again emerged in the early 1600s as the dominant and most enduring basis of contact between the two countries, though the scale of both had been dramatically augmented. Consequently, by 1610, Ireland and its inhabitants were known to an immeasurably larger section of French society than had been the case 100 years before. Yet in spite of the intensification of their contacts, the intricacies of Irish domestic, political, religious and ideological tensions still eluded the vast majority of cultivated Frenchmen, even those in government. In their minds Ireland remained an exotic, wild country with a population that they found to be just as slothful, dirty, prolific and uncouth in the streets of their cities and towns as they were portrayed in the French scholarly tracts read by the French elite in their leisure time.[11]

11 For a detailed discussion of a limited selection of early seventeenth-century French scholarly tracts see Lyons, 'Franco-Irish relations', ch. vi.

Bibliography

Unpublished primary sources

ENGLAND
London, British Library

MS Add. 30,666 'Traité d'alliance entre Roy François premier et Jacques, comte de Eymonie [Desmond], prince en Hybernie, contre le roy d'Angleterre', 1523 (NLI microfilm, n. 861, p. 743)

MS Cotton Titus B.XI (extract) 'Articles agreed upon between François Ier, king of France, and James, earl of Desmond, for making war against Henry VlIl', 1523 (NLI microfilm, n. 3642, p. 3260)

MS Stowe 154 (extract) Copy of a letter of Henri II of France to Con Bacagh O'Neill, earl of Tyrone, accrediting envoys, 11 oct. 1549 (NLI microfilm, n. 1924, p. 1458)

London, Public Record Office

SP 52, 60, 61, 62, 63, 68, 70 (consulted on microfilm in NLI)

FRANCE
Paris, Archives Nationales

Arch. Priv. 159 Fourquevaux papers

J. 960, no. 34 Acquits sur l'épargne: 300 *écus* sent to O'Donnell of Ireland, 17 mai 1531

J. 960³, no. 40, anc. J. 960, no. 2 Acquits sur l'epargne: undated grant of 50 *écus* by François I to Balthazar Lynch

E. 8a, fo. 161r Arrêts du conseil d'état, Henri IV, 8 fév. 1605

E. 8a, fo. 214r Arrêt relatif au procès intenté par un marchand de Limerick à Messire Antoine, comte de Gramont, gouverneur de Bayonne, au sujet de la vente de ses marchandises autorisé par le juge de l'Amirauté au siège de Bayonne

E. 12b, fo. 177r Arrêts du conseil d'état, Henri IV, 27 mars 1607

V. 6 11, no. 129 Arrêts du conseil privé, 7 mai 1607

Paris, Bibliothèque Nationale

Fonds français

MSS Fr. 2085–6 Traité du commerce de l'étranger avec la France (3e et 4e vol.)

MS Fr. 3208, fo. 1r Lettre de Catherine de Médicis à Monsieur de Montmorency, maréchal de France, 31 juill. 1564

MS Fr. 3484, fo. 30. Henri IV to M. de Bethune, 9 nov. 1601

MS Fr. 4128 Recueil de copies de lettres adressées et reçue, de 1598 à 1601, par le sieur de Boissize, ambassadeur de France en Angleterre

MS Fr. 5819 'Remonstrance au roy (Charles IX) sur le présent état d'Angleterre
. . . sept. 1569'

MS Fr. 5873 (ançien fonds) 'Le livre de la description des pays de Gilles Le
Bouvier, dit Berry'

MS Fr. 7024 Seventeenth-century copy, in Latin, of the treaty of alliance
between Francis I, king of France, and James, eleventh earl of Desmond, June
1523

MS Fr. 10751, fo. 8 Letter of Manus O'Donnell to Henri II

MS Fr. 15466 Mélanges

MS Fr. 15466r 316 'Melanges De l'État d'Allemaigne et aucuns royaumes et estats
voisins, par M. Godeffroy, historiographie du roy'

MS Fr. 15578, fo. 246 Lettre de Bellièvre à Villeroy, 2 nov. 1605

MS Fr. 15975, fos 11, 22, 37,46 Correspondance de Monsieur de Beaumont, 1602

MS Fr. 15976, fo. 210 Correspondance de Monsieur de Beaumont, 1603

MS Fr. 18168, fo. 66r Arrêts du conseil d'état, Henri IV, 8 fév. 1605

MS Fr. 18170, fo. 91v (see AN, E. 8a, fo. 214r)

MS Fr. 18171, fo. 221r Arrêts du conseil d'état, Henri IV

MS Fr. 20457, fo. 265 Lettre de Marie de Guise

MS Fr. 20530, fo. 9 'Un mémoire sur l'Angleterre, l'Écosse et l'Irlande'

MS Fr. 20793, xxiii, fo. 3 Pièces sur la guerre d'Irlande, 1568

Paris, Collège des Irlandais
File 3 B2, A no. 1 (3) Accounts of the establishment of the Collège des Irlandais,
Paris

Paris, Ministère des Affaires Étrangères, Quai d'Orsay
Correspondance politique, sous-série: Angleterre, vols xii, xiii, xiv

Copies des dépêches et mémoires des ambassades de MM Antoine, François et
Gilles de Noailles

Correspondance politique, sous-série: Angleterre, vol. iii
Ambassade de M. de Castillon

Correspondance politique, sous-serie: Angleterre, vol. ix
Correspondance d'Antoine, François et Gilles de Noailles

Rennes, Archives Départmentales, Ille-et-Vilaine
Sous-série 5J Fonds Henri Bourde de La Rogerie, 5J 70, 71, 74

Rouen, Archives Départementales, Seine-Maritime
Série G.2308 (1620), G.2187 (9 avr. 1627), G.2315 (1628), G.2319 (30 mai
1630), G.2320 (19 avr. 1631), G.8777 (1633–6)

Guides to primary sources

Published guides

Beaurepaire, C. de Robillard de, *Inventaire-sommaire des archives communales antérieures à 1790, ville de Rouen*, I: *Déliberations*, Rouen 1887

Burckhard, François, *Guide des archives de la Seine-Maritime*, I: *Généralités, archives antérieures à 1790, ville de Rouen*, i: *Déliberations*, Rouen 1887

Département d'Ille-et-Vilaine, ville de Saint-Malo: inventaire sommaire des archives communales, 1393–1800, n.p. 1991

Ducaunnès-Duval, Gaston and Jean-Auguste Brutails, *Inventaire-sommaire des archives départementales antérieures à 1790, Gironde, série E supplément*, ii (nos 2164–3697), Bordeaux 1901

Dumont, François, Solange Bertheau and Elizabeth Kustner, *Inventaire des arrêts du conseil privé (règnes de Henri III et de Henri IV)*, 2 vols, 4 fascs, Paris 1969–78, ii, fascs 1, 3

État numerique des fonds de la correspondance politique de l'origin à 1871, Paris 1936

Hauser, Henri, *Les Sources de l'histoire de France XVIe siècle (1494–1610)*, 4 vols; i–ii, 2nd edn Paris 1967; iii–iv, Paris 1912

Hayes, R. J., *Manuscript sources for the history of Irish civilisation*, 11 vols, Boston, Mass. 1965

Hohl, Claude, *Guide des archives de la Seine-Maritime*, II: *Séries F et I, archives postérieures à 1790, sources complémentaires*, Rouen 1993

Inventaire-sommaire des archives du département des affaires étrangères, mémoires et documents, France, Paris 1883

Inventaire-sommaire des archives hospitalières antérieures à 1790, Hôtel-Dieu, ii, repr. Paris 1884

Maitre, Léon, *Inventaire sommaire des archives départementales antérieurs à 1790*, Nantes 1902

Pesseau, [?] and [?] Havard, *Département d'Ille-et-Vilaine, ville de Saint-Malo, inventaire-sommaire des archives communales antérieures à 1790*, Saint-Malo 1883, repr. 1991

Teiieiro, S. de la Nicollière, *Inventaire-sommaire des archives communales antérieures à 1790*, I: *Séries AA, BB, CC, DD, ville de Nantes*, Nantes 1888

Valois, Noel, *Inventaire des arrêts du conseil d'état (règne de Henri IV)*, 2 vols, Paris 1886–93

Unpublished guides

'Collection des inventaires-sommaires des archives départementales antérieures à 1790, première partie, archives civiles, série C & D', typescript, Bibliothèque Nationale, Paris

Mauduech, Gérard, 'Archives départementales de la Seine-Maritime: série B, sous-série 216 B, amirauté du Havre, inventaire-sommaire', 1975, typescript, Archives Départementales, Seine-Maritime, Rouen

'Sécretariat de la maison du roi: inventaire des registres 0_11 à 0_1128 23 vols x (H–I)', typescript, Archives Nationales, Paris

Published primary sources

Accounts of the lord high treasurer of Scotland, ed. Thomas Dickson and Sir James Balfour-Paul, 11 vols, Edinburgh 1877–1916, x

Acts of the privy council of England, new ser., 46 vols, London 1890–1964, iv

Advertisements for Ireland, ed. George O'Brien, Dublin 1923

Ambassades de MM. de Noailles en Angleterre, ed. Rene Aubert de Vertot, 5 vols, Paris 1763, iii–v

Anciens Registres paroissiaux de Bretagne (baptêmes–mariages–sépultures): Saint-Malo, ed. Paul Paris-Jallobert, 15 vols, Rennes 1893–1907; first fasc., Rennes 1898, iii

'An Englishman's view of the court of Henri III, 1584–1585: Richard Cook's "description of the court of France" ', ed. D. L. Potter and P. R. Roberts, *French History* ii (1988), 312–44

Annála Connacht: the Annals of Connacht, A.D. 1224–1544, ed. A. M. Freeman, Dublin 1944

Annála ríoghachta Éireann: Annals of the kingdom of Ireland by the Four Masters from the earliest period to the year 1616, ed. and trans. John O'Donovan, 5 vols, Dublin 1846–51, iii

Annála Uladh: Annals of Ulster . . .: a chronicle of Irish affairs, 431–1131, 1155–1541, ed. W. M. Hennessy and Bartholomew MacCarthy, 4 vols, Dublin 1887–1901

'Annales breves Hiberniae auctore Thaddaeo Dowling', in *The annals of Ireland by Friar John Clyn and Thady Dowling, together with the Annals of Ross*, ed. Richard Butler, Dublin 1849

Annales de Nantes, comp. F. C. Meuret, 2 vols, Paris 1830–1, ii

Ansélme, D., *Histoire de la maison royale de France et des grands officiers de la couronne*, continued by Caille du Fourny, 9 vols, 3rd edn, Paris 1726–1879

Beacon, Richard, *Solon his follie, or A politique discourse, touching the reformation of common-weales conquered, declined or corrupted*, Oxford 1594

Boorde, Andrew, *The fyrst boke of the introduction of knowledge [1548?]*, ed. F. J. Furnivall, London 1870

Calendar of the Carew manuscripts preserved in the archiepiscopal library at Lambeth, 1515–1624, 6 vols, London 1867–73

Calendar of fiants, Henry VIII to Elizabeth: in Public Record Office of Ireland, report of the Deputy Keeper, 7–22, Dublin 1875–90

Calendar of material relating to Ireland from the High Court of Admiralty examinations, 1536–1641, ed. John C. Appleby, Dublin 1992

Calendar of the patent and close rolls of chancery in Ireland, ed. James Morrin, 3 vols, Dublin 1861–3, i

Calendar of the patent and close rolls preserved in the Public Record Office, Henry VII, 2 vols, London 1914–16, ii

Calendar of state papers preserved in the Public Record Office, London, domestic series, 12 vols, London 1855–72

Calendar of state papers preserved in the Public Record Office, foreign series, 1547–89, 23 vols, London 1896–1950

Calendar of the state papers relating to Ireland, 1509–1670, 24 vols, London 1860–1912

Calendar of state papers relating to Scotland and Mary, Queen of Scots, 1547–1603, *preserved in the Public Record Office, the British Museum and elsewhere in England*, 13 vols, London 1898–1969

Calendar of state papers, Spanish, London 1862–95

Camden, William, *Britannia, sive florentissimorum regnorum Angliae, Scotiae, Hiberniae et insularum adjacentium ex intima antiquitate chorographica descriptio*, trans. Philemon Holland, London 1610

——— *Remaines concerning Britain*, 7th edn, London 1674

——— *The history of the most renowned and victorious princess Elizabeth late queen of England*, ed. W. T. MacCaffrey, Chicago 1970

Campion, Edmund, *Two bokes of the histories of Ireland compiled by Edmund Campion*, ed. A. F. Vossen, Assen 1963

Captain Cuellar's adventures in Connacht and Ulster A.D. 1588: a picture of the times, drawn from contemporary sources, ed. Robert Crawford, London 1897

Catalogue des actes de François Ier, 9 vols, Paris 1887–1907, ii (1888); vii, second supplement (1896)

Chronique bordelaise, comp. Jean de Gaufreteau, 2 vols, Bordeaux 1876–8

Collection of documents relating to Jacques Carrier and the sieur de Roberval, ed. H. P. Biggar, Ottawa 1930

Commerce d'importation en France au milieu du XVIe siècle: document inédit, ed. Albert Chamberland, Paris 1894

Complete works in verse and prose of Edmund Spenser, ed. A. B. Grosart, 9 vols, London 1882–4, ix

Comptes rendus des échevins de Rouen avec des documents relatifs à leur élection, 1409–1701, ed. Julien Félix, Rouen 1890

'Confession Catholique du sieur de Sancy', in *Oeuvres complétès de Théodore Agrippa d'Aubigné*, ed. Eugène Réaume and François de Caussade, 6 vols, Paris 1873–92, ii

Correspondance diplomatique de Bertrand de Salignac de La Mothe Fénélon, ambassadeur de France en Angleterre de 1568 à 1575, ed. Auguste Teulet, 7 vols, Paris 1838–40, iii–vii

Correspondance du duc de Mercoeur et des Ligeurs bretons avec l'Éspagne extraite des archives nationales, ed. Gaston de Carné, 2 vols, Vannes 1899, i

Correspondance du nonce en France, Anselmo Dandino (1578–81), ed. Juan Cloulas, Rome 1970

Correspondance du nonce en France, Antonio Maria Salviati (1572–8), ed. Pierre Hurtubise, 2 vols, Rome 1975

Correspondance du nonce en France, Fabio Mirto Frangipani, 1568–72, 1586–7, nonce extraordinaire en 1574, 1575–6 et 1578, ed. A. Lynn Martin and Robert Taupin, Rome 1984

Correspondance du nonce en France, Giovanni Battista Castelli, 1581–3, ed. Robert Toupin, Rome 1967

Correspondance des nonces en France, Dandino, Della Torre et Trivultio (1546–51) avec des documents relatifs à la rupture des relations diplomatiques, 1551–52, ed. Jean Lestocquoy, Rome 1966

Correspondance politique de M. de Lanssac (Louis de Saint-Gelais), 1548–57, ed. C. Sauzé de l'Humeau, Poitiers 1904

Correspondance politique de MM de Castillon et de Marillac, ambassadeurs de France en Angleterre (1537–42), ed. Jean Kaulek, Louis Farges and Gennain Léfèvre-Pontalis, Paris 1885

Correspondance politique de Odet de Selve, ambassadeur de France en Angleterre (1546–9), ed. Germain Léfèvre-Pontalis, Paris 1888

Davies, Sir John, 'A discoverie of the state of Ireland with the true causes why that kingdom was never entirely subdued . . . 1613', in *A collection of tracts and treatises illustrative of the natural history, antiquities, and of the political and social state of Ireland*, 2 vols, Dublin 1870, i

Derricke, John, *The image of Irelande, with a discoverie of woodkarne*, London 1581, ed. John Small, Edinburgh 1883

Documents authentiques et inédits pour servir à l'histoire de la marine normande et du commerce rouennais pendant les XVIe et XVIIe siècles, ed. Edouard Gosselin, Rouen 1876

'Documents concerning the negotiation of the Anglo-French treaty of March 1550', ed. D. L. Potter, *Camden Miscellany XXVIII* (Camden 4th ser. xxix, 1984), 58–180

'Documents relating to the Irish in the West Indies', ed. Aubrey Gwynn, *Analecta Hibernica* iv (1932), 139–286

Dymmok, John, 'A treatise of Ireland, ed. Richard Butler, in *Tracts relating to Ireland*, ii/1 (1843), 1–90

Falkiner, C. L., *Illustrations of Irish history and topography, mainly of the seventeenth century*, London 1904

First version of the topography of Ireland by Giraldus Cambrensis, trans. John O'Meara, Dundalk 1951

Foreign correspondence with Marie de Lorraine, queen of Scotland, from the originals in the Balcarres papers, 1537–48, ed. Marguerite Wood, Edinburgh 1923

Gernon, Luke, 'A discourse of Ireland [c. 1620]', in Falkiner, *Illustrations*, 345–64

Girolamo Ragazzoni évêque de Bergame, nonce de France, correspondance de sa nonciature, 1583–6, ed. Pierre Blet, Paris 1962

Hamilton papers: letters and papers illustrating the political relations of England and Scotland in the XVI century, ed. Joseph Bain, 2 vols, Edinburgh 1892, ii

Histoire générale de Paris, registre des délibérations du Bureau de la ville de Paris, ed. Paul Le Guérin, François Bonnardot, Alexandre Tuetey, Léon Le Grand, Suzanne Clémencet and others, 20 vols, Paris 1883–1984, xiv

Histoire de la Ligue: oeuvre inédite d'un contemporain anonyme (1574–93), ed. Charles Valois, Paris 1814

Histoire universelle par Agrippa d'Aubigné, 1553–1602, ed. Alphonse de Ruble, 9 vols, Paris 1886–97; supplément, Paris 1886–1925, ix

HMC, *Calendar of the manuscripts of the . . . marquess of Salisbury presented at Hatfield House*, 23 vols, London 1883–1973, i–v, ix, xii

HMC, *Report on the manuscripts of Lord de l'Isle and Dudley preserved at Penshurst Place*, 6 vols, London 1925–66, ii

HMC, *Thirteenth report, appendix, part iv: the manuscripts of Rye and Hereford corporations*, London 1892

Holinshed, Raphael, *The historie of Irelande*, continued by Richard Stanihurst, London 1577

Ibernia Ignatiana; seu Ibernorum Societatis Jesu patrum monumenta collecta, ed. Edmund Hogan, Dublin 1880

Instructions sur le faict de la guerre of Raymond de Beccarie de Pavie, sieur de Fourquevaux, ed. Gladys Dickinson, London 1954

'Instructions to the French ambassador, 20 March 1550', ed. Gladys Dickinson, *SHR* xxvi (1947), 154–67

'The Irish at Paris in 1605', ed. David Buisseret, *IHS* xiv (1964–5), 58–60

Jacques Cartier: documents, ed. Frédéric Joüon Des Longrais, Paris 1984

Lascelles, Rowley, *Liber munerum publicorum Hiberniae*, 2 vols, London 1852, pt v

Lebeuf, l'abbé, *Histoire de la ville et de tout le diocèse de Paris*, new edn, 5 vols, Paris 1864

Letters, despatches, and state papers, relating to the negotiations between England and Spain, preserved in the archives at Vienna, Brussels, Simancas, and elsewhere, 13 vols, London 1873–1954

Letters of James V, collected and calendared by the late Robert Kerr Hannay, ed. Denys Hay, Edinburgh 1954

Letters of John Chamberlain, ed. N. E. McClure, 2 vols, Philadelphia 1939, i

Letters and papers, foreign and domestic, Henry VIII, 21 vols, London 1862–1932

Letters and state papers relating to English affairs, preserved in the archives of Simancas, 4 vols, London 1892–9

Lettres du Cardinal Charles de Lorraine (1525–1574), ed. Daniel Cuisiat, Geneva 1998

Lettres de Catherine de Médicis, ed. Hector de la Ferrière and Gustave Baguenault de Puchesse, 10 vols, Paris 1880–1943, ii, v, vii

Lettres de Henri III, roi de France, ed. Pierre Champion, Bernard Barbiche and Henri Zuber, 4 vols, Paris 1959–84

Lettres inédites du roi Henri IV à M. de Bethune, ambassadeur de France à Rome du 2 janvier au 25 janvier 1602, ed. Eugène Halphen, Paris 1890

Lettres et mémoires d'estat, ed. Guillaume Ribier, 2 vols, Paris 1666, ii

Livre de la description des pays de Gilles le Bouvier, dit Berry, ed. E. T. Hamy, Paris 1908

Maxwell, Constantia, *Irish history from contemporary sources (1509–1610)*, Dublin 1923

Melvil, Jacques, *Memoirs of Sir James Melvil of Hal Hall: containing an important account of the most remarkable affairs of state . . .*, ed. George Scott, London 1683 edn

—— *Mémoires historiques, contenant plusieurs evenemens tres importans, & qui ne se trouvent point dans les autres histoires*, ed. George Scott, 2 vols, Paris 1694, i

Mémoires authentiques de Jacques Nompar de Caumont, duc de la Force, ed. le marquis de la Grange, Paris 1843

Mémoires de la Ligue, contenant les évenements les plus remarquables depuis 1576, jusqu'à la paix accordée entre le roi de France et le roi d'Espagne, en 1598, 6 vols, Amsterdam 1758, i

'Mémoires de Messire Claude Groulard, premier président du parlement de Normandie ou voyages par lui faits en cour', in *Collection complète des mémoires relatifs à l'histoire de France*, xlix, ed. Claude-Bernard Petitot, Paris 1826

Memorials of affairs of state, ed. Edmund Sawyer, 3 vols, London 1725 (*Miscellany of the Maitland Club*, 1837), i

Mission de Beccarie de Pavie, baron de Fourquevaux, en Écosse, 1549, ed. Gladys Dickinson, Oxford 1949

Mission de Christophe de Harlay, comte de Beaumont, 1602–05, ed. Pierre-Paul Laffleur de Kermaingant, 2 vols, Paris 1895

Montaigne, Michel de, *Les Essais*, ed. Fortunat Strowski, 5 vols, New York 1981, i

Moryson, Fynes, 'The commonwealth of Ireland', in Falkiner, *Illustrations*
——— *An itinerary . . .* 3 pts, London 1617; new edn in 4 vols, Glasgow 1907–8
Négociations, lettres et pièces diverses relatives au règne de François II, ed. Louis Paris, Paris 1841
Nouvelle Collection des mémoires pour servir à l'histoire de France depuis le XIIIe siècle jusqu'à la fin du XVIII, ed. Jean-François Michaud and Jean-Joseph François Poujoulat, 32 vols, Paris 1836–9, i (1837) (Pierre L'Estoile's journal); ix (1838) (memoirs of de Castelnau)
Nouvelles Additions aux memoires de Michel de Castelnau, seigneur de Mauvissiere, ed. Jean Le Laboureur, 2 vols, Paris 1659–60, i (1660); 3 vols, Brussels 1731–2, i–iii
Ó Cianáin, Tadhg, *The flight of the earls*, ed. Paul Walsh, Dublin 1916
Ó Cléirigh, Lughaigh, *Beatha Aodha Ruaidh Uí Domhnaill. The life of Hugh Roe O'Donnell, prince of Tirconnell (1586–1602)*, trans. with notes and illustrations by Denis Murphy, Dublin 1895
Ó Cléirigh, Lughaidh, *The life of Aodh Ruaidh Uí Domhnaill, transcribed from the book of Lughaidh Ó Clerigh*, ed. Paul Walsh, 2 pts, Dublin 1948–57
Oeconomies royales de Sully, ed. David Buisseret and Bernard Barbiche, 2 vols, Paris 1970–88, ii
Oeuvres complètes de Pierre de Bourdeille, seigneur de Brantome, ed. Ludovic Lalanne, 11 vols, Paris 1865–82, iii
Ordonnances des rois de France, règne de François Ier, 9 vols, Paris 1902–92, v, viii
O'Sullivan Beare, Don Philip, *Ireland under Elizabeth*, trans. Matthew J. Byrne, Dublin 1903
Papiers d'état, pièces et documents inédits ou peu connus relatifs à l'histoire de l'Écosse au XVIe siècle, ed. Alexandre Teulet, 3 vols, Paris 1852–60, iii
Parker, Matthew, *Correspondence*, ed. John Bruce and T. T. Peroune, Cambridge 1833
Payne, Robert, *A briefe description of Ireland: made in this yeare 1589*, London 1589, 1590, repr. in *Tracts relating to Ireland*, i/2 (1841)
Rabelais, François, *Les Oeuvres de Maistre François Rabelais*, ed. Ch. Marty-Laveaux, 6 vols, Paris 1868–1903, i–iv
Recueil des lettres missives de Henri IV, ed. Jules Berger de Xivrey, 11 vols, Paris 1843–76, iii–vi
'Registre journal de Henri IV et de Louis XIII', in *Nouvelle Collection* i, 2nd. ser. (1837)
Relations des ambassadeurs vénitiens sur les affaires de France au XVIe siècle, ed. and trans. Niccolo Tommaseo, 2 vols, Paris 1838, i
Relations entre la France et l'Allemagne au milieu du XVIe siècle, d'après des documents inédits, ed. Jean-Daniel Pariset, Strassburg 1981
Relations politiques de la France et de l'Éspagne avec l'Écosse au XVIe siècle, ed. Alexandre Teulet, 5 vols, new edn, Paris 1862, i, ii
Rich, Barnaby. *A new description of Ireland*, London 1610
Rymer, Thomas, *Foedera*, 17 vols, London 1704–17, xvi
Scottish correspondence of Mary of Guise, including some three hundred letters from 20 February to 15 May 1560, ed. Annie Cameron, Edinburgh 1927
'Select documents, XVI: The Irish wine trade, 1614–15', ed. H. F. Kearney, *IHS* ix (Sept. 1955), 400–42

Smith, Thomas, 'Information for Ireland (1561)', *Ulster Journal of Archaeology* vi (1858), 165–7

Spicilegium Ossoriense, being a collection of original letters and papers illustrative of the history of the Irish Church from the Reformation to the year 1800, ed. P. F. Moran, 3 vols, Dublin 1874–84, i

Stanihurst, Richard, 'A treatise conteining a plaine and perfect description of Ireland . . .', in *The second volume of chronicles . . . first collected by Raphael Holinshed . . .*, ed. John Hooker, London 1586

State papers, Henry VIII, 11 vols, London 1830–52

State papers and manuscripts relating to English affairs, existing in the archives and collections of Venice, and in other libraries of Northern Italy, 38 vols, London 1864–1947

State papers, relating to English affairs, in the Vatican archives and library, 2 vols, London 1916–26

Tracts relating to Ireland, 2 vols, Dublin 1841–3

Tudor royal proclamations, ed. P. L. Hughes and J. F. Larkin, 3 vols, New Haven 1969, ii

Valois, Noel, *Inventaire des arrêts du conseil d'état (règne de Henri IV)*, 2 vols, Paris 1886–93

Walsingham letter-book or register of Ireland, May, 1578 to December, 1579, ed. James Hogan and N. McNeill O'Farrell, Dublin 1959

Secondary sources

Agnew, David, *Protestant exiles from France chiefly in the reign of Louis XIV*, 2 vols, 3rd edn. n.p. 1886, i (published for private circulation)

Anderson, S., *The rise of modern diplomacy, 1450–1919*, Harlow 1993

——— *The origins of the modern European state system, 1494–1618*, Harlow 1998

Babelon, Jean-Pierre, *Henri IV*, Paris 1982

Bagwell, Richard. *Ireland under the Tudors: with a succinct account of the earlier history*, 3 vols, London 1885–90

Banéat, Paul, *Le Département d'Ille-et-Vilaine: histoire, archaéologie, monuments*, 4 vols, Mayenne 1994, iii

Baudouin-Matuszek, Marie-Noelle, 'Henri II et les expéditions françaises en Écosse', *Bibliothèque de l'École de chartes* cxlv (1987), 339–82

——— 'Un Ambassadeur en Écosse au XVIe siècle: Henri Clutin d'Oisel', *RH* cclxxxi (1989), 77–131

Baumgartner, Frédéric, *Radical reactionaries: the political thought of the French Catholic League*, Geneva 1976

Beaurepaire, Charles de, 'Expulsion des irlandais, 1606', *Bulletin de la Société de l'histoire de Normandie* ix (1900–4), 42–4

Behrens, Betty, 'Treatises on the ambassador written in the fifteenth and early sixteenth centuries', *EHR* li (1936), 616–27

Beier, A. L., *Masterless men: the vagrancy problem in England, 1560–1640*, London 1985

Bell, Gary (comp.), *A handlist of British diplomatic representatives, 1509–1688*, London 1990

Benedict, Philip, *Rouen during the wars of religion*, Cambridge 1981

Bernard, Jacques, *Navires et gens de mer à Bordeaux, vers 1400–vers 1550*, 3 vols, Paris 1968

———— 'The maritime intercourse between Bordeaux and Ireland, c. 1450–c. 1520', *IESH* vii (1980), 1–21

Bertrand, Antoine-Louis, *Histoire des seminaires de Bordeaux et de Bazas*, 3 vols, Bordeaux 1894, i

Betts, R. R., 'Constitutional development and political thought in western Europe', in Elton, *New Cambridge modern history*, ii. 438–63

Bideaux, Michel, 'Jacques Cartier, découvreur en mission', *ASHAA Saint-Malo* (1984), 205–16

Billot, Claudine, 'L'Assimilation des étrangers dans le royaume de France aux XIVe et XVe siècles', *RH* dxlviii (oct.–déc. 1983), 225–96

Biographie universelle (Michaud) ancienne et moderne, new edn, 45 vols, Paris 1843–

Biraben, Jean-Noël, *Les Hommes et la peste en France, dans les pays européens et méditeranéens*, Paris 1975

Birch, Thomas, *An historical view of the negotiations between the courts of England, France and Brussels from the year 1592 to 1617*, London 1749

Bois, Paul, *Histoire de Nantes*, Toulouse 1977

Boissonade, Prosper, Le Mouvement commerciale entre la France et les Iles Britanniques au XVI siècle', *RH* cxxxiv (mai–août 1920), 193–228; cxxxv (sept.–déc. 1920), 1–27

Bonnenfant, Chanoine, *Les Séminaires normandes du XVIIe et XVIIIe siècle*, Paris 1915

Bonney, Richard, *The European dynastic states, 1494–1660*, Oxford 1991

Boüard, Michel de, *Histoire de la Normandie*, Toulouse 1970

Bourdais, F., 'L'Industrie et le commerce de la toile en Bretagne du XV au XIX siècle', *Annales de Bretagne* xxii (1907), 264–70

Boutruche, Robert, *Histoire de Bordeaux de 1453 à 1715*, Bordeaux 1966

Boyle, Patrick, *The Irish college in Paris, 1578–1901*, Dublin 1901

———— 'The Irish college at Paris, 1578–1901', *IER* 4th ser. xi (Jan.–June 1902), 193–210

———— 'The Irish college at Bordeaux, 1603–1792', *IER* 4th ser. xxii (July–Dec. 1907), 127–45

Bradshaw, Brendan, *The Irish constitutional revolution of the sixteenth century*, Cambridge 1979

———— 'Manus "The Magnificent": O'Donnell as Renaissance prince', in Cosgrove and McCartney, *Studies in Irish history*, 15–36

———— and John Morrill (eds), *The British problem, c. 1534–1707: state formation in the Atlantic archipelago*, London 1996

Brady, Ciaran, *Faction and the origins of the Desmond rebellion of 1579*, IHS xxii (Sept. 1980), 289–312

———— *The chief governors: the rise and fall of reform government in Tudor Ireland, 1536–1588*, Cambridge 1994

———— *Shane O' Neill*, Dublin 1996

———— 'Shane O'Neill departs from the court of Elizabeth: Irish, English, Scottish perspectives and the paralysis of policy, July 1559 to April 1562', in Connolly, *Kingdoms united?*, 13–28

Braudel, Fernand and Ernest Labrousse, *Histoire économique et sociale de la France au XVIe siècle*, Paris 1977, i

Briggs, Robin, *Early modern France, 1560–1715*, Oxford 1977

Brockliss, L. W. B. and Patrick Ferté, 'Irish clerics in France in the seventeenth and eighteenth centuries: a statistical survey', *PRIA* lxxxvii C (1987), 527–72

Buisseret, David, *Sully and the growth of centralised government in France, 1598–1610*, Paris 1968

Burns, J. H., 'Scotland and England: culture and nationality, 1500–1800', in J. S. Bromley and E. H. Kossman (eds), *Metropolis, dominion and province: Britain and the Netherlands*, iv, The Hague 1971

Butler, W. F. T., 'The barony of Carbery', in *Journal of Cork Historical and Archaeological Society* x (Jan.–Mar. 1904), 1–10

Cailleteau, Jacques, *La Rochelle*, Paris 1978

Canny, N. P., 'Identity formation in Ireland: the emergence of the Anglo-Irish', in N. P. Canny and Anthony Pagden (eds), *Colonial identity and the Atlantic world, 1500–1800*, Princeton 1987, 159–212

—————— (ed.), *Europeans on the move: studies on European migration, 1500–1800*, Oxford 1994

Carey, Vincent, *Surviving the Tudors: the 'Wizard' earl of Kildare and English rule in Ireland, 1537–1586*, Dublin 2002

Carré, Henri, *Essai sur le fonctionnement du parlement de Bretagne après la Ligue, 1598–1610*, Paris 1888

Carroll, Stuart, *Noble power during the French wars of religion: the Guise affinity and the Catholic cause in Normandy*, Cambridge 1998

Casway, Jerrold, 'Henry O'Neill and the formation of the Irish regiment in the Netherlands, 1605', *IHS* xviii (Sept. 1973), 481–8

Charlevoix, P. F. X. de, *History and general description of New France*, trans. with notes, John Gilmary Shea, 6 vols, New York 1866–72, i

Chastelain, Jean-Didier, *Imposture de Perkin Warbeck*, Brussels 1952

Childs, Wendy, 'Ireland's trade with England in the later Middle Ages', *IESH* ix (1982), 5–33

—————— and Timothy O'Neill, 'Overseas trade', in Art Cosgrove (ed.), *A new history of Ireland, II: Medieval Ireland, 1169–1534*, Oxford 1987, 492–524

Clarke, Aidan, 'The Irish economy, 1600–60', in Moody, Martin and Byrne, *A new history of Ireland*, iii. 168–86

Cloulas, Ivan, 'Les Ibériques dans la société rouennaise dea XVIe et XVIIe siècles', *Revue des sociétés savants de Haute Normandie* lx (1970), 11–30

Comerford, Michael, *Collections relating to the diocese of Kildare and Leighlin*, 3 vols, Dublin 1883–6, i

Connolly, S. J. (ed.), *Kingdoms united?: Great Britain and Ireland since 1500*, Dublin 1999

Constant, Jean-Marie, *Les Guise*, Paris 1984

Corson, Guillotin de, *Les Grandes Seigneuries de Haute Bretagne*, 3rd edn, Rennes 1899

Cosgrove, Art and Donal McCartney (eds), *Studies in Irish history presented to R. Dudley Edwards*, Dublin 1979

Croft, Pauline, 'Trading with the enemy, 1585–1604', *HJ* xxxii (1989), 281–302

Croix, Alain, *Nantes et le pays nantais au XVI siècle*, Paris 1974

—————— *L'Âge d'or de la Bretagne, 1532–1675*, Rennes 1993

Crowson, Paul, *Tudor foreign policy*, London 1973

Cullen, L. M., *An economic history of Ireland since 1660*, 2nd edn, London 1987
———— 'The Irish diaspora of the seventeenth and eighteenth centuries', in Canny, *Europeans on the move*, 113–49
Darsel, Joachim, *Histoire de Morlaix des origines à la révolution*, Rennes 1942
Daumesnil, Joseph, *Histoire de Morlaix*, Morlaix 1976
Daumet, George, 'Notices sur les établissements réligieux anglais, écossais et irlandais fondés à Paris avant la révolution: fin', *Mémoires de la Société de l'histoire de Paris et de l'Ile de France* xxxix (1912), 88–124
Davies, Godfrey, *The early Stuarts, 1603–1660*, repr. Oxford 1976
Dawson, Jane, 'Two kingdoms or three? Ireland in Anglo-Scottish relations in the middle of the sixteenth century', in R. A. Mason (ed.), *Scotland and England, 1286–1815*, Edinburgh 1987, 113–38
———— 'The fifth earl of Argyle, Gaelic lordship and political power in sixteenth-century Scotland', *SHS* lxvii (1988), 1–27
———— 'Sir William Cecil and the British dimension of early Elizabethan foreign policy', *History* lxxiv (1989), 196–216
———— 'Anglo-Scottish Protestant culture and integration in sixteenth-century Britain', in Ellis and Barber, *Conquest and union*, 87–114
Decrue, Francis. *Anne de Montmorency, grand maître et connétable de France à la cour, aux armies et au conseil du roi François Ier*, Paris 1885
———— *Anne duc de Montmorency, connétable et pair de France sous les rois Henri II, François II et Charles IX*, Paris 1889
Deloison, Charles Giry, 'La Naissance de la diplomatie moderne en France et en Angleterre du XVIe siècle, 1475–1520', *Nouvelle Revue du seizième siècle* v (1987), 41–58
Dickinson, W. Croft, *Scotland from the earliest times to 1603*, 3rd edn, rev. and ed. Archibald Duncan, Oxford 1977
Dictionnaire de la biographie français, comp. Prévost D'Amat and Roman D'Amat, fasc. xxxvii, Paris 1954
Dictionnaire des biographies, III: *La France moderne*, comp. Jean-Maurice Bizière and Jacques Solé, Paris 1993
Dictionnaire général de biographie et d'histoire, comp. Charles Dezobry and Theodore Bochelet, 9th edn, Paris 1873
Dictionnaire de la noblesse, comp. François-Alexandre Aubert de La Chenaye-Desbois and [?] Badier, 19 vols, 3rd edn, Paris 1863–76
Dictionary of national biography, London 1885–
Donaldson, Gordon, *Scotland: James V to James VII*, Edinburgh 1971
———— *All the queen's men: power and politics in Mary Stuart's Scotland*, London 1983
Dubost, Jean-François, *Les Étrangers en France, XVIe siècle–1789*, Paris 1993
———— *La France italienne, XVIe–XVIIe siècle*, Paris 1997
———— and Peter Sahlins, *Et si on faisait payer les étrangers? Louis XIV, les immigrés et quelques autres*, Paris 1999
Durkin, John, 'Robert Wauchop', *Innes Review* i (1950), 48–85
Elliott, J. H., *Europe divided, 1559–98*, London 1968
———— 'The Spanish monarchy and the kingdom of Portugal, 1580–1640', in Greengrass, *Conquest and coalescence*, 48–67
Ellis, S. G., 'England in the Tudor state', *HJ* xxvi (1983), 201–12

——— *Tudor Ireland: crown, community and the conflict of cultures, 1470–1603*, London 1985

——— *Tudor frontiers and noble power: the making of the British state*, Oxford 1995

——— *Ireland in the age of the Tudors, 1447–1603: English expansion and the end of Gaelic rule*, Harlow 1999

——— and Sarah Barber (ed.), *Conquest and union: fashioning a British state, 1485–1725*, London 1995

Elton, G. R. *England under the Tudors*, 2nd edn, London 1989

——— (ed.), *The new Cambridge modern history*, II: *The Reformation, 1520–1559*, Cambridge 1958

Fagniez, Gustave, *Le Commerce extérieur de la France sous Henri IV, 1589–1610*, Paris 1881

Farin, François, *Histoire de la ville de Rouen*, 2 vols, Marseille 1976, i

Féliban, Michel, *Histoire de la ville de Paris*, reviewed, augmented and updated by D. G. A. Lobineau, 5 vols, Paris 1725, ii, iv

Finot, Jules, *Étude historique sur les relations commerciales entre la Flandre et l'Éspagne au moyen âge*, Paris 1899

Fitzgerald, Brian, *The Geraldines: an experiment in Irish government, 1169–1601*, London 1951

Fitzgerald, C. W., *The earls of Kildare and their ancestors from 1057 to 1773*, 2nd edn, Dublin 1858

Fitzgerald, Patrick, ' "Like crickets to the crevice of a brew house": poor Irish migrants in England, 1560–1640', in Patrick O'Sullivan (ed.), *Patterns of migration*, i, London 1992, 13–35

Flynn, T. S., *The Irish Dominicans, 1536–1641*, Dublin 1993

Foletier, François de Vaux de, 'Les Portugais à Rouen du XVIIe au XVIIIe siècle', in *Revue des sociétés de Haute Normandie* vii (1957), 33–42

Foucqueron, Gilles, 'Jacques Cartier, témoin de son temps', *ASHAA Saint-Malo* (1984), 121–33

Françoise, Marcel, *La Navigation en Seine au fil de l'histoire*, Rouen n.d.

Fréville, Ernest de, *Mémoire sur le commerce maritime de Rouen depuis les temps les plus reculés jusqu'à la fin du XVIe siècle*, 2 vols, Rouen 1857

Frondeville, Henri de, *Les Présidents du parlement de Normandie, 1499–1790: recueil généalogique*, Rouen 1953

Gabriel, Astrik, 'Les Étudiants étrangers à l'Université de Paris au XVe siècle', *Annales de l'Université de Paris* xxix (juill.–dec. 1959), 377–400

Ganier, G., *La Politique du connétable Anne de Montmorency, 1547–59*, Le Havre 1957

Garrisson, Janine, *Guerre civile et compromis, 1559–98*, Paris 1991

——— *A history of sixteenth-century France, 1483–1598: Renaissance, Reformation and rebellion*, trans. Richard Rex, Basingstoke 1995

Gaulle, Julien-Philippe de, *Nouvelle Histoire de Paris et de ses environs*, 5 vols, Paris 1839–42, iii

Gayet, Jacques Lacour, *Histoire du commerce*, IV: *Le Commerce du XVe siècle et au milieu du XV siècle*, Paris 1951

Gillespie, Raymond, *The transformation of the Irish economy, 1550–1700*, Dublin 1991

Giry, Arthur, *Les Établissements de Rouen*, Paris 1975

Goubert, Pierre, *The ancien régime: French society, 1600–1750*, repr. Paris 1976

Gouhier, Pierre, 'Mercinaires irlandais au service de la France, 1635–1664', *Revue d'histoire moderne et contemporaine* xv (jan.–mars 1968), 672–90

Gourvil, F., 'Familles irlandaises en Bretagne aux XVIIe et XVIIIe siècles', *Nouvelle Revue de Bretagne* i (jan.–fév. 1949), supplément, 125–31

Grant, A. and K. Stringer (eds), *Uniting the kingdom? The enigma of British history*, London 1995

Green, Alice Stopford, *The making of Ireland and its undoing, 1200–1600*, London 1913

Greengrass, Mark (ed.), *Conquest and coalescence: the shaping of the state in early modern Europe*, New York 1991

——— *France in the age of Henri IV: the struggle for stability*, 2nd edn, Paris 1995

Gueriff, Fernand, 'Recherches sur les "étrangers" à Saint-Nazaire sous l'ancien régime', *Bulletin de la Société archéologique et historique de Nantes et de Loire-Atlantique* ciii (1964), 15–34

Gutton, Jean-Pierre, *La Société et les pauvres en Europe XVIe–XVIIIe siècles*, Vendôme 1974

Gwyn, Peter, 'Wolsey's foreign policy: the conferences at Calais and Bruges re-considered', *HJ* xxiii (1980), 755–72

Harbison, E. H., 'French intrigue at the court of Queen Mary', *AHA* xlv (1940), 533–51

——— *Rival ambassadors at the court of Queen Mary*, London 1940

Hayes, Richard, 'Irish footprints in Rouen', *Studies* xxvi (1937), 418–28

——— 'Irish links with Bordeaux', *Studies* xxvii (1938), 291–306

——— *Old Irish links with France*, Dublin 1940

——— 'Irish associations with Nantes', *Studies* xxxvii (1948), 115–26

——— *Biographical dictionary of Irishmen in France*, Dublin 1949

——— Christopher Preston and Jacques Weygand (eds), *Les Irlandais en Aquitaine*, Bordeaux 1971

Head, David, 'Henry VIII's Scottish policy: a reassessment', *SHR* lxi (1982), 1–24

Henry, Gráinne, *The Irish military community in Spanish Flanders, 1586–1621*, Dublin 1992

Herpin, E., 'Les Nobles bourgeois de Saint-Malo (du XIIe au XVIIe siècle)', *ASHAA Saint-Malo* (1925–6), 83–96

Herval, René, *Histoire de Rouen*, 3 vols, Rouen 1949, ii

Hewitt, George, *Scotland under Morton, 1572–80*, Edinburgh 1982

Hogan, James, *Ireland in the European system*, London 1920

Ireland, John de Courcy, *Ireland and the Irish in maritime history*, Dublin 1986

Jeannin, Pierre, *Les Marchands au XVIe siècle*, Paris 1957

——— 'Les Pratiques commerciales des colonies marchands étrangères dans les ports français XVIe–XVIIIe siècles', in L. M. Cullen and Paul Butel (eds), *Négoce et industrie en France et en Irlande aux XVIIIe et XIXe siècles*, Paris 1980, 9–16

Jennings, Brendan, 'Irish swordsmen in Flanders, 1586–1610', *Studies* xxxvi (1947), 402–10; xxxvii (1948), 189–202

Jonquière, le marquis de la, 'Une Ambassade en Angleterre au XVIe siècle: M. de Castillon à la cour d'Henri VIII', *Revue des Deux Mondes* xcviii (mars 1890), 123–58

Jütte, Robert, *Poverty and deviance in early modern Europe*, repr. Cambridge 1996

Kelley, Donald, 'France', in Roy Porter and Mikulás Teich (eds), *The Renaissance in national context*, Cambridge 1992, 123–45

Kermaingant, Pierre-Paul Laffleur de, *L'Ambassade de France en Angleterre sous Henri IV: mission de Jean de Thumery, sieur de Boissise, 1598–1602*, Paris 1886

Kerney Walsh, Micheline, *'Destruction by peace': Hugh O'Neill after Kinsale*, Monaghan 1986

———— *An exile of Ireland: Hugh O'Neill, prince of Ulster*, Dublin 1996

Kilroy, Phil, 'Women and the Reformation in seventeenth-century Ireland', in Margaret MacCurtain and Mary O'Dowd (eds), *Women in early modern Ireland*, Dublin 1991, 179–96

Knecht, R. J. *French Renaissance monarchy: Francis I and Henri II*, New York 1984

———— *The French wars of religion, 1559–1598*, 2nd edn, Harlow 1999

Koenigsberger, H. G., G. L. Mosse and G. Q. Bowler, *Europe in the sixteenth century*, 2nd edn, London 1989

Labatut, Jean-Pierre, *Les Ducs et pairs de France au XVIIe siècle*, Paris 1972

Laisney, Georges, *Histoire de Normandie*, Rouen 1944

Laurent, Catherine and Helen Davis (eds), *Irlande et Bretagne: vingt siècles d'histoire*, Rennes 1994

Lécureux, Bernadette, *Histoire de Morlaix des origines à la révolution*, Morlaix 1983

Lemonnier, Henry, *Histoire de la France et de la Renaissance, 1492–1598*, Switzerland 1983 edn

Lennon, Colm, *Richard Stanihurst: the Dubliner, 1547–1618*, Dublin 1981

———— *Sixteenth-century Ireland: the incomplete conquest*, Dublin 1994

Le Parquier, E., *Contribution à l'histoire de Rouen: une année de l'administration municipale au XVIe siècle (année 1515)*, Rouen 1895

Lequin, Yves, *La Mosaïque France: histoire des étrangers et de l'immigration en France*, Paris 1988

Lescarbot, Marc, *The history of New France*, with an English translation, notes and appendices by W. L. Grant and an introduction by H. F. Biggar, 3 vols, Toronto 1907–14, i

L'Éspagnol, André, *Histoire de Saint-Malo et du pays malouin*, Toulouse 1984

———— 'Les Relations commerciales entre l'Irlande et la Bretagne aux temps modernes, XVe et XVIIIe siècles: complémentarité ou concurrence?', in Laurent and Davis, *Irlande et Bretagne*, 166–77

Levack, B. P., *The formation of the British state: England, Scotland and the Union, 1603–1707*, Oxford 1987

Longfield, A. K., 'Anglo-Irish trade in the sixteenth century as illustrated by the English customs accounts and port books', *PRIA* xxxvi C (1924), 317–32

———— *Anglo-Irish trade in the sixteenth century*, London 1929

Lynch, Michael (ed.), *Mary Stewart, queen in three kingdoms*, Oxford 1988

Lyons, Mary Ann, *Gearóid Óge Fitzgerald, ninth earl of Kildare*, Dundalk 1998

———— *Church and society in County Kildare, c. 1470–c. 1547*, Dublin 2000

———— 'The emergence of an Irish community in Saint-Malo, 1550–1710', in O'Connor, *The Irish in Europe*, 107–26

———— 'Maritime relations between France and Ireland, c. 1480–c. 1630', *IESH* xxvii (2000), 1–21

———— ' "Vagabonds", "mendiants", "gueux": French reaction to Irish immigration in the early seventeenth century', *French History* xiv (2000), 363–82

———— 'Reluctant collaborators: French reaction to the Nine Years' War and the flight of the earls, 1594–1608', *Seanchas Ard Mhacha* xix (2002), 70–90

MacCaffrey, Wallace, 'The Anjou match and the making of Elizabethan foreign policy', in Peter Clark, A. G. R. Smith and Nicholas Tyacke (eds), *The English Commonwealth, 1547–1640: essays in politics and society*, New York 1979, 59–75

———— *Queen Elizabeth and the making of policy, 1572–88*, Princeton 1981

MacCaughan, Michael and John Appleby (eds), *The Irish sea: aspects of maritime history*, Belfast 1989

McCorristine, Laurence, *The revolt of Silken Thomas: a challenge to Henry VIII*, Dublin 1987

McCoy, G. A. Hayes, 'The completion of the Tudor conquest and the advance of the Counter-Reformation, 1571–1603', in Moody, Martin and Byrne, *New history of Ireland*, iii. 94–141

MacCraith, Micheál, 'The Gaelic reaction to the Reformation', in Ellis and Barber, *Conquest and union*, 139–61

MacCurtain, Margaret, 'The fall of the house of Desmond', *Journal of the Kerry Archaeological and Historical Society* viii (1975), 28–44

MacDougall, Norman, *The Stewart dynasty in Scotland: James IV*, East Lothian 1997

McGurk, J. N. N., 'The fall of the noble house of Desmond, 1579–83', *History Today* xxix (1979), 578–85, 670–75

Mackie. J. D., 'Henry VIII and Scotland', *TRHS* 4th ser. xxix (1947), 93–114

———— *A history of Scotland*, 2nd edn, rev. Bruce Lenman and Geoffrey Parker, Middlesex 1978

Mandrou, Robert, *Introduction to modern France, 1500–1640: an essay in historical psychology*, trans. R. E. Hallmark, London 1975

Mariotte, Jean-Yves, 'François Ier et la ligue de Smalkalde de la trêve de Nice à la paix de Crespy, 1538–44', *Schweizerische Zeitschrift für Geschichte* xvi (1966), 206–42

Martin, F. X., 'Confusion abounding: Bernard O'Higgins, O.S.A., bishop of Elphin, 1542–61', in Cosgrove and McCartney, *Studies in Irish history*, 38–84

Mason, Roger (ed.), *Scotland and England, 1286–1815*, Edinburgh 1987

Mathew, David, *The Celtic peoples and Renaissance Europe*, London 1933

Mathorez, Jules, 'Notes sur les prêtres irlandais refugiés à Nantes aux XVIIe et XVIIIe siècles', *Revue d'histoire de l'église de France* xiii (jan.–fév. 1912), 164–73

———— *Notes sur la colonie irlandaise de Nantes du XVIe au XVIIIe siècles*, Nantes 1913

Mattingly, Garrett, *Renaissance diplomacy*, London 1955

———— 'International diplomacy and international law', in R. B. Wernham (ed.), *The new Cambridge modern history*, III: *The Counter-Reformation and the price revolution, 1559–1610*, Cambridge 1971, 149–70

Maugis, Edouard, *Histoire du parlement de Paris*, 3 vols, Geneva 1977

Meehan, C. P., *The fate and fortunes of Hugh O'Neill, earl of Tyrone and Rory O'Donnel, earl of Tyrconnell: their flight from Ireland and death in exile*, 3rd edn, Dublin 1886

Michel, Roland Francisque, *Les Écossais en France et les français en Écosse*, 2 vols, London 1862

———— *Histoire du commerce et de la navigation à Bordeaux, principalement sous l'administration anglaise*, 2 vols, Bordeaux 1867–70

———— *Les Portugais en France: les français en Portugal*, Paris 1882

Millett, Benignus, 'The pastoral zeal of Robert Wauchop', *Seanchas Ard Mhaca* ii (1956), 32–60

Millier, Bernard, 'Jacques Cartier et la decouverte du Canada: le miracle canadien', *ASHAA Saint-Malo* (1973), 61–78

Mollat, Michel, *Le Commerce de la Haute Normandie au XVe siècle et au début du XVIe siècle*, Paris 1952

———— *Le Commerce maritime normand à la fin du moyen âge*, Paris 1952

———— *Histoire de Rouen*, Toulouse 1979

Moody, T. W., *The Londonderry plantation, 1609–41: the city of London and the plantation in Ulster*, Belfast 1939

———— F. X. Martin and F. J. Byrne (eds), *A new history of Ireland*, III: *Early modern Ireland, 1534–1691*, Oxford 1976

Morgan, Hiram, 'British policies before the British state', in Bradshaw and Morrill, *The British problem*, 66–88

Morrill, John, 'The fashioning of Britain', in Ellis and Barber, *Conquest and union*, 8–39

———— 'The British problem, c. 1534–1707', in Bradshaw and Morrill, *The British problem*, 1–38

Morton, Grenfell, *Elizabethan Ireland*, London 1971

Nahon, Gérard, 'La Nation juive portugaise en France XVIème–XVIIIème siècle: espaces et pouvoirs', *Revue des études juives* cliii (juill.–déc. 1944), 353–82

Nicholls, Mark, *A history of the modern British Isles, 1529–1603*, Oxford 1999

Nouvelle Biographie générale depuis les temps les plus reculés jusqu'à 1850–60, comp. Firmin Didot, Paris 1963–

O'Boyle, James, *The Irish colleges on the continent*, Dublin 1935

O'Brien, A. F., 'Commercial relations between Aquitaine and Ireland, c. 1000 to c. 1550', in Jean-Michel Picard (ed.), *Aquitaine and Ireland in the Middle Ages*, Dublin 1995, 31–80

Obry, Olga, 'Saint-Malo porte d'un monde nouveau', *ASHAA Saint-Malo* (1979), 223–9

Ó Ciosáin, Éamon, 'Les Irlandais en Bretagne, 1603–1780: "invasion", accueil, intégration', in Laurent and Davis, *Irlande et Bretagne*, 152–66

———— 'A hundred years of Irish migration to France, 1590–1688', in O'Connor, *The Irish in Europe*, 93–106

O'Connor, Thomas, 'Ireland and Europe, 1580–1815: some historiographical remarks', in O'Connor, *The Irish in Europe*, 9–26

———— (ed.), *The Irish in Europe, 1580–1815*, Dublin 2000

———— and Mary Ann Lyons (eds), *Irish migrants in Europe after Kinsale, 1602–1820*, Dublin 2003

Ó Cuív, Brian, 'The earl of Thomond and the poets, A.D. 1572', *Celtica* xii (1977), 125–45

Ó Danachair, Caoimhín, 'Irish tower houses and their regional distribution', *Béaloideas* xlv–xlvii (1977–90), 158–63

Ó Fiaich, Tomás, *The Irish colleges in France*, Dublin 1990

Ohlmeyer, Jane, 'Ireland independent: confederate foreign policy and international relations during the mid-seventeenth century', in Jane Ohlmeyer (ed.), *Ireland from independence to occupation, 1641–1660*, Cambridge 1995, 89–111

O'Neill, Timothy, *Merchants and mariners*, Dublin 1987

O'Scea, Ciaran, 'The devotional world of the Irish Catholic exile in early-modern Galicia, 1598–1666', in O'Connor, *The Irish in Europe*, 27–49

Palliser, D. M., *The age of Elizabeth: England under the later Tudors, 1547–1603*, New York 1983

Palmer, William, *The problem of Ireland in Tudor foreign policy, 1485–1603*, Woodbridge 1994

Pariset, Jean-Daniel, 'La France et les princes allemands: documents et commentaires, 1545–57', *Francia* x (1982), 229–301

Parker, David, *The making of French absolutism*, London 1983

Periaux. Nicétas, *Histoire sommaire et chronologique de la ville de Rouen*, Rouen 1874

Petout, Philippe, *Hôtels et maisons de Saint-Malo XVIe, XVIIe et XVIIIe siècles*, Paris 1985

Pillorget, René, 'Louis XIV and Ireland', in Bernadette Whelan (ed.), *The last of the great wars: essays on the war of the three kings in Ireland, 1688–1691*, Limerick 1995, 1–16

Plaisse, André, 'Le Commerce du port de Brest à la fin du XVIe siècle', *Revue d'histoire économique et sociale* xiii (1964), 499–545

Pocock, J. G. A., 'British history: a plea for a new subject', *JMH* xlvii (1975), 601–28

——— 'The limits and divisions of British history', *AHR* lxxxviii (1982), 311–36

Poete, Marcel, *Une Vie de cité: Paris et sa naissance à nos jours*, 3 vols, Paris 1924–31

Pollen, J. H., 'The Irish expedition of 1579', *The Month* ci (1903), 69–85

Potter, D. L., 'Foreign policy in the age of the Reformation: French involvement in the Schmalkaldic war, 1544–47', *HJ* xx (1977), 525–44

——— 'The Treaty of Boulogne and European diplomacy, 1549–50', *BIHR* lv (1982), 50–65

——— 'French intrigue in Ireland during the reign of Henri II, 1547–59', *IHR* v (May 1983), 159–80

——— *A history of France, 1460–1560: the emergence of a nation state*, Basingstoke 1995

Pyne, Peter, 'Irish soldiers in Barcelona, 1653–4', *Irish Sword* xix (winter 1995), 277–89.

Quinn, D. B., *The Elizabethans and the Irish*, New York 1965

Ramsay, G. D., 'The foreign policy of Elizabeth I', in Christopher Haigh (ed.). *The reign of Elizabeth I*, London 1984, 147–68

Ravenez, L.-W., *Histoire du Cardinal François de Sourdis*, Bordeaux 1867

Read, Conyers, 'English foreign trade under Elizabeth', *EHR* xxix (1914), 515–24

Reneault, A., *La Paroisse Saint-Patrice de Rouen*, Fécamp 1942

Ricateau, Maurice, *La Rochelle 200 ans Huguenot, 1500–1700*, Ave. des Ondines 1970

Sauval, Henri, *Histoire de recherches des antiquitiés de la ville de Paris*, 3 vols, Paris 1724, i

Scarisbrick, J. J., *Henry VIII*, 4th edn, London 1970

Schalk, Ellery, 'The court as "civilizer" of the nobility: noble attitudes and the court in France in the late sixteenth and early seventeenth centuries', in Ronald Asch and Adolf Birke (eds), *Princes, patronage, and the nobility: the court at the beginning of the modem age* c. *1450–1650*, Oxford 1991, 245–63

Scheurer, R., 'Les Relations franco-anglaises pendant la négociation de la paix', in Pauline Smith and I. D. McFarlane (eds), *Literature and the arts in the reign of Francis I: essays presented to C. A. Mayer*, Lexington 1985, 142–62

Schüller, Karin, *Die beziehungen zwischen Spanien und Irland im 16. und 17. Jahrhundert: diplomatie, handel und die soziale integration Katholischer exulanten*, Münster 1999

Sée, Henri, 'Le Commerce en France au XVIe siècle', in *Annales d'histoire économique et sociale* i (1929), 551–61

Shennan. J. H., *The origins of the modern European state, 1450–1725*, London 1974

Silke, J. J., *Ireland and Europe, 1559–1607*, Dundalk 1966 (Dublin Historical Association, Irish History Series, no. 7)

―――― 'The Irish abroad, 1534–1691', in Moody, Martin and Byrne, *A new history of Ireland*, iii. 587–633

Smith, Alan G. R., *The emergence of a nation state: the commonwealth of England, 1529–1660*, Essex 1984

Smout, T. C., 'The culture of migration: Scots as Europeans, 1500–1800', *History Workshop Journal* xl (1995), 108–17

―――― N. C. Landsman and T. M. Devine, 'Scottish emigration in the seventeenth and eighteenth centuries', in Canny, *Europeans on the move*, 76–112

Spooner, F. C., 'The Hapsburg–Valois struggle', in Elton, *New Cambridge modern history*, ii. 334–58

Swords, Liam, *The Irish-French connection, 1578–1978*, Paris 1978

―――― *Soldiers, scholars, priests: a short history of the Irish college, Paris*, Paris 1985

Tanguy, Jean, *Le Commerce du port de Nantes au milieu du XVIe siècle*, Paris 1956

Thorp, Malcolm, 'Catholic conspiracy in early Elizabethan foreign policy', *Sixteenth Century Journal* xv (1984), 431–48

Touchard, Henri, *Le Commerce maritime breton à la fin du moyen âge*, Paris 1967

Travers, Nicolas, *Histoire civile, politique et religieuse de la ville et du comté de Nantes*, 3 vols, Nantes 1836–41, iii

Trocmé, Etienne and Marcel Delafosse, *Le Commerce rochelais de la fin du XVe siècle au début du XVIIe*, Paris 1953

Tytler, Patrick Fraser, *History of Scotland*, 6 vols, Edinburgh 1828–37

―――― *England under the reigns of Edward VI and Mary, with the contemporary history of Europe, illustrated in a series of original letters never before printed*, 2 vols, London 1839, i

Valkenburg, Augustine, 'A study in diplomacy: Gerald, eleventh earl of Kildare, 1525–85', *Journal of the Kildare Archaeological Society* xiv (1968), 294–315

Vassiere, Pierre de, *Charles de Marillac, ambassadeur et homme politique sous les règnes de François Ier, Henry II et François II, 1510–60*, Geneva 1971

Veyrat, Maurice, 'Les Gouverneurs de Normandie du XVe siècle à la Revolution', *Études normandes* (1953), 557–88

Vindry, Fleury, *Les Ambassadeurs français permanents au XVIe siècle*, Paris 1903

Walsh, A., 'Irish exiles in Brittany', *IER* 4th ser. i (Jan.–June 1897), 311–22

Walsh, Helen Coburn, 'The rebellion of William Nugent, 1581', in R. V. Comerford, Mary Cullen, J. R. Hill and Colm Lennon (eds), *Religion, conflict and coexistence in Ireland: essays presented to Monsignor Patrick J. Corish*, Dublin 1990, 26–52

Walsh, T. J., *The Irish continental college movement: the colleges at Bordeaux, Toulouse and Lille*, Dublin 1973

Warren, John, *Elizabeth I: religion and foreign affairs*, London 1993

Went, Arthur, 'Foreign fishing fleets along the Irish coasts', *Journal of the Cork Historical and Archaeological Society* liv (1949), 7–24

Wernham, R. B., *Before the Armada: the growth of English foreign policy*, London 1966

White, D. G., 'Henry VIII's Irish kerne in France and Scotland, 1544–5', *Irish Sword* iii (1957–8), 213–24

———— 'The reign of Edward VI in Ireland: some political, social and economic aspects', *IHS* xiv no. 55 (Mar. 1965), 199–203

Wilson, Philip, *The beginnings of modern Ireland*, Dublin 1912

Wood, Herbert, 'Commercial intercourse with Ireland in the Middle Ages', *Studies* iv (Mar. 1915), 250–66

Woodward, Donald, 'Irish sea trades and shipping from the later Middle Ages to c. 1660', in McCaughan and Appleby, *The Irish sea*, 35–46

Wormald, Jenny, *Lords and men*, Edinburgh 1985

———— *Mary Queen of Scots: a study in failure*, London 1988

———— 'The creation of Britain: multiple kingdoms or core and colonies?', *TRHS* 6th ser. (1992), 175–94

Zeller, Gaston, *Les Institutions de la France au XVIe siècle*, Paris 1948

Unpublished theses etc.

Bonner, Elizabeth, 'The first phase of the politique of Henri II in Scotland', PhD diss. Sydney 1993

Brockliss, L. W. B. and Patrick Ferté, 'A prosopography of Irish clerics who studied in France in the seventeenth and eighteenth centuries, in particular at the universities of Paris and Toulouse', typescript, Royal Irish Academy Library, Dublin, and Russell Library, Maynooth, County Kildare

Carey, Vincent, 'Local elite and central authority: Gerald XI earl of Kildare and Tudor rule in Ireland, 1547–1586', PhD diss. New York Stony Brook

Downey, M., 'Culture and diplomacy: the Spanish–Habsburg dimension in the Irish counter-Reformation movement, c. 1529–c. 1629', PhD diss. Cambridge 1994

Holte, P., 'Tradition, reform and diplomacy: Anglo-Scottish relations, 1528–42', PhD diss. Cambridge 1992

Lennon, Colm, 'Poverty, disease and welfare in Dublin, 1540–1640', unpubl. paper delivered at the annual conference of the Economic and Social History Society of Ireland, Queen's University, Belfast 1994

Lyons, Mary Ann, 'Franco-Irish relations in the sixteenth century', PhD diss. National University of Ireland 1997

Potter, D. L., 'Diplomacy in the mid-sixteenth century: England and France, 1536–1550', PhD diss. Cambridge 1973

Richardson, Glenn John, 'Anglo-French political and cultural relations during the reign of Henry VIII', PhD diss. London 1995

Sasso, C. R., 'The Desmond rebellions, 1569–73 and 1579–83', PhD diss. Chicago Loyola 1980

Glossary

booleying	A form of transhumance practiced in Gaelic society
écu	The value of this coin, originally 3 *livres*, was increased by Richelieu to 4 *livres* 14 *sous*
galloglas	Gaelic professional soldiers, of Scottish descent, who were armed with a distinctive axe
hôtel-dieu	A hospice for the destitute sick
idlemen	A term used by English officials in describing professional soldiers who apparently transgressed the statutes against poverty and vagrancy
kerne	Unarmoured Gaelic foot-soldiers, equipped with a sword, bow or javelin
livre tournois	Common unit of money, divided into 20 *sols* and each sol into 12 *deniers*
sol	A form of *sou*
vidame	The nobleman appointed to administer and protect the temporal possessions of a church or monastery

Index